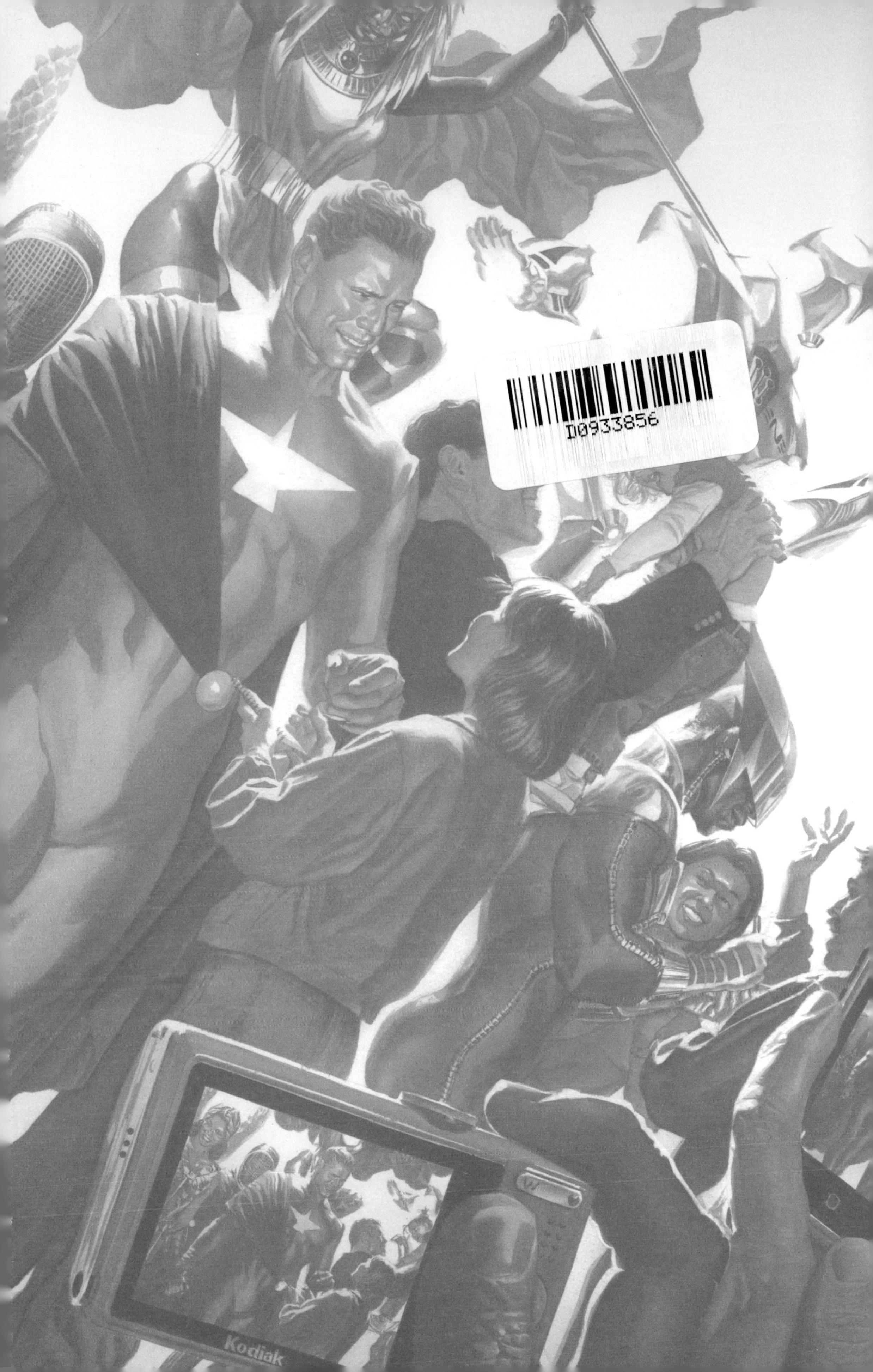
Kodiak

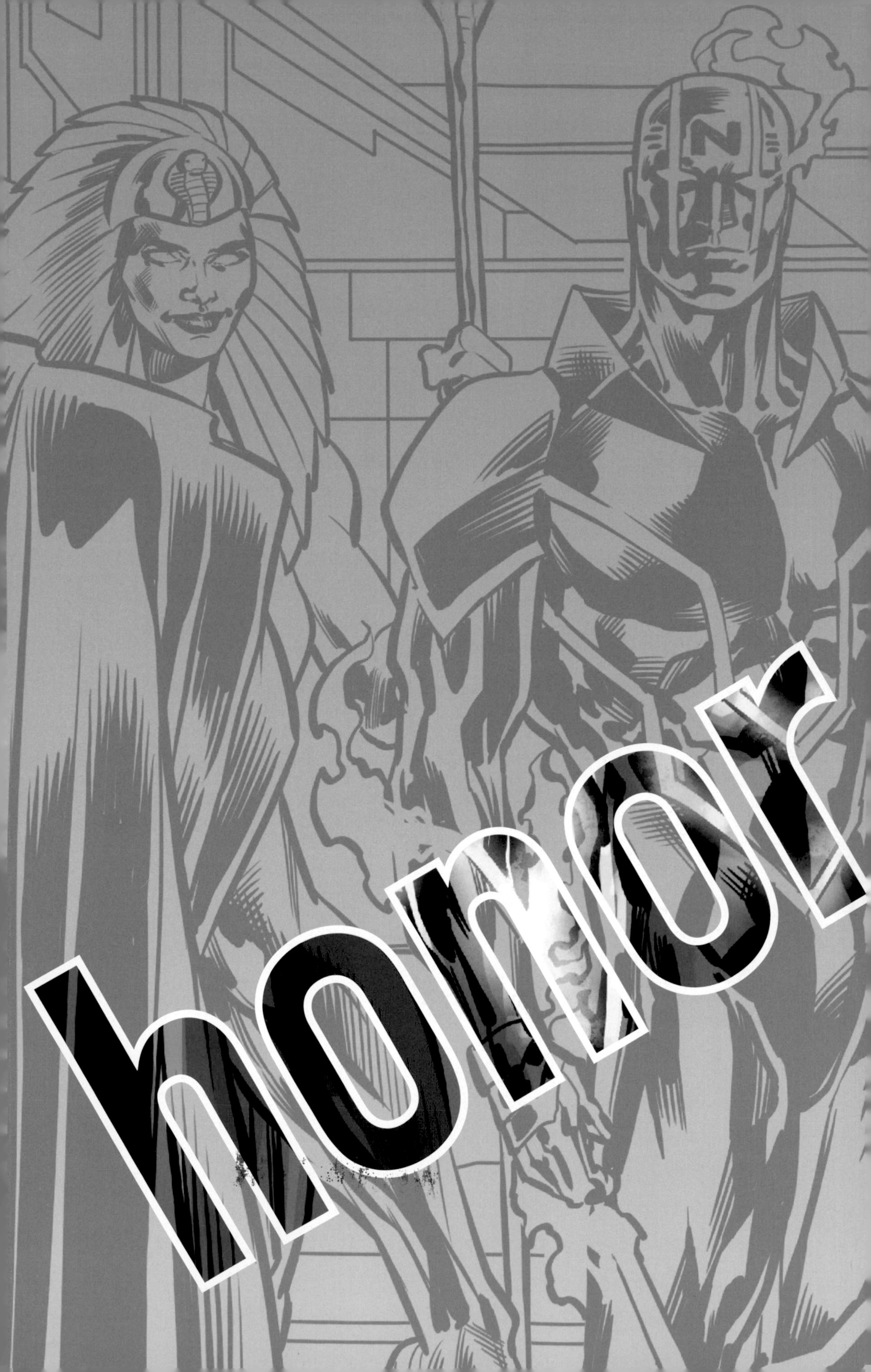
honor

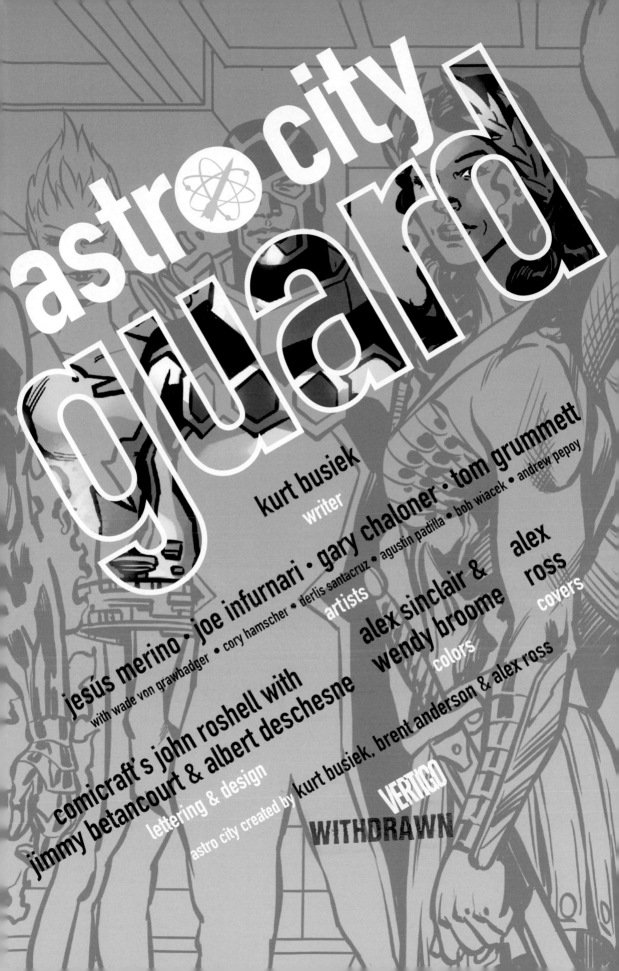

astro city guard

kurt busiek
writer

jesús merino · joe infurnari · gary chaloner · tom grummett
with wade von grawbadger · cory hamscher · derlis santacruz · agustín padilla · bob wiacek · andrew pepoy
artists

alex sinclair & wendy broome
colors

alex ross
covers

comicraft's john roshell with jimmy betancourt & albert deschesne
lettering & design

astro city created by kurt busiek, brent anderson & alex ross

VERTIGO

WITHDRAWN

VERTIGO

Kristy Quinn — Editors – Original Series
Molly Mahan — Assistant Editor – Original Series
Jessica Chen — Group Editor – Collected Editions
Jeb Woodard — Editor – Collected Edition
Liz Erickson —

Steve Cook — Design Director – Books

Bob Harras — Senior VP – Editor-in-Chief, DC Comics

Diane Nelson — President
Dan DiDio and Jim Lee — Co-Publishers
Geoff Johns — Chief Creative Officer
Amit Desai — Senior VP – Marketing & Global Franchise Management
Nairi Gardiner — Senior VP – Finance
Sam Ades — VP – Digital Marketing
Bobbie Chase — VP – Talent Development
Mark Chiarello — Senior VP – Art, Design & Collected Editions
John Cunningham — VP – Content Strategy
Anne DePies — VP – Strategy Planning & Reporting
Don Falletti — VP – Manufacturing Operations
Lawrence Ganem — VP – Editorial Administration & Talent Relations
Alison Gill — Senior VP – Manufacturing & Operations
Hank Kanalz — Senior VP – Editorial Strategy & Administration
Jay Kogan — VP – Legal Affairs
Derek Maddalena — Senior VP – Sales & Business Development
Jack Mahan — VP – Business Affairs
Dan Miron — VP – Sales Planning & Trade Development
Nick Napolitano — VP – Manufacturing Administration
Carol Roeder — VP – Marketing
Eddie Scannell — VP – Mass Account & Digital Sales
Courtney Simmons — Senior VP – Publicity & Communications
Jim (Ski) Sokolowski — VP – Comic Book Specialty & Newsstand Sales
Sandy Yi — Senior VP – Global Franchise Management

JUKE BOX PRODUCTIONS

COMICRAFT SINCE 1992

RICHARD STARKINGS
Art Director

ASTRO CITY VOL. 13: HONOR GUARD

Published by DC Comics. Compilation, cover and all new material
Copyright © 2016 Juke Box Productions. All Rights Reserved.

Originally published in single magazine form as ASTRO CITY 17, 22,
23, 27-28, 31 © 2014, 2015, 2016 Juke Box Productions. All Rights
Reserved. Astro City, its logos, symbols, prominent characters
featured in this volume and the distinctive likenesses thereof are
trademarks of Juke Box Productions. VERTIGO is a trademark of
DC Comics. The stories, characters and incidents featured in this
publication are entirely fictional. DC Comics does not read or
accept unsolicited submissions of ideas, stories or artwork.

DC Comics, 2900 West Alameda Ave., Burbank, CA 91505
Printed by RR Donnelley, Salem, VA, USA. 7/8/16.
First Printing.
ISBN: 978-1-4012-6387-4

Library of Congress Cataloging-in-Publication Data

Names: Busiek, Kurt, author. | Ross, Alex, 1970- illustrator. | Merino,
Jesus, illustrator.
Title: Astro City : honor guard / Kurt Busiek, writer ; Alex Ross, Jesus
Merino, artists.
Description: Burbank, CA : DC Comics/Vertigo, [2016]
Identifiers: LCCN 2016018386 | ISBN 9781401263874 (hardback) |
Subjects: LCSH: Comic books, strips, etc. | BISAC: COMICS & GRAPHIC NOVELS /
Superheroes.
Classification: LCC PN6728.A79 B75 2016 | DDC 741.5/973—dc23
LC record available at https://lccn.loc.gov/2016018386

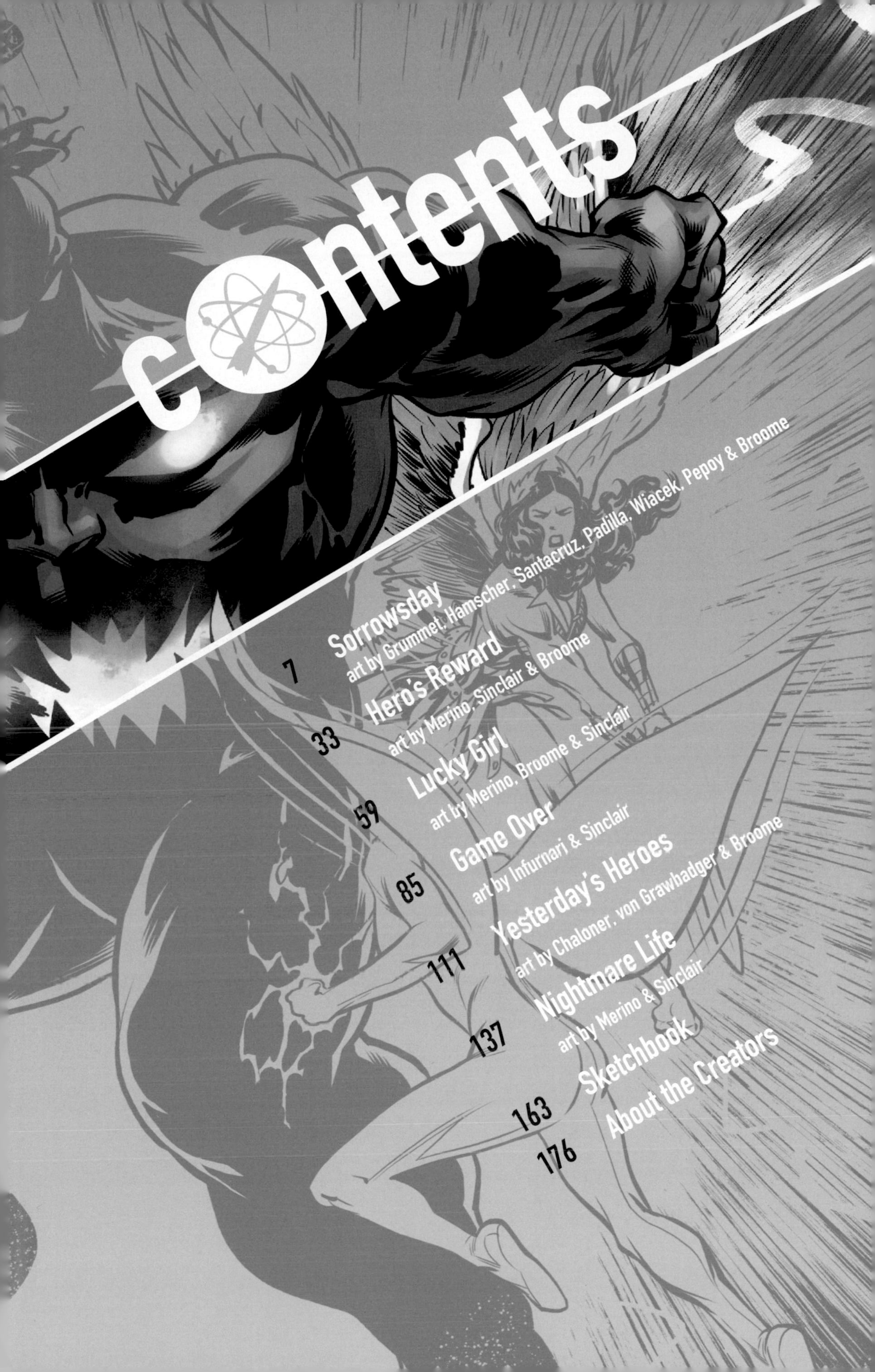

Contents

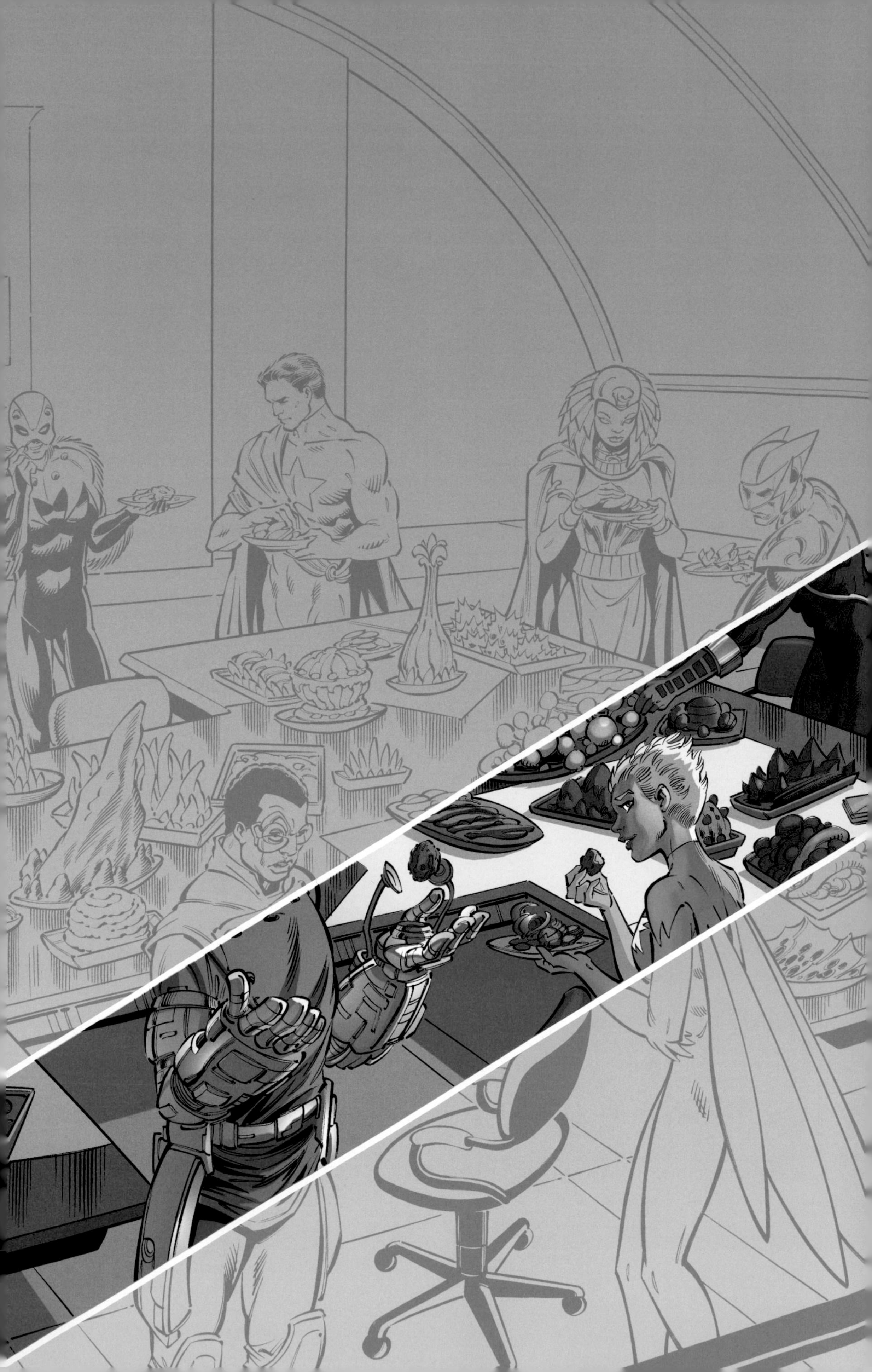

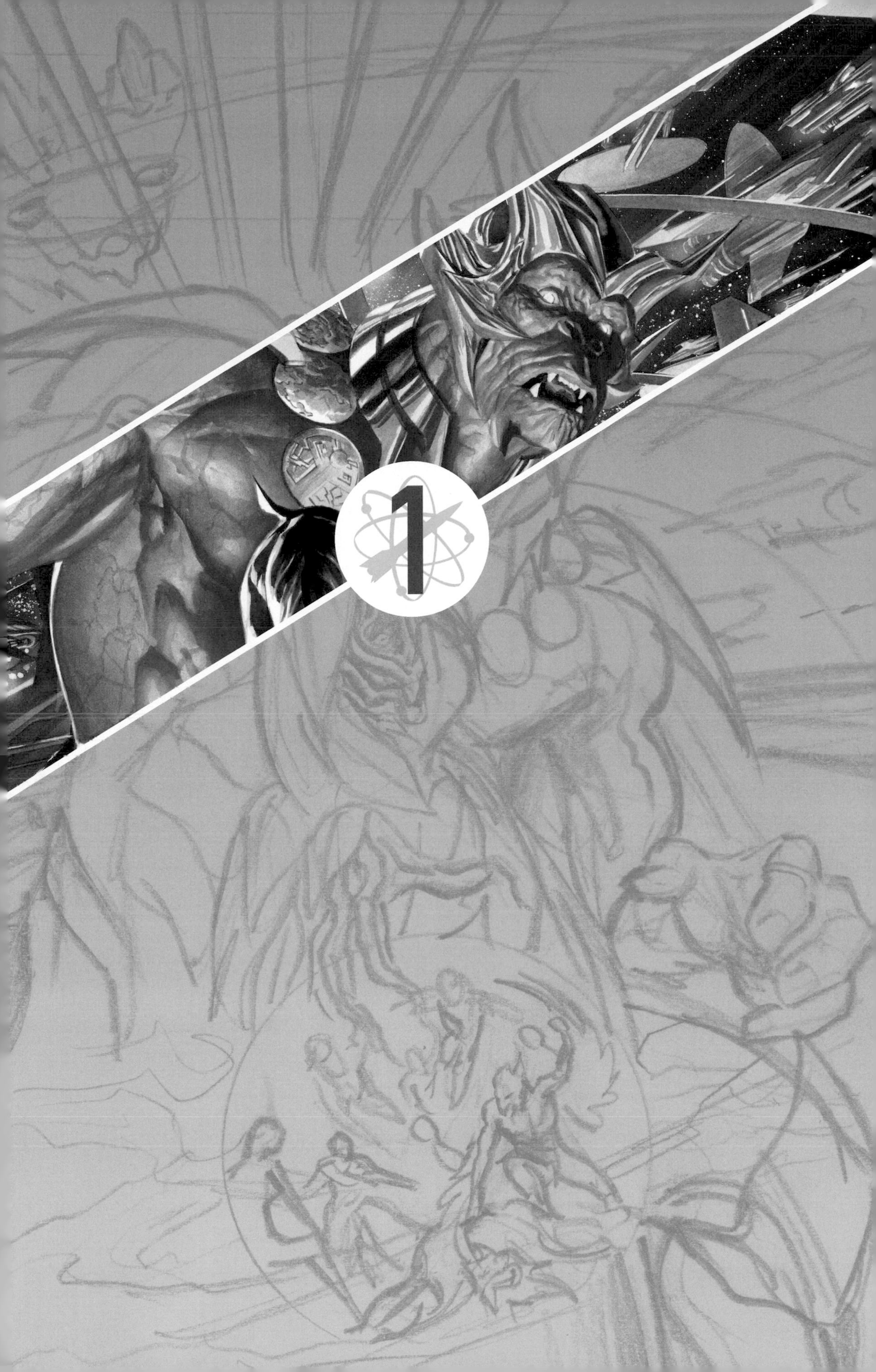
1

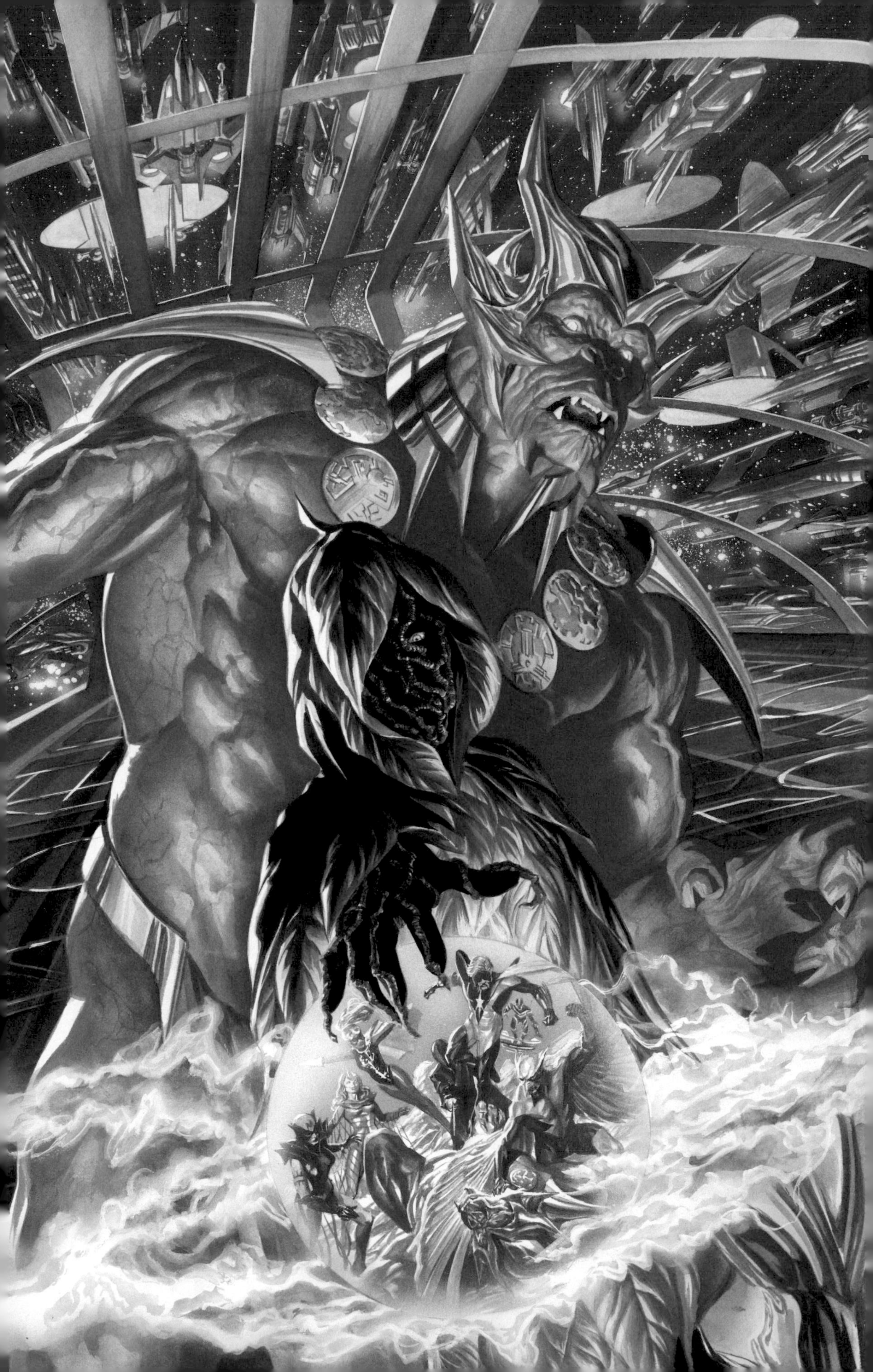

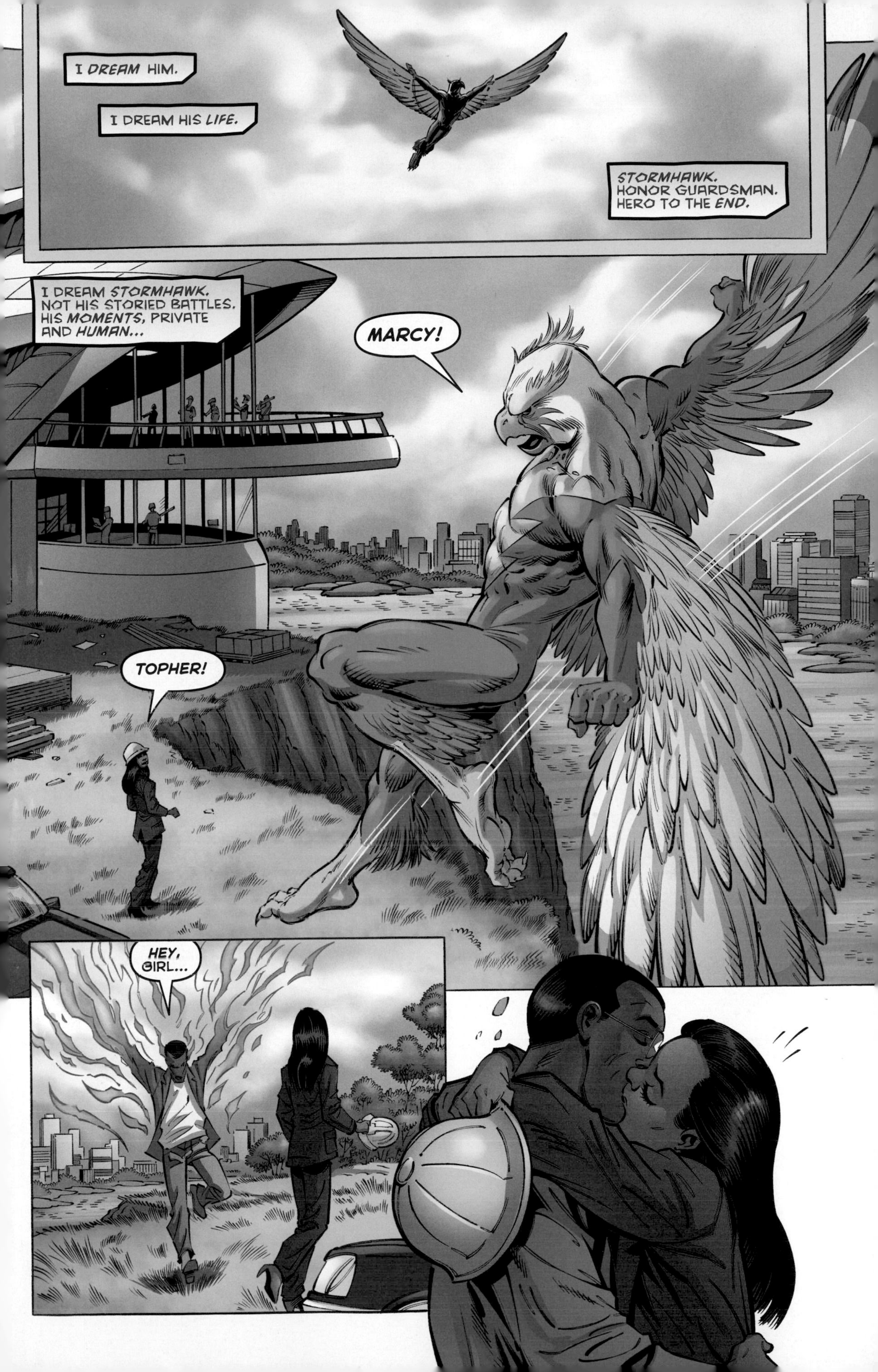
I DREAM HIM.
I DREAM HIS LIFE.
STORMHAWK. HONOR GUARDSMAN. HERO TO THE END.
I DREAM STORMHAWK. NOT HIS STORIED BATTLES. HIS MOMENTS, PRIVATE AND HUMAN...
MARCY!
TOPHER!
HEY, GIRL...

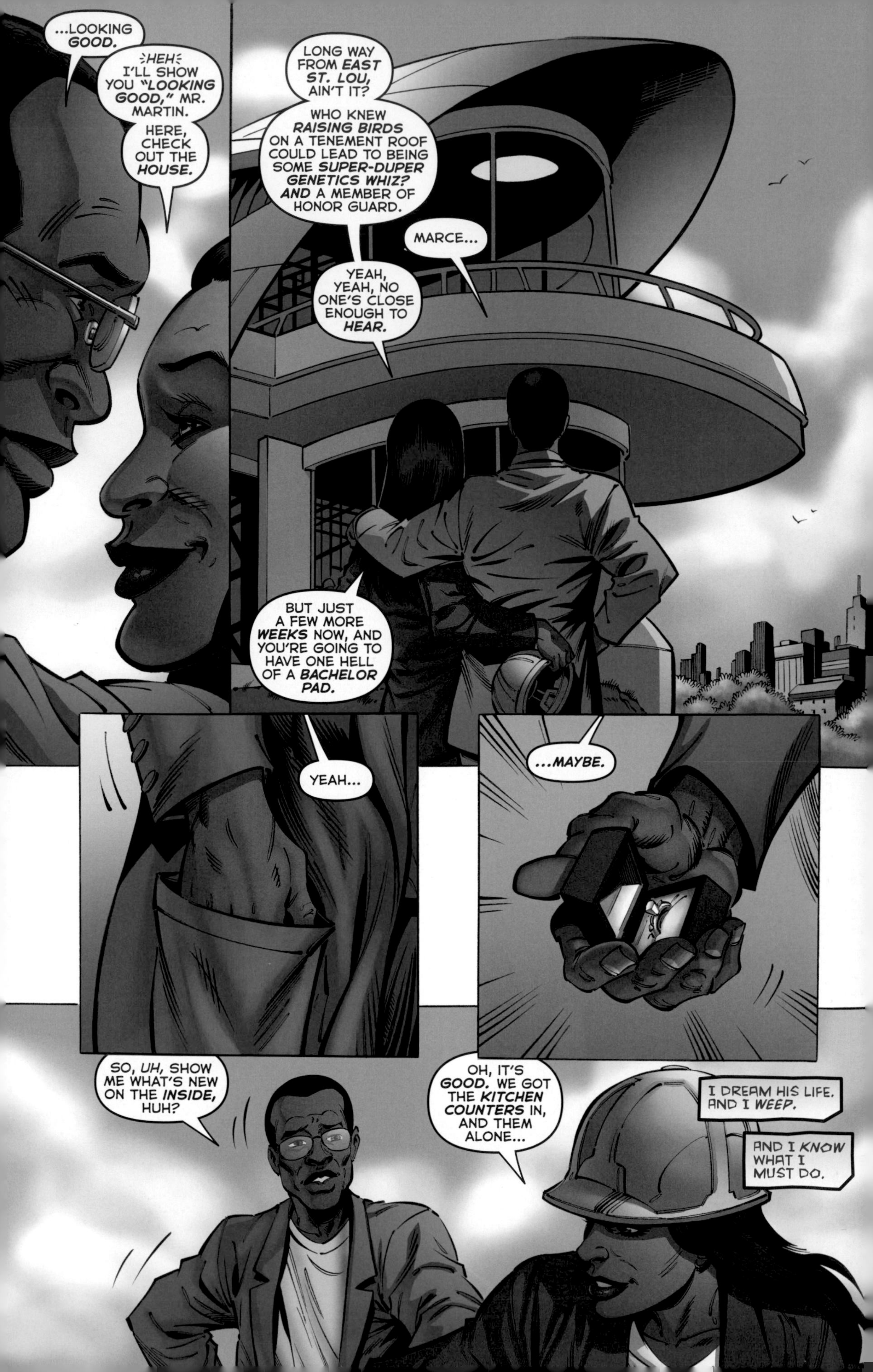
...LOOKING GOOD.
HEH I'LL SHOW YOU "LOOKING GOOD," MR. MARTIN.
HERE, CHECK OUT THE HOUSE.
LONG WAY FROM EAST ST. LOU, AIN'T IT?
WHO KNEW RAISING BIRDS ON A TENEMENT ROOF COULD LEAD TO BEING SOME SUPER-DUPER GENETICS WHIZ? AND A MEMBER OF HONOR GUARD.
MARCE...
YEAH, YEAH, NO ONE'S CLOSE ENOUGH TO HEAR.
BUT JUST A FEW MORE WEEKS NOW, AND YOU'RE GOING TO HAVE ONE HELL OF A BACHELOR PAD.
YEAH...
...MAYBE.
SO, UH, SHOW ME WHAT'S NEW ON THE INSIDE, HUH?
OH, IT'S GOOD. WE GOT THE KITCHEN COUNTERS IN, AND THEM ALONE...
I DREAM HIS LIFE. AND I WEEP.
AND I KNOW WHAT I MUST DO.

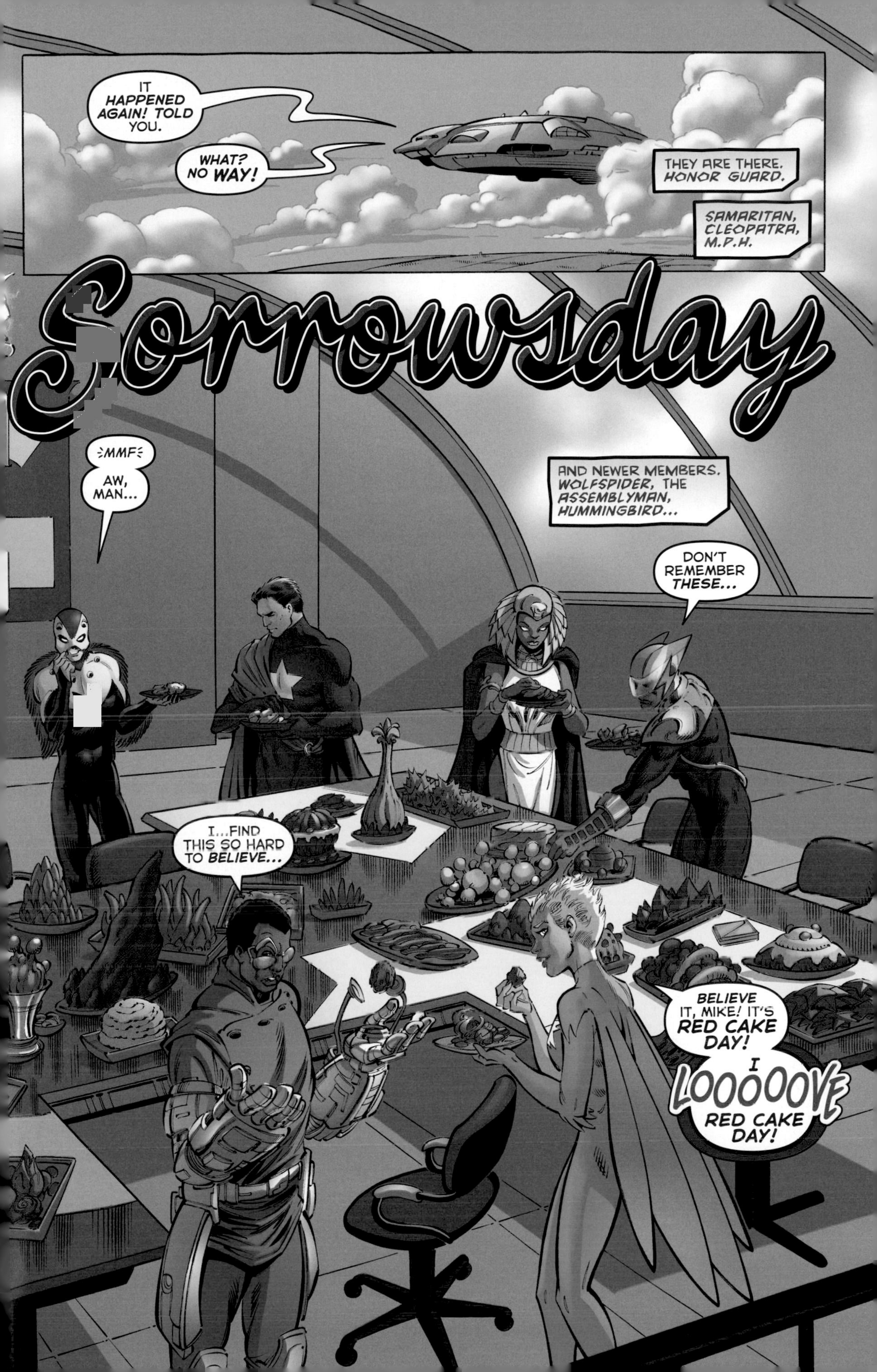

IT HAPPENED AGAIN! TOLD YOU.
WHAT? NO WAY!
THEY ARE THERE. HONOR GUARD.
SAMARITAN, CLEOPATRA, M.P.H.
Sorrowsday
MMF
AW, MAN...
AND NEWER MEMBERS. WOLFSPIDER, THE ASSEMBLYMAN, HUMMINGBIRD...
DON'T REMEMBER THESE...
I...FIND THIS SO HARD TO BELIEVE...
BELIEVE IT, MIKE! IT'S RED CAKE DAY!
I LOOOOOVE RED CAKE DAY!

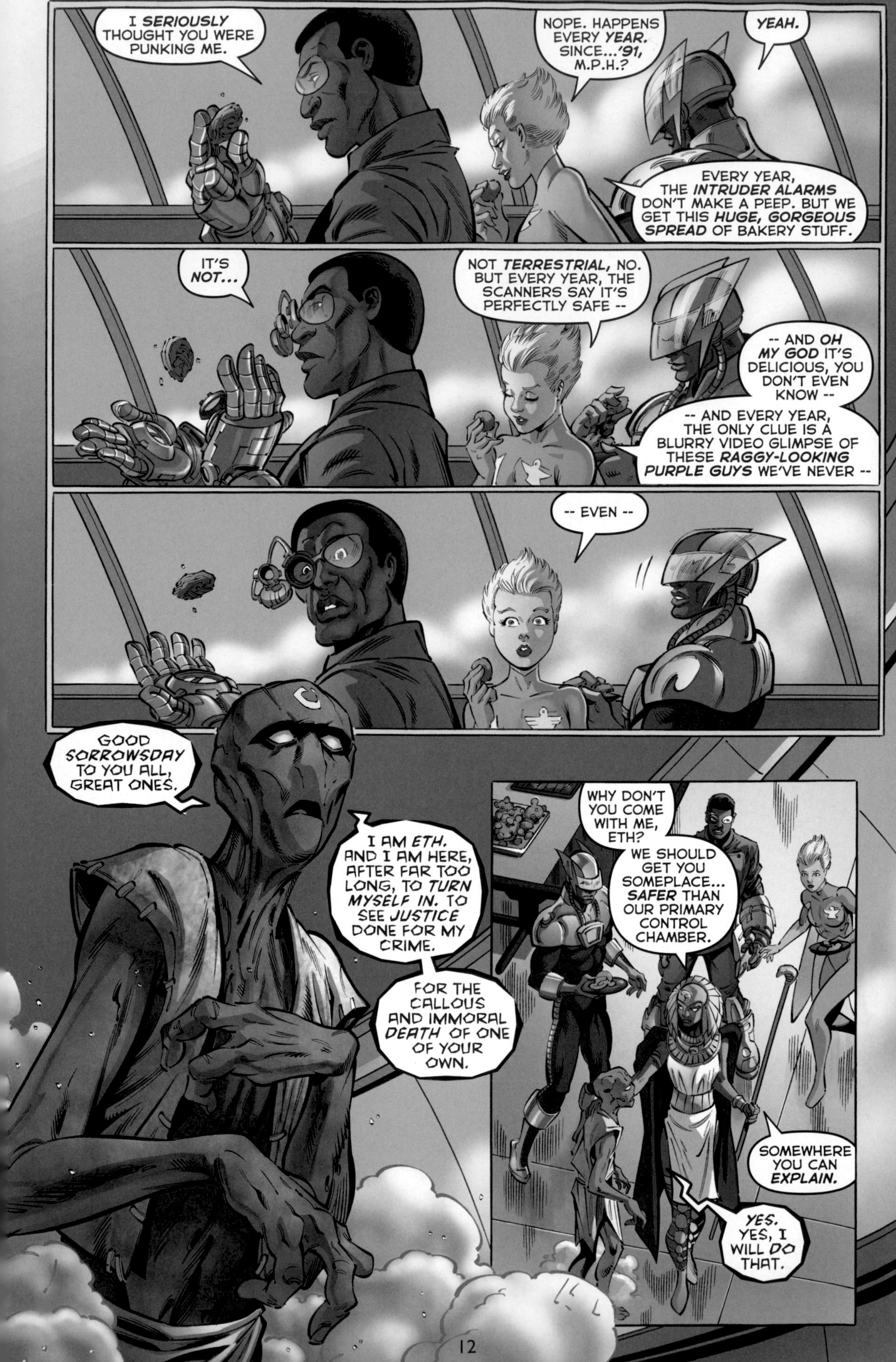

I *SERIOUSLY* THOUGHT YOU WERE PUNKING ME.
NOPE. HAPPENS EVERY *YEAR.* SINCE...'91, M.P.H.?
YEAH.
EVERY YEAR, THE *INTRUDER ALARMS* DON'T MAKE A PEEP. BUT WE GET THIS *HUGE, GORGEOUS SPREAD* OF BAKERY STUFF.
IT'S *NOT...*
NOT *TERRESTRIAL,* NO. BUT EVERY YEAR, THE SCANNERS SAY IT'S PERFECTLY SAFE --
-- AND *OH MY GOD* IT'S DELICIOUS, YOU DON'T EVEN KNOW --
-- AND EVERY YEAR, THE ONLY CLUE IS A BLURRY VIDEO GLIMPSE OF THESE *RAGGY-LOOKING PURPLE GUYS* WE'VE NEVER --
-- EVEN --
GOOD *SORROWSDAY* TO YOU ALL, GREAT ONES.
I AM *ETH.* AND I AM HERE, AFTER FAR TOO LONG, TO *TURN MYSELF IN.* TO SEE *JUSTICE* DONE FOR MY CRIME.
FOR THE CALLOUS AND IMMORAL *DEATH* OF ONE OF YOUR OWN.
WHY DON'T YOU COME WITH ME, ETH?
WE SHOULD GET YOU SOMEPLACE... *SAFER* THAN OUR PRIMARY CONTROL CHAMBER.
SOMEWHERE YOU CAN *EXPLAIN.*
YES. YES, I WILL *DO* THAT.

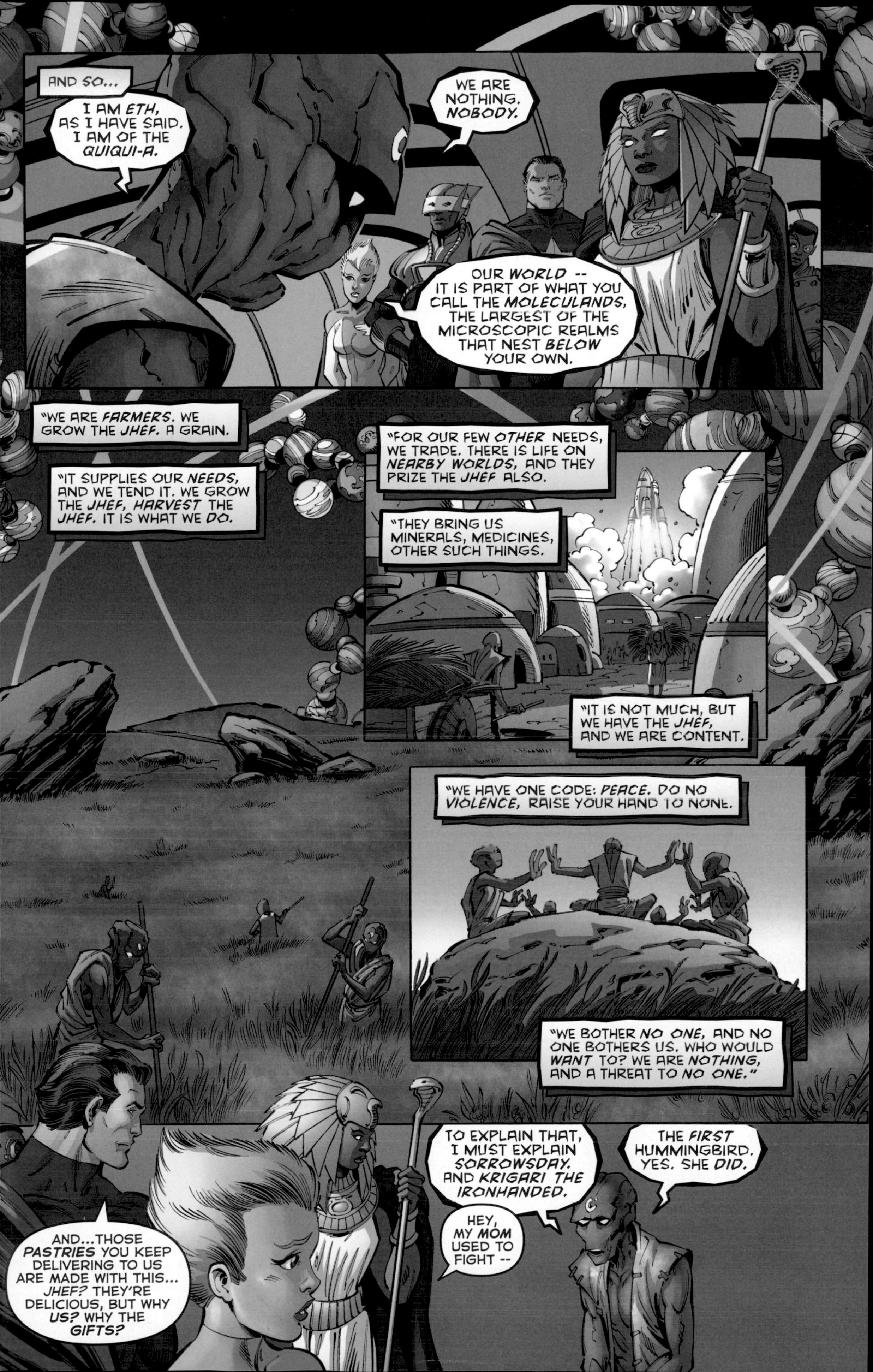
AND SO...
I AM ETH, AS I HAVE SAID. I AM OF THE QUIQUI-A.
WE ARE NOTHING. NOBODY.
OUR WORLD -- IT IS PART OF WHAT YOU CALL THE MOLECULANDS, THE LARGEST OF THE MICROSCOPIC REALMS THAT NEST BELOW YOUR OWN.
"WE ARE FARMERS. WE GROW THE JHEF. A GRAIN.
"IT SUPPLIES OUR NEEDS, AND WE TEND IT. WE GROW THE JHEF, HARVEST THE JHEF. IT IS WHAT WE DO.
"FOR OUR FEW OTHER NEEDS, WE TRADE. THERE IS LIFE ON NEARBY WORLDS, AND THEY PRIZE THE JHEF ALSO.
"THEY BRING US MINERALS, MEDICINES, OTHER SUCH THINGS.
"IT IS NOT MUCH, BUT WE HAVE THE JHEF, AND WE ARE CONTENT.
"WE HAVE ONE CODE: PEACE. DO NO VIOLENCE, RAISE YOUR HAND TO NONE.
"WE BOTHER NO ONE, AND NO ONE BOTHERS US. WHO WOULD WANT TO? WE ARE NOTHING, AND A THREAT TO NO ONE."
AND...THOSE PASTRIES YOU KEEP DELIVERING TO US ARE MADE WITH THIS... JHEF? THEY'RE DELICIOUS, BUT WHY US? WHY THE GIFTS?
TO EXPLAIN THAT, I MUST EXPLAIN SORROWSDAY. AND KRIGARI THE IRONHANDED.
HEY, MY MOM USED TO FIGHT --
THE FIRST HUMMINGBIRD. YES. SHE DID.

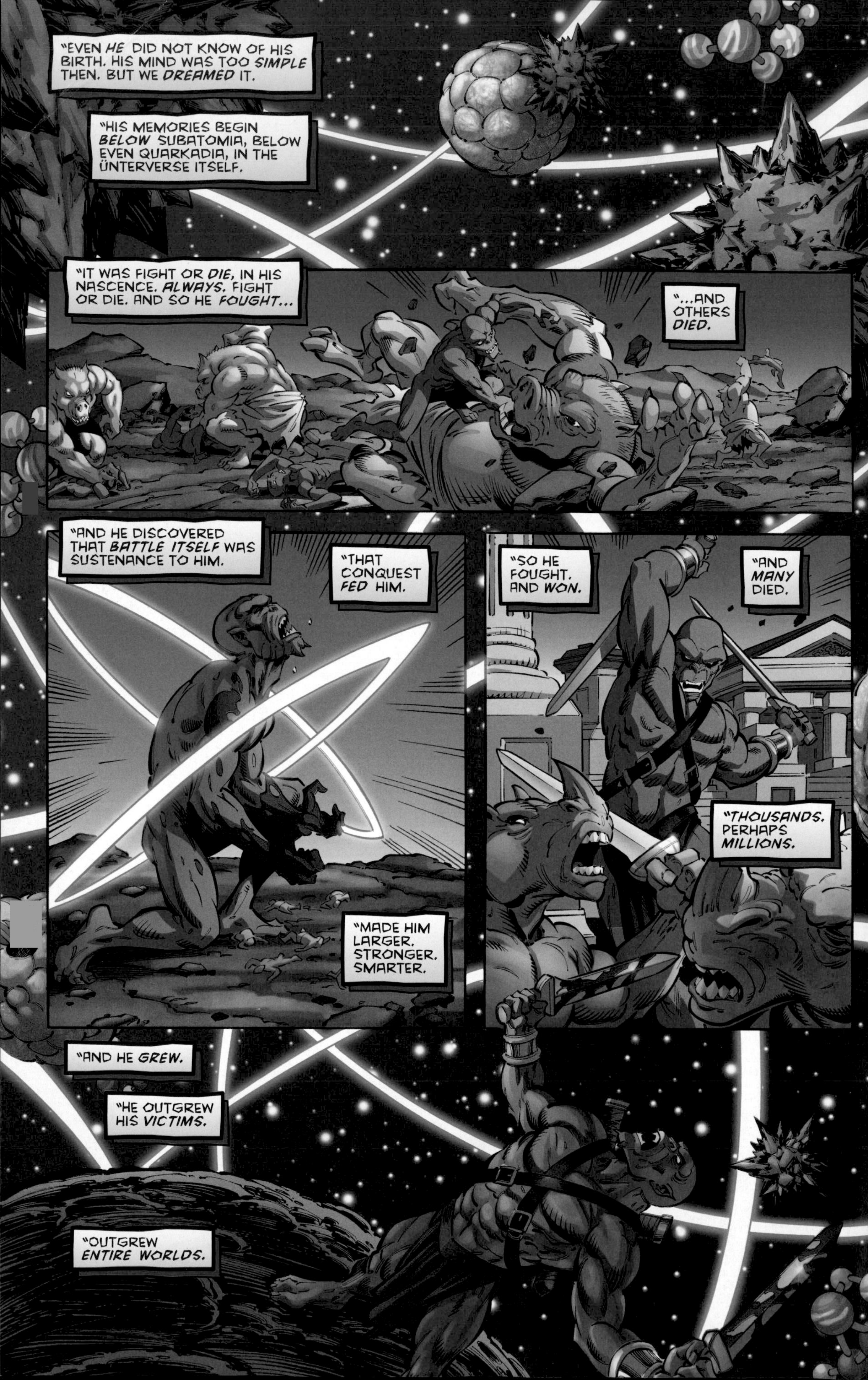
"EVEN HE DID NOT KNOW OF HIS BIRTH. HIS MIND WAS TOO SIMPLE THEN. BUT WE DREAMED IT.
"HIS MEMORIES BEGIN BELOW SUBATOMIA, BELOW EVEN QUARKADIA, IN THE ÜNTERVERSE ITSELF.
"IT WAS FIGHT OR DIE, IN HIS NASCENCE. ALWAYS. FIGHT OR DIE. AND SO HE FOUGHT...
"...AND OTHERS DIED.
"AND HE DISCOVERED THAT BATTLE ITSELF WAS SUSTENANCE TO HIM.
"THAT CONQUEST FED HIM.
"MADE HIM LARGER. STRONGER. SMARTER.
"SO HE FOUGHT. AND WON.
"AND MANY DIED.
"THOUSANDS. PERHAPS MILLIONS.
"AND HE GREW.
"HE OUTGREW HIS VICTIMS.
"OUTGREW ENTIRE WORLDS.

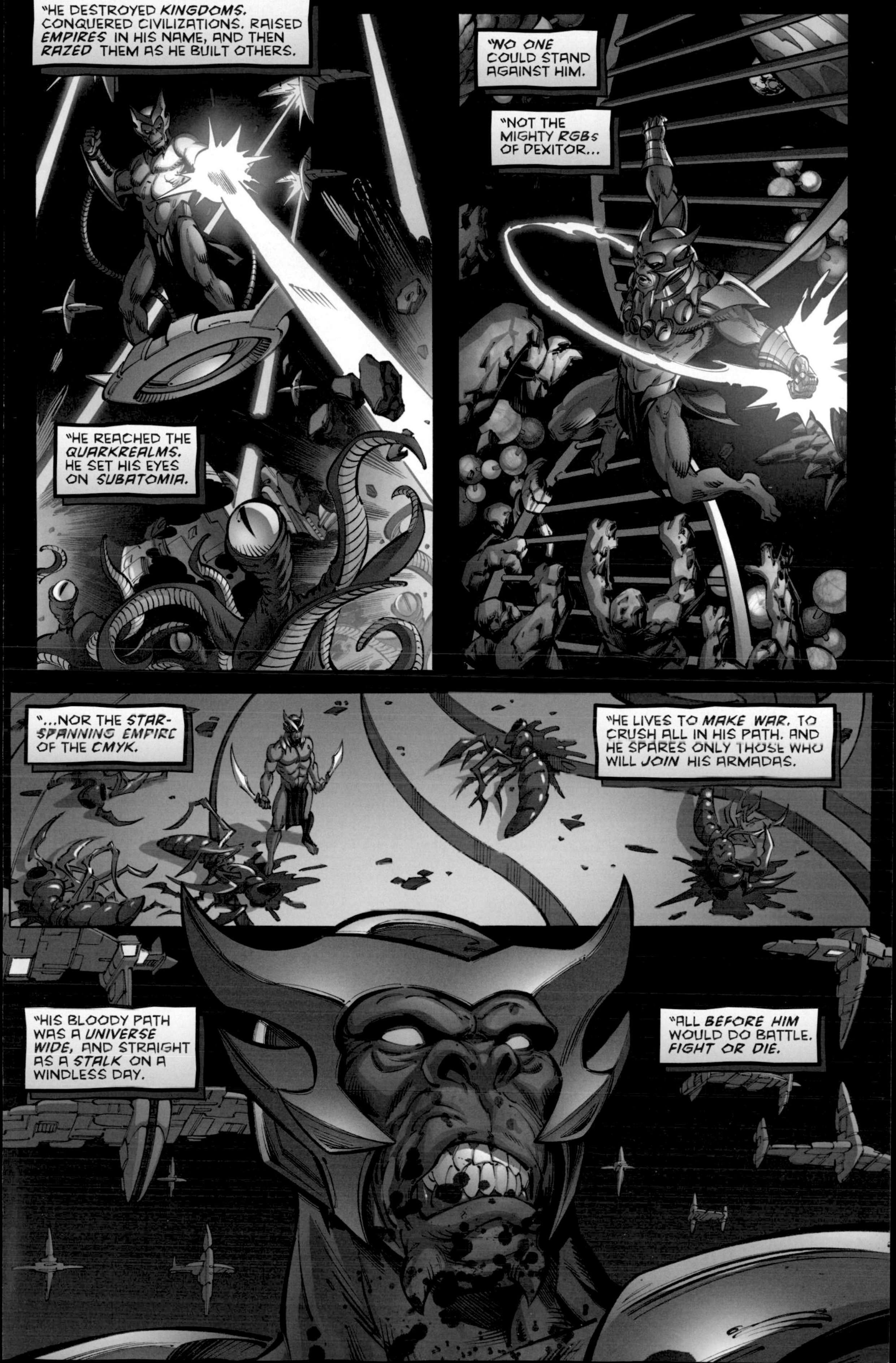
"HE DESTROYED KINGDOMS. CONQUERED CIVILIZATIONS. RAISED EMPIRES IN HIS NAME, AND THEN RAZED THEM AS HE BUILT OTHERS.
"HE REACHED THE QUARKREALMS. HE SET HIS EYES ON SUBATOMIA.
"NO ONE COULD STAND AGAINST HIM.
"NOT THE MIGHTY RGBs OF DEXITOR...
"...NOR THE STAR-SPANNING EMPIRE OF THE CMYK.
"HE LIVES TO MAKE WAR. TO CRUSH ALL IN HIS PATH. AND HE SPARES ONLY THOSE WHO WILL JOIN HIS ARMADAS.
"HIS BLOODY PATH WAS A UNIVERSE WIDE, AND STRAIGHT AS A STALK ON A WINDLESS DAY.
"ALL BEFORE HIM WOULD DO BATTLE. FIGHT OR DIE.

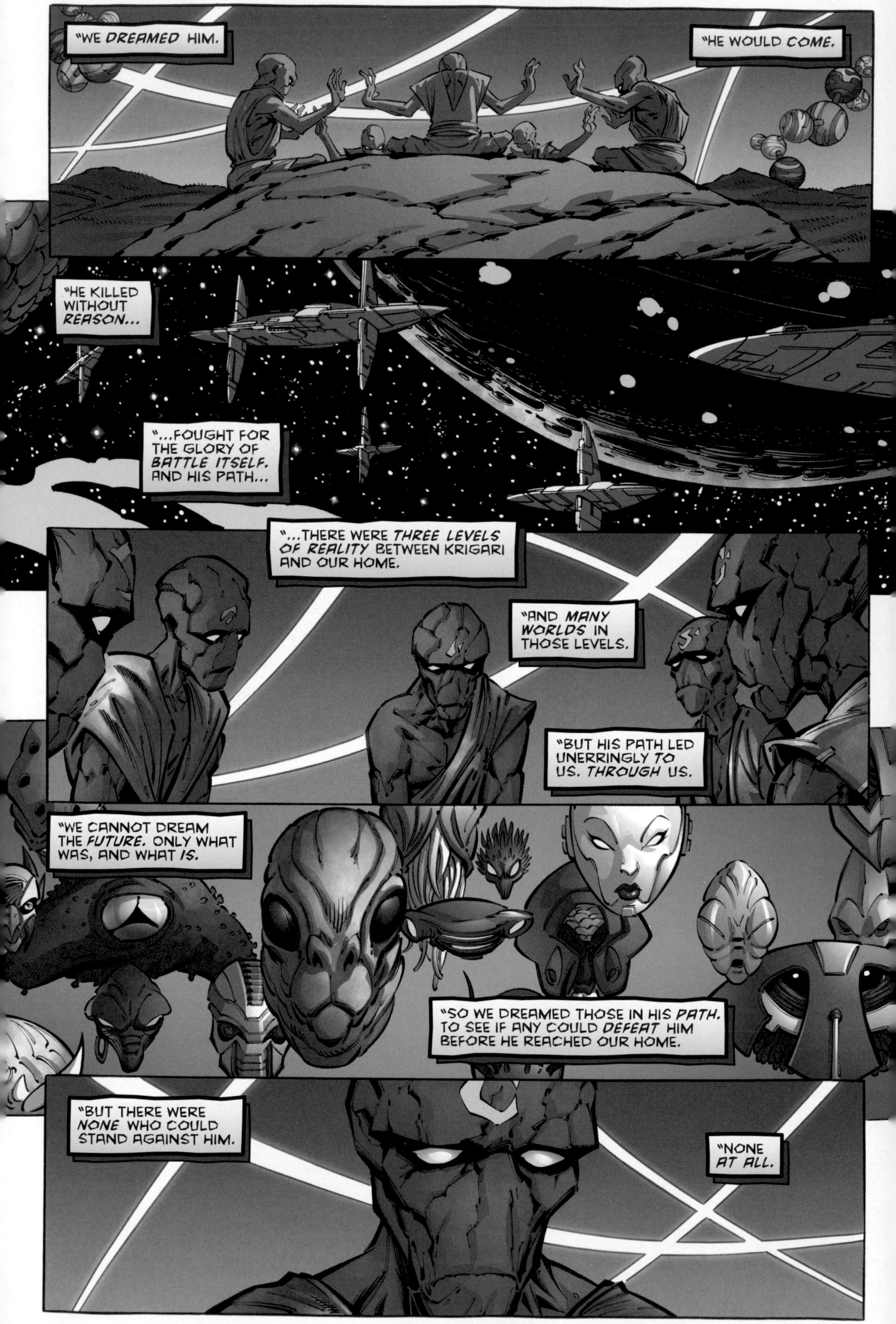
"WE DREAMED HIM.
"HE WOULD COME.
"HE KILLED WITHOUT REASON...
"...FOUGHT FOR THE GLORY OF BATTLE ITSELF. AND HIS PATH...
"...THERE WERE THREE LEVELS OF REALITY BETWEEN KRIGARI AND OUR HOME.
"AND MANY WORLDS IN THOSE LEVELS.
"BUT HIS PATH LED UNERRINGLY TO US. THROUGH US.
"WE CANNOT DREAM THE FUTURE. ONLY WHAT WAS, AND WHAT IS.
"SO WE DREAMED THOSE IN HIS PATH. TO SEE IF ANY COULD DEFEAT HIM BEFORE HE REACHED OUR HOME.
"BUT THERE WERE NONE WHO COULD STAND AGAINST HIM.
"NONE AT ALL.

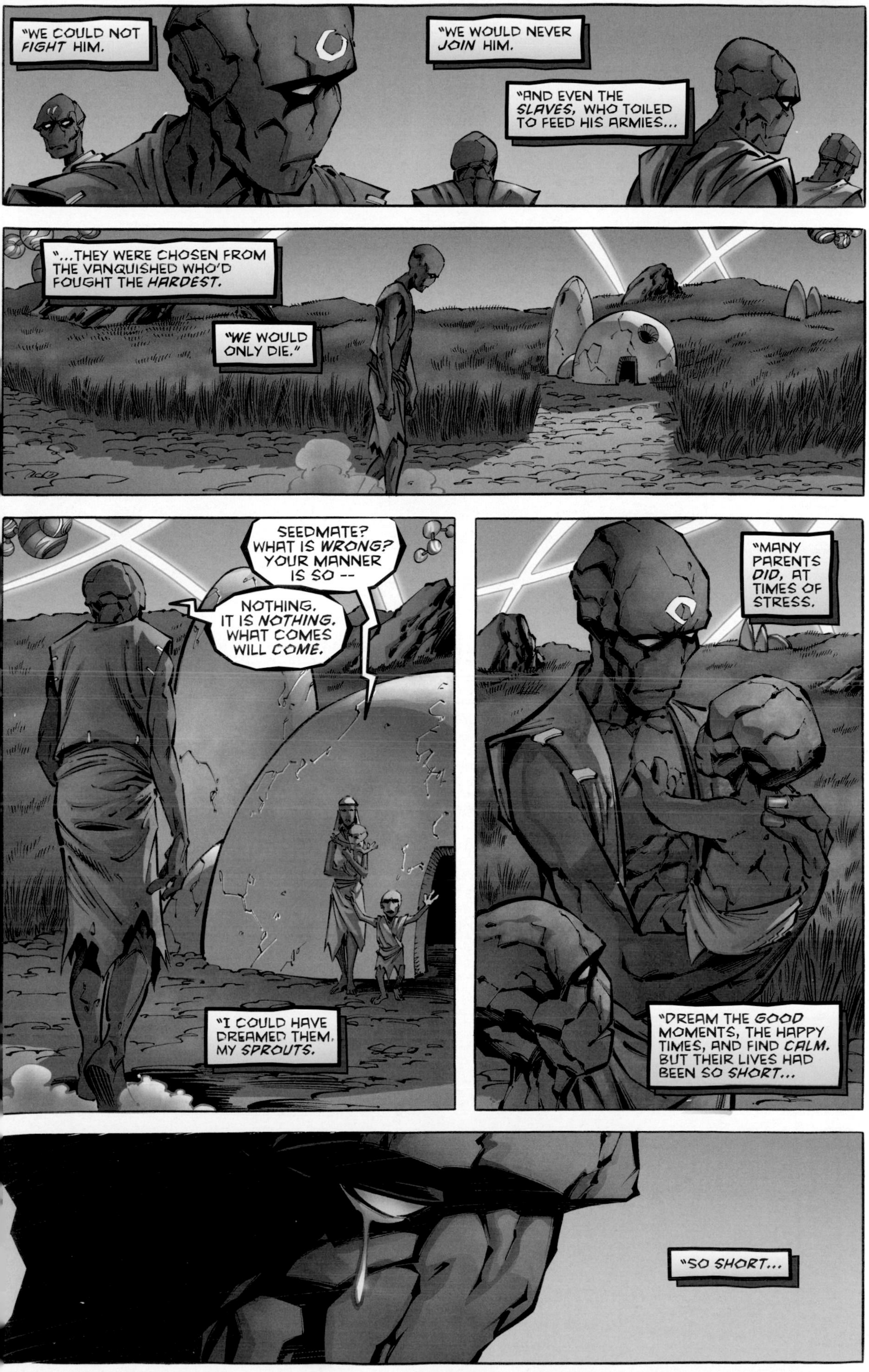
"WE COULD NOT FIGHT HIM.
"WE WOULD NEVER JOIN HIM.
"AND EVEN THE SLAVES, WHO TOILED TO FEED HIS ARMIES...
"...THEY WERE CHOSEN FROM THE VANQUISHED WHO'D FOUGHT THE HARDEST.
"WE WOULD ONLY DIE."
SEEDMATE? WHAT IS WRONG? YOUR MANNER IS SO --
NOTHING. IT IS NOTHING. WHAT COMES WILL COME.
"I COULD HAVE DREAMED THEM, MY SPROUTS.
"MANY PARENTS DID, AT TIMES OF STRESS.
"DREAM THE GOOD MOMENTS, THE HAPPY TIMES, AND FIND CALM. BUT THEIR LIVES HAD BEEN SO SHORT...
"SO SHORT...

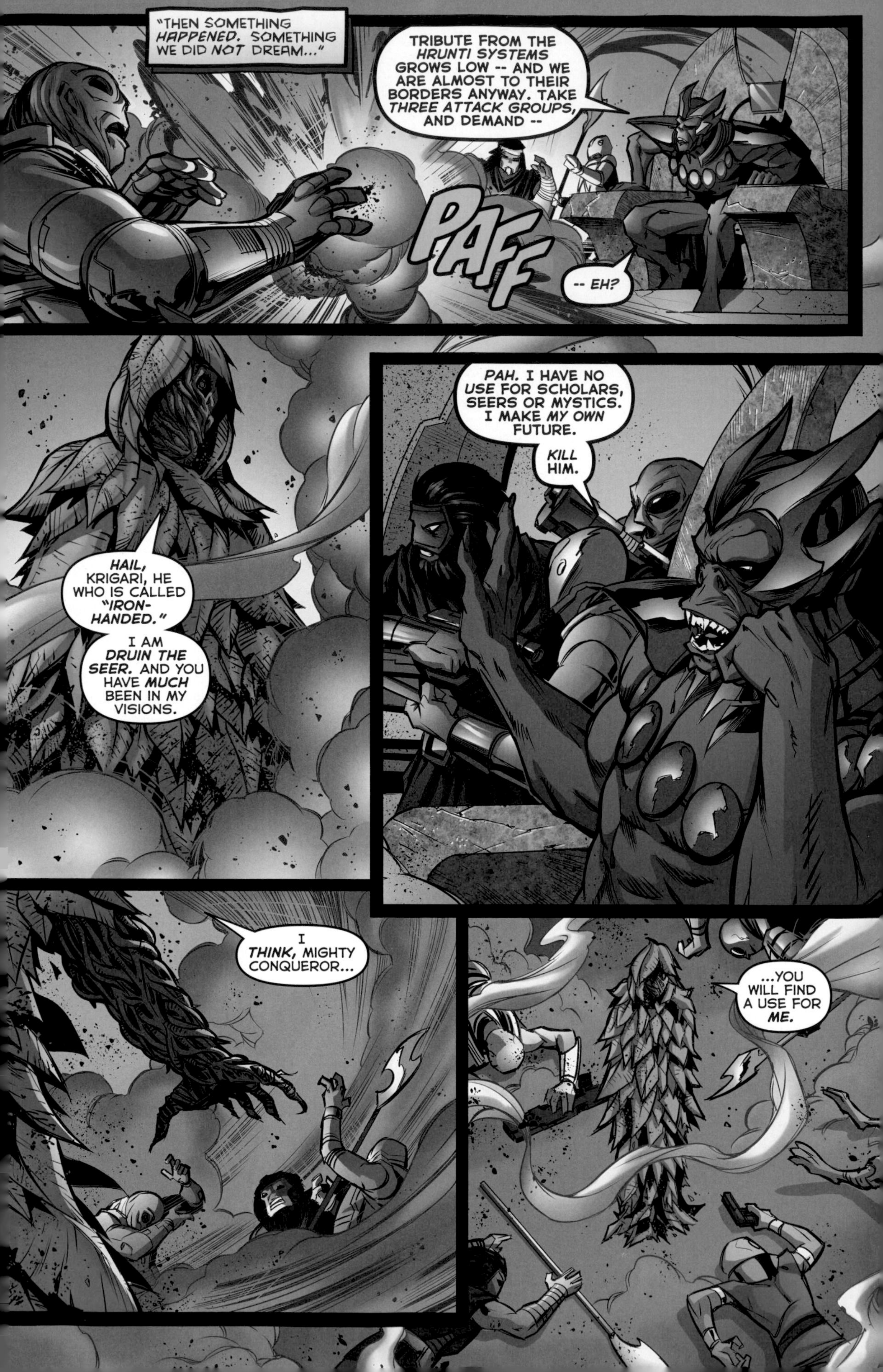
"THEN SOMETHING HAPPENED. SOMETHING WE DID NOT DREAM..."
TRIBUTE FROM THE HRUNTI SYSTEMS GROWS LOW -- AND WE ARE ALMOST TO THEIR BORDERS ANYWAY. TAKE THREE ATTACK GROUPS, AND DEMAND --
PAFF
-- EH?
HAIL, KRIGARI, HE WHO IS CALLED "IRON-HANDED."
I AM DRUIN THE SEER. AND YOU HAVE MUCH BEEN IN MY VISIONS.
PAH. I HAVE NO USE FOR SCHOLARS, SEERS OR MYSTICS. I MAKE MY OWN FUTURE.
KILL HIM.
I THINK, MIGHTY CONQUEROR...
...YOU WILL FIND A USE FOR ME.

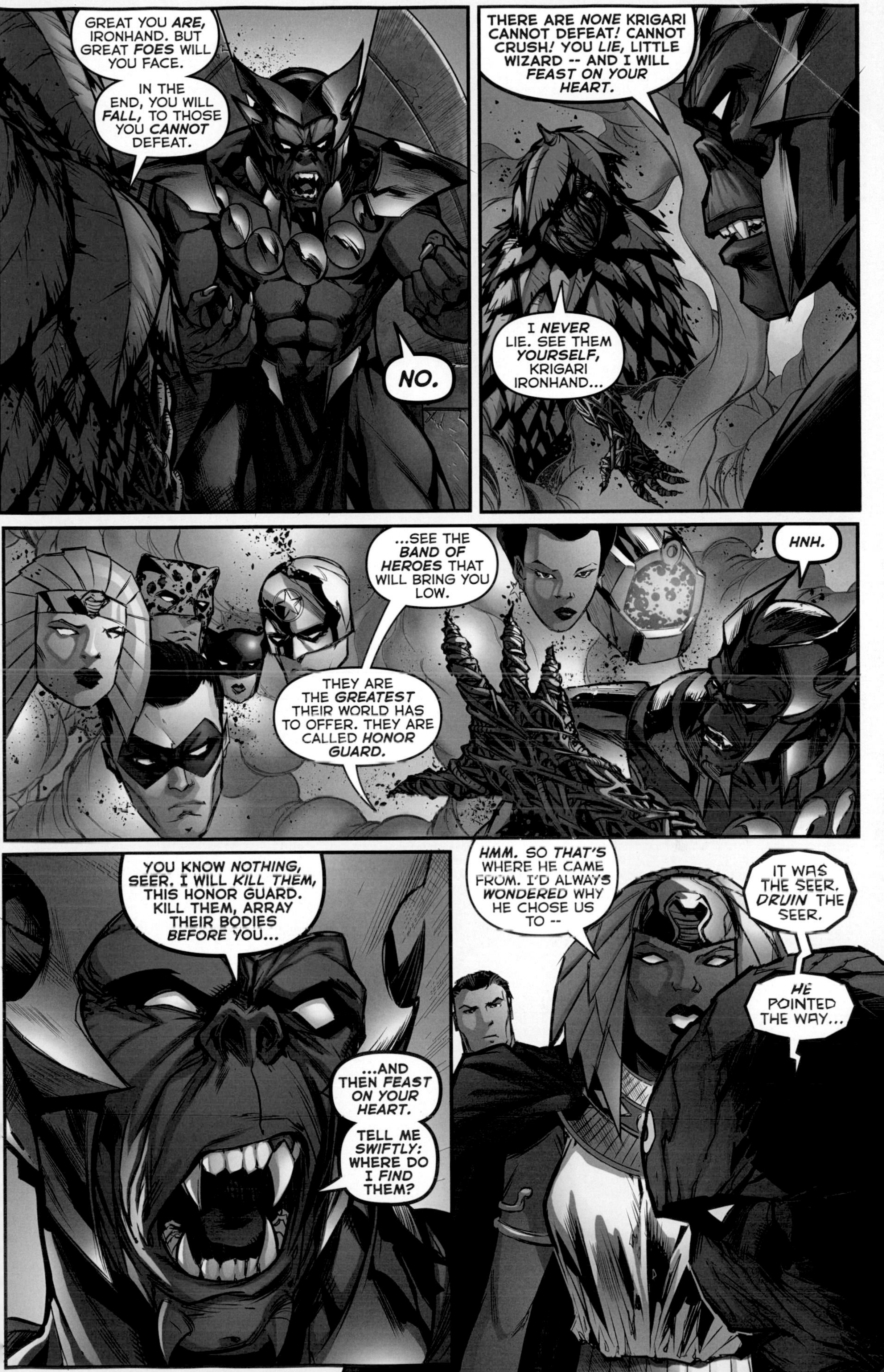
GREAT YOU ARE, IRONHAND. BUT GREAT FOES WILL YOU FACE.
IN THE END, YOU WILL FALL, TO THOSE YOU CANNOT DEFEAT.
NO.
THERE ARE NONE KRIGARI CANNOT DEFEAT! CANNOT CRUSH! YOU LIE, LITTLE WIZARD -- AND I WILL FEAST ON YOUR HEART.
I NEVER LIE. SEE THEM YOURSELF, KRIGARI IRONHAND...
...SEE THE BAND OF HEROES THAT WILL BRING YOU LOW.
THEY ARE THE GREATEST THEIR WORLD HAS TO OFFER. THEY ARE CALLED HONOR GUARD.
HNH.
YOU KNOW NOTHING, SEER. I WILL KILL THEM, THIS HONOR GUARD. KILL THEM, ARRAY THEIR BODIES BEFORE YOU...
...AND THEN FEAST ON YOUR HEART.
TELL ME SWIFTLY: WHERE DO I FIND THEM?
HMM. SO THAT'S WHERE HE CAME FROM. I'D ALWAYS WONDERED WHY HE CHOSE US TO --
IT WAS THE SEER. DRUIN THE SEER.
HE POINTED THE WAY...

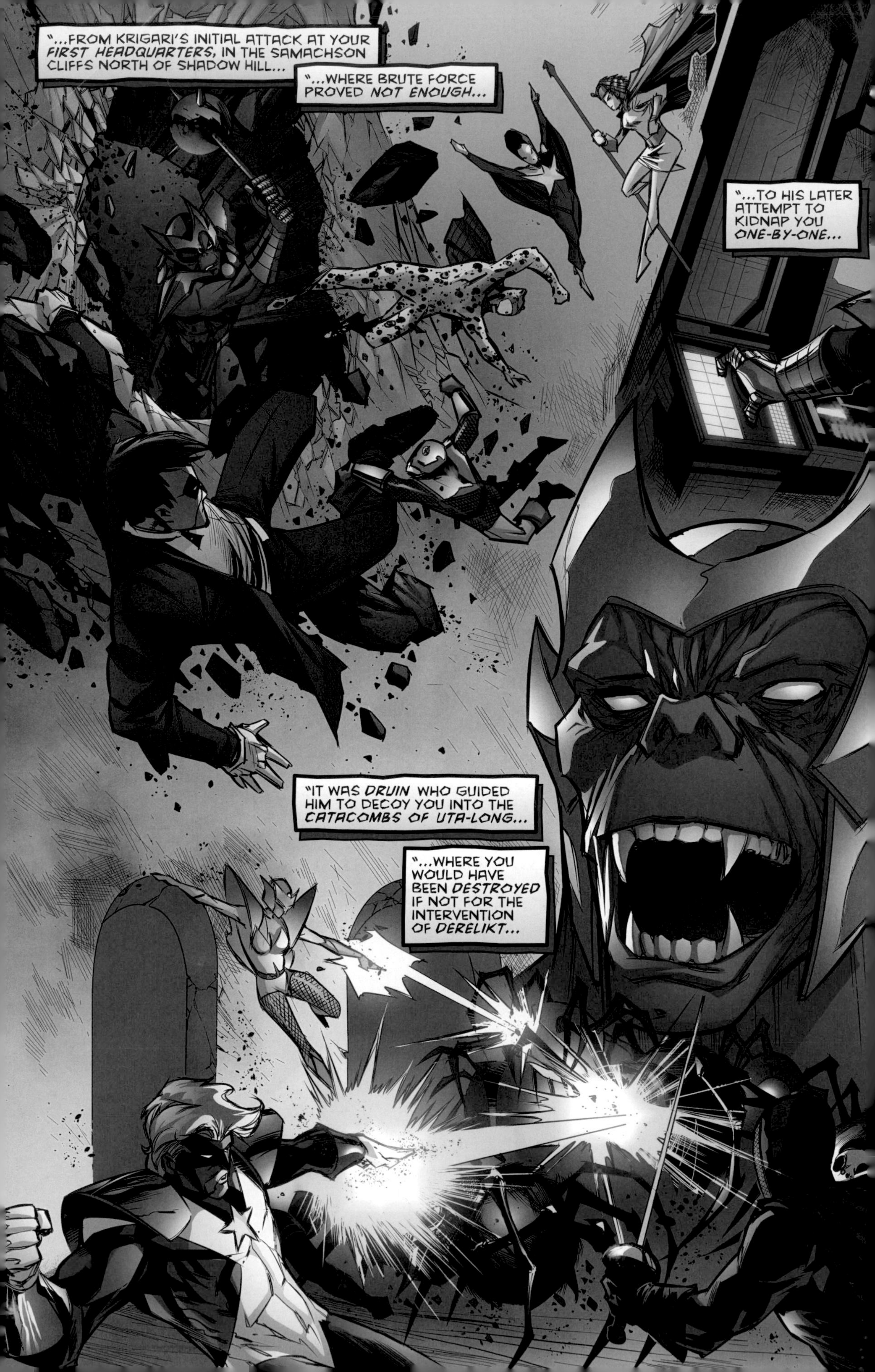
"...FROM KRIGARI'S INITIAL ATTACK AT YOUR FIRST HEADQUARTERS, IN THE SAMACHSON CLIFFS NORTH OF SHADOW HILL...
"...WHERE BRUTE FORCE PROVED NOT ENOUGH...
"...TO HIS LATER ATTEMPT TO KIDNAP YOU ONE-BY-ONE...
"IT WAS DRUIN WHO GUIDED HIM TO DECOY YOU INTO THE CATACOMBS OF UTA-LONG...
"...WHERE YOU WOULD HAVE BEEN DESTROYED IF NOT FOR THE INTERVENTION OF DERELIKT...

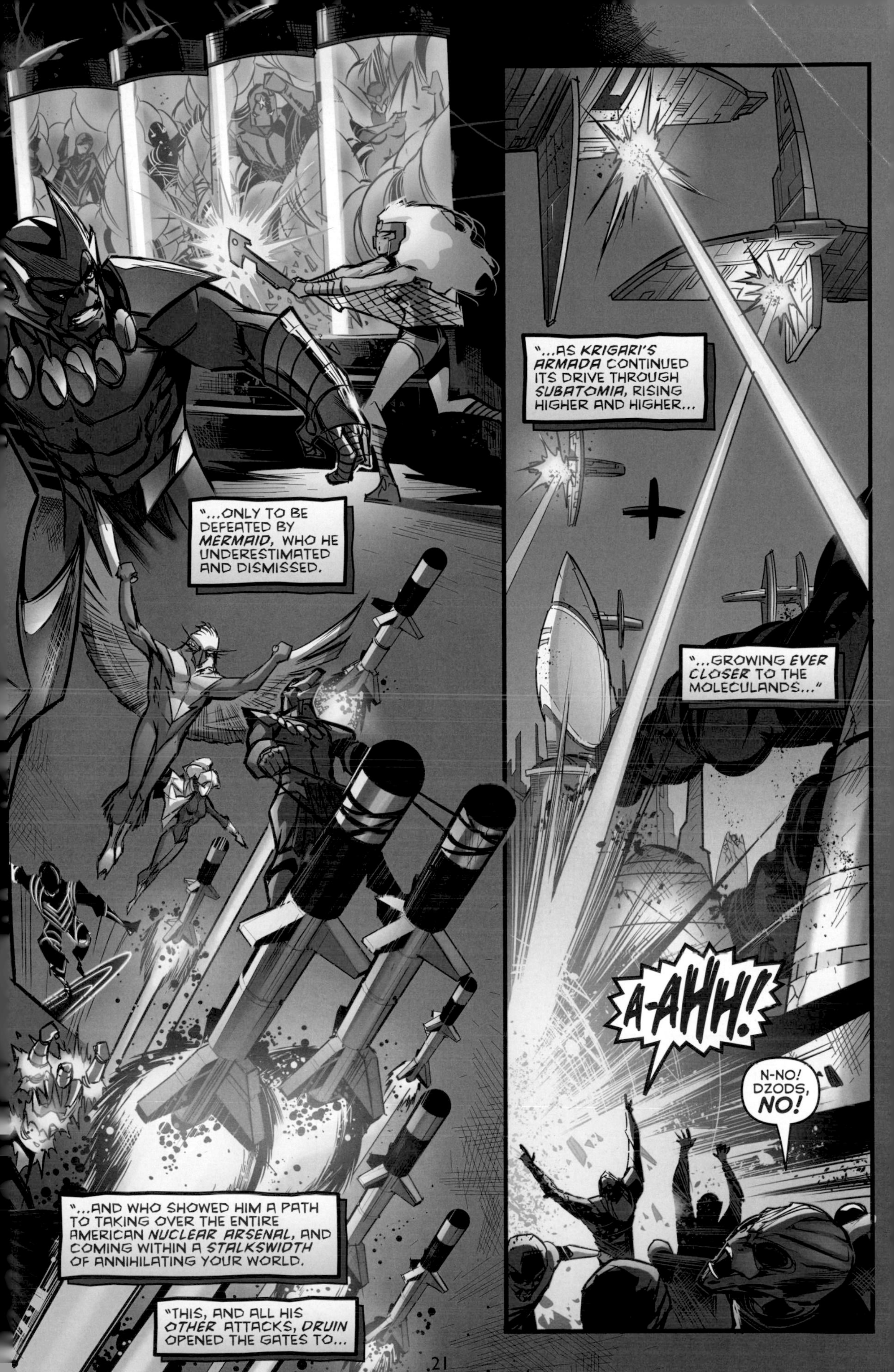
"...ONLY TO BE DEFEATED BY MERMAID, WHO HE UNDERESTIMATED AND DISMISSED.
"...AND WHO SHOWED HIM A PATH TO TAKING OVER THE ENTIRE AMERICAN NUCLEAR ARSENAL, AND COMING WITHIN A STALKSWIDTH OF ANNIHILATING YOUR WORLD.
"THIS, AND ALL HIS OTHER ATTACKS, DRUIN OPENED THE GATES TO...
"...AS KRIGARI'S ARMADA CONTINUED ITS DRIVE THROUGH SUBATOMIA, RISING HIGHER AND HIGHER...
"...GROWING EVER CLOSER TO THE MOLECULANDS..."
A-AHH!
N-NO! DZODS, NO!

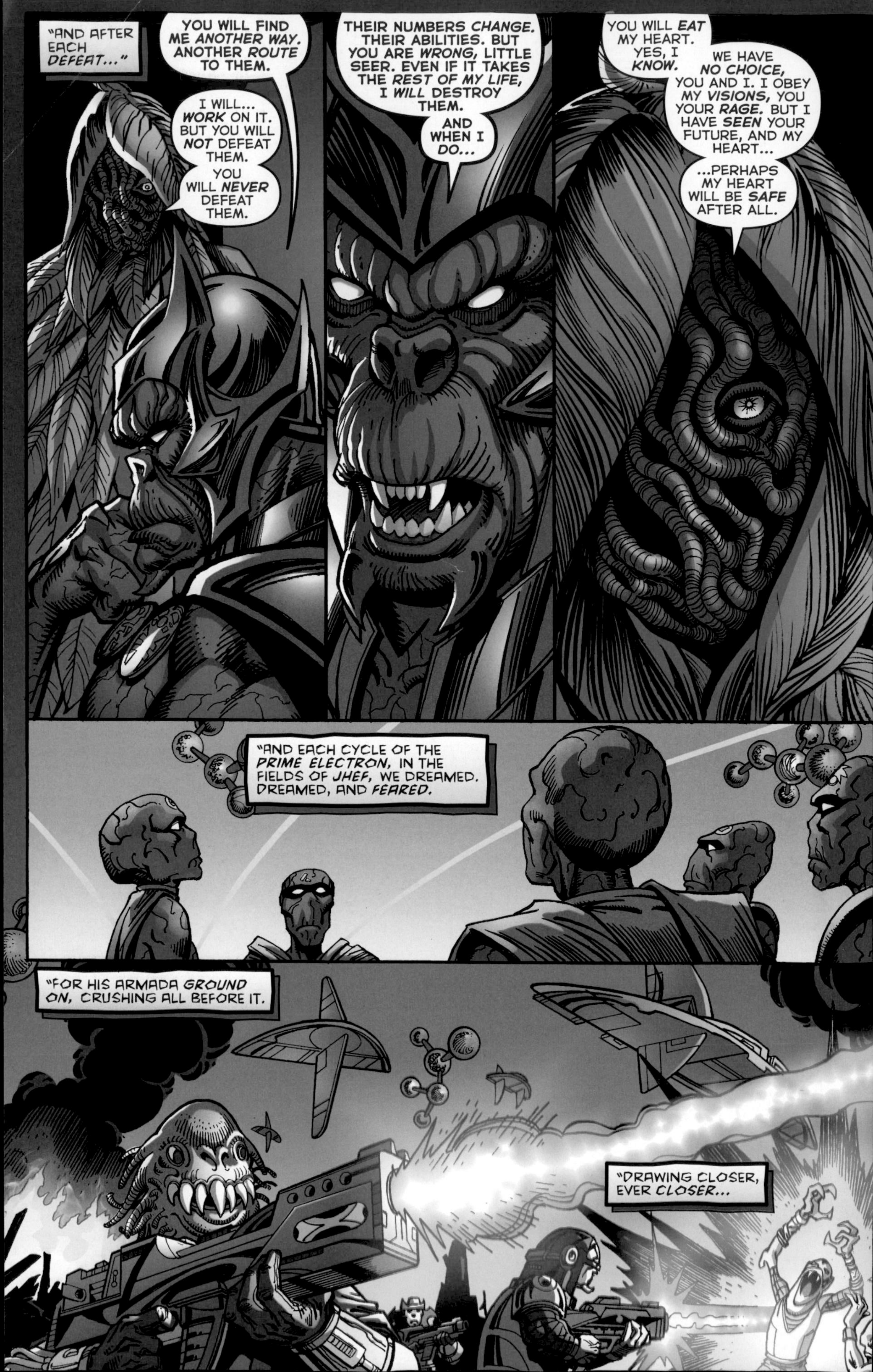
"AND AFTER EACH DEFEAT..."
YOU WILL FIND ME ANOTHER WAY. ANOTHER ROUTE TO THEM.
I WILL... WORK ON IT. BUT YOU WILL NOT DEFEAT THEM.
YOU WILL NEVER DEFEAT THEM.
THEIR NUMBERS CHANGE. THEIR ABILITIES. BUT YOU ARE WRONG, LITTLE SEER. EVEN IF IT TAKES THE REST OF MY LIFE, I WILL DESTROY THEM.
AND WHEN I DO...
YOU WILL EAT MY HEART. YES, I KNOW.
WE HAVE NO CHOICE, YOU AND I. I OBEY MY VISIONS, YOU YOUR RAGE. BUT I HAVE SEEN YOUR FUTURE, AND MY HEART...
...PERHAPS MY HEART WILL BE SAFE AFTER ALL.
"AND EACH CYCLE OF THE PRIME ELECTRON, IN THE FIELDS OF JHEF, WE DREAMED. DREAMED, AND FEARED.
"FOR HIS ARMADA GROUND ON, CRUSHING ALL BEFORE IT.
"DRAWING CLOSER, EVER CLOSER...

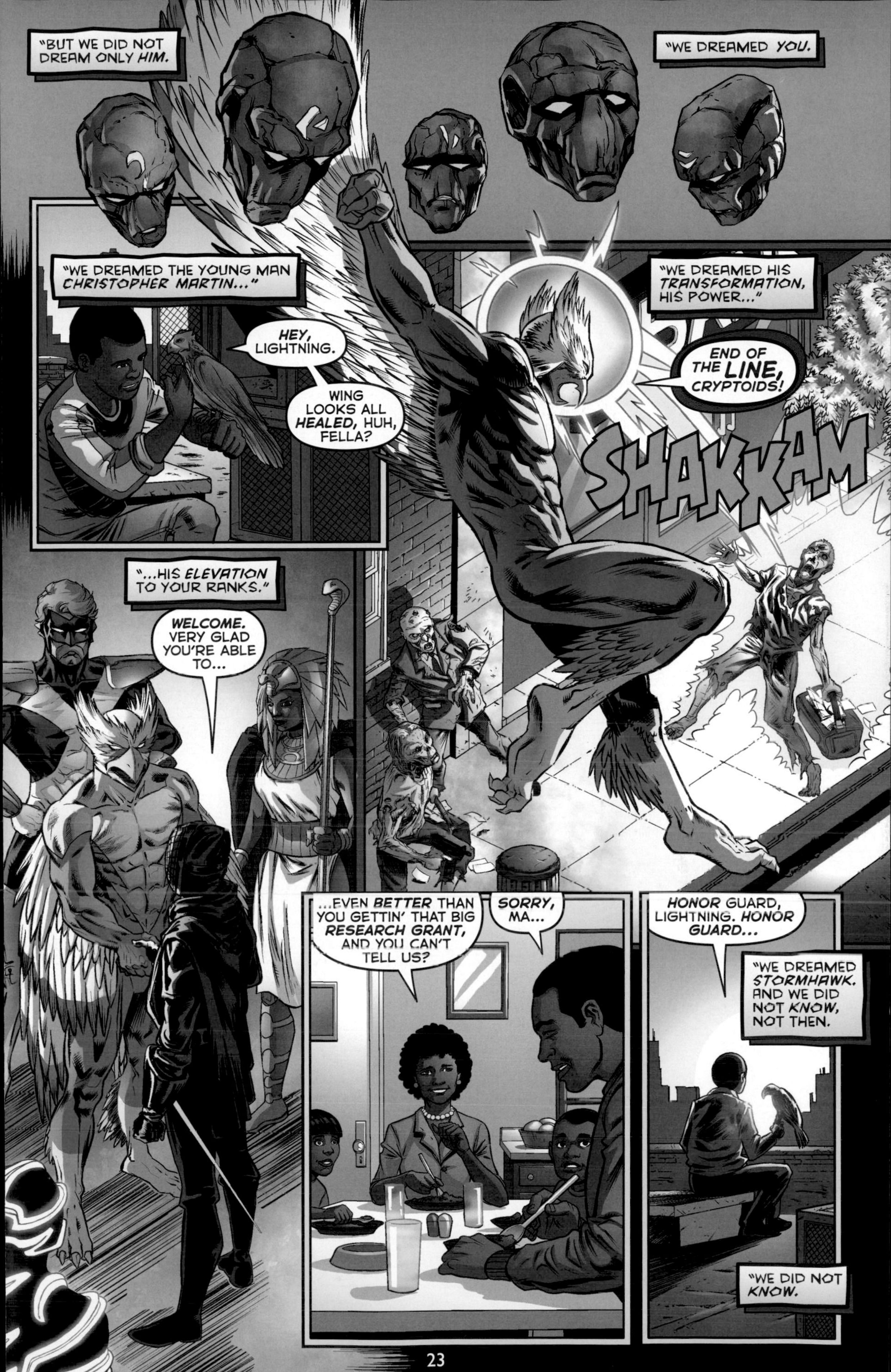
"BUT WE DID NOT DREAM ONLY HIM.
"WE DREAMED YOU.
"WE DREAMED THE YOUNG MAN CHRISTOPHER MARTIN..."
HEY, LIGHTNING.
WING LOOKS ALL HEALED, HUH, FELLA?
"WE DREAMED HIS TRANSFORMATION, HIS POWER..."
END OF THE LINE, CRYPTOIDS!
SHAKKAM
"...HIS ELEVATION TO YOUR RANKS."
WELCOME. VERY GLAD YOU'RE ABLE TO...
...EVEN BETTER THAN YOU GETTIN' THAT BIG RESEARCH GRANT, AND YOU CAN'T TELL US?
SORRY, MA...
HONOR GUARD, LIGHTNING. HONOR GUARD...
"WE DREAMED STORMHAWK. AND WE DID NOT KNOW, NOT THEN.
"WE DID NOT KNOW.

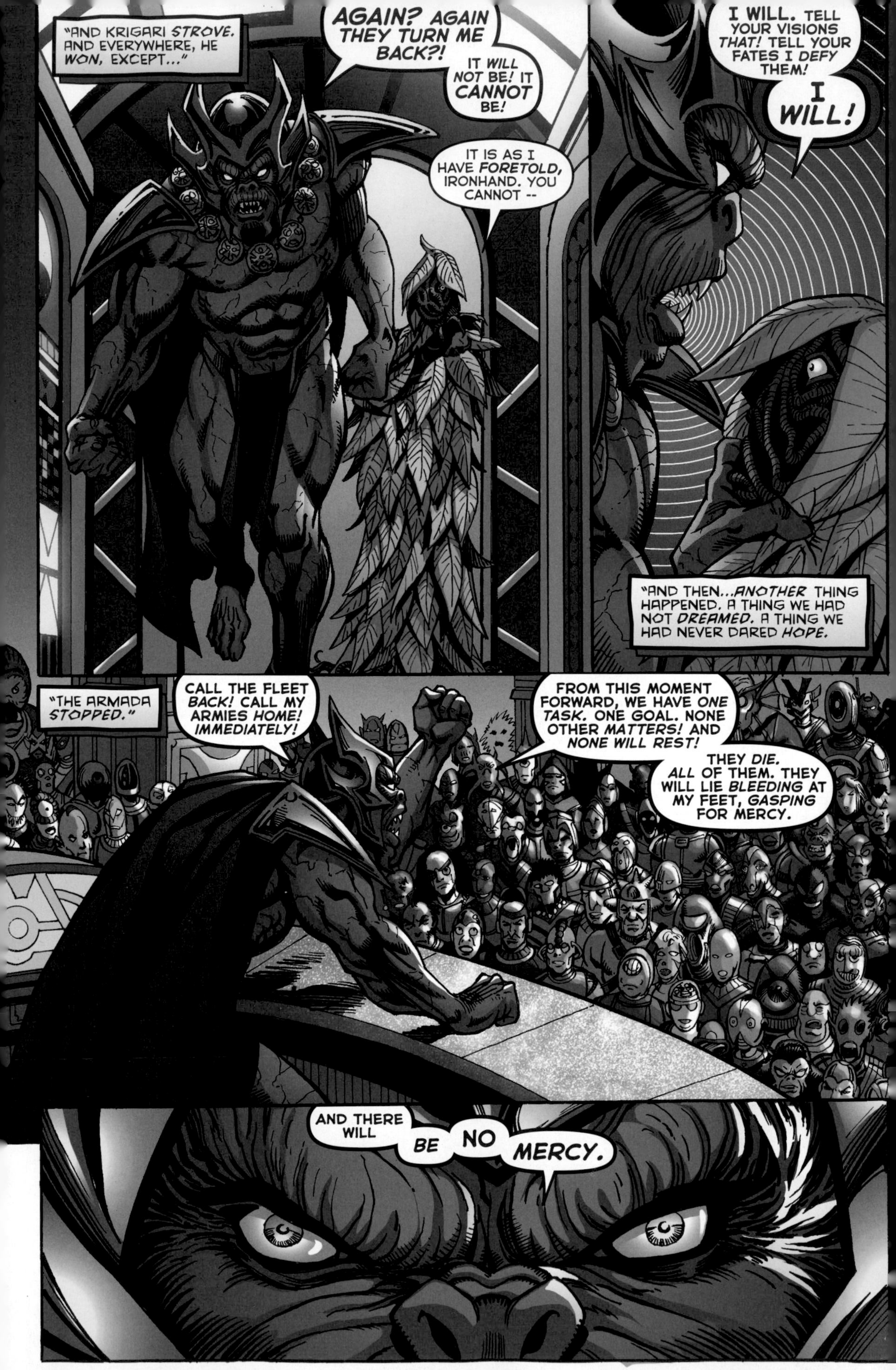
"AND KRIGARI STROVE. AND EVERYWHERE, HE WON, EXCEPT..."
AGAIN? AGAIN THEY TURN ME BACK?!
IT WILL NOT BE! IT CANNOT BE!
IT IS AS I HAVE FORETOLD, IRONHAND. YOU CANNOT --
I WILL. TELL YOUR VISIONS THAT! TELL YOUR FATES I DEFY THEM!
I WILL!
"AND THEN...ANOTHER THING HAPPENED. A THING WE HAD NOT DREAMED. A THING WE HAD NEVER DARED HOPE.
"THE ARMADA STOPPED."
CALL THE FLEET BACK! CALL MY ARMIES HOME! IMMEDIATELY!
FROM THIS MOMENT FORWARD, WE HAVE ONE TASK. ONE GOAL. NONE OTHER MATTERS! AND NONE WILL REST!
THEY DIE. ALL OF THEM. THEY WILL LIE BLEEDING AT MY FEET, GASPING FOR MERCY.
AND THERE WILL BE NO MERCY.

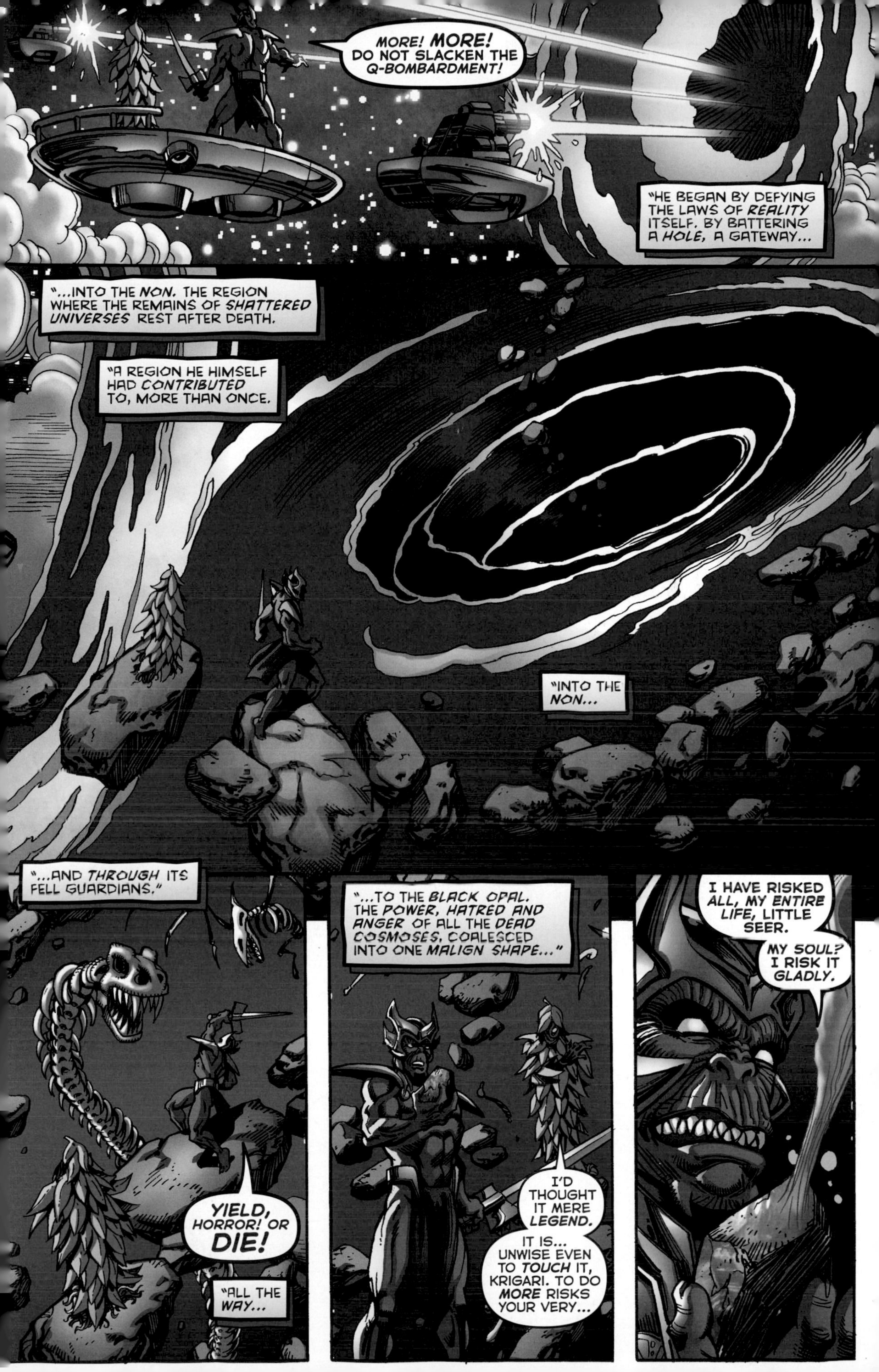
MORE! MORE! DO NOT SLACKEN THE Q-BOMBARDMENT!
"HE BEGAN BY DEFYING THE LAWS OF REALITY ITSELF. BY BATTERING A HOLE, A GATEWAY...
"...INTO THE NON. THE REGION WHERE THE REMAINS OF SHATTERED UNIVERSES REST AFTER DEATH.
"A REGION HE HIMSELF HAD CONTRIBUTED TO, MORE THAN ONCE.
"INTO THE NON...
"...AND THROUGH ITS FELL GUARDIANS."
YIELD, HORROR! OR DIE!
"ALL THE WAY...
"...TO THE BLACK OPAL. THE POWER, HATRED AND ANGER OF ALL THE DEAD COSMOSES, COALESCED INTO ONE MALIGN SHAPE..."
I'D THOUGHT IT MERE LEGEND.
IT IS... UNWISE EVEN TO TOUCH IT, KRIGARI. TO DO MORE RISKS YOUR VERY...
I HAVE RISKED ALL, MY ENTIRE LIFE, LITTLE SEER.
MY SOUL? I RISK IT GLADLY.

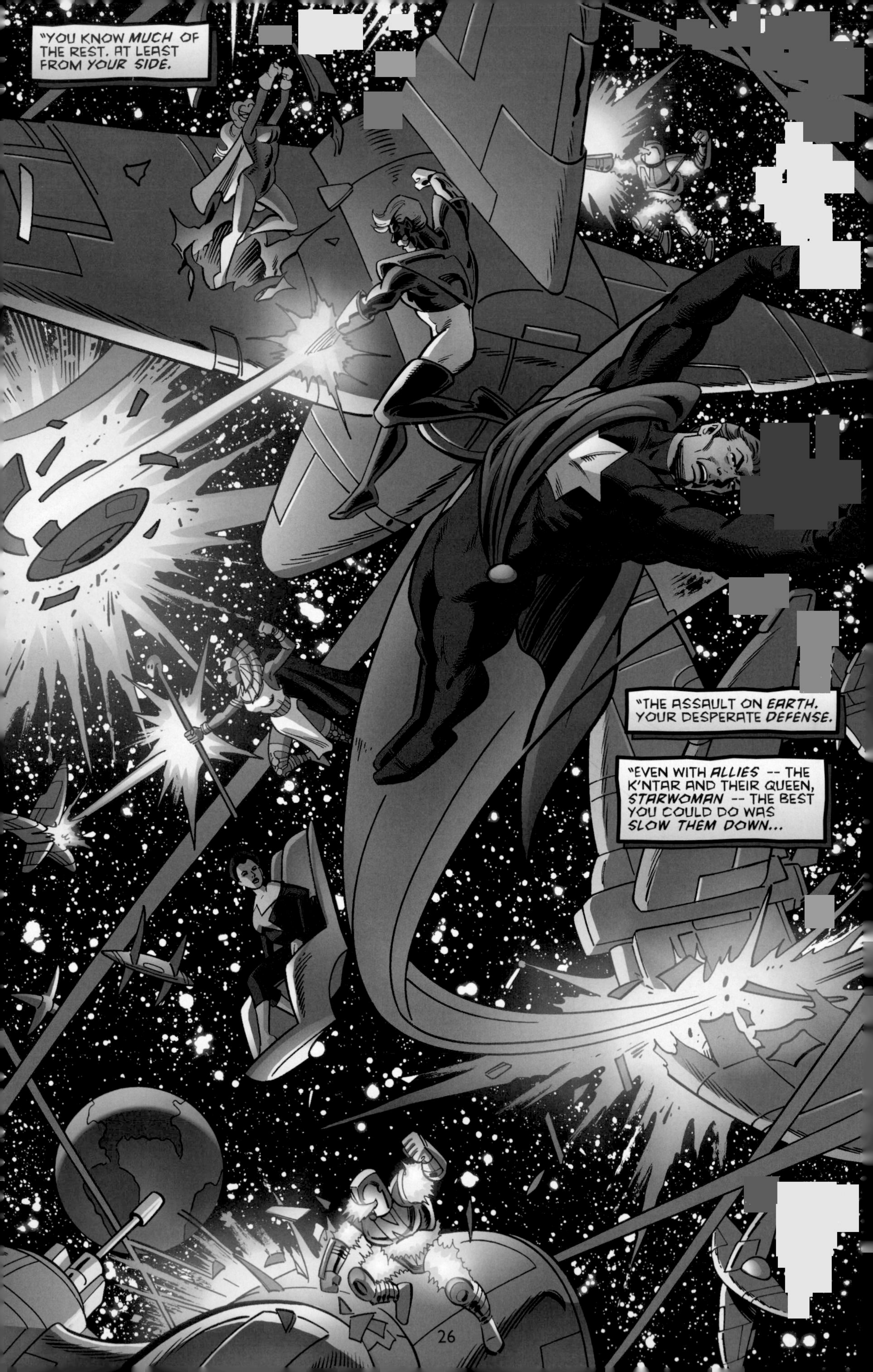
"YOU KNOW MUCH OF THE REST. AT LEAST FROM YOUR SIDE.
"THE ASSAULT ON EARTH. YOUR DESPERATE DEFENSE.
"EVEN WITH ALLIES -- THE K'NTAR AND THEIR QUEEN, STARWOMAN -- THE BEST YOU COULD DO WAS SLOW THEM DOWN...

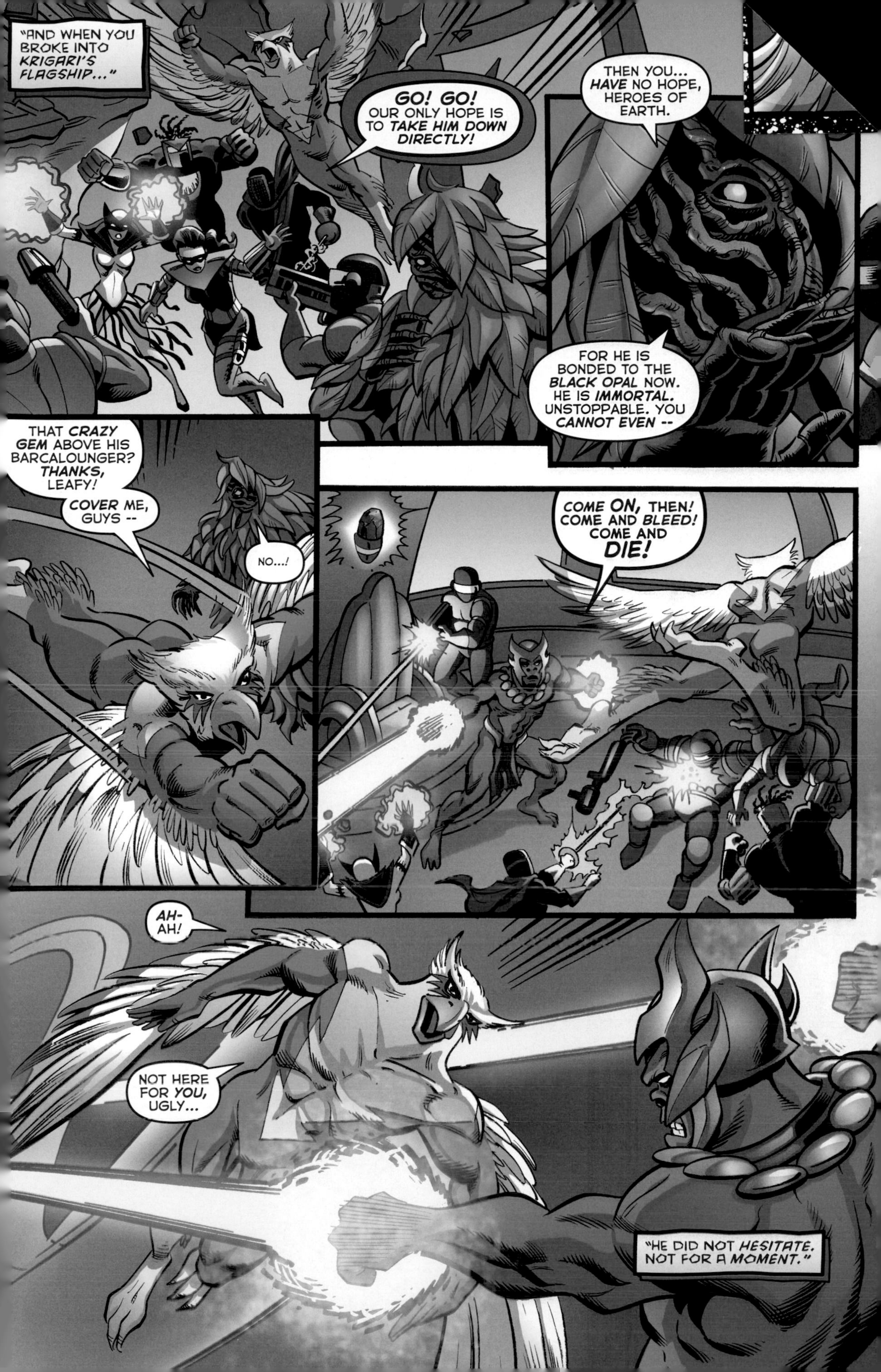
"AND WHEN YOU BROKE INTO KRIGARI'S FLAGSHIP..."
GO! GO! OUR ONLY HOPE IS TO TAKE HIM DOWN DIRECTLY!
THEN YOU... HAVE NO HOPE, HEROES OF EARTH.
FOR HE IS BONDED TO THE BLACK OPAL NOW. HE IS IMMORTAL. UNSTOPPABLE. YOU CANNOT EVEN --
THAT CRAZY GEM ABOVE HIS BARCALOUNGER? THANKS, LEAFY!
COVER ME, GUYS --
NO...!
COME ON, THEN! COME AND BLEED! COME AND DIE!
AH-AH!
NOT HERE FOR YOU, UGLY...
"HE DID NOT HESITATE. NOT FOR A MOMENT."

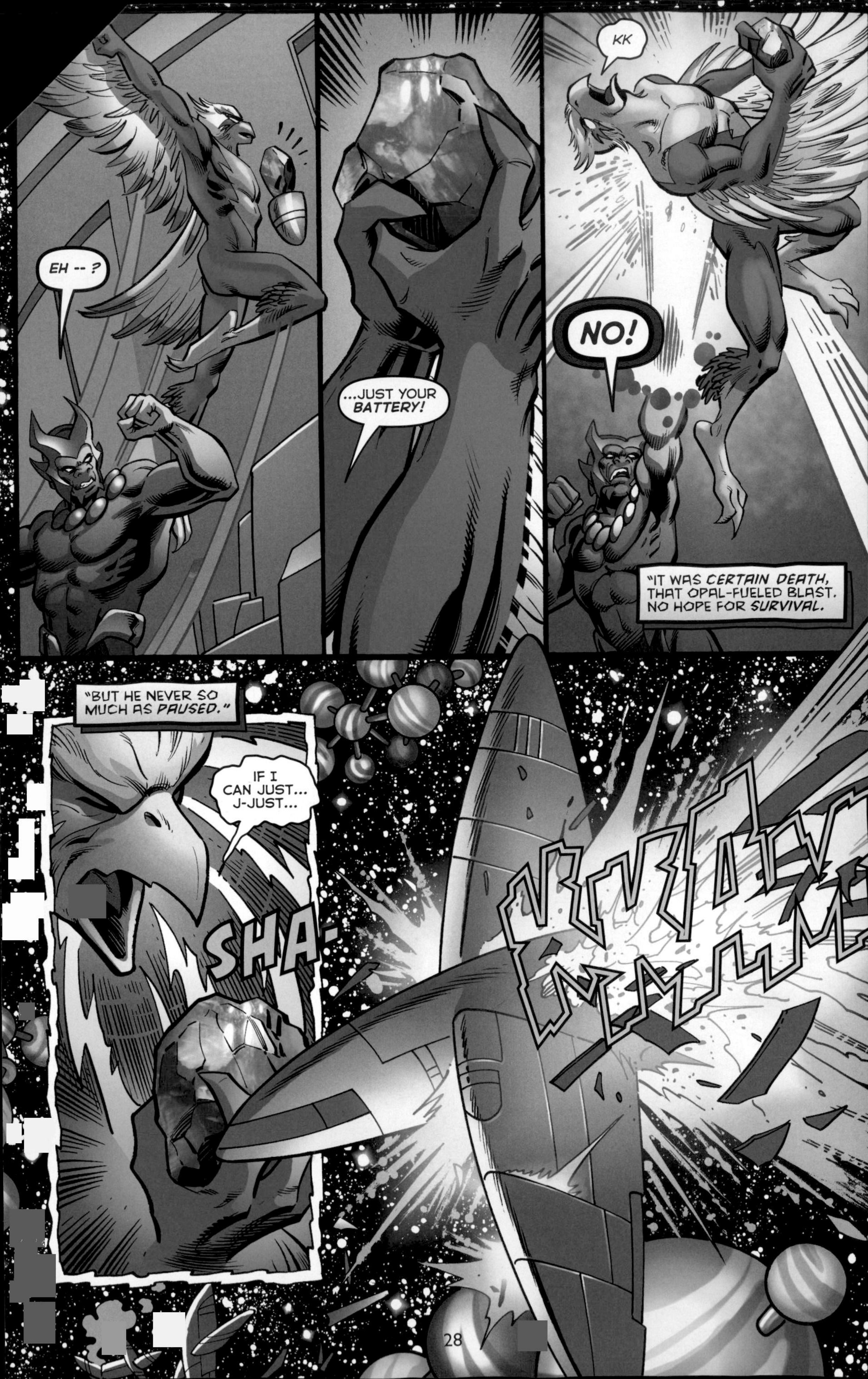
EH -- ?
...JUST YOUR BATTERY!
KK
NO!
"IT WAS CERTAIN DEATH, THAT OPAL-FUELED BLAST. NO HOPE FOR SURVIVAL.
"BUT HE NEVER SO MUCH AS PAUSED."
IF I CAN JUST... J-JUST...
SHA-

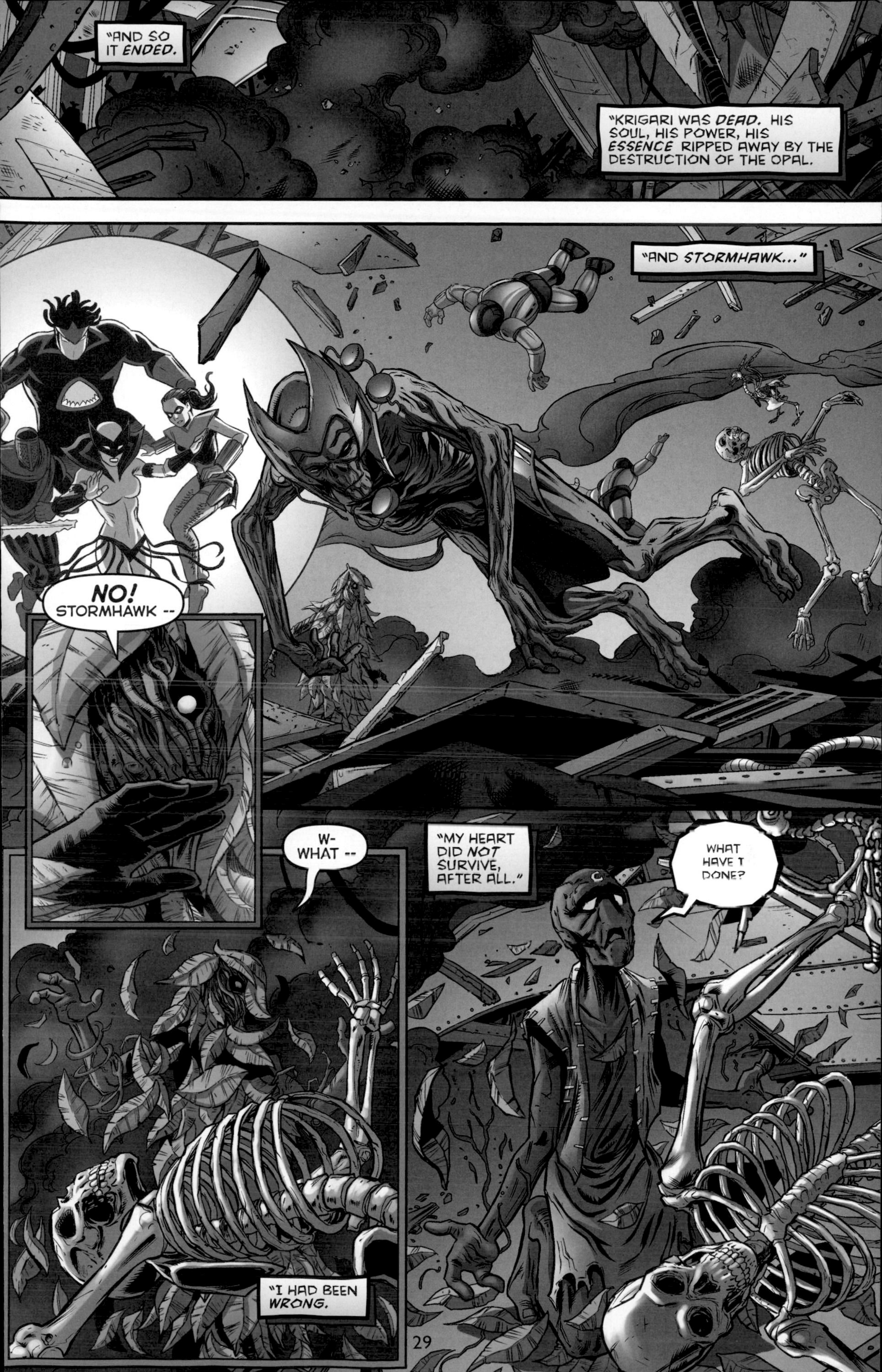
"AND SO IT ENDED.
"KRIGARI WAS DEAD. HIS SOUL, HIS POWER, HIS ESSENCE RIPPED AWAY BY THE DESTRUCTION OF THE OPAL.
"AND STORMHAWK..."
NO! STORMHAWK --
W- WHAT --
"MY HEART DID NOT SURVIVE, AFTER ALL."
WHAT HAVE I DONE?
"I HAD BEEN WRONG.

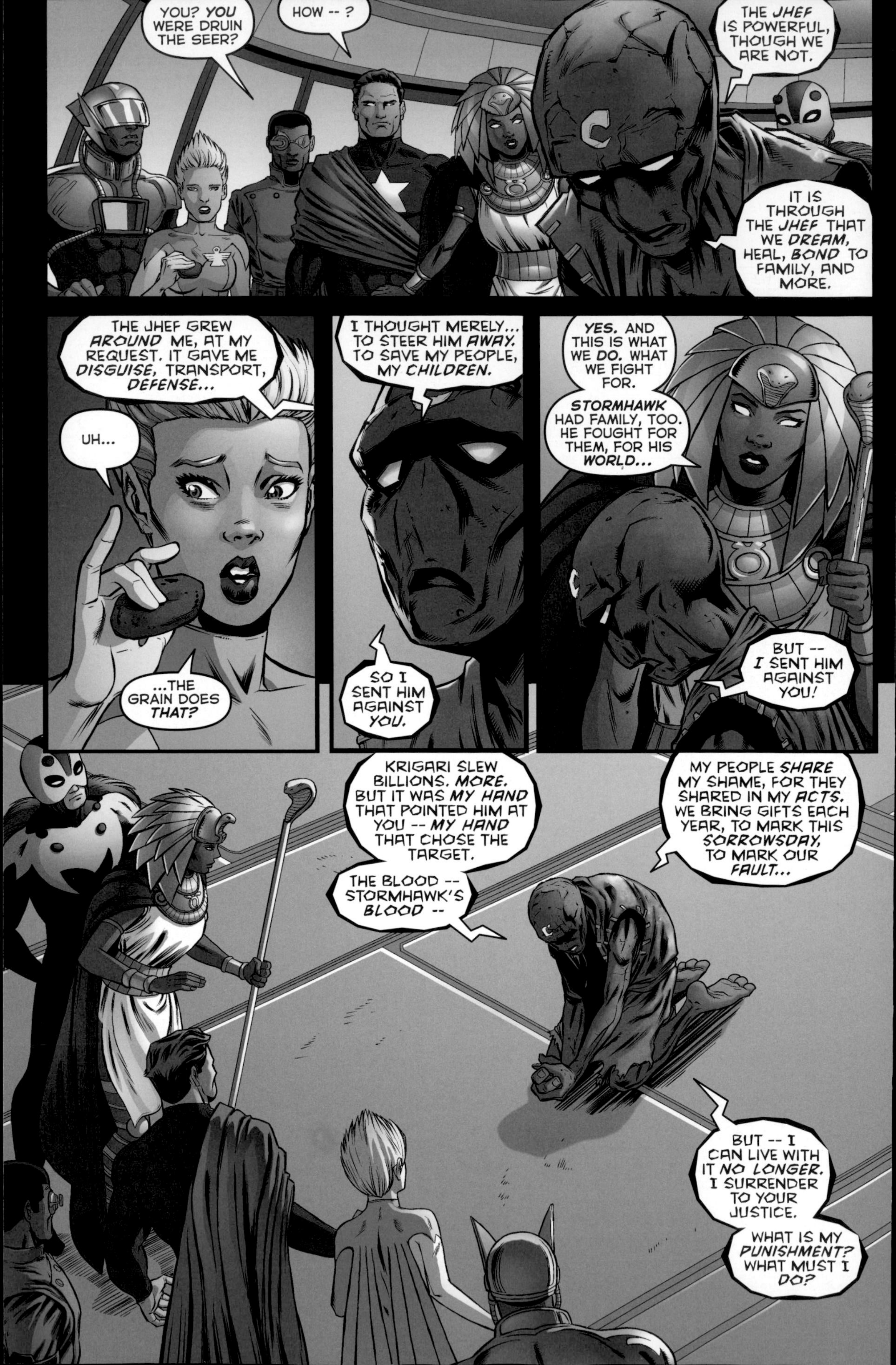
YOU? YOU WERE DRUIN THE SEER?
HOW -- ?
THE JHEF IS POWERFUL, THOUGH WE ARE NOT.
IT IS THROUGH THE JHEF THAT WE DREAM, HEAL, BOND TO FAMILY, AND MORE.
THE JHEF GREW AROUND ME, AT MY REQUEST. IT GAVE ME DISGUISE, TRANSPORT, DEFENSE...
UH...
...THE GRAIN DOES THAT?
I THOUGHT MERELY... TO STEER HIM AWAY. TO SAVE MY PEOPLE, MY CHILDREN.
SO I SENT HIM AGAINST YOU.
YES. AND THIS IS WHAT WE DO. WHAT WE FIGHT FOR.
STORMHAWK HAD FAMILY, TOO. HE FOUGHT FOR THEM, FOR HIS WORLD...
BUT -- I SENT HIM AGAINST YOU!
KRIGARI SLEW BILLIONS. MORE. BUT IT WAS MY HAND THAT POINTED HIM AT YOU -- MY HAND THAT CHOSE THE TARGET.
THE BLOOD -- STORMHAWK'S BLOOD --
MY PEOPLE SHARE MY SHAME, FOR THEY SHARED IN MY ACTS. WE BRING GIFTS EACH YEAR, TO MARK THIS SORROWSDAY, TO MARK OUR FAULT...
BUT -- I CAN LIVE WITH IT NO LONGER. I SURRENDER TO YOUR JUSTICE.
WHAT IS MY PUNISHMENT? WHAT MUST I DO?

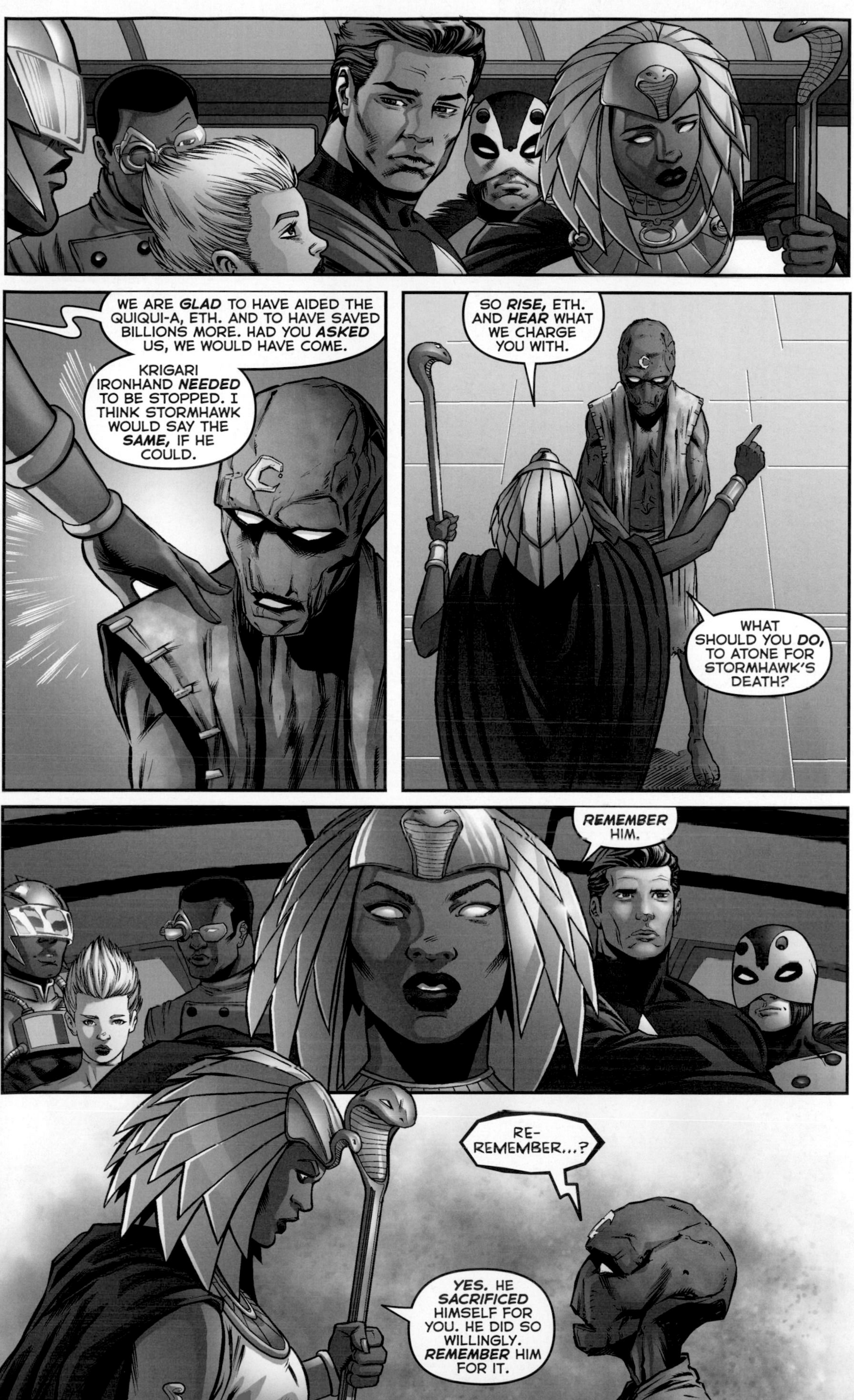
WE ARE GLAD TO HAVE AIDED THE QUIQUI-A, ETH. AND TO HAVE SAVED BILLIONS MORE. HAD YOU ASKED US, WE WOULD HAVE COME.
KRIGARI IRONHAND NEEDED TO BE STOPPED. I THINK STORMHAWK WOULD SAY THE SAME, IF HE COULD.
SO RISE, ETH. AND HEAR WHAT WE CHARGE YOU WITH.
WHAT SHOULD YOU DO, TO ATONE FOR STORMHAWK'S DEATH?
REMEMBER HIM.
RE-REMEMBER...?
YES. HE SACRIFICED HIMSELF FOR YOU. HE DID SO WILLINGLY. REMEMBER HIM FOR IT.

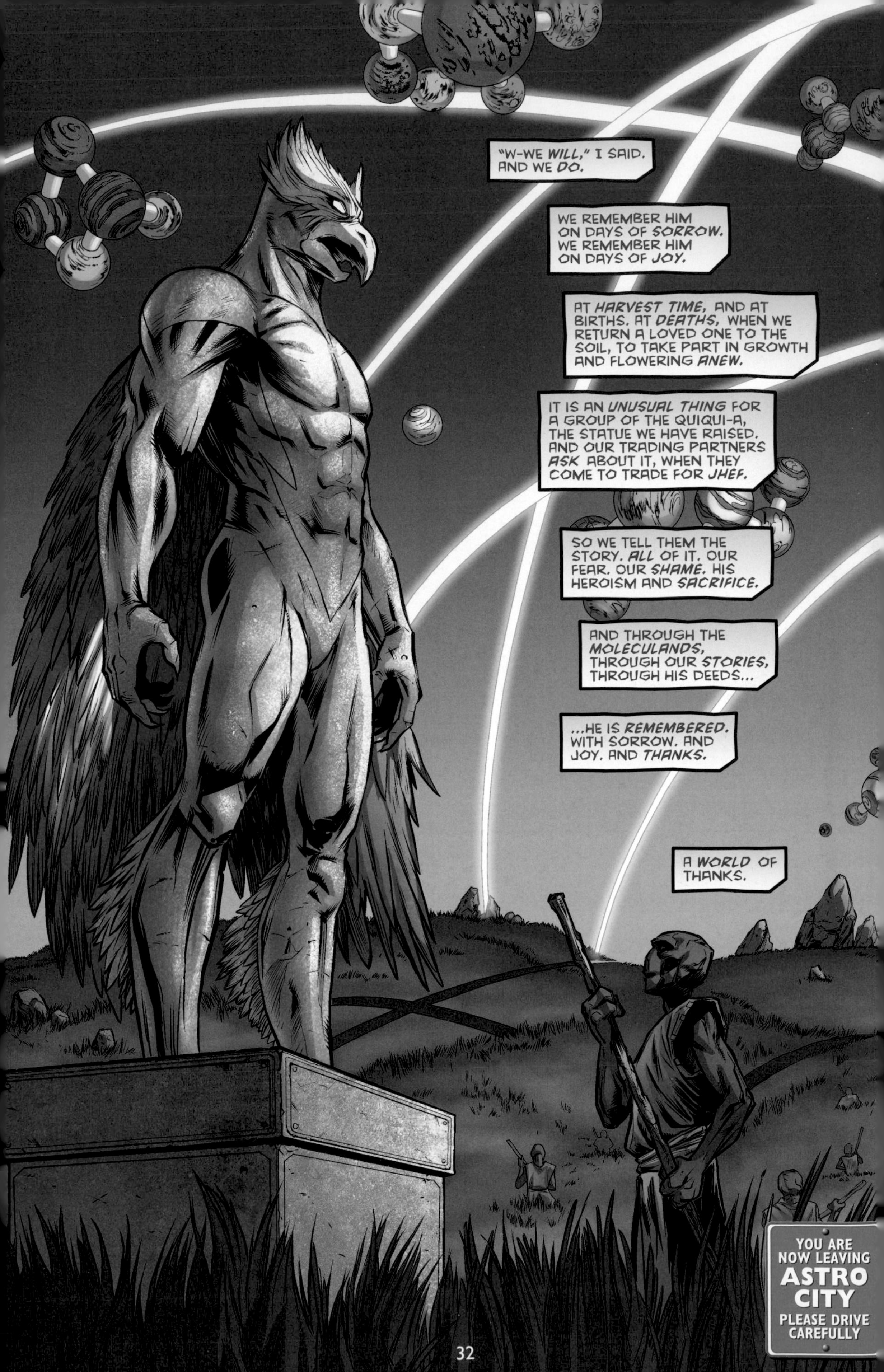
"W-WE WILL," I SAID. AND WE DO.
WE REMEMBER HIM ON DAYS OF SORROW. WE REMEMBER HIM ON DAYS OF JOY.
AT HARVEST TIME, AND AT BIRTHS. AT DEATHS, WHEN WE RETURN A LOVED ONE TO THE SOIL, TO TAKE PART IN GROWTH AND FLOWERING ANEW.
IT IS AN UNUSUAL THING FOR A GROUP OF THE QUIQUI-A, THE STATUE WE HAVE RAISED. AND OUR TRADING PARTNERS ASK ABOUT IT, WHEN THEY COME TO TRADE FOR JHEF.
SO WE TELL THEM THE STORY. ALL OF IT. OUR FEAR. OUR SHAME. HIS HEROISM AND SACRIFICE.
AND THROUGH THE MOLECULANDS, THROUGH OUR STORIES, THROUGH HIS DEEDS...
...HE IS REMEMBERED. WITH SORROW. AND JOY. AND THANKS.
A WORLD OF THANKS.
YOU ARE NOW LEAVING ASTRO CITY PLEASE DRIVE CAREFULLY

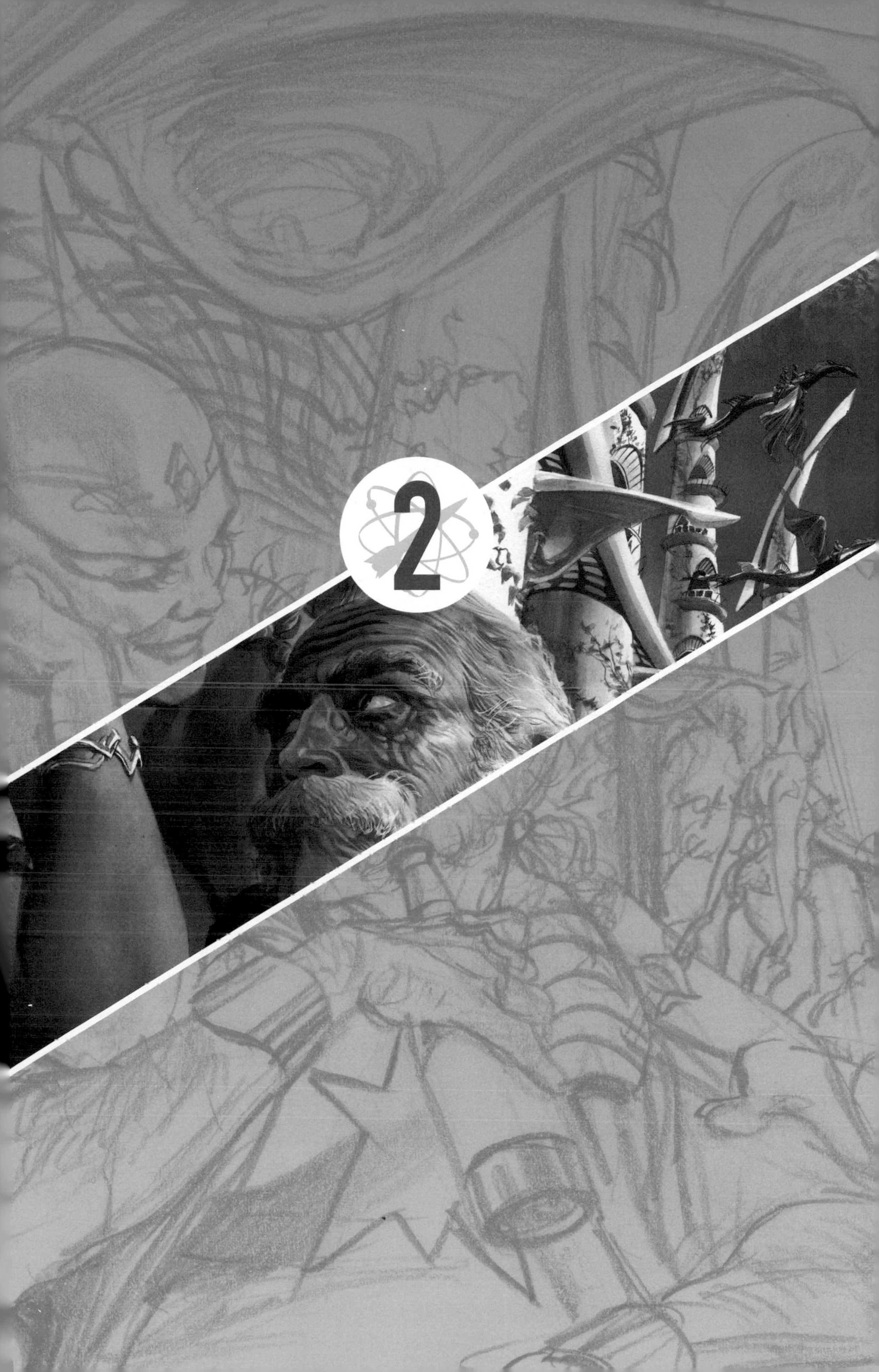
2

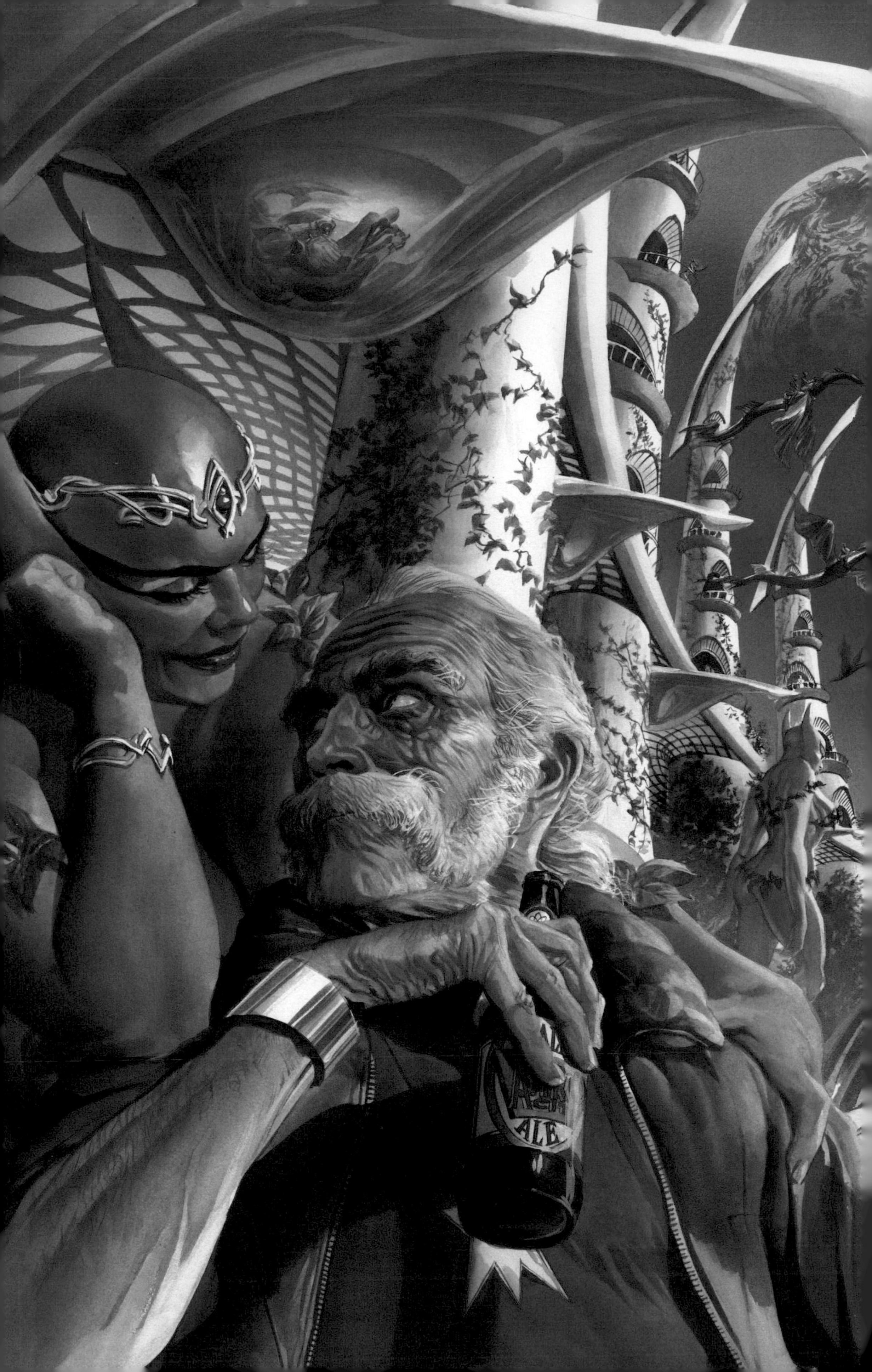
ALE

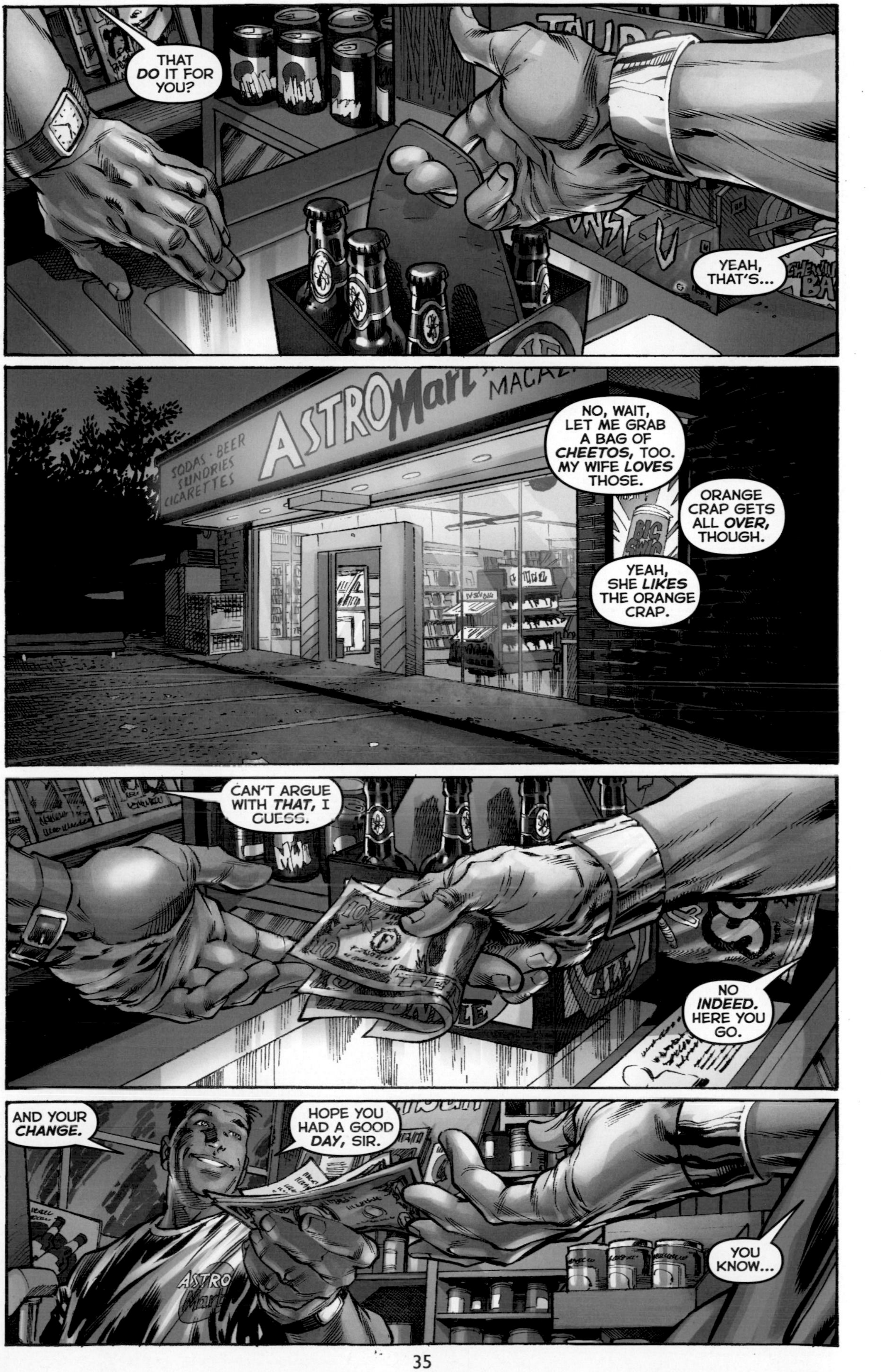
THAT DO IT FOR YOU?
YEAH, THAT'S...
ASTROMart
SODAS · BEER SUNDRIES CIGARETTES
NO, WAIT, LET ME GRAB A BAG OF CHEETOS, TOO. MY WIFE LOVES THOSE.
ORANGE CRAP GETS ALL OVER, THOUGH.
YEAH, SHE LIKES THE ORANGE CRAP.
CAN'T ARGUE WITH THAT, I GUESS.
NO INDEED. HERE YOU GO.
AND YOUR CHANGE.
HOPE YOU HAD A GOOD DAY, SIR.
YOU KNOW...

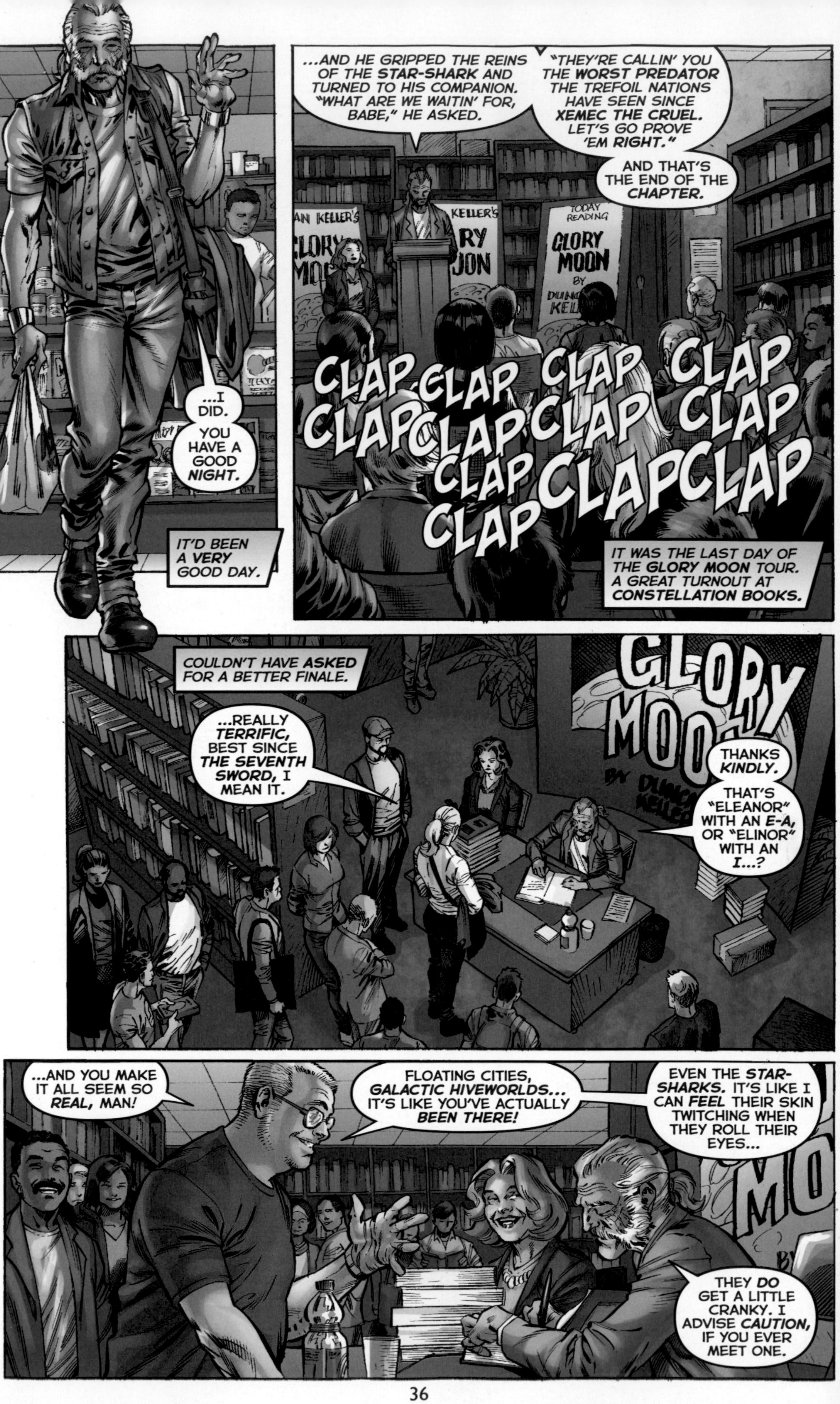
...I DID. YOU HAVE A GOOD NIGHT.
IT'D BEEN A VERY GOOD DAY.
...AND HE GRIPPED THE REINS OF THE STAR-SHARK AND TURNED TO HIS COMPANION. "WHAT ARE WE WAITIN' FOR, BABE," HE ASKED.
"THEY'RE CALLIN' YOU THE WORST PREDATOR THE TREFOIL NATIONS HAVE SEEN SINCE XEMEC THE CRUEL. LET'S GO PROVE 'EM RIGHT."
AND THAT'S THE END OF THE CHAPTER.
TODAY READING GLORY MOON
CLAP CLAP CLAP CLAP CLAP CLAP CLAP CLAP CLAP CLAP CLAP CLAP CLAP
IT WAS THE LAST DAY OF THE GLORY MOON TOUR. A GREAT TURNOUT AT CONSTELLATION BOOKS.
COULDN'T HAVE ASKED FOR A BETTER FINALE.
GLORY
...REALLY TERRIFIC, BEST SINCE THE SEVENTH SWORD, I MEAN IT.
THANKS KINDLY.
THAT'S "ELEANOR" WITH AN E-A, OR "ELINOR" WITH AN I...?
...AND YOU MAKE IT ALL SEEM SO REAL, MAN!
FLOATING CITIES, GALACTIC HIVEWORLDS... IT'S LIKE YOU'VE ACTUALLY BEEN THERE!
EVEN THE STAR-SHARKS. IT'S LIKE I CAN FEEL THEIR SKIN TWITCHING WHEN THEY ROLL THEIR EYES...
THEY DO GET A LITTLE CRANKY. I ADVISE CAUTION, IF YOU EVER MEET ONE.

EVEN THE Q&A WENT WELL.

...AT LEAST, I *THOUGHT* IT WAS SUSHI!

HA HA HA HA HA HA

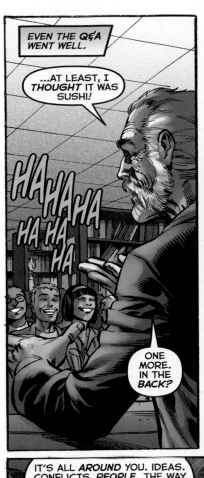

ONE MORE. IN THE *BACK?*

UM...I KNOW IT'S A *CLICHÉ* QUESTION, BUT I'D STILL LIKE TO KNOW.

YOUR BOOKS ARE FULL OF SUCH *CONSTANT INVENTION,* SUCH *FULLY-REALIZED* WORLDS. WHERE DO YOU GET *IDEAS* FOR ALL OF THAT?

LORY OON

KELLER

I *COULD* GIVE YOU A JOKE ANSWER. THERE ARE PLENTY. BUT FOR REAL...

IT'S ALL *AROUND* YOU. IDEAS. CONFLICTS. *PEOPLE.* THE WAY THEY TALK. WHAT THEY LOVE. AND HATE. YOU GOTTA GET OUT THERE, AND JUST *SEE* IT.

THE MOST *ASTONISHING SIGHTS,* FROM *JUNGLE VILLAGES* TO THE HIGH *DESERT.*

SEE WHAT THE UNIVERSE HAS TO OFFER. FOLLOW THE ROAD IN *FRONT* OF YOU. SEE WHERE IT LEADS, WHERE YOU *END UP.*

AND ONCE YOU'VE SEEN *ENOUGH,* WELL...THAT'S WHEN YOU CHANGE ALL THE *NAMES* AND *HAIRDOS,* AND MESS IT AROUND INTO A STORY.

THEN COMES THE *EASY* PART. YOU KNOW, WRITING IT, FINDING AN AGENT, ALL *THAT* GOOD STUFF...

AHAHA HA HA HAHAHA HA HAHAHA HA

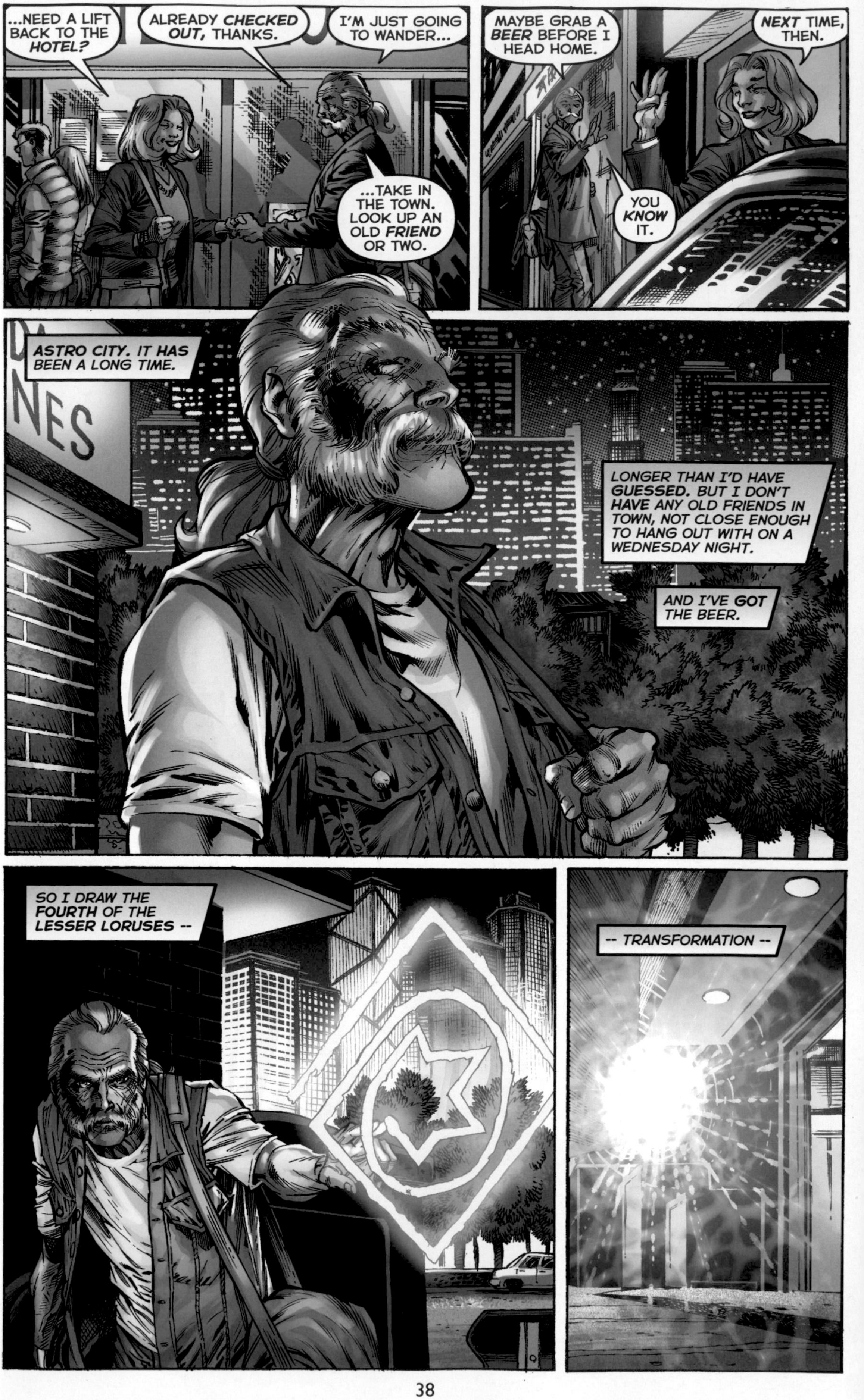
...NEED A LIFT BACK TO THE HOTEL?
ALREADY CHECKED OUT, THANKS.
I'M JUST GOING TO WANDER...
...TAKE IN THE TOWN. LOOK UP AN OLD FRIEND OR TWO.
MAYBE GRAB A BEER BEFORE I HEAD HOME.
NEXT TIME, THEN.
YOU KNOW IT.
NES
ASTRO CITY. IT HAS BEEN A LONG TIME.
LONGER THAN I'D HAVE GUESSED. BUT I DON'T HAVE ANY OLD FRIENDS IN TOWN, NOT CLOSE ENOUGH TO HANG OUT WITH ON A WEDNESDAY NIGHT.
AND I'VE GOT THE BEER.
SO I DRAW THE FOURTH OF THE LESSER LORUSES --
-- TRANSFORMATION --

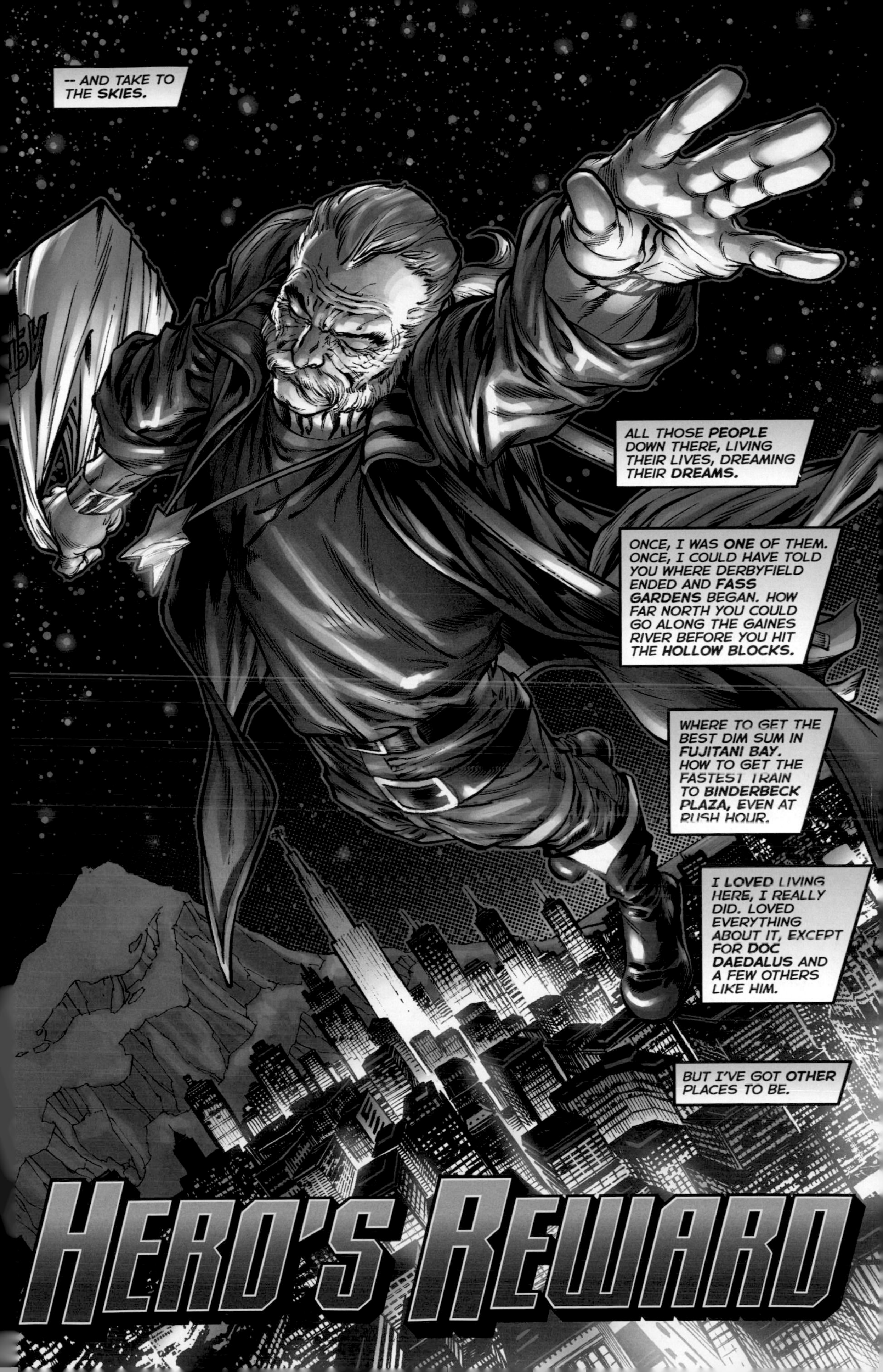
-- AND TAKE TO THE SKIES.
ALL THOSE PEOPLE DOWN THERE, LIVING THEIR LIVES, DREAMING THEIR DREAMS.
ONCE, I WAS ONE OF THEM. ONCE, I COULD HAVE TOLD YOU WHERE DERBYFIELD ENDED AND FASS GARDENS BEGAN. HOW FAR NORTH YOU COULD GO ALONG THE GAINES RIVER BEFORE YOU HIT THE HOLLOW BLOCKS.
WHERE TO GET THE BEST DIM SUM IN FUJITANI BAY. HOW TO GET THE FASTEST TRAIN TO BINDERBECK PLAZA, EVEN AT RUSH HOUR.
I LOVED LIVING HERE, I REALLY DID. LOVED EVERYTHING ABOUT IT, EXCEPT FOR DOC DAEDALUS AND A FEW OTHERS LIKE HIM.
BUT I'VE GOT OTHER PLACES TO BE.
HERO'S REWARD

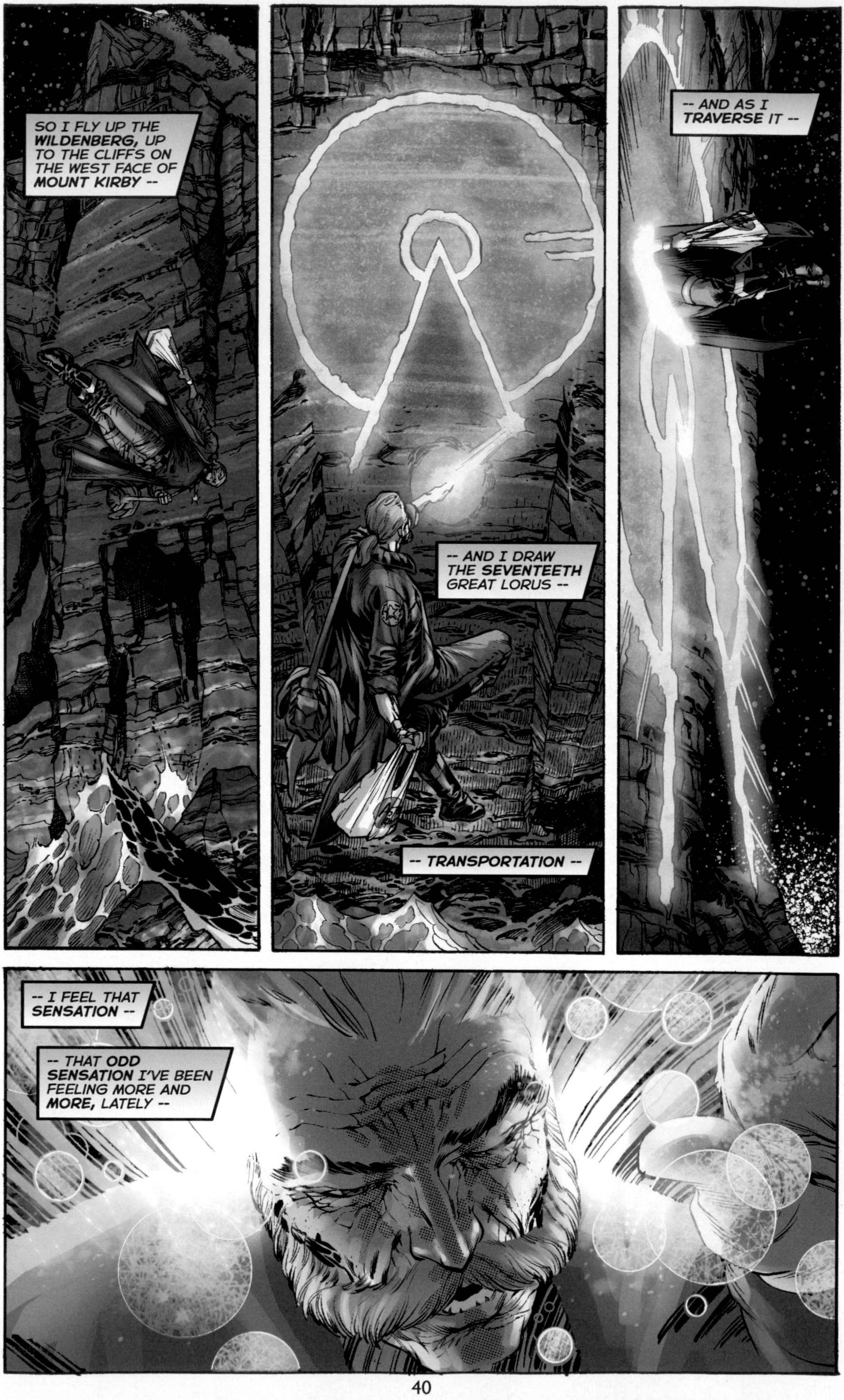
SO I FLY UP THE WILDENBERG, UP TO THE CLIFFS ON THE WEST FACE OF MOUNT KIRBY --
-- AND I DRAW THE SEVENTEETH GREAT LORUS --
-- TRANSPORTATION --
-- AND AS I TRAVERSE IT --
-- I FEEL THAT SENSATION --
-- THAT ODD SENSATION I'VE BEEN FEELING MORE AND MORE, LATELY --

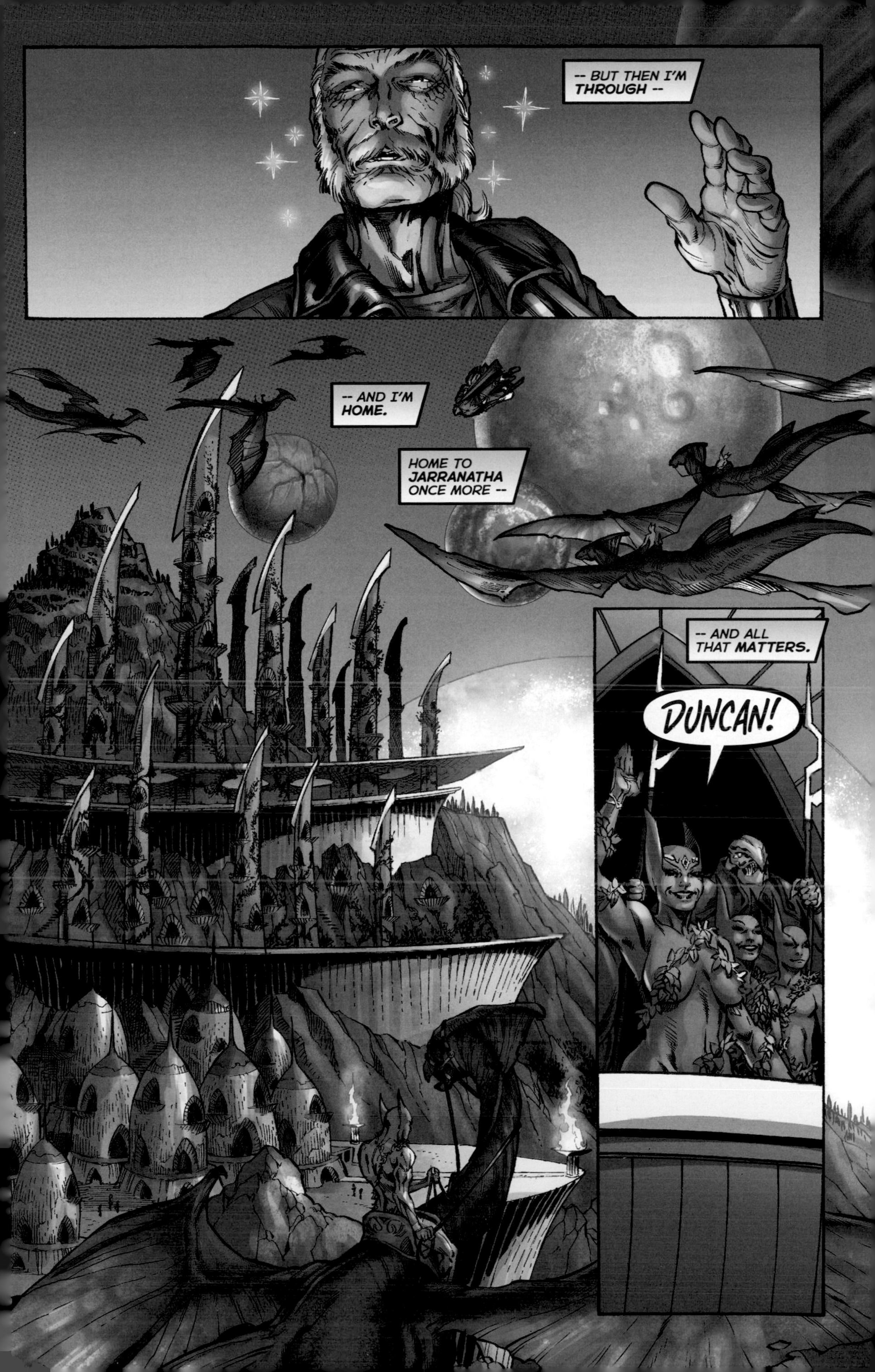
-- BUT THEN I'M THROUGH --
-- AND I'M HOME.
HOME TO JARRANATHA ONCE MORE --
-- AND ALL THAT MATTERS.
DUNCAN!

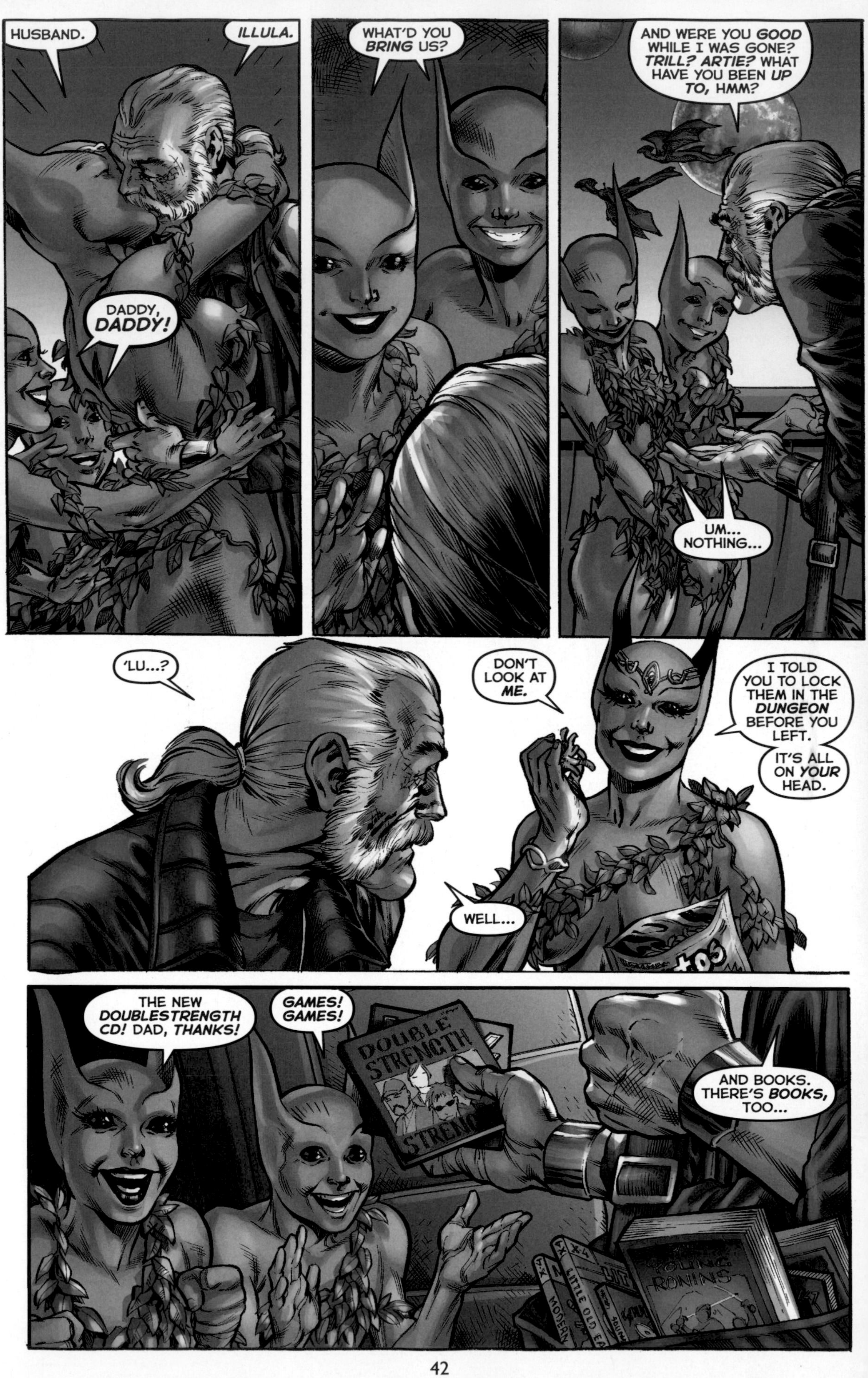
HUSBAND.
ILLULA.
DADDY, DADDY!
WHAT'D YOU BRING US?
AND WERE YOU GOOD WHILE I WAS GONE? TRILL? ARTIE? WHAT HAVE YOU BEEN UP TO, HMM?
UM... NOTHING...
'LU...?
DON'T LOOK AT ME.
I TOLD YOU TO LOCK THEM IN THE DUNGEON BEFORE YOU LEFT.
IT'S ALL ON YOUR HEAD.
WELL...
THE NEW DOUBLESTRENGTH CD! DAD, THANKS!
GAMES! GAMES!
DOUBLE STRENGTH
AND BOOKS. THERE'S BOOKS, TOO...
LITTLE OLD
MODERN
RONINS

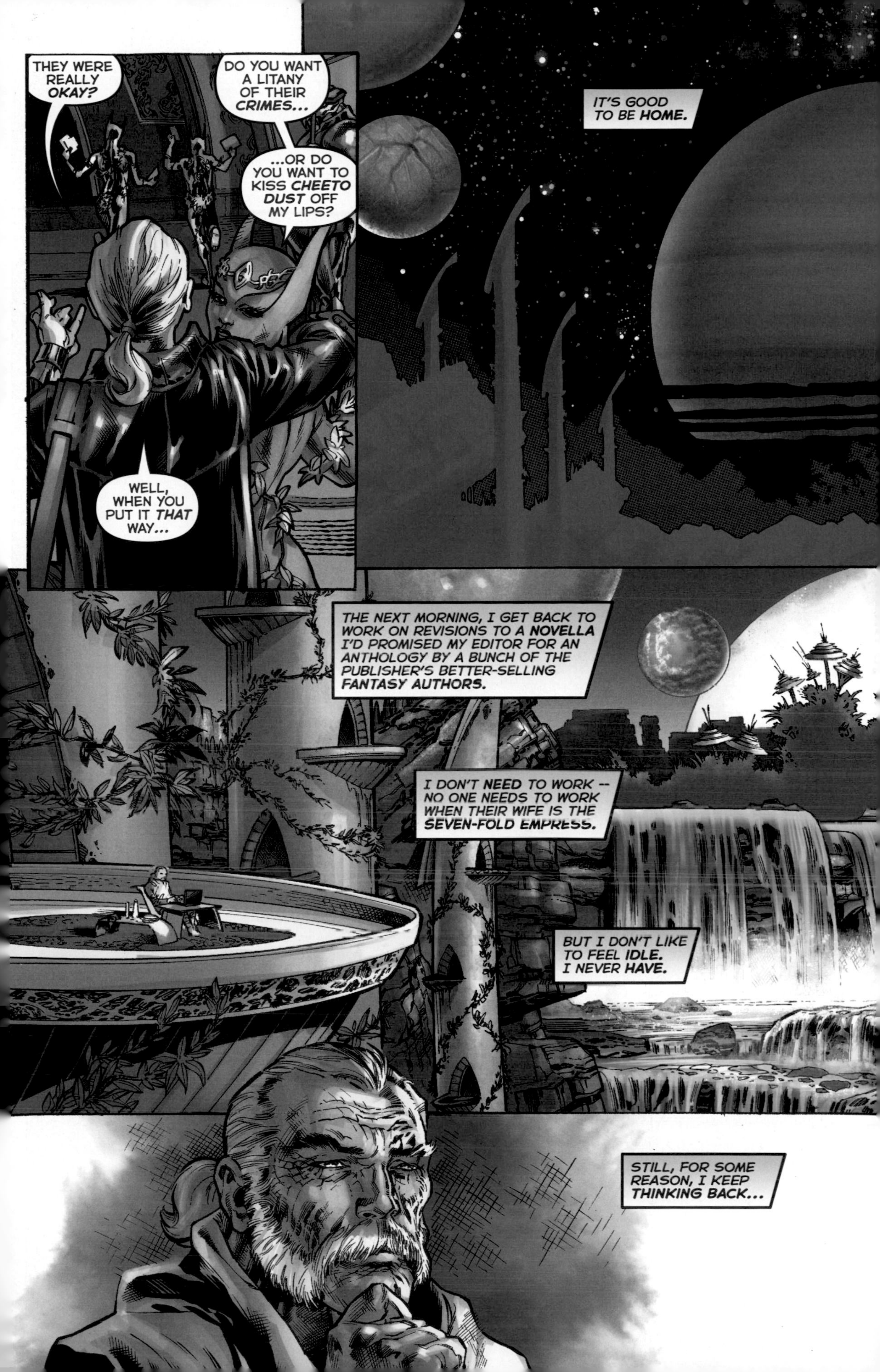

THEY WERE REALLY OKAY?
DO YOU WANT A LITANY OF THEIR CRIMES...
...OR DO YOU WANT TO KISS CHEETO DUST OFF MY LIPS?
WELL, WHEN YOU PUT IT THAT WAY...
IT'S GOOD TO BE HOME.
THE NEXT MORNING, I GET BACK TO WORK ON REVISIONS TO A NOVELLA I'D PROMISED MY EDITOR FOR AN ANTHOLOGY BY A BUNCH OF THE PUBLISHER'S BETTER-SELLING FANTASY AUTHORS.
I DON'T NEED TO WORK -- NO ONE NEEDS TO WORK WHEN THEIR WIFE IS THE SEVEN-FOLD EMPRESS.
BUT I DON'T LIKE TO FEEL IDLE. I NEVER HAVE.
STILL, FOR SOME REASON, I KEEP THINKING BACK...

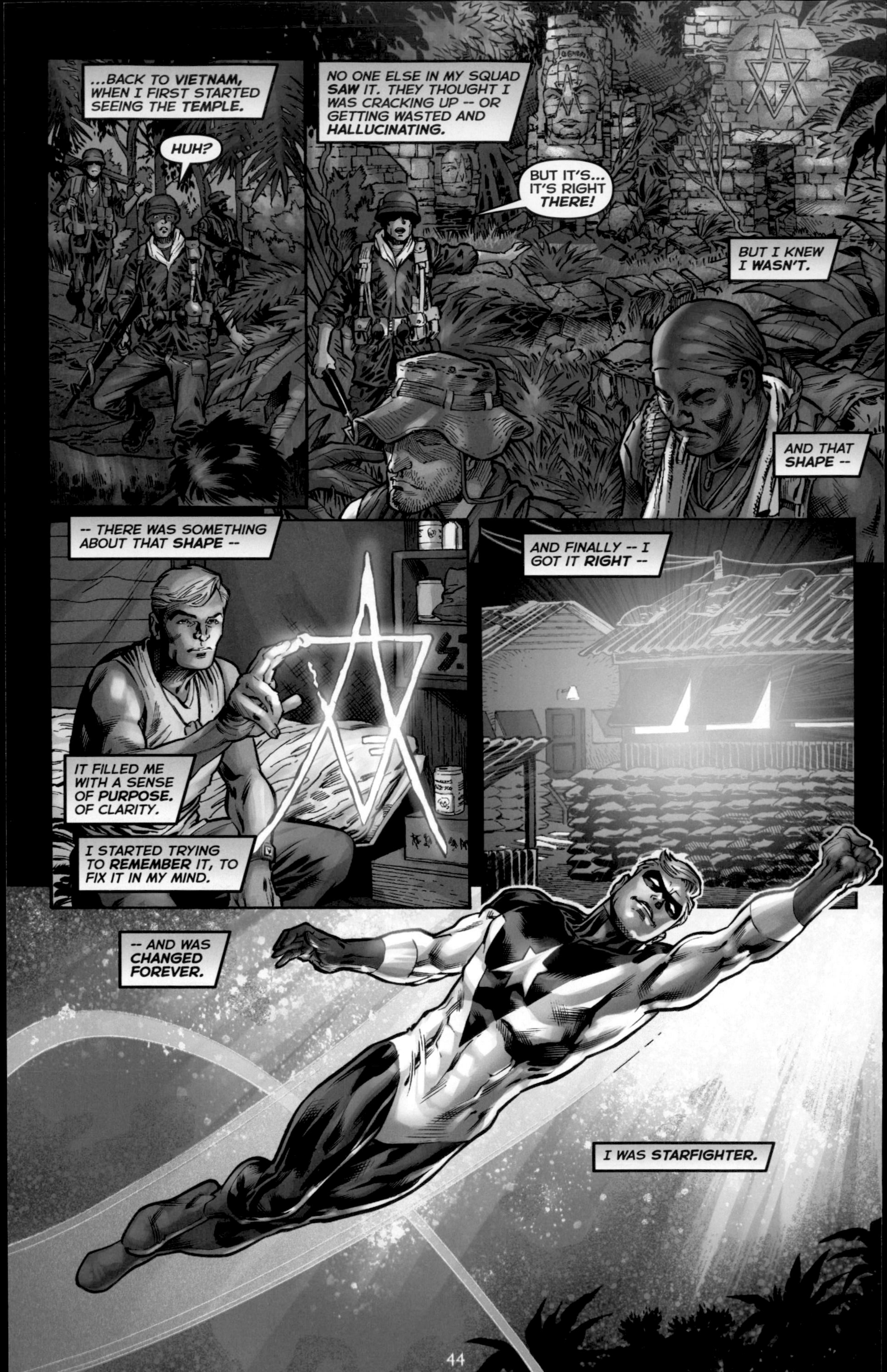

...BACK TO VIETNAM, WHEN I FIRST STARTED SEEING THE TEMPLE.
HUH?
NO ONE ELSE IN MY SQUAD SAW IT. THEY THOUGHT I WAS CRACKING UP -- OR GETTING WASTED AND HALLUCINATING.
BUT IT'S... IT'S RIGHT THERE!
BUT I KNEW I WASN'T.
AND THAT SHAPE --
-- THERE WAS SOMETHING ABOUT THAT SHAPE --
IT FILLED ME WITH A SENSE OF PURPOSE. OF CLARITY.
I STARTED TRYING TO REMEMBER IT, TO FIX IT IN MY MIND.
AND FINALLY -- I GOT IT RIGHT --
-- AND WAS CHANGED FOREVER.
I WAS STARFIGHTER.

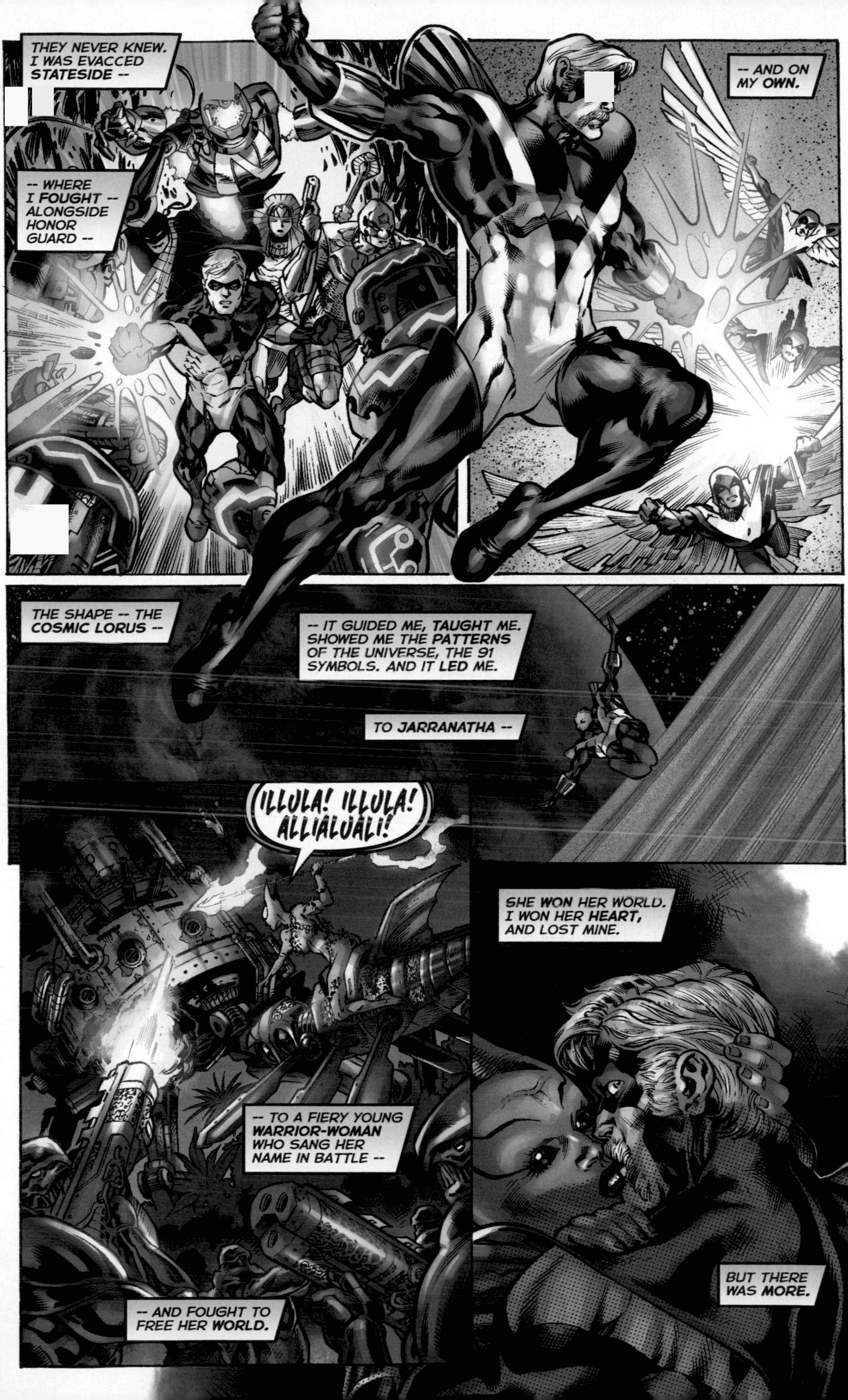
THEY NEVER KNEW. I WAS EVACCED STATESIDE --
-- WHERE I FOUGHT -- ALONGSIDE HONOR GUARD --
-- AND ON MY OWN.
THE SHAPE -- THE COSMIC LORUS --
-- IT GUIDED ME, TAUGHT ME. SHOWED ME THE PATTERNS OF THE UNIVERSE, THE 91 SYMBOLS. AND IT LED ME.
TO JARRANATHA --
ILLULA! ILLULA! ALLIALUALI!
-- TO A FIERY YOUNG WARRIOR-WOMAN WHO SANG HER NAME IN BATTLE --
-- AND FOUGHT TO FREE HER WORLD.
SHE WON HER WORLD. I WON HER HEART, AND LOST MINE.
BUT THERE WAS MORE.

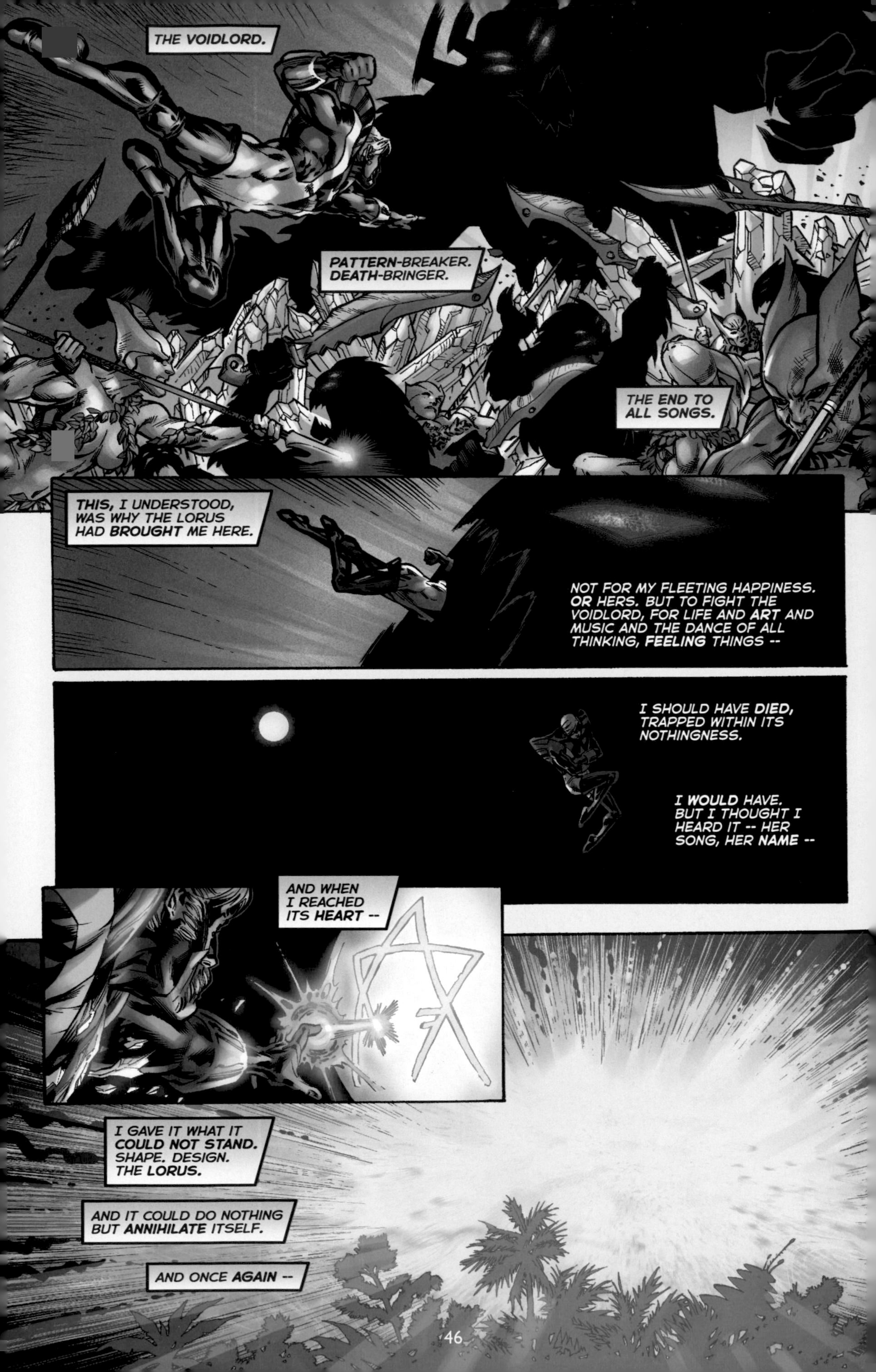
THE VOIDLORD.
PATTERN-BREAKER. DEATH-BRINGER.
THE END TO ALL SONGS.
THIS, I UNDERSTOOD, WAS WHY THE LORUS HAD BROUGHT ME HERE.
NOT FOR MY FLEETING HAPPINESS. OR HERS. BUT TO FIGHT THE VOIDLORD, FOR LIFE AND ART AND MUSIC AND THE DANCE OF ALL THINKING, FEELING THINGS --
I SHOULD HAVE DIED, TRAPPED WITHIN ITS NOTHINGNESS.
I WOULD HAVE. BUT I THOUGHT I HEARD IT -- HER SONG, HER NAME --
AND WHEN I REACHED ITS HEART --
I GAVE IT WHAT IT COULD NOT STAND. SHAPE. DESIGN. THE LORUS.
AND IT COULD DO NOTHING BUT ANNIHILATE ITSELF.
AND ONCE AGAIN --

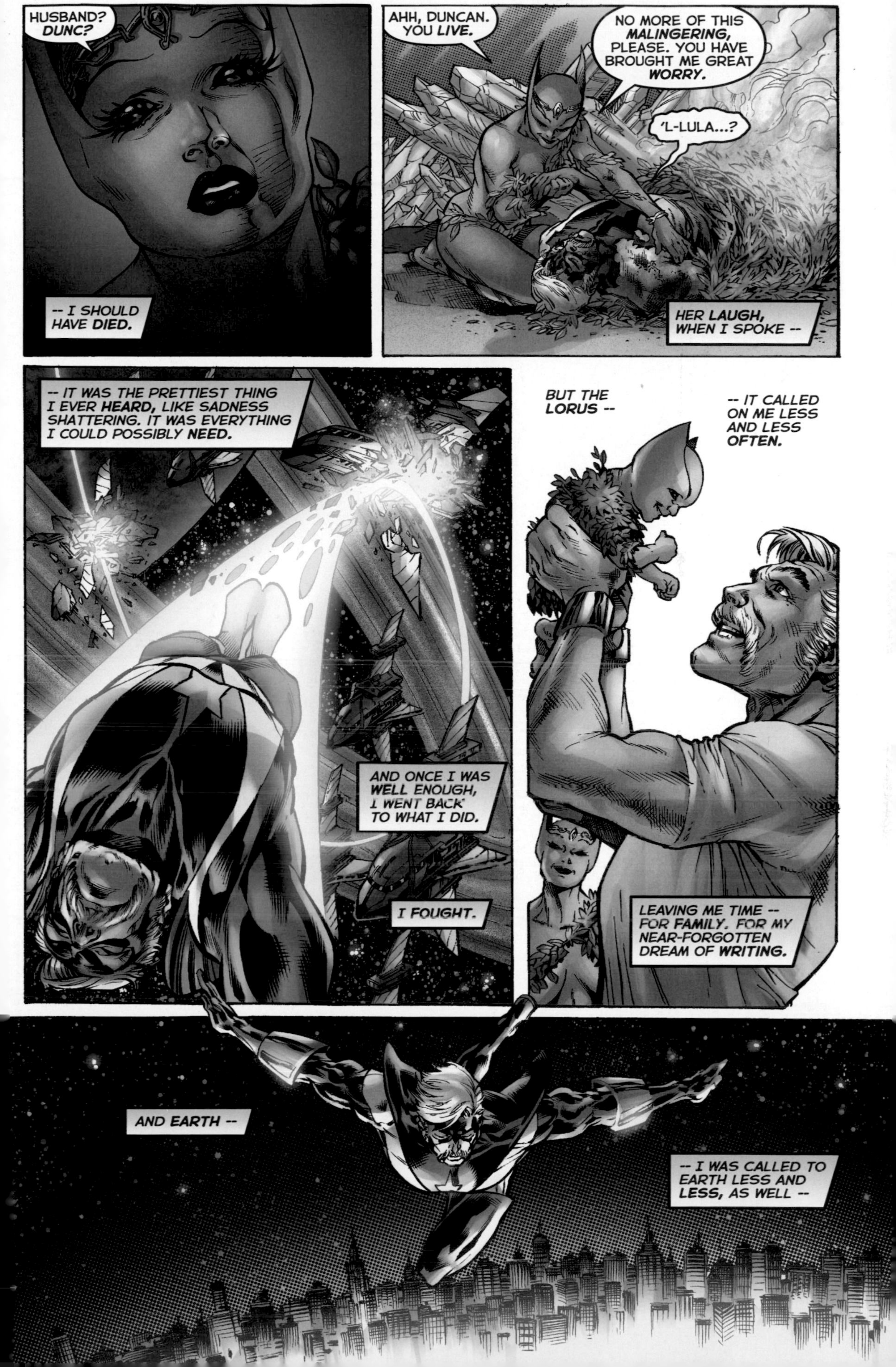
HUSBAND? DUNC?
-- I SHOULD HAVE DIED.
AHH, DUNCAN. YOU LIVE.
NO MORE OF THIS MALINGERING, PLEASE. YOU HAVE BROUGHT ME GREAT WORRY.
'L-LULA...?
HER LAUGH, WHEN I SPOKE --
-- IT WAS THE PRETTIEST THING I EVER HEARD, LIKE SADNESS SHATTERING. IT WAS EVERYTHING I COULD POSSIBLY NEED.
AND ONCE I WAS WELL ENOUGH, I WENT BACK TO WHAT I DID.
I FOUGHT.
BUT THE LORUS --
-- IT CALLED ON ME LESS AND LESS OFTEN.
LEAVING ME TIME -- FOR FAMILY. FOR MY NEAR-FORGOTTEN DREAM OF WRITING.
AND EARTH --
-- I WAS CALLED TO EARTH LESS AND LESS, AS WELL --

YOU ARE...LOST IN A *DREAM*, DUNCAN?

I'M JUST -- IT'S --

SOMETHING'S *WRONG*, HON. SOMETHING'S... *OFF*, IN THE UNIVERSE. ON A GRAND SCALE. I FEEL IT EVERY TIME I INVOKE ONE OF THE *MAJOR LORI*.

WHAT *IS* IT?

I...DON'T KNOW. I CAN'T *FOCUS* ON IT, SOMEHOW. IT'S THERE...

...BUT THEN IT SLIPS AWAY.

AND YOU HAVE ASKED THE *LORUS* ABOUT IT? WHAT DOES IT *TELL* YOU?

NOTHING. NOT A *FEELING*, NOT A HINT, NOT A *DIRECTION.* NOT EVEN A DAMN *ECHO.*

THEN --

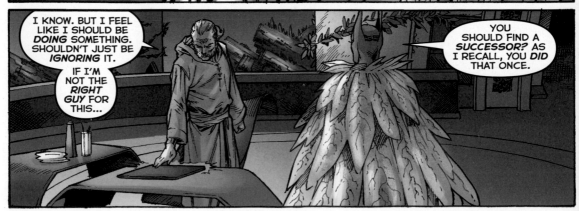

I KNOW. BUT I FEEL LIKE I SHOULD BE *DOING* SOMETHING. SHOULDN'T JUST BE *IGNORING* IT.

IF I'M NOT THE *RIGHT GUY* FOR THIS...

YOU SHOULD FIND A *SUCCESSOR?* AS I RECALL, YOU *DID* THAT ONCE.

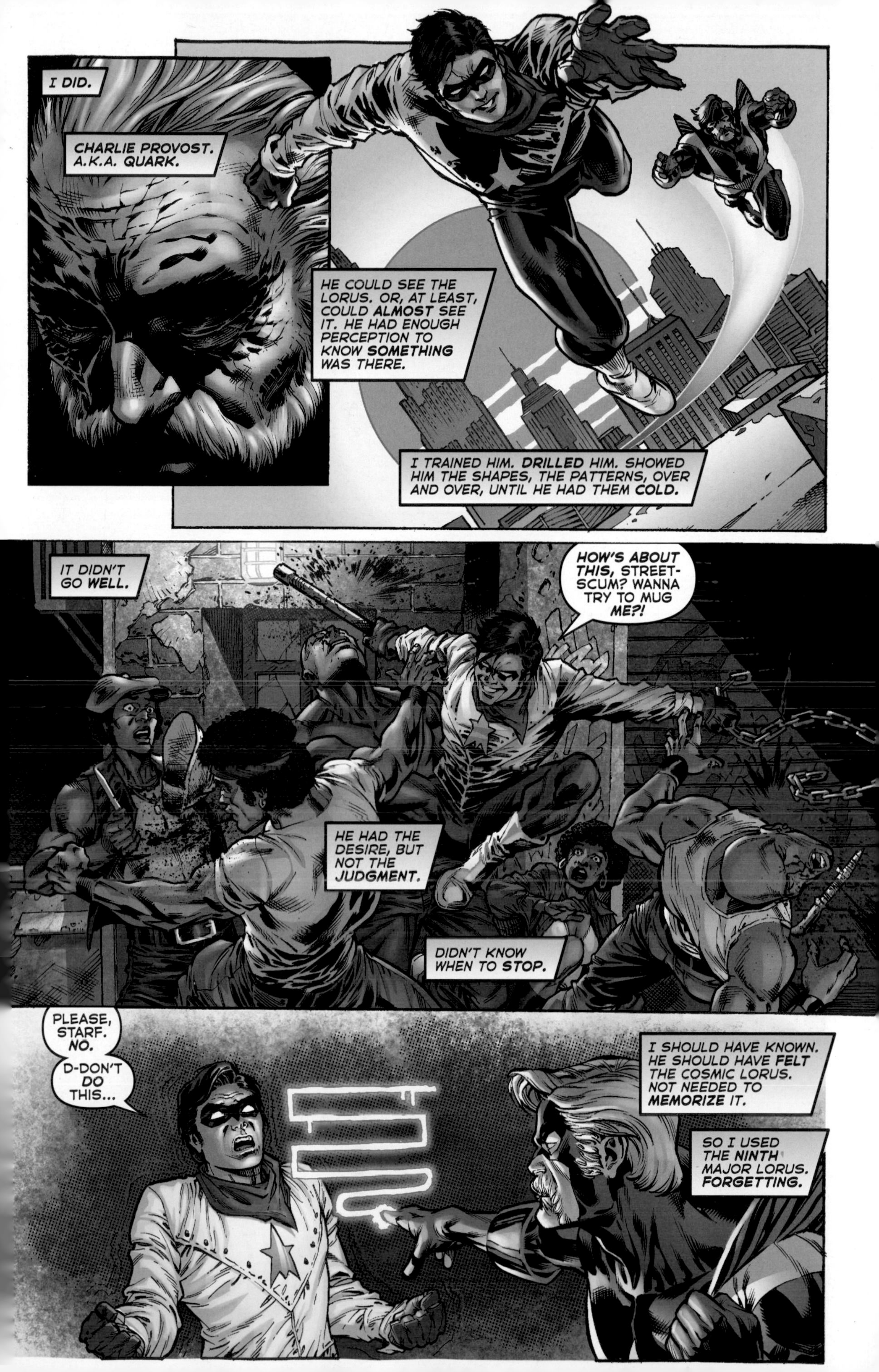
I DID.
CHARLIE PROVOST. A.K.A. QUARK.
HE COULD SEE THE LORUS. OR, AT LEAST, COULD ALMOST SEE IT. HE HAD ENOUGH PERCEPTION TO KNOW SOMETHING WAS THERE.
I TRAINED HIM. DRILLED HIM. SHOWED HIM THE SHAPES, THE PATTERNS, OVER AND OVER, UNTIL HE HAD THEM COLD.
IT DIDN'T GO WELL.
HOW'S ABOUT THIS, STREET-SCUM? WANNA TRY TO MUG ME?!
HE HAD THE DESIRE, BUT NOT THE JUDGMENT.
DIDN'T KNOW WHEN TO STOP.
PLEASE, STARF. NO.
D-DON'T DO THIS...
I SHOULD HAVE KNOWN. HE SHOULD HAVE FELT THE COSMIC LORUS. NOT NEEDED TO MEMORIZE IT.
SO I USED THE NINTH MAJOR LORUS. FORGETTING.

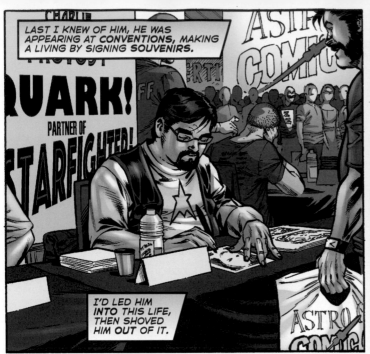

LAST I KNEW OF HIM, HE WAS APPEARING AT *CONVENTIONS*, MAKING A LIVING BY SIGNING *SOUVENIRS*.

QUARK!
PARTNER OF STARFIGHTER!

ASTRO COMICS

I'D LED HIM INTO THIS LIFE, THEN SHOVED HIM *OUT* OF IT.

AND HE COULDN'T LET GO.

I'LL *REMEMBER!* I'LL REMEMBER -- AN' I'LL BE *BACK!*

DAMN YOU, STARFIGHTER -- I'LL BE *BACK!*

YEAH, I REALLY *CRAPPED THE BED* WITH THAT ONE, HUH? POOR *KID*.

HE SOUNDS LIKE A *HORROR*, TO ME.

YOU FEEL GUILTY FOR NOT HAVING DONE *BETTER* BY HIM? AND NOW YOU FEEL THAT YOU HAVE NOT DONE ENOUGH FOR THE *UNIVERSE?*

I THINK I'VE PROBABLY DONE *ENOUGH* FOR THE UNIVERSE. I THINK THE SCORE'S *PRETTY GOOD* IN MY FAVOR.

BUT JUST BECAUSE I'VE DONE ENOUGH DOESN'T MEAN THERE ISN'T *MORE* TO DO.

THERE'S SOMETHING *OUT* THERE...

I SEE. I *THINK*.

50

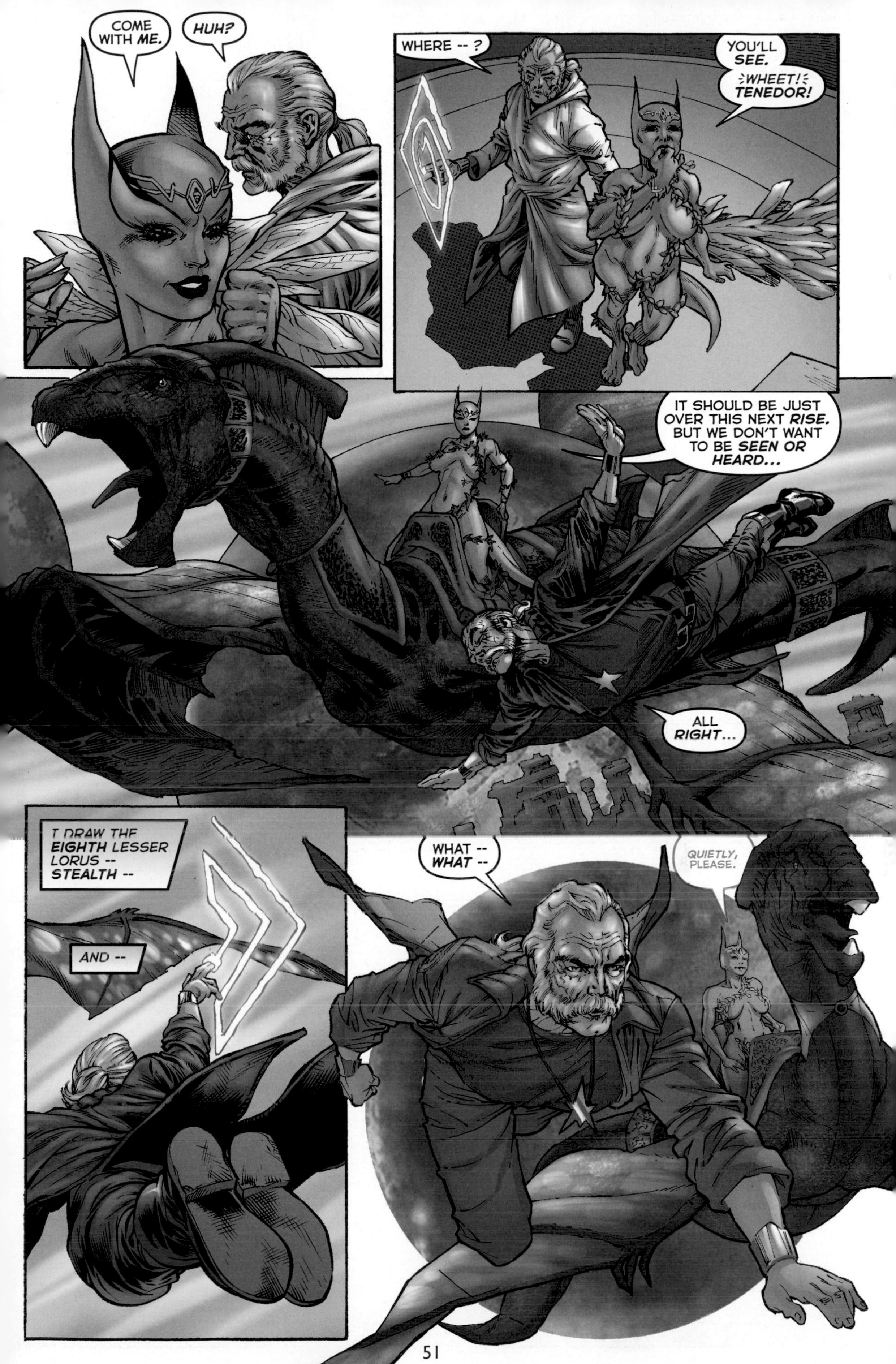
COME WITH ME.
HUH?
WHERE -- ?
YOU'LL SEE.
WHEET! TENEDOR!
IT SHOULD BE JUST OVER THIS NEXT RISE. BUT WE DON'T WANT TO BE SEEN OR HEARD...
ALL RIGHT...
I DRAW THE EIGHTH LESSER LORUS -- STEALTH --
AND --
WHAT -- WHAT --
QUIETLY, PLEASE.

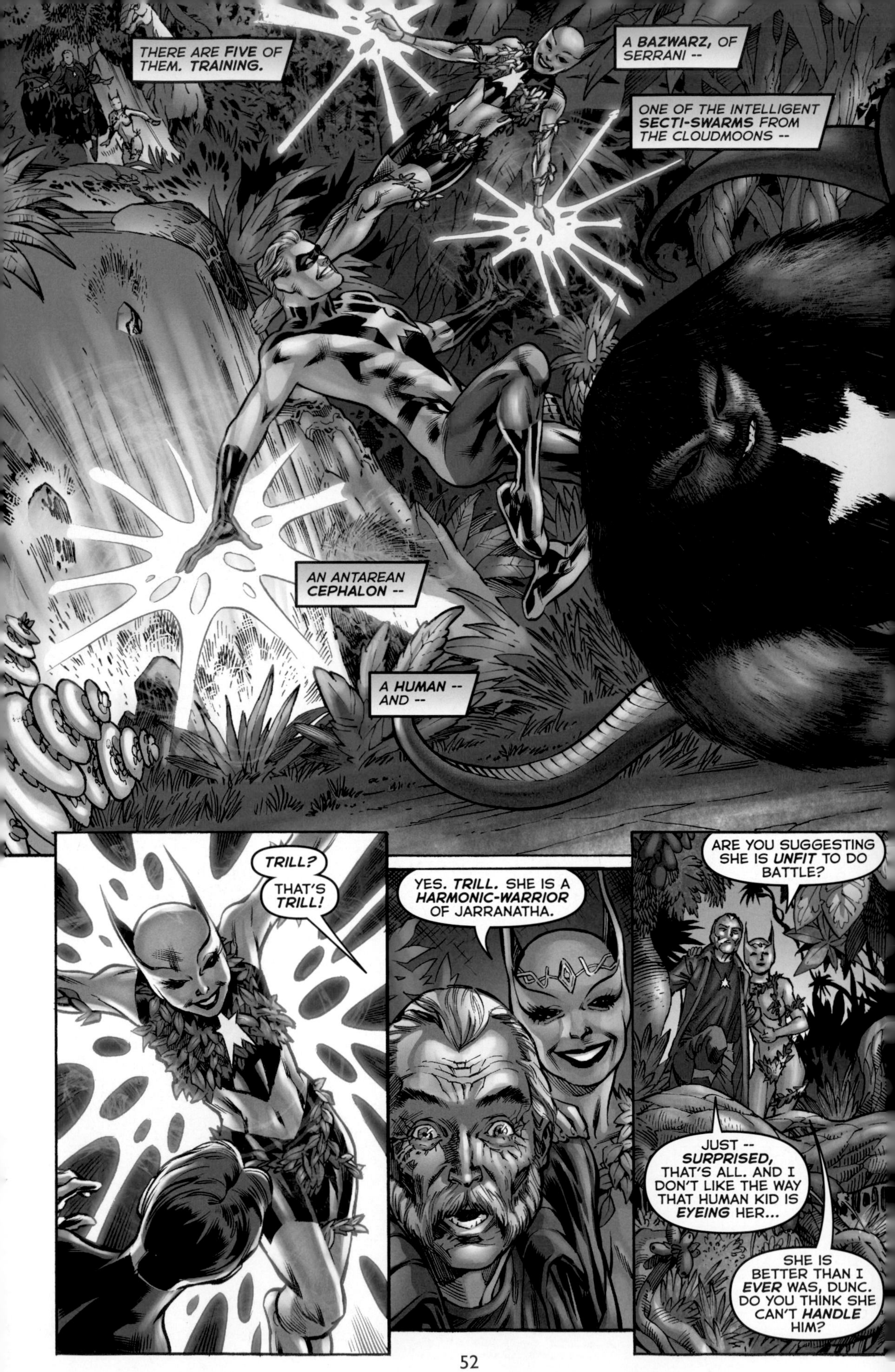
THERE ARE FIVE OF THEM. TRAINING.
A BAZWARZ, OF SERRANI --
ONE OF THE INTELLIGENT SECTI-SWARMS FROM THE CLOUDMOONS --
AN ANTAREAN CEPHALON --
A HUMAN -- AND --
TRILL?
THAT'S TRILL!
YES. TRILL. SHE IS A HARMONIC-WARRIOR OF JARRANATHA.
ARE YOU SUGGESTING SHE IS UNFIT TO DO BATTLE?
JUST -- SURPRISED, THAT'S ALL. AND I DON'T LIKE THE WAY THAT HUMAN KID IS EYEING HER...
SHE IS BETTER THAN I EVER WAS, DUNC. DO YOU THINK SHE CAN'T HANDLE HIM?

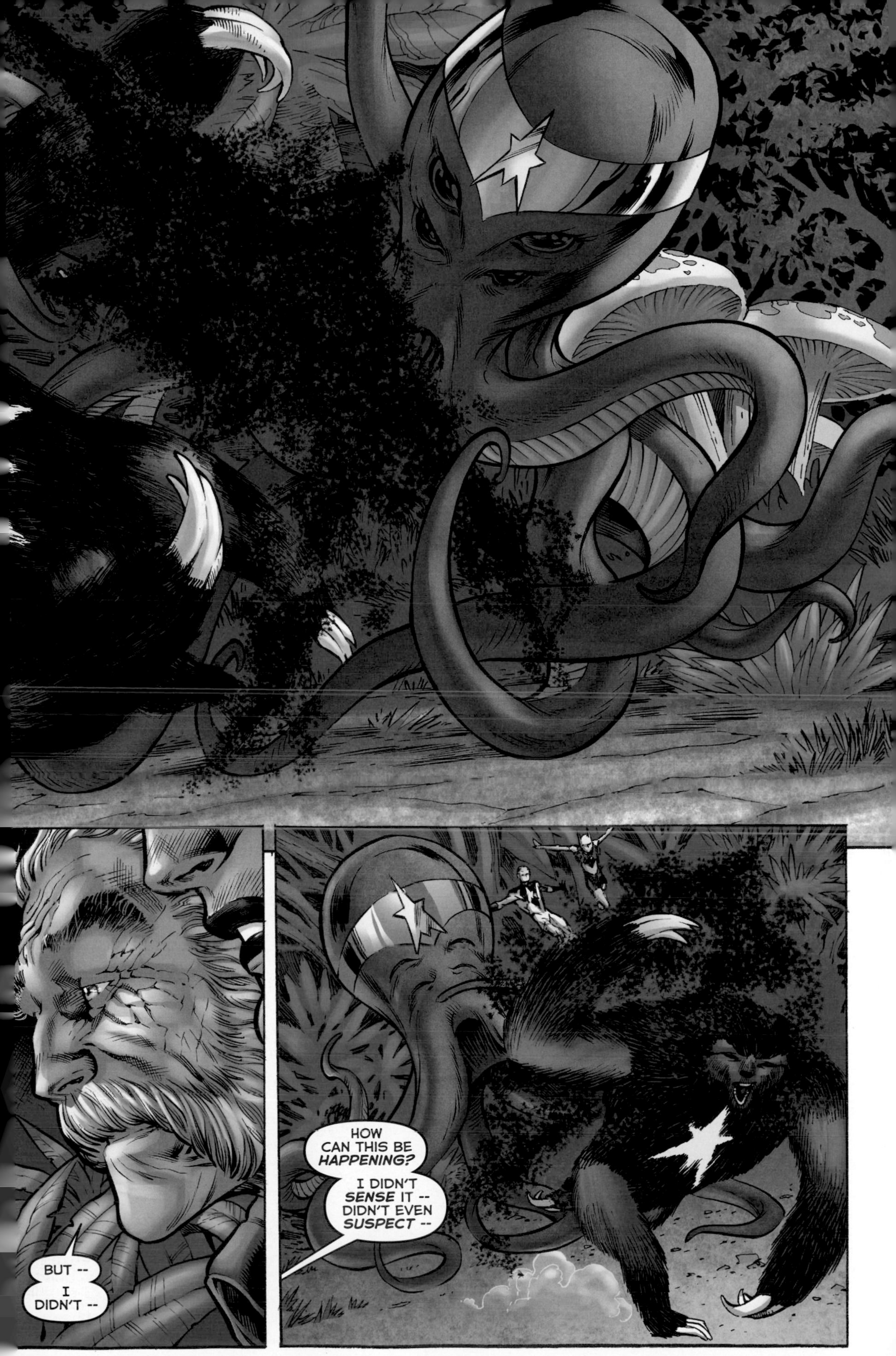
BUT -- I DIDN'T --
HOW CAN THIS BE *HAPPENING?*
I DIDN'T *SENSE* IT -- DIDN'T EVEN *SUSPECT* --

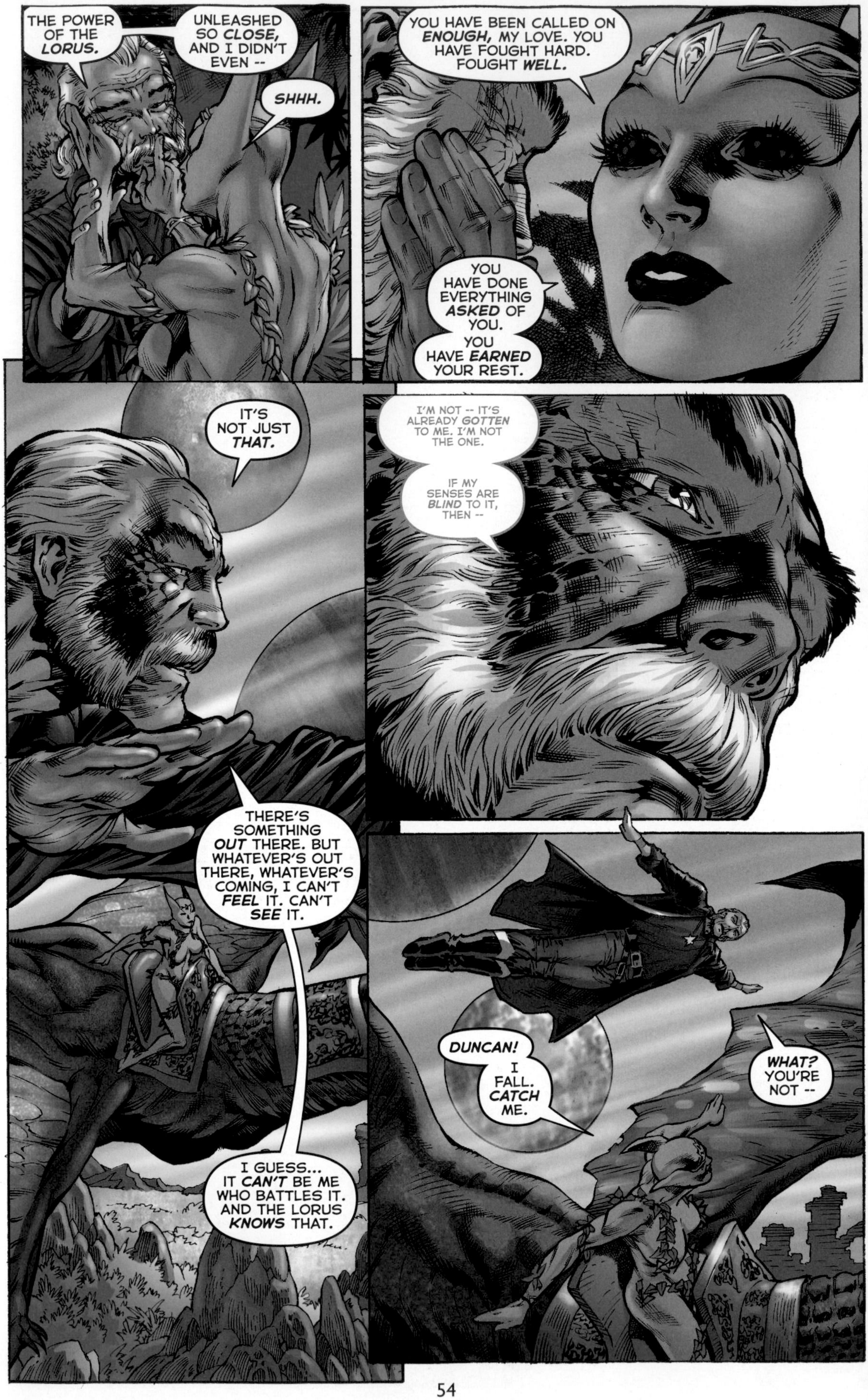
THE POWER OF THE LORUS.
UNLEASHED SO CLOSE, AND I DIDN'T EVEN --
SHHH.
YOU HAVE BEEN CALLED ON ENOUGH, MY LOVE. YOU HAVE FOUGHT HARD. FOUGHT WELL.
YOU HAVE DONE EVERYTHING ASKED OF YOU.
YOU HAVE EARNED YOUR REST.
IT'S NOT JUST THAT.
I'M NOT -- IT'S ALREADY GOTTEN TO ME. I'M NOT THE ONE.
IF MY SENSES ARE BLIND TO IT, THEN --
THERE'S SOMETHING OUT THERE. BUT WHATEVER'S OUT THERE, WHATEVER'S COMING, I CAN'T FEEL IT. CAN'T SEE IT.
I GUESS... IT CAN'T BE ME WHO BATTLES IT. AND THE LORUS KNOWS THAT.
DUNCAN!
I FALL. CATCH ME.
WHAT? YOU'RE NOT --

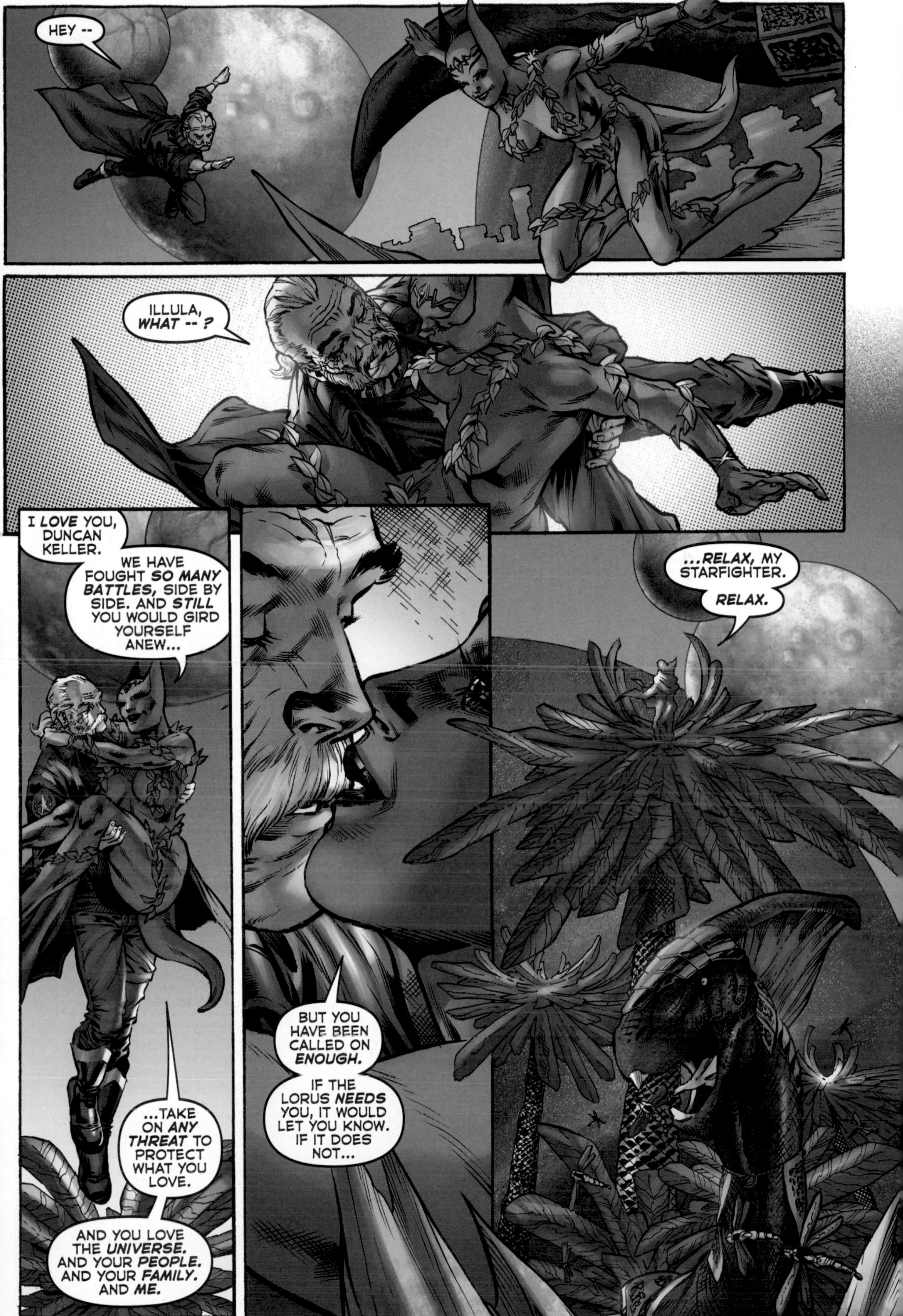
HEY --
ILLULA, WHAT -- ?
I LOVE YOU, DUNCAN KELLER.
WE HAVE FOUGHT SO MANY BATTLES, SIDE BY SIDE. AND STILL YOU WOULD GIRD YOURSELF ANEW...
...TAKE ON ANY THREAT TO PROTECT WHAT YOU LOVE.
AND YOU LOVE THE UNIVERSE. AND YOUR PEOPLE. AND YOUR FAMILY. AND ME.
BUT YOU HAVE BEEN CALLED ON ENOUGH.
IF THE LORUS NEEDS YOU, IT WOULD LET YOU KNOW. IF IT DOES NOT...
...RELAX, MY STARFIGHTER.
RELAX.

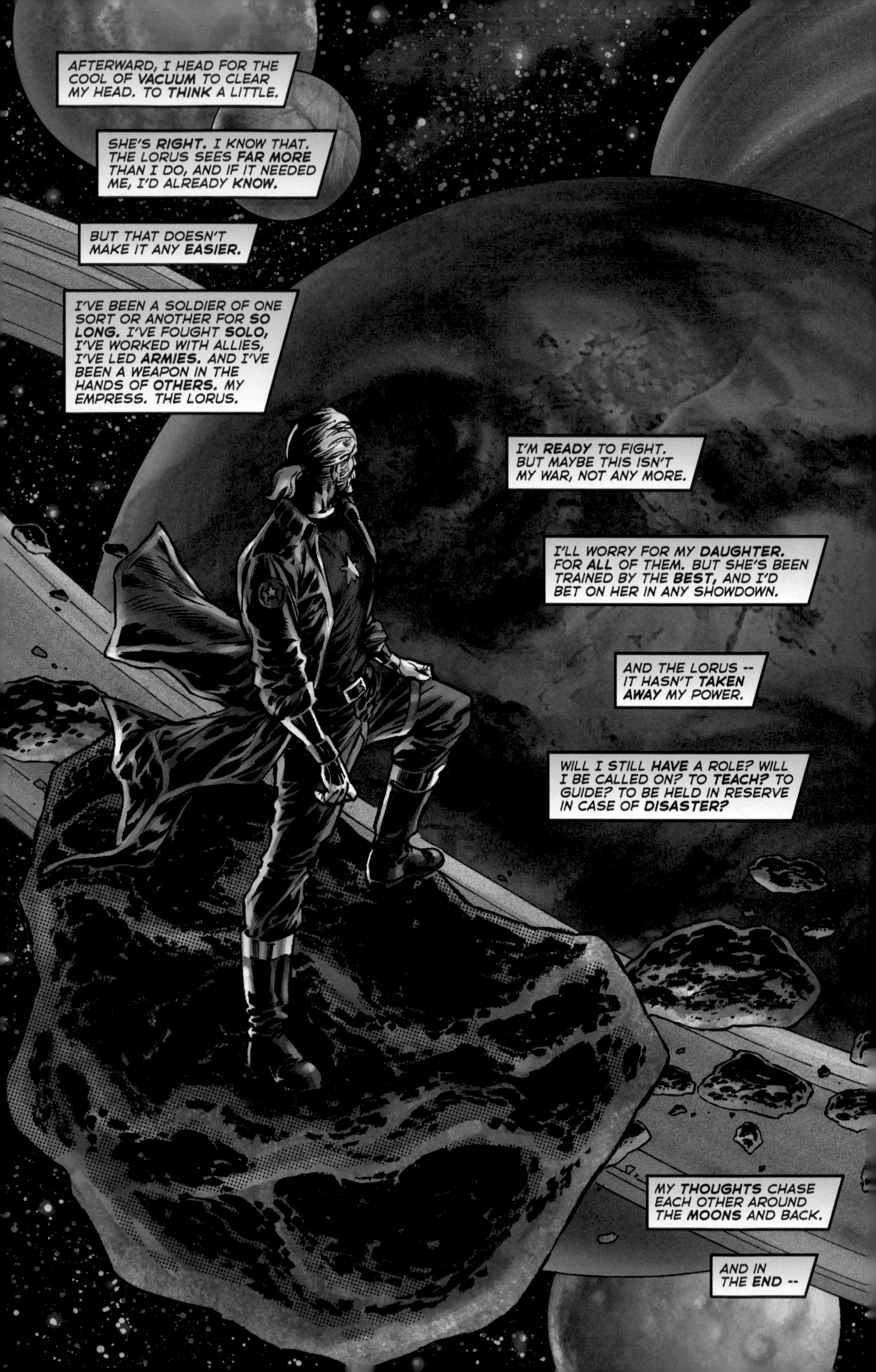
AFTERWARD, I HEAD FOR THE COOL OF VACUUM TO CLEAR MY HEAD. TO THINK A LITTLE.
SHE'S RIGHT. I KNOW THAT. THE LORUS SEES FAR MORE THAN I DO, AND IF IT NEEDED ME, I'D ALREADY KNOW.
BUT THAT DOESN'T MAKE IT ANY EASIER.
I'VE BEEN A SOLDIER OF ONE SORT OR ANOTHER FOR SO LONG. I'VE FOUGHT SOLO, I'VE WORKED WITH ALLIES, I'VE LED ARMIES. AND I'VE BEEN A WEAPON IN THE HANDS OF OTHERS. MY EMPRESS. THE LORUS.
I'M READY TO FIGHT. BUT MAYBE THIS ISN'T MY WAR, NOT ANY MORE.
I'LL WORRY FOR MY DAUGHTER. FOR ALL OF THEM. BUT SHE'S BEEN TRAINED BY THE BEST, AND I'D BET ON HER IN ANY SHOWDOWN.
AND THE LORUS -- IT HASN'T TAKEN AWAY MY POWER.
WILL I STILL HAVE A ROLE? WILL I BE CALLED ON? TO TEACH? TO GUIDE? TO BE HELD IN RESERVE IN CASE OF DISASTER?
MY THOUGHTS CHASE EACH OTHER AROUND THE MOONS AND BACK.
AND IN THE END --

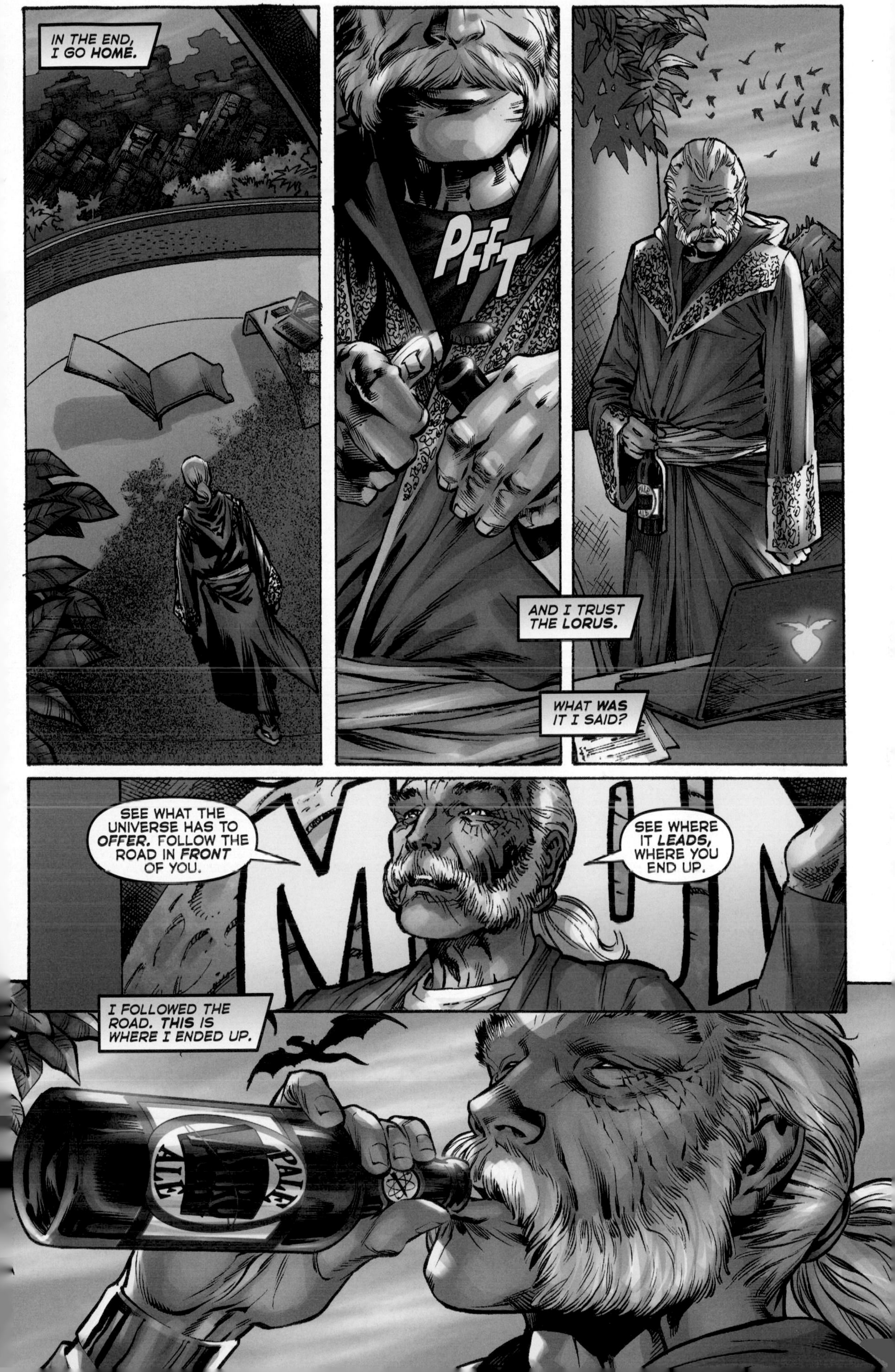
IN THE END, I GO HOME.
PFFT
AND I TRUST THE LORUS.
WHAT WAS IT I SAID?
SEE WHAT THE UNIVERSE HAS TO OFFER. FOLLOW THE ROAD IN FRONT OF YOU.
SEE WHERE IT LEADS, WHERE YOU END UP.
I FOLLOWED THE ROAD. THIS IS WHERE I ENDED UP.
PALE ALE

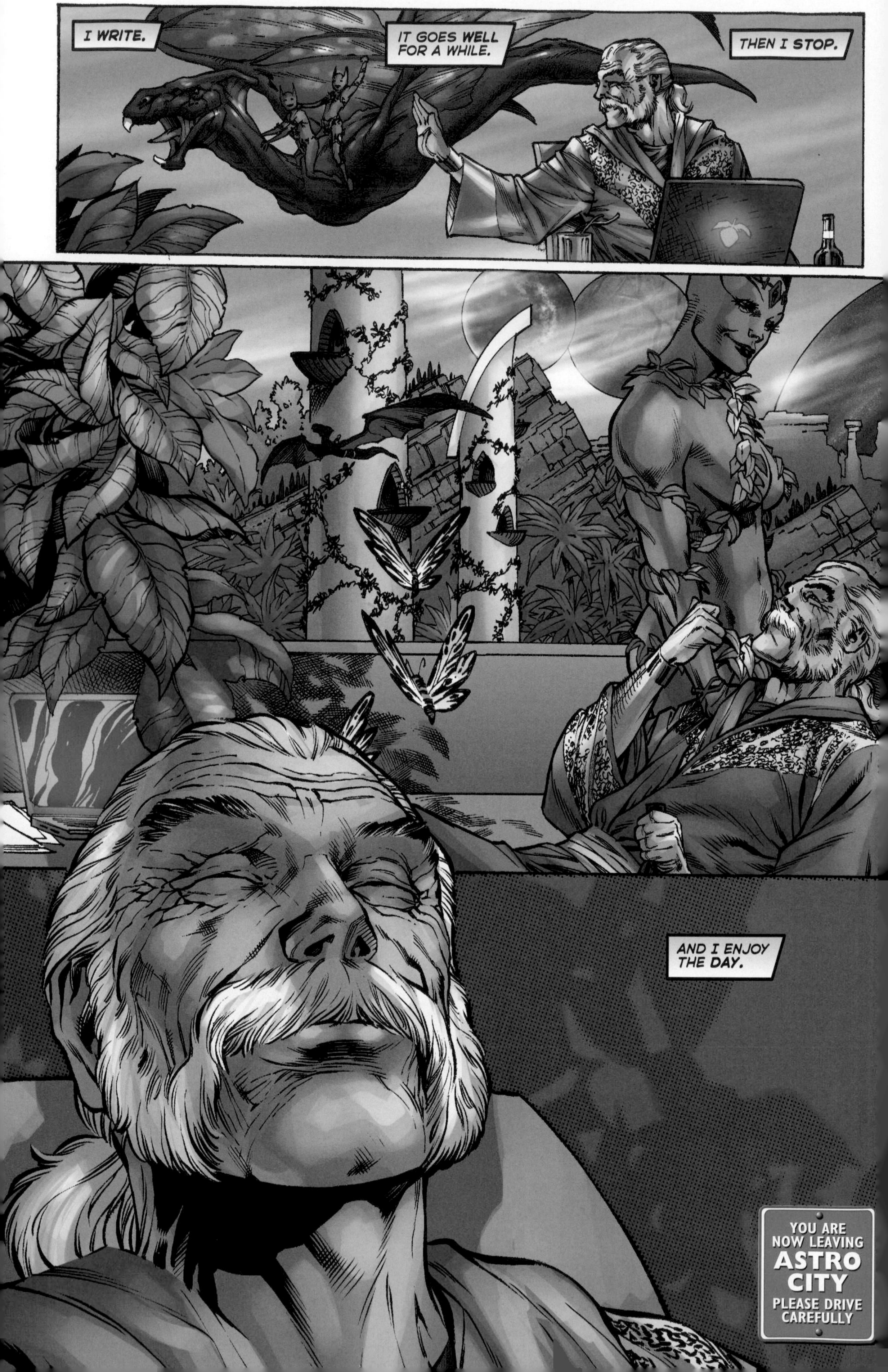
I WRITE.
IT GOES WELL FOR A WHILE.
THEN I STOP.
AND I ENJOY THE DAY.
YOU ARE NOW LEAVING ASTRO CITY PLEASE DRIVE CAREFULLY

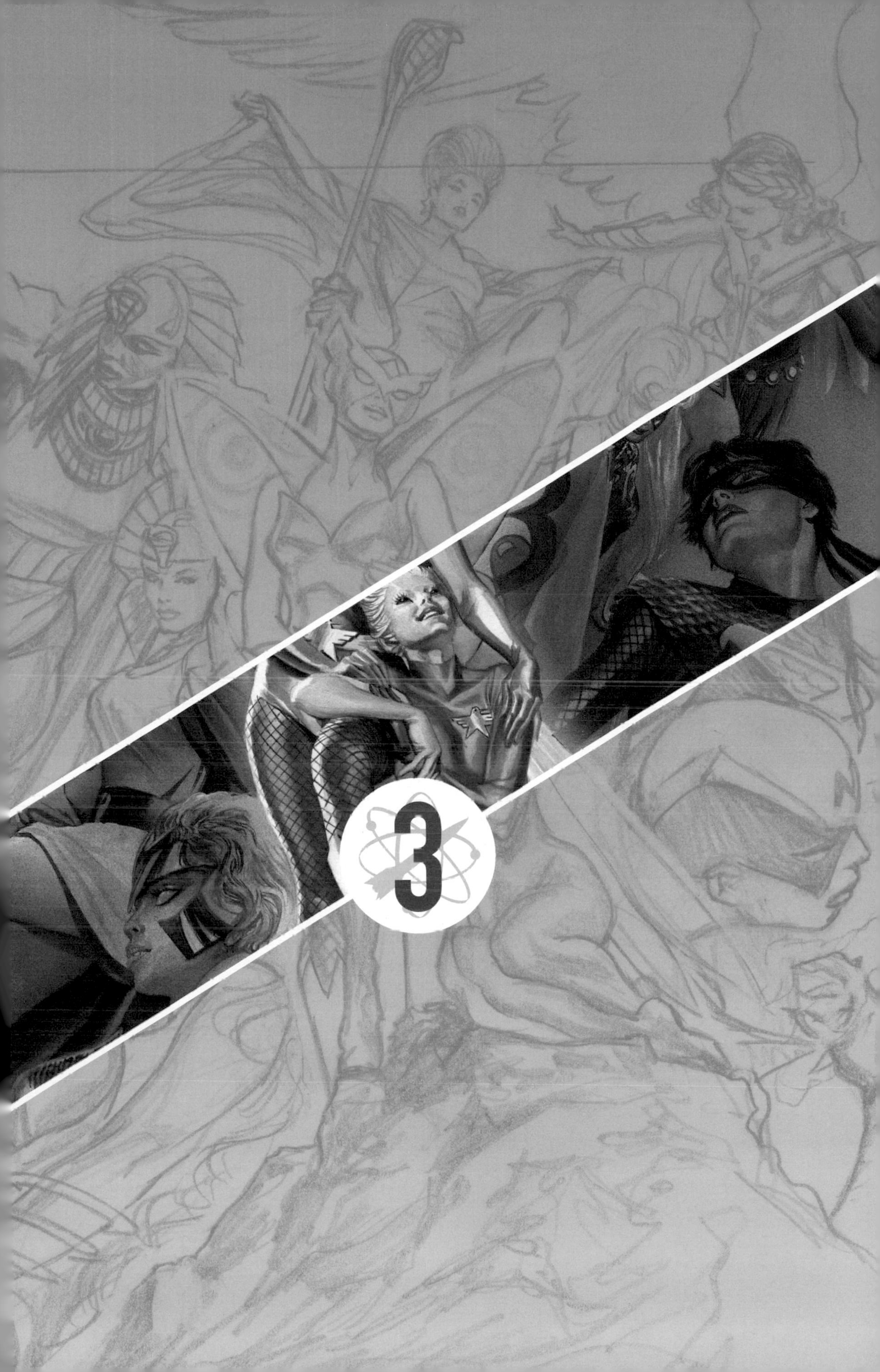
3

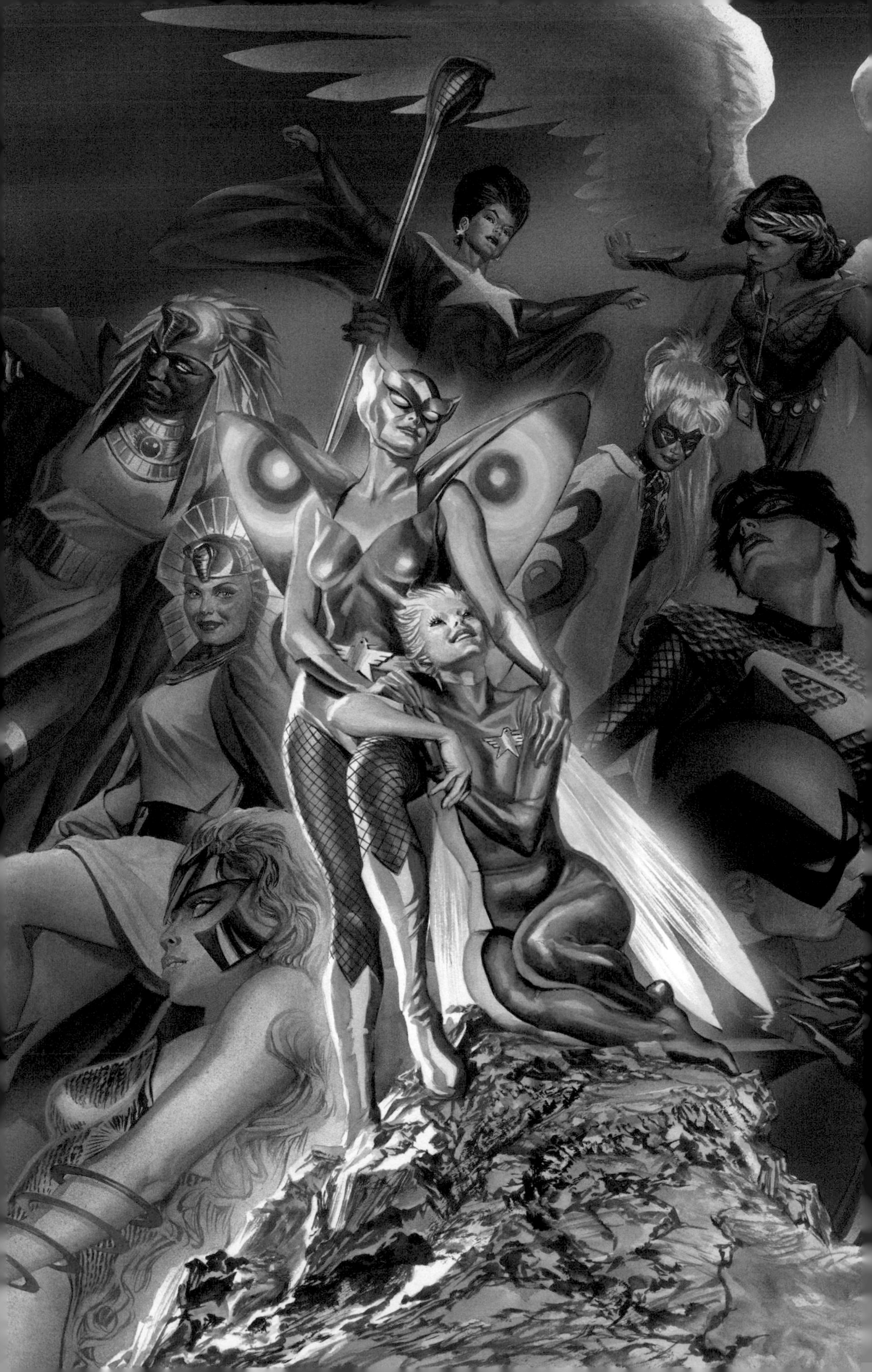

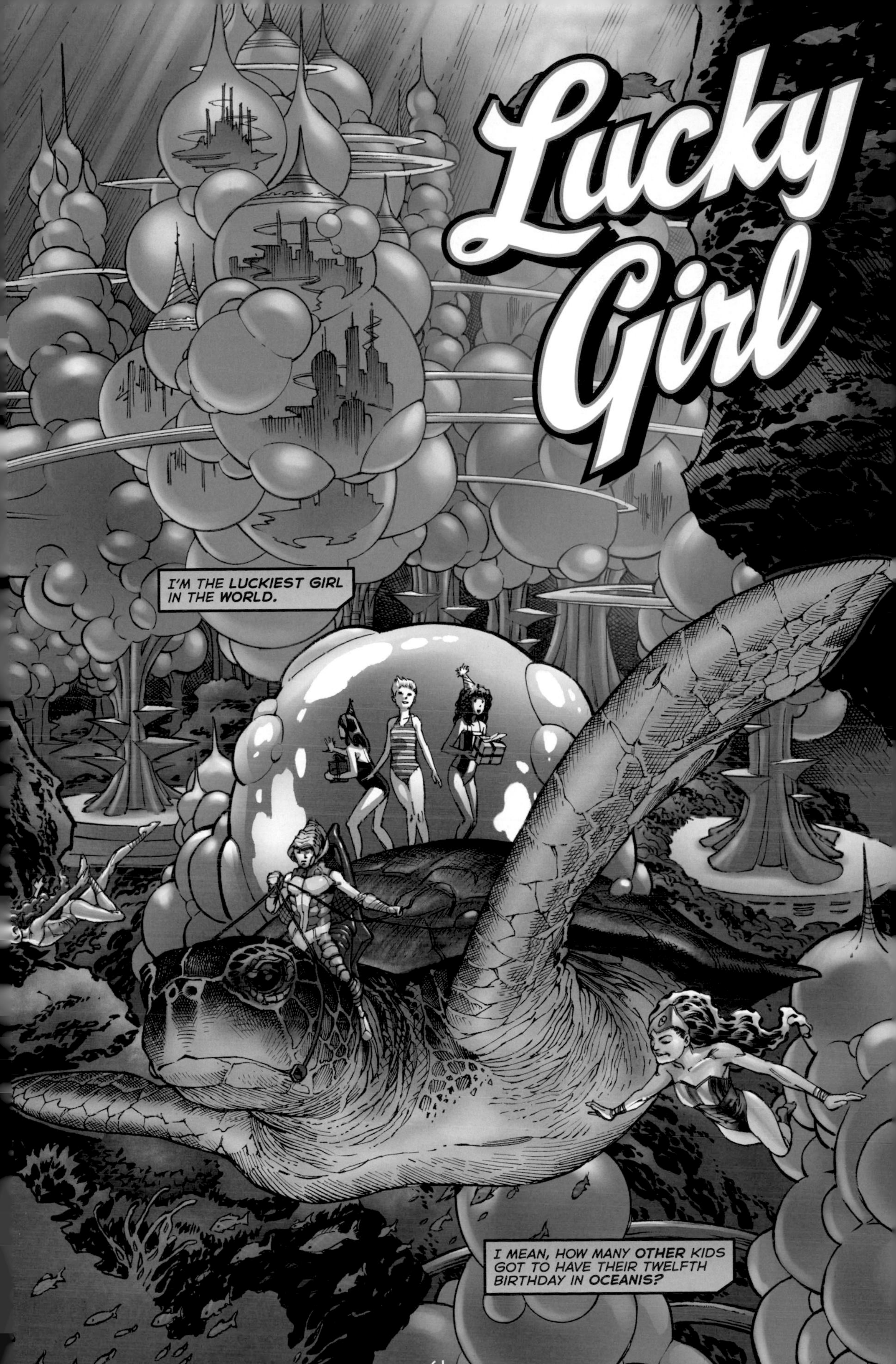
Lucky Girl
I'M THE LUCKIEST GIRL IN THE WORLD.
I MEAN, HOW MANY OTHER KIDS GOT TO HAVE THEIR TWELFTH BIRTHDAY IN OCEANIS?

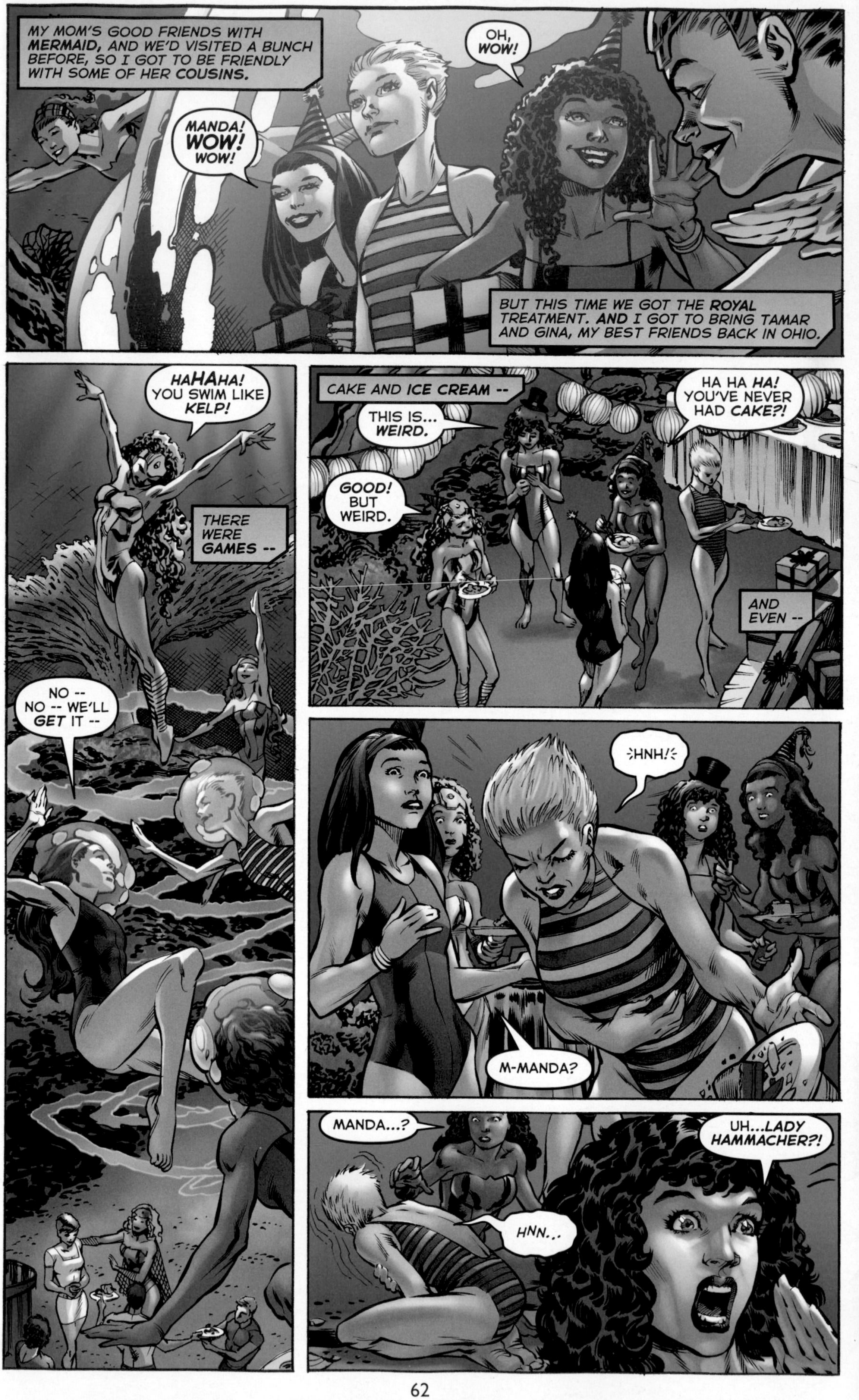
MY MOM'S GOOD FRIENDS WITH MERMAID, AND WE'D VISITED A BUNCH BEFORE, SO I GOT TO BE FRIENDLY WITH SOME OF HER COUSINS.
OH, WOW!
MANDA! WOW! WOW!
BUT THIS TIME WE GOT THE ROYAL TREATMENT. AND I GOT TO BRING TAMAR AND GINA, MY BEST FRIENDS BACK IN OHIO.
HAHAHA! YOU SWIM LIKE KELP!
THERE WERE GAMES --
NO -- NO -- WE'LL GET IT --
CAKE AND ICE CREAM --
THIS IS... WEIRD.
HA HA HA! YOU'VE NEVER HAD CAKE?!
GOOD! BUT WEIRD.
AND EVEN --
HNH!
M-MANDA?
MANDA...?
UH...LADY HAMMACHER?!
HNN...

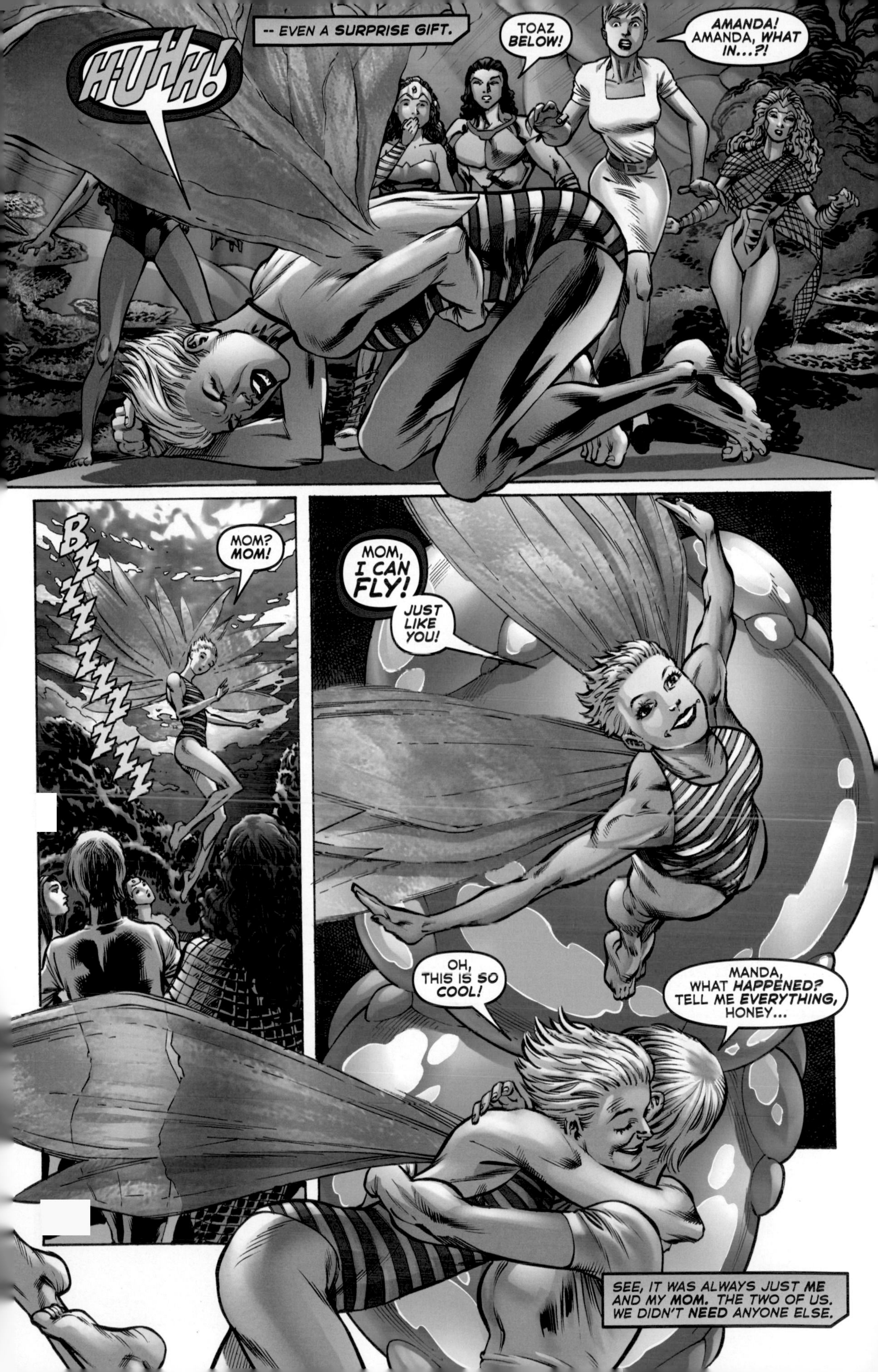
-- EVEN A SURPRISE GIFT.
H-UHH!
TOAZ BELOW!
AMANDA! AMANDA, WHAT IN...?!
BZZZZZZZZZ
MOM? MOM!
MOM, I CAN FLY!
JUST LIKE YOU!
OH, THIS IS SO COOL!
MANDA, WHAT HAPPENED? TELL ME EVERYTHING, HONEY...
SEE, IT WAS ALWAYS JUST ME AND MY MOM. THE TWO OF US. WE DIDN'T NEED ANYONE ELSE.

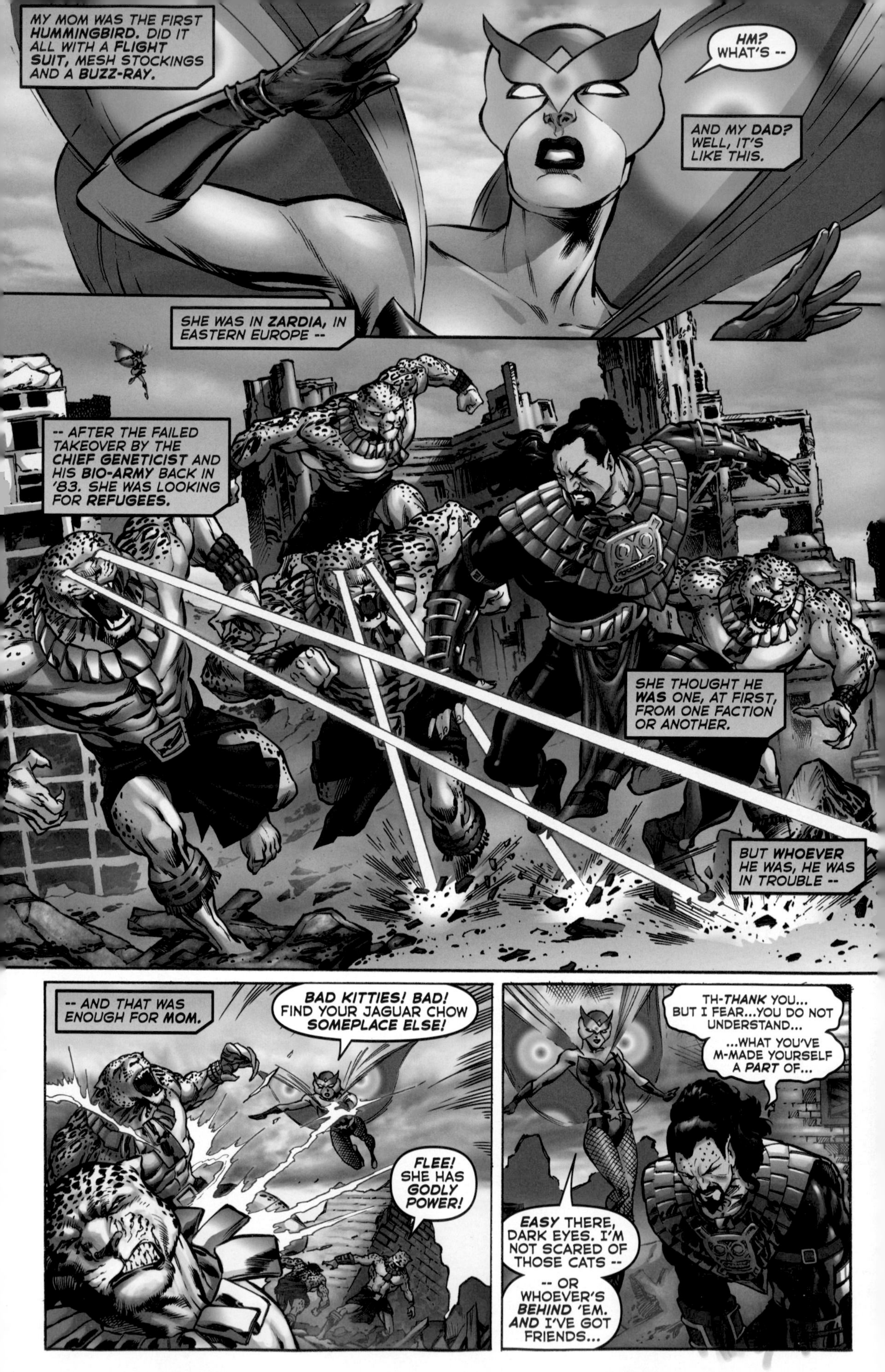
MY MOM WAS THE FIRST HUMMINGBIRD. DID IT ALL WITH A FLIGHT SUIT, MESH STOCKINGS AND A BUZZ-RAY.
HM? WHAT'S --
AND MY DAD? WELL, IT'S LIKE THIS.
SHE WAS IN ZARDIA, IN EASTERN EUROPE --
-- AFTER THE FAILED TAKEOVER BY THE CHIEF GENETICIST AND HIS BIO-ARMY BACK IN '83. SHE WAS LOOKING FOR REFUGEES.
SHE THOUGHT HE WAS ONE, AT FIRST, FROM ONE FACTION OR ANOTHER.
BUT WHOEVER HE WAS, HE WAS IN TROUBLE --
-- AND THAT WAS ENOUGH FOR MOM.
BAD KITTIES! BAD! FIND YOUR JAGUAR CHOW SOMEPLACE ELSE!
FLEE! SHE HAS GODLY POWER!
TH-THANK YOU... BUT I FEAR...YOU DO NOT UNDERSTAND...
...WHAT YOU'VE M-MADE YOURSELF A PART OF...
EASY THERE, DARK EYES. I'M NOT SCARED OF THOSE CATS --
-- OR WHOEVER'S BEHIND 'EM. AND I'VE GOT FRIENDS...

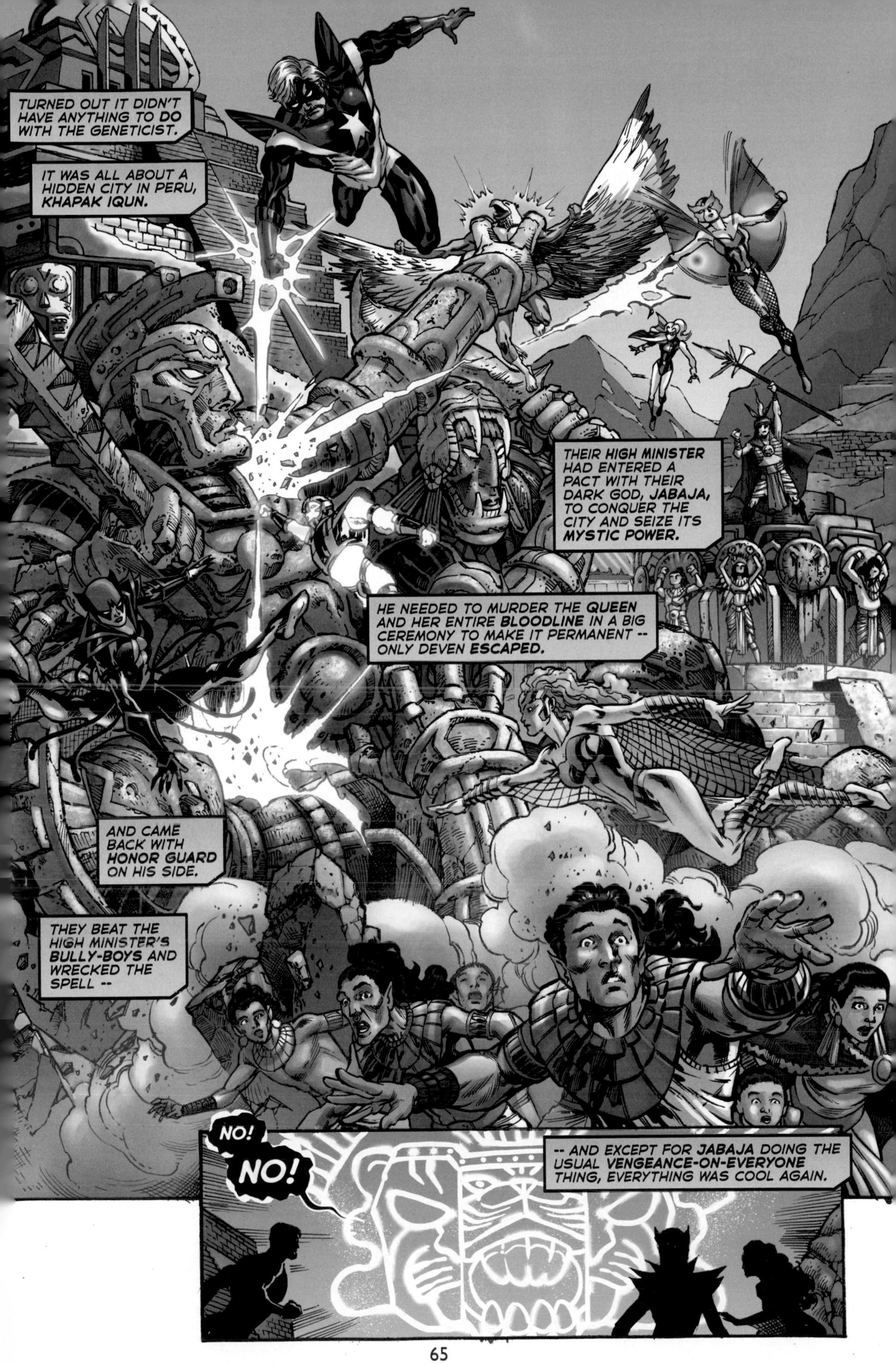
TURNED OUT IT DIDN'T HAVE ANYTHING TO DO WITH THE GENETICIST.
IT WAS ALL ABOUT A HIDDEN CITY IN PERU, KHAPAK IQUN.
THEIR HIGH MINISTER HAD ENTERED A PACT WITH THEIR DARK GOD, JABAJA, TO CONQUER THE CITY AND SEIZE ITS MYSTIC POWER.
HE NEEDED TO MURDER THE QUEEN AND HER ENTIRE BLOODLINE IN A BIG CEREMONY TO MAKE IT PERMANENT -- ONLY DEVEN ESCAPED.
AND CAME BACK WITH HONOR GUARD ON HIS SIDE.
THEY BEAT THE HIGH MINISTER'S BULLY-BOYS AND WRECKED THE SPELL --
NO!
NO!
-- AND EXCEPT FOR JABAJA DOING THE USUAL VENGEANCE-ON-EVERYONE THING, EVERYTHING WAS COOL AGAIN.

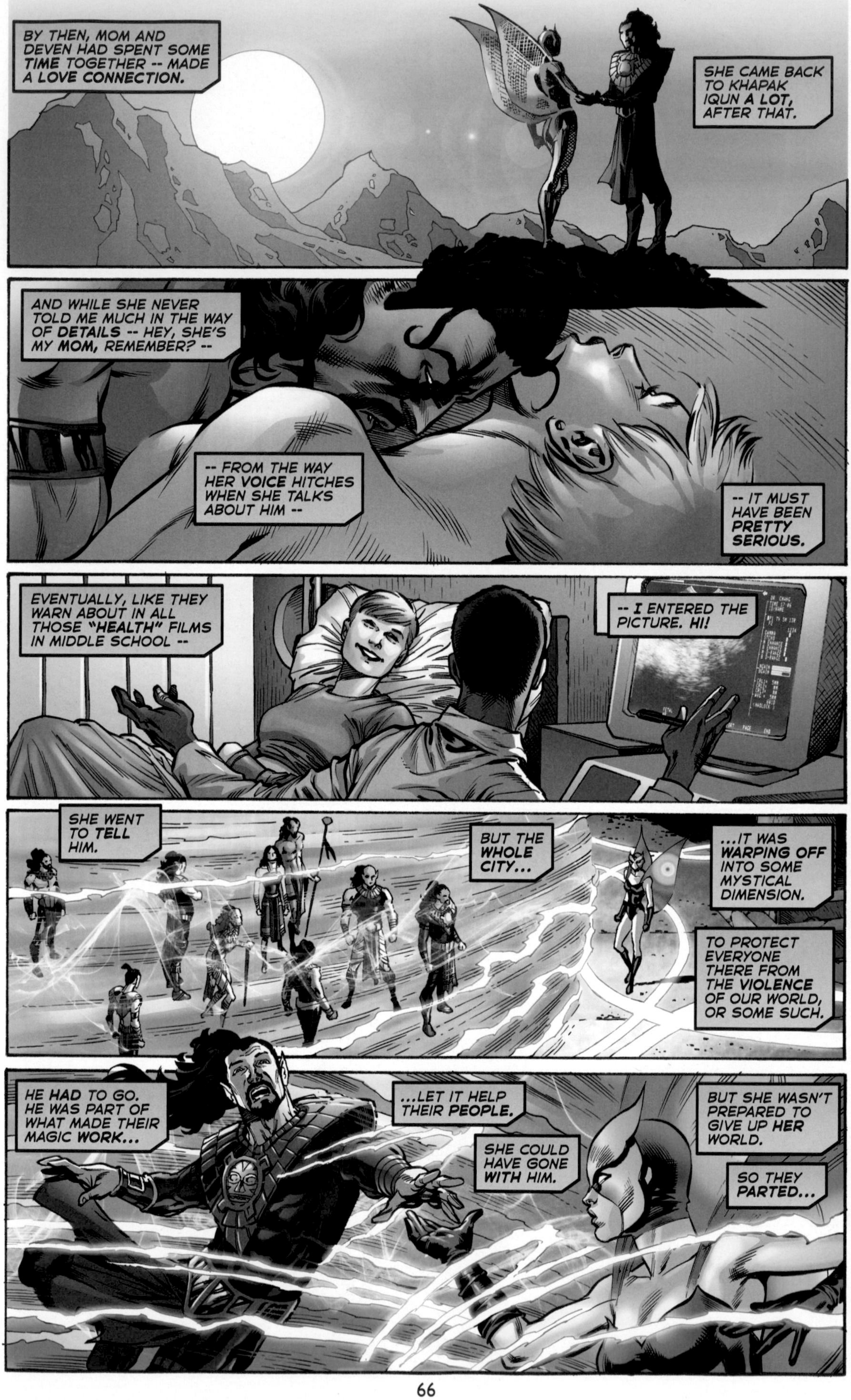
BY THEN, MOM AND DEVEN HAD SPENT SOME TIME TOGETHER -- MADE A LOVE CONNECTION.
SHE CAME BACK TO KHAPAK IQUN A LOT, AFTER THAT.
AND WHILE SHE NEVER TOLD ME MUCH IN THE WAY OF DETAILS -- HEY, SHE'S MY MOM, REMEMBER? --
-- FROM THE WAY HER VOICE HITCHES WHEN SHE TALKS ABOUT HIM --
-- IT MUST HAVE BEEN PRETTY SERIOUS.
EVENTUALLY, LIKE THEY WARN ABOUT IN ALL THOSE "HEALTH" FILMS IN MIDDLE SCHOOL --
-- I ENTERED THE PICTURE. HI!
SHE WENT TO TELL HIM.
BUT THE WHOLE CITY...
...IT WAS WARPING OFF INTO SOME MYSTICAL DIMENSION.
TO PROTECT EVERYONE THERE FROM THE VIOLENCE OF OUR WORLD, OR SOME SUCH.
HE HAD TO GO. HE WAS PART OF WHAT MADE THEIR MAGIC WORK...
...LET IT HELP THEIR PEOPLE.
SHE COULD HAVE GONE WITH HIM.
BUT SHE WASN'T PREPARED TO GIVE UP HER WORLD.
SO THEY PARTED...

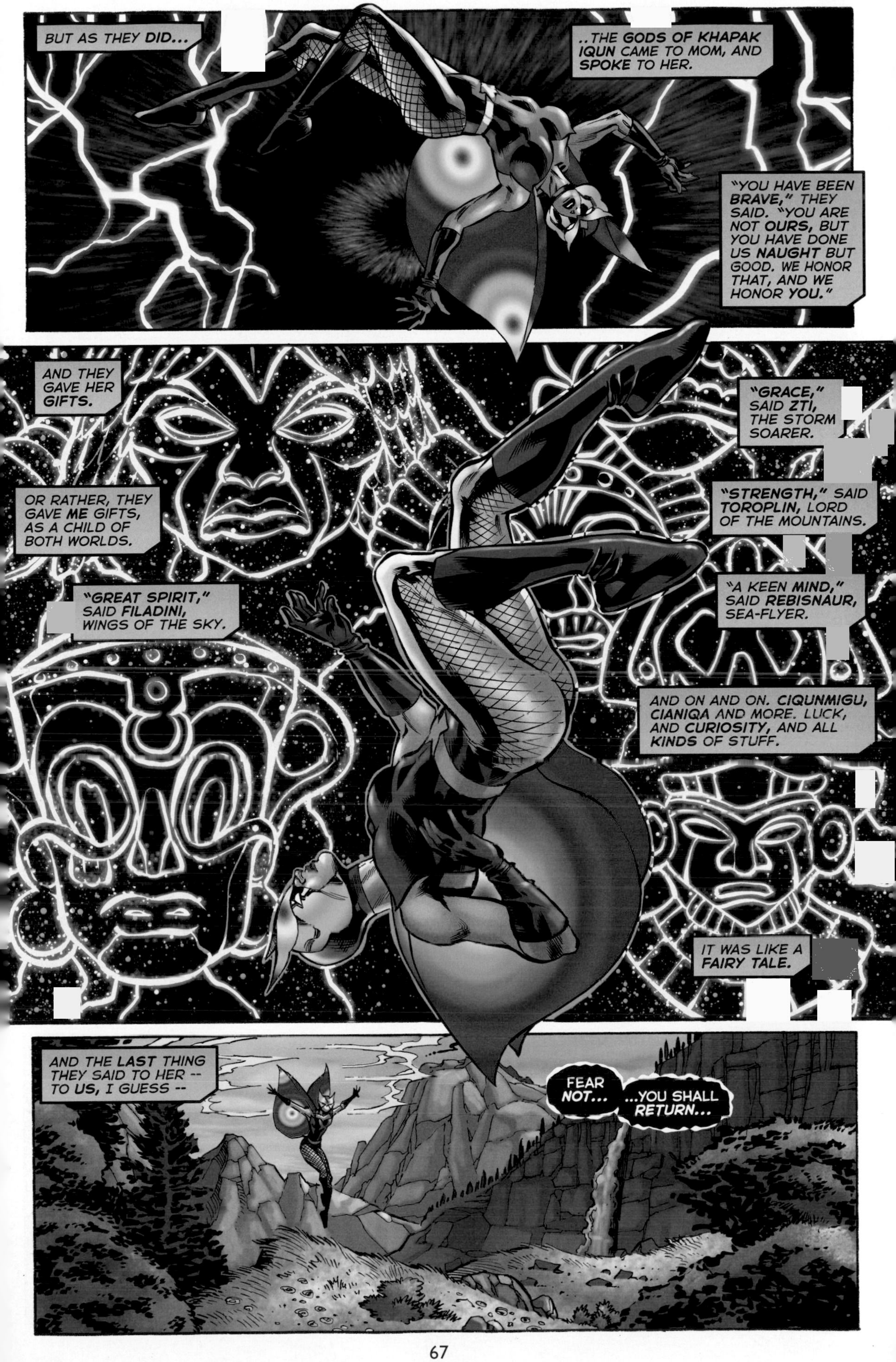
BUT AS THEY DID...
..THE GODS OF KHAPAK IQUN CAME TO MOM, AND SPOKE TO HER.
"YOU HAVE BEEN BRAVE," THEY SAID. "YOU ARE NOT OURS, BUT YOU HAVE DONE US NAUGHT BUT GOOD. WE HONOR THAT, AND WE HONOR YOU."
AND THEY GAVE HER GIFTS.
OR RATHER, THEY GAVE ME GIFTS, AS A CHILD OF BOTH WORLDS.
"GREAT SPIRIT," SAID FILADINI, WINGS OF THE SKY.
"GRACE," SAID ZTI, THE STORM SOARER.
"STRENGTH," SAID TOROPLIN, LORD OF THE MOUNTAINS.
"A KEEN MIND," SAID REBISNAUR, SEA-FLYER.
AND ON AND ON. CIQUNMIGU, CIANIQA AND MORE. LUCK, AND CURIOSITY, AND ALL KINDS OF STUFF.
IT WAS LIKE A FAIRY TALE.
AND THE LAST THING THEY SAID TO HER -- TO US, I GUESS --
FEAR NOT...
...YOU SHALL RETURN...

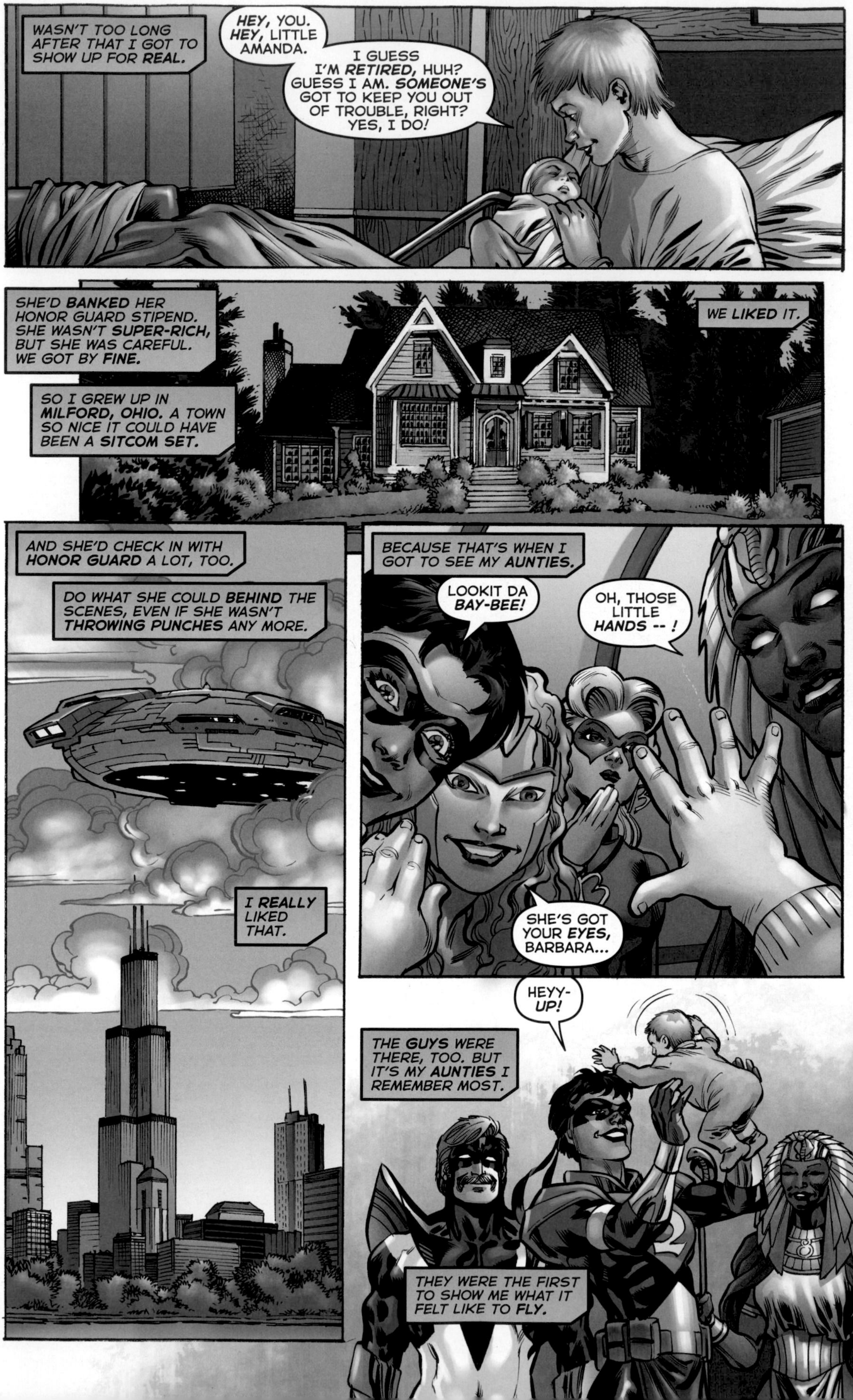
WASN'T TOO LONG AFTER THAT I GOT TO SHOW UP FOR REAL.
HEY, YOU. HEY, LITTLE AMANDA.
I GUESS I'M RETIRED, HUH? GUESS I AM. SOMEONE'S GOT TO KEEP YOU OUT OF TROUBLE, RIGHT? YES, I DO!
SHE'D BANKED HER HONOR GUARD STIPEND. SHE WASN'T SUPER-RICH, BUT SHE WAS CAREFUL. WE GOT BY FINE.
SO I GREW UP IN MILFORD, OHIO. A TOWN SO NICE IT COULD HAVE BEEN A SITCOM SET.
WE LIKED IT.
AND SHE'D CHECK IN WITH HONOR GUARD A LOT, TOO.
DO WHAT SHE COULD BEHIND THE SCENES, EVEN IF SHE WASN'T THROWING PUNCHES ANY MORE.
I REALLY LIKED THAT.
BECAUSE THAT'S WHEN I GOT TO SEE MY AUNTIES.
LOOKIT DA BAY-BEE!
OH, THOSE LITTLE HANDS -- !
SHE'S GOT YOUR EYES, BARBARA...
HEYY-UP!
THE GUYS WERE THERE, TOO. BUT IT'S MY AUNTIES I REMEMBER MOST.
THEY WERE THE FIRST TO SHOW ME WHAT IT FELT LIKE TO FLY.

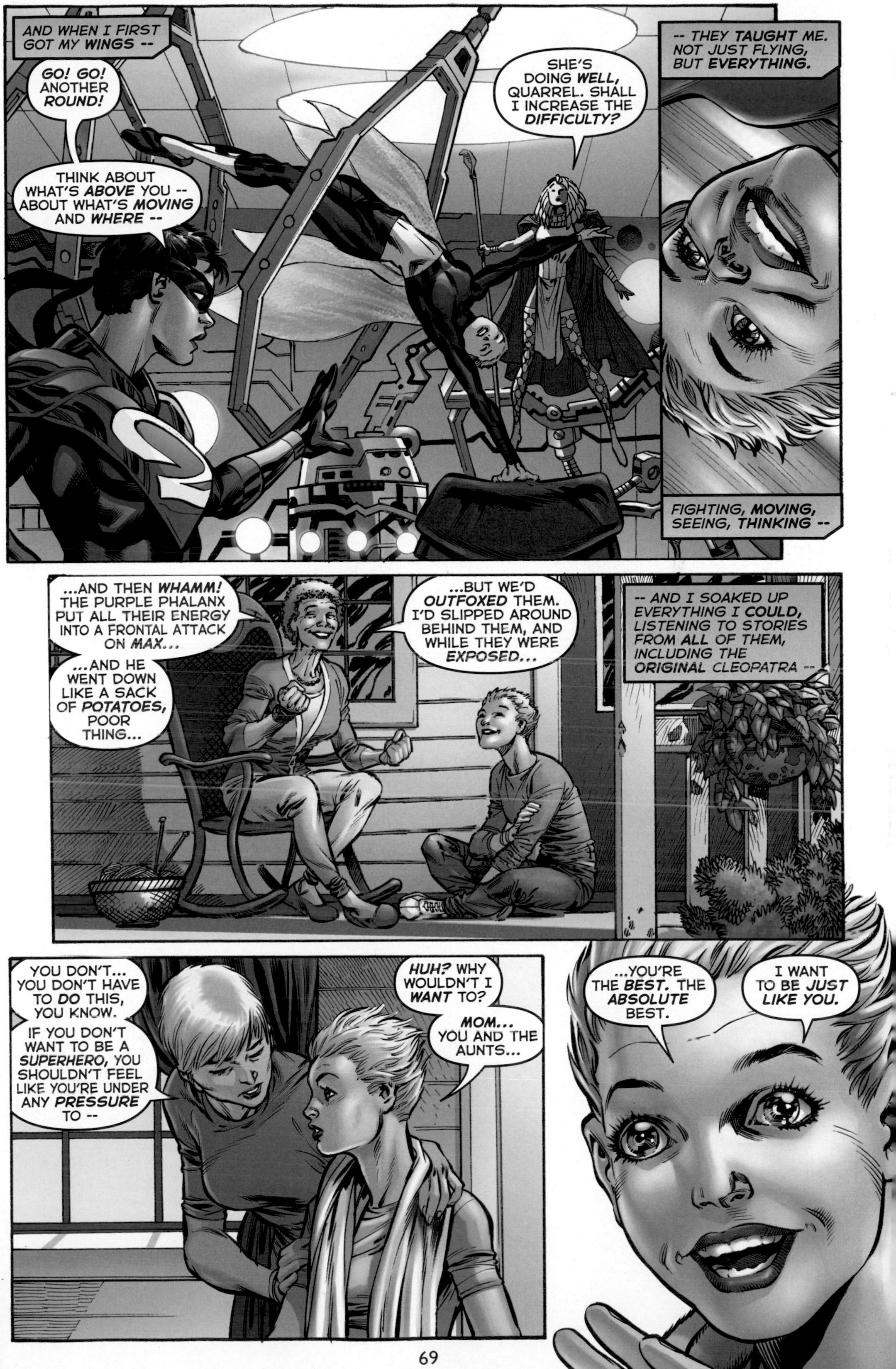
AND WHEN I FIRST GOT MY WINGS --
GO! GO! ANOTHER ROUND!
THINK ABOUT WHAT'S ABOVE YOU -- ABOUT WHAT'S MOVING AND WHERE --
SHE'S DOING WELL, QUARREL. SHALL I INCREASE THE DIFFICULTY?
-- THEY TAUGHT ME. NOT JUST FLYING, BUT EVERYTHING.
FIGHTING, MOVING, SEEING, THINKING --
...AND THEN WHAMM! THE PURPLE PHALANX PUT ALL THEIR ENERGY INTO A FRONTAL ATTACK ON MAX...
...AND HE WENT DOWN LIKE A SACK OF POTATOES, POOR THING...
...BUT WE'D OUTFOXED THEM. I'D SLIPPED AROUND BEHIND THEM, AND WHILE THEY WERE EXPOSED...
-- AND I SOAKED UP EVERYTHING I COULD, LISTENING TO STORIES FROM ALL OF THEM, INCLUDING THE ORIGINAL CLEOPATRA --
YOU DON'T... YOU DON'T HAVE TO DO THIS, YOU KNOW.
IF YOU DON'T WANT TO BE A SUPERHERO, YOU SHOULDN'T FEEL LIKE YOU'RE UNDER ANY PRESSURE TO --
HUH? WHY WOULDN'T I WANT TO?
MOM... YOU AND THE AUNTS...
...YOU'RE THE BEST. THE ABSOLUTE BEST.
I WANT TO BE JUST LIKE YOU.

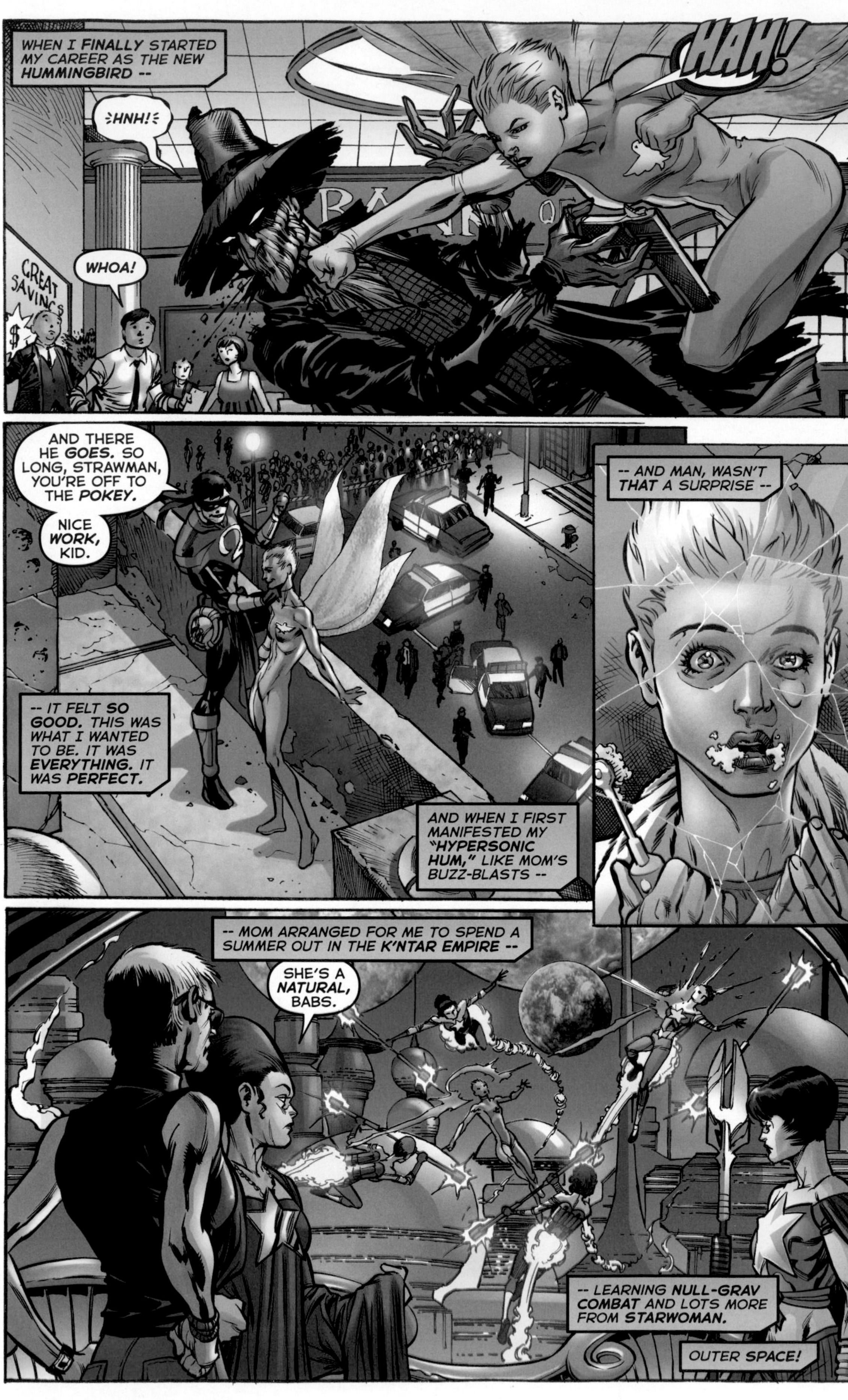
WHEN I FINALLY STARTED MY CAREER AS THE NEW HUMMINGBIRD --
HAH!
HNH!
WHOA!
GREAT SAVINGS
AND THERE HE GOES. SO LONG, STRAWMAN, YOU'RE OFF TO THE POKEY.
NICE WORK, KID.
-- IT FELT SO GOOD. THIS WAS WHAT I WANTED TO BE. IT WAS EVERYTHING. IT WAS PERFECT.
AND WHEN I FIRST MANIFESTED MY "HYPERSONIC HUM," LIKE MOM'S BUZZ-BLASTS --
-- AND MAN, WASN'T THAT A SURPRISE --
-- MOM ARRANGED FOR ME TO SPEND A SUMMER OUT IN THE K'NTAR EMPIRE --
SHE'S A NATURAL, BABS.
-- LEARNING NULL-GRAV COMBAT AND LOTS MORE FROM STARWOMAN.
OUTER SPACE!

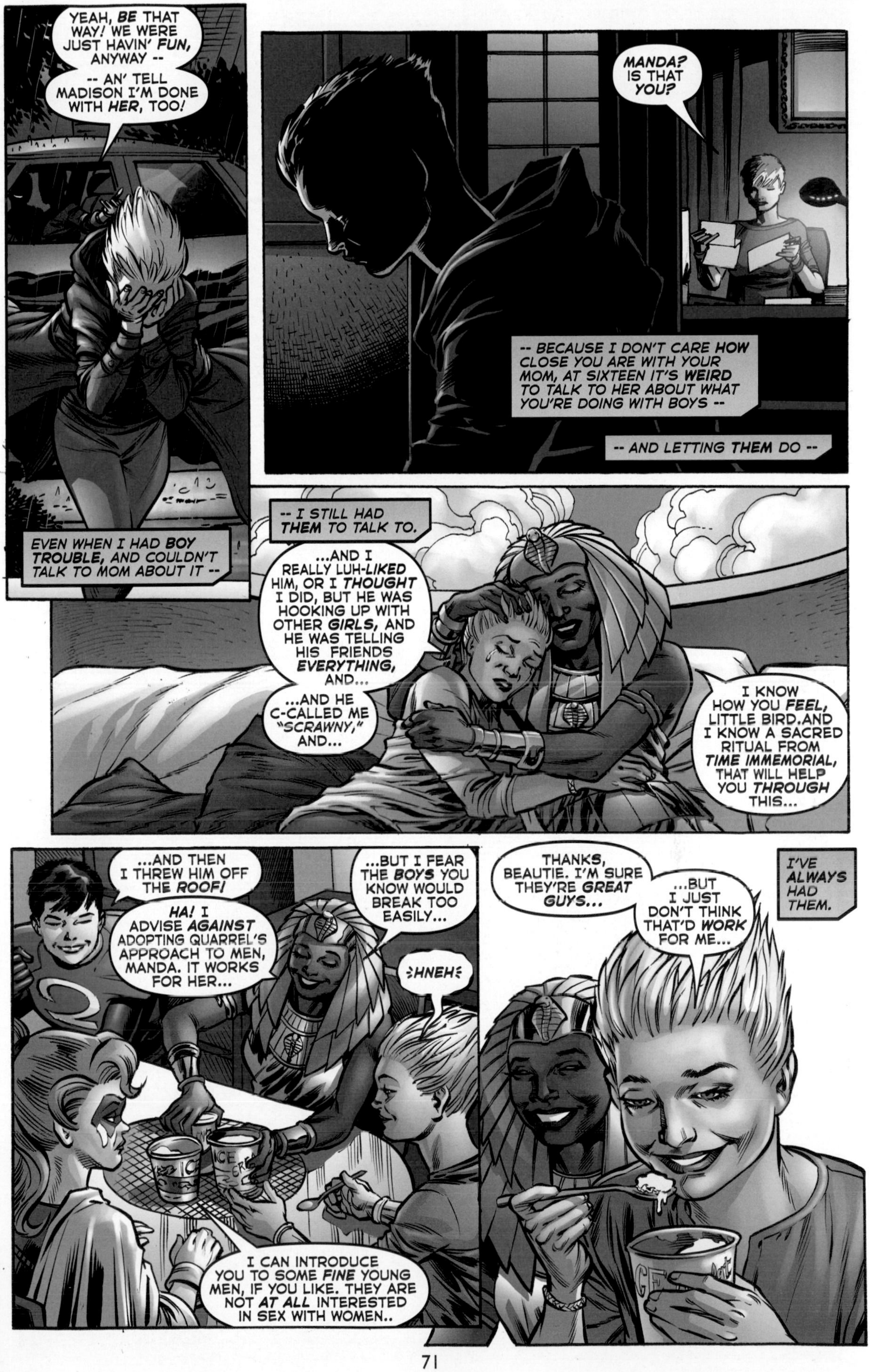
YEAH, BE THAT WAY! WE WERE JUST HAVIN' FUN, ANYWAY --
-- AN' TELL MADISON I'M DONE WITH HER, TOO!
MANDA? IS THAT YOU?
-- BECAUSE I DON'T CARE HOW CLOSE YOU ARE WITH YOUR MOM, AT SIXTEEN IT'S WEIRD TO TALK TO HER ABOUT WHAT YOU'RE DOING WITH BOYS --
-- AND LETTING THEM DO --
EVEN WHEN I HAD BOY TROUBLE, AND COULDN'T TALK TO MOM ABOUT IT --
-- I STILL HAD THEM TO TALK TO.
...AND I REALLY LUH-LIKED HIM, OR I THOUGHT I DID, BUT HE WAS HOOKING UP WITH OTHER GIRLS, AND HE WAS TELLING HIS FRIENDS EVERYTHING, AND...
...AND HE C-CALLED ME "SCRAWNY," AND...
I KNOW HOW YOU FEEL, LITTLE BIRD.AND I KNOW A SACRED RITUAL FROM TIME IMMEMORIAL, THAT WILL HELP YOU THROUGH THIS...
...AND THEN I THREW HIM OFF THE ROOF!
HA! I ADVISE AGAINST ADOPTING QUARREL'S APPROACH TO MEN, MANDA. IT WORKS FOR HER...
...BUT I FEAR THE BOYS YOU KNOW WOULD BREAK TOO EASILY...
HNEH
I CAN INTRODUCE YOU TO SOME FINE YOUNG MEN, IF YOU LIKE. THEY ARE NOT AT ALL INTERESTED IN SEX WITH WOMEN..
THANKS, BEAUTIE. I'M SURE THEY'RE GREAT GUYS...
...BUT I JUST DON'T THINK THAT'D WORK FOR ME...
I'VE ALWAYS HAD THEM.

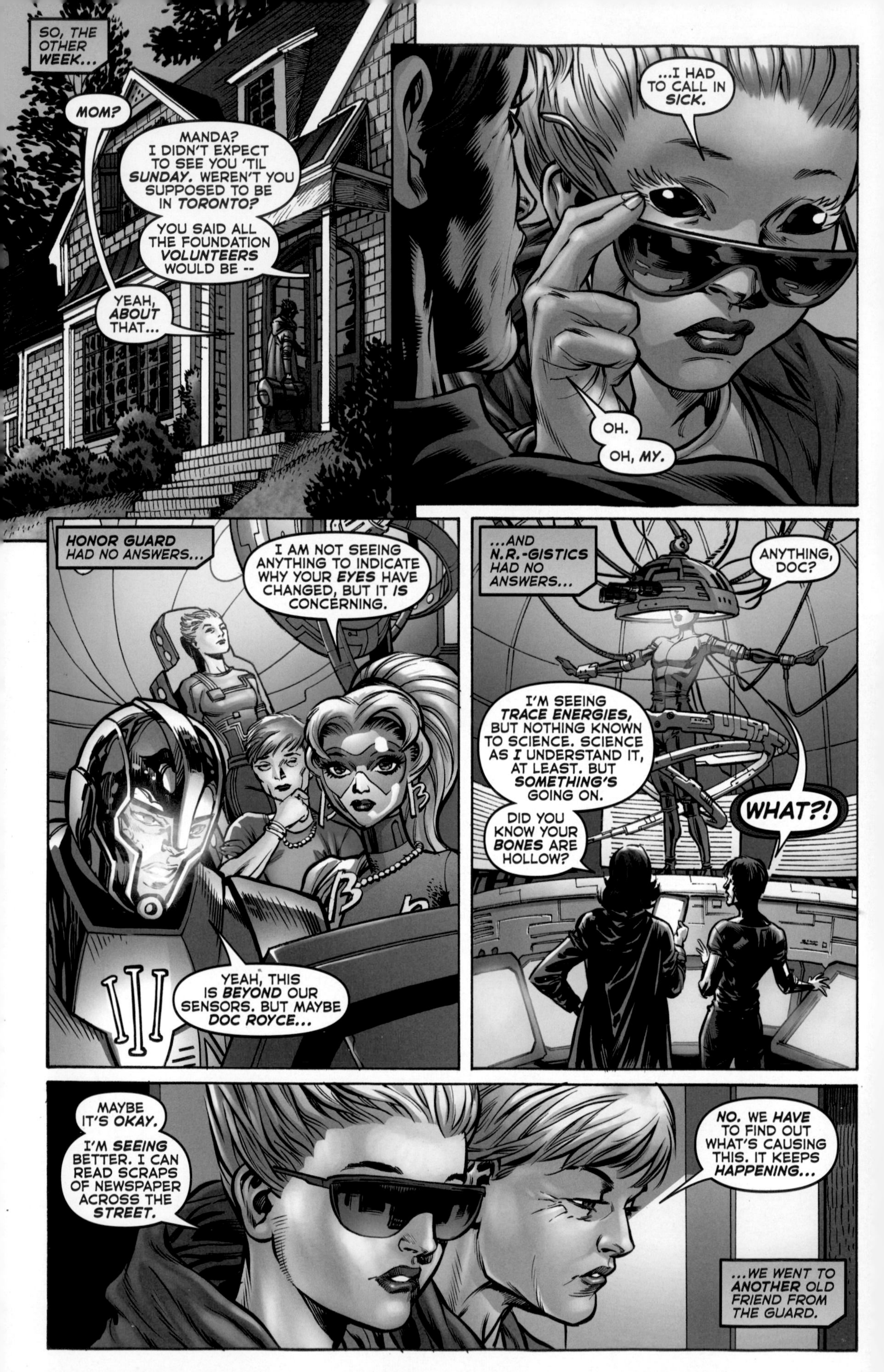
SO, THE OTHER WEEK...
MOM?
MANDA? I DIDN'T EXPECT TO SEE YOU 'TIL SUNDAY. WEREN'T YOU SUPPOSED TO BE IN TORONTO?
YOU SAID ALL THE FOUNDATION VOLUNTEERS WOULD BE --
YEAH, ABOUT THAT...
...I HAD TO CALL IN SICK.
OH.
OH, MY.
HONOR GUARD HAD NO ANSWERS...
I AM NOT SEEING ANYTHING TO INDICATE WHY YOUR EYES HAVE CHANGED, BUT IT IS CONCERNING.
YEAH, THIS IS BEYOND OUR SENSORS. BUT MAYBE DOC ROYCE...
...AND N.R.-GISTICS HAD NO ANSWERS...
ANYTHING, DOC?
I'M SEEING TRACE ENERGIES, BUT NOTHING KNOWN TO SCIENCE. SCIENCE AS I UNDERSTAND IT, AT LEAST. BUT SOMETHING'S GOING ON.
DID YOU KNOW YOUR BONES ARE HOLLOW?
WHAT?!
MAYBE IT'S OKAY.
I'M SEEING BETTER. I CAN READ SCRAPS OF NEWSPAPER ACROSS THE STREET.
NO. WE HAVE TO FIND OUT WHAT'S CAUSING THIS. IT KEEPS HAPPENING...
...WE WENT TO ANOTHER OLD FRIEND FROM THE GUARD.

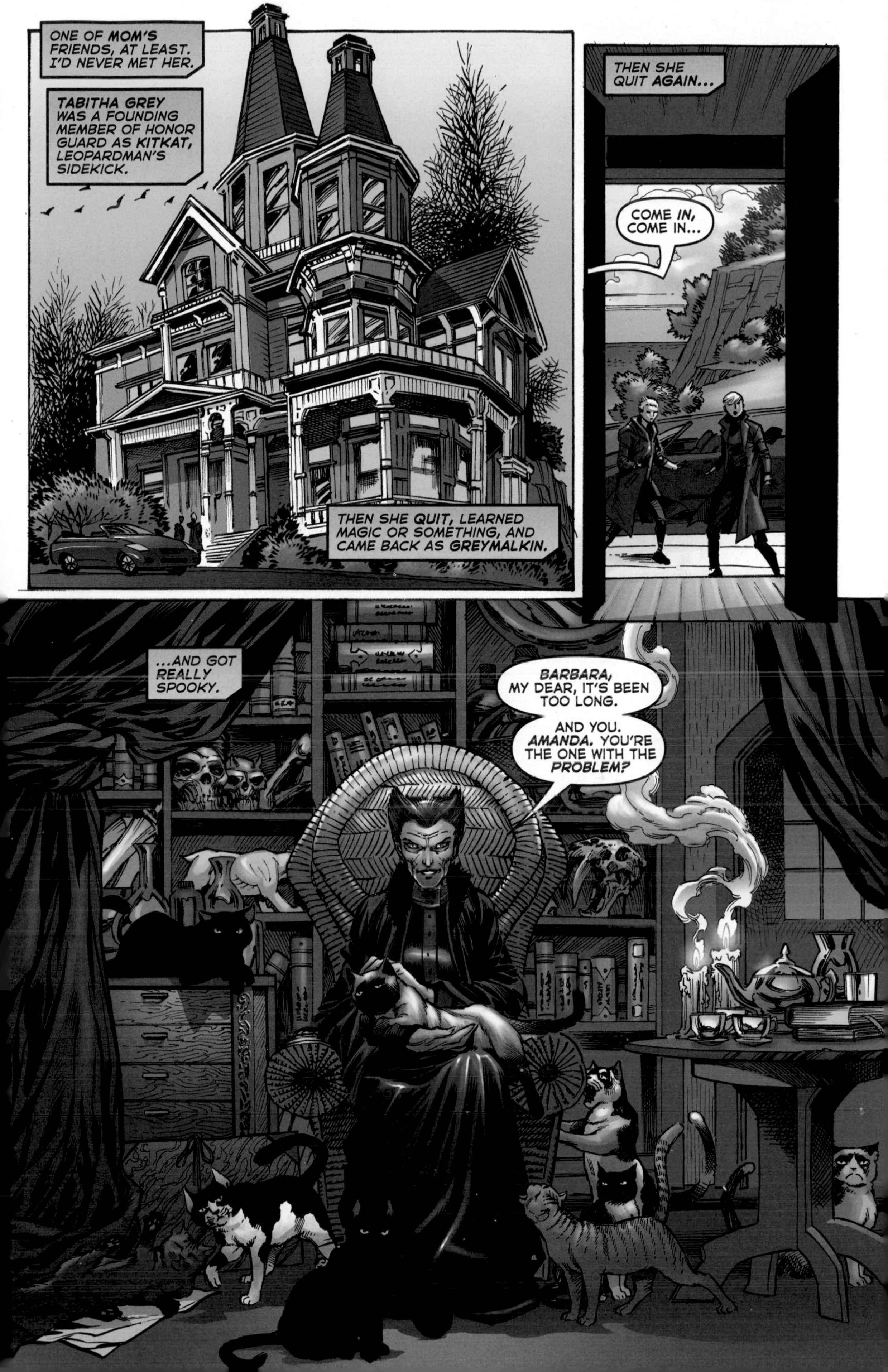
ONE OF MOM'S FRIENDS, AT LEAST. I'D NEVER MET HER.
TABITHA GREY WAS A FOUNDING MEMBER OF HONOR GUARD AS KITKAT, LEOPARDMAN'S SIDEKICK.
THEN SHE QUIT, LEARNED MAGIC OR SOMETHING, AND CAME BACK AS GREYMALKIN.
THEN SHE QUIT AGAIN...
COME IN, COME IN...
...AND GOT REALLY SPOOKY.
BARBARA, MY DEAR, IT'S BEEN TOO LONG.
AND YOU. AMANDA. YOU'RE THE ONE WITH THE PROBLEM?

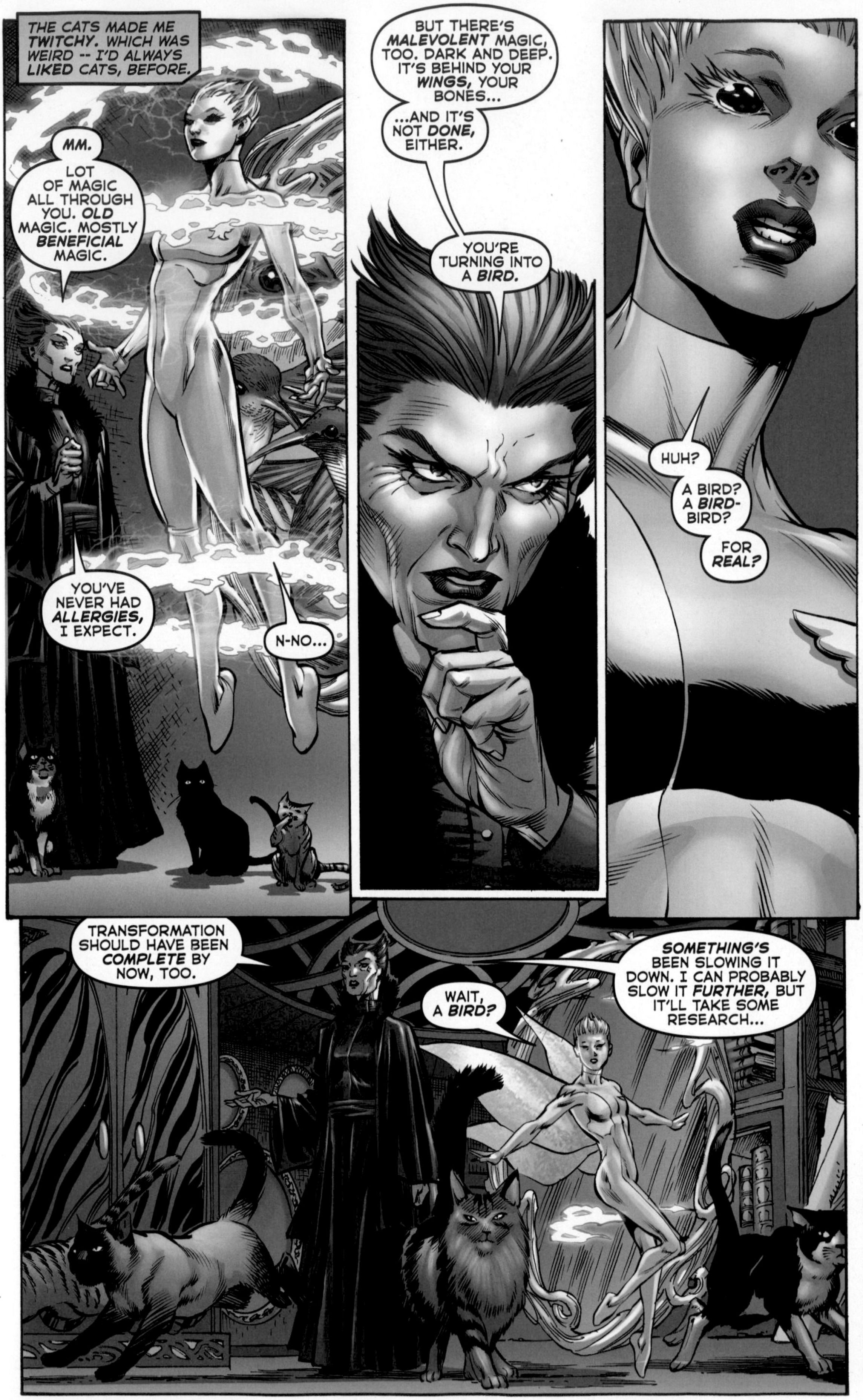
THE CATS MADE ME TWITCHY. WHICH WAS WEIRD -- I'D ALWAYS LIKED CATS, BEFORE.
MM.
LOT OF MAGIC ALL THROUGH YOU. OLD MAGIC. MOSTLY BENEFICIAL MAGIC.
YOU'VE NEVER HAD ALLERGIES, I EXPECT.
N-NO...
BUT THERE'S MALEVOLENT MAGIC, TOO. DARK AND DEEP. IT'S BEHIND YOUR WINGS, YOUR BONES...
...AND IT'S NOT DONE, EITHER.
YOU'RE TURNING INTO A BIRD.
HUH?
A BIRD? A BIRD-BIRD?
FOR REAL?
TRANSFORMATION SHOULD HAVE BEEN COMPLETE BY NOW, TOO.
WAIT, A BIRD?
SOMETHING'S BEEN SLOWING IT DOWN. I CAN PROBABLY SLOW IT FURTHER, BUT IT'LL TAKE SOME RESEARCH...

A BIRD?

I KNOW I'VE GOT BIRD-LIKE *POWERS*, BUT --

IT'LL BE OKAY, HONEY, YOU'LL SEE. TABBY'S *VERY* GOOD. SHE'LL GET TO THE BOTTOM OF WHATEVER'S --

MANDA?!

MEET YOU BACK *HOME*, MOM.

I'VE JUST GOT TO -- GOT TO THINK THIS *THROUGH* --

THERE WAS A GUARD *"DOORWAY"* IN BANGOR I COULD USE.

BUT I WASN'T *THINKING* ABOUT THAT, I WAS JUST --

WAS THIS *BAD?* ALL MY LIFE, I'D THOUGHT MY POWERS WERE A *GIFT.* PART OF THE FAIRY TALE.

BUT -- WERE THEY A *CURSE?* DID I HAVE *THAT* PART OF THE FAIRY TALE, TOO?

EVERYTHING I WAS -- EVERYTHING I'D *WANTED* TO BE -- IT WAS ALL TIED UP IN MY GIFTS --

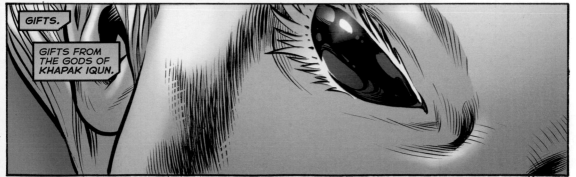

GIFTS.

GIFTS FROM THE GODS OF KHAPAK IQUN.

75

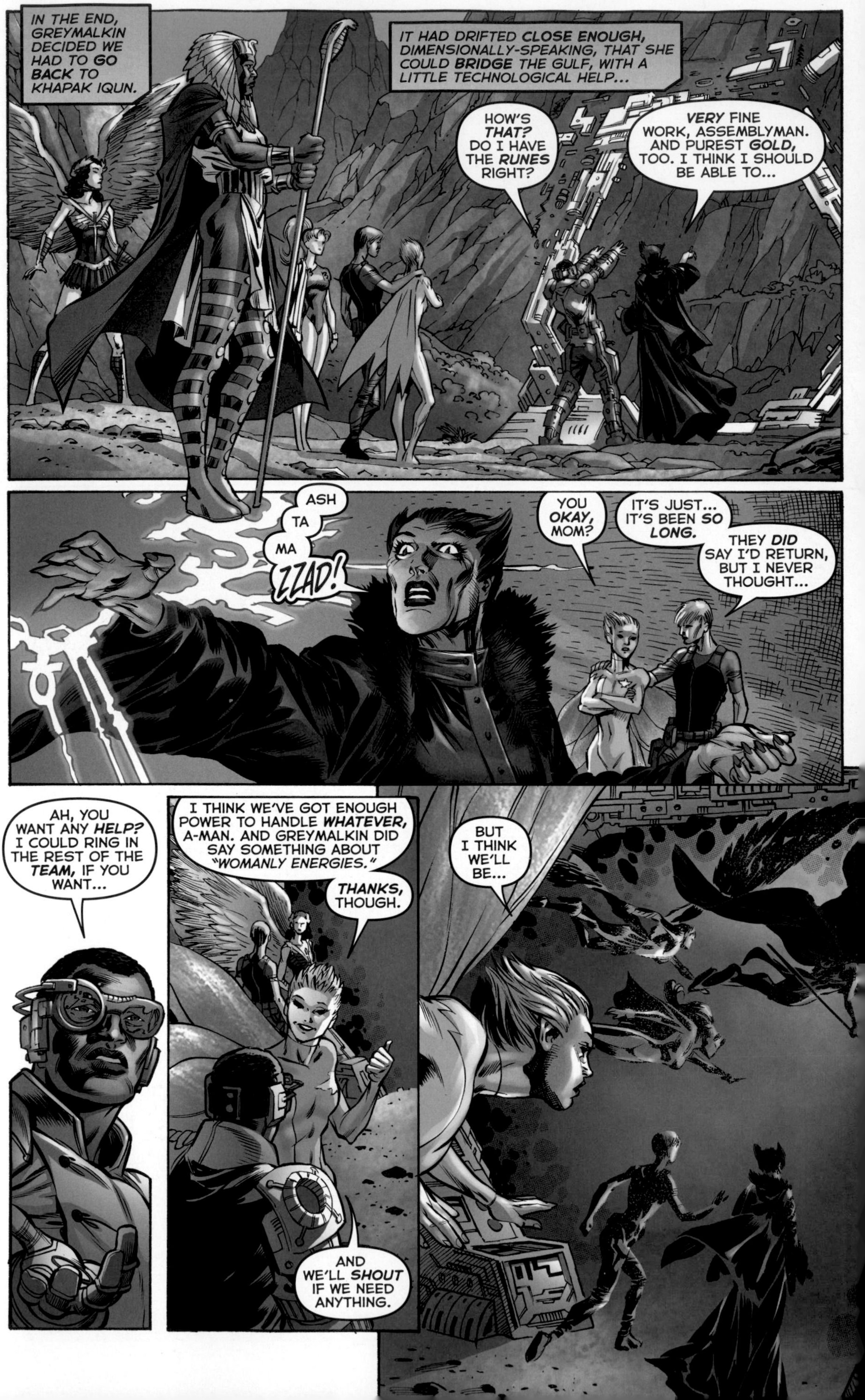

IN THE END, GREYMALKIN DECIDED WE HAD TO GO BACK TO KHAPAK IQUN.
IT HAD DRIFTED CLOSE ENOUGH, DIMENSIONALLY-SPEAKING, THAT SHE COULD BRIDGE THE GULF, WITH A LITTLE TECHNOLOGICAL HELP...
HOW'S THAT? DO I HAVE THE RUNES RIGHT?
VERY FINE WORK, ASSEMBLYMAN. AND PUREST GOLD, TOO. I THINK I SHOULD BE ABLE TO...
ASH
TA
MA
ZZAD!
YOU OKAY, MOM?
IT'S JUST... IT'S BEEN SO LONG.
THEY DID SAY I'D RETURN, BUT I NEVER THOUGHT...
AH, YOU WANT ANY HELP? I COULD RING IN THE REST OF THE TEAM, IF YOU WANT...
I THINK WE'VE GOT ENOUGH POWER TO HANDLE WHATEVER, A-MAN. AND GREYMALKIN DID SAY SOMETHING ABOUT "WOMANLY ENERGIES."
THANKS, THOUGH.
AND WE'LL SHOUT IF WE NEED ANYTHING.
BUT I THINK WE'LL BE...

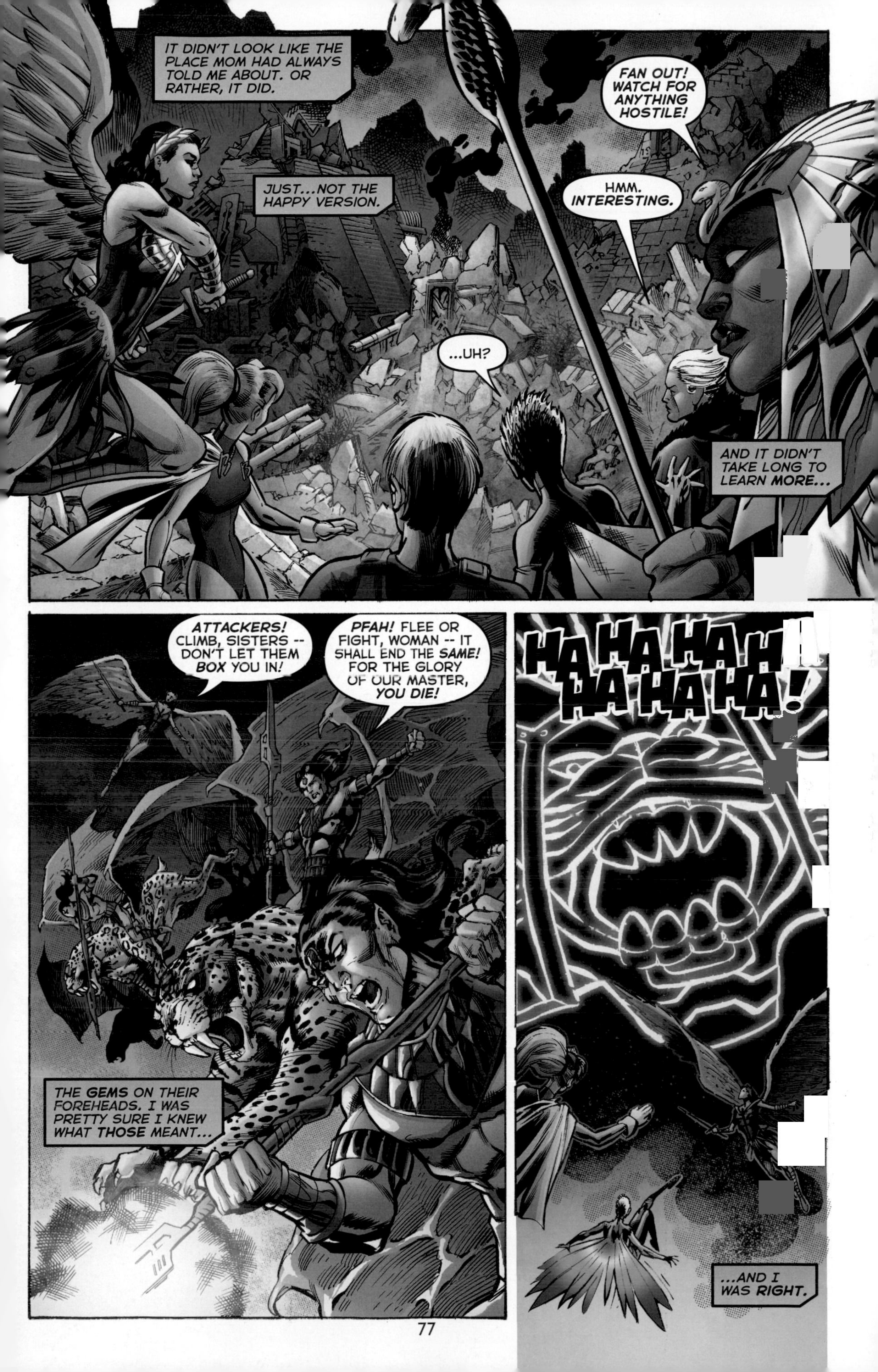
IT DIDN'T LOOK LIKE THE PLACE MOM HAD ALWAYS TOLD ME ABOUT. OR RATHER, IT DID.
JUST...NOT THE HAPPY VERSION.
FAN OUT! WATCH FOR ANYTHING HOSTILE!
HMM. INTERESTING.
...UH?
AND IT DIDN'T TAKE LONG TO LEARN MORE...
ATTACKERS! CLIMB, SISTERS -- DON'T LET THEM BOX YOU IN!
PFAH! FLEE OR FIGHT, WOMAN -- IT SHALL END THE SAME! FOR THE GLORY OF OUR MASTER, YOU DIE!
THE GEMS ON THEIR FOREHEADS. I WAS PRETTY SURE I KNEW WHAT THOSE MEANT...
HA HA HA HA HA HA HA HA!
...AND I WAS RIGHT.

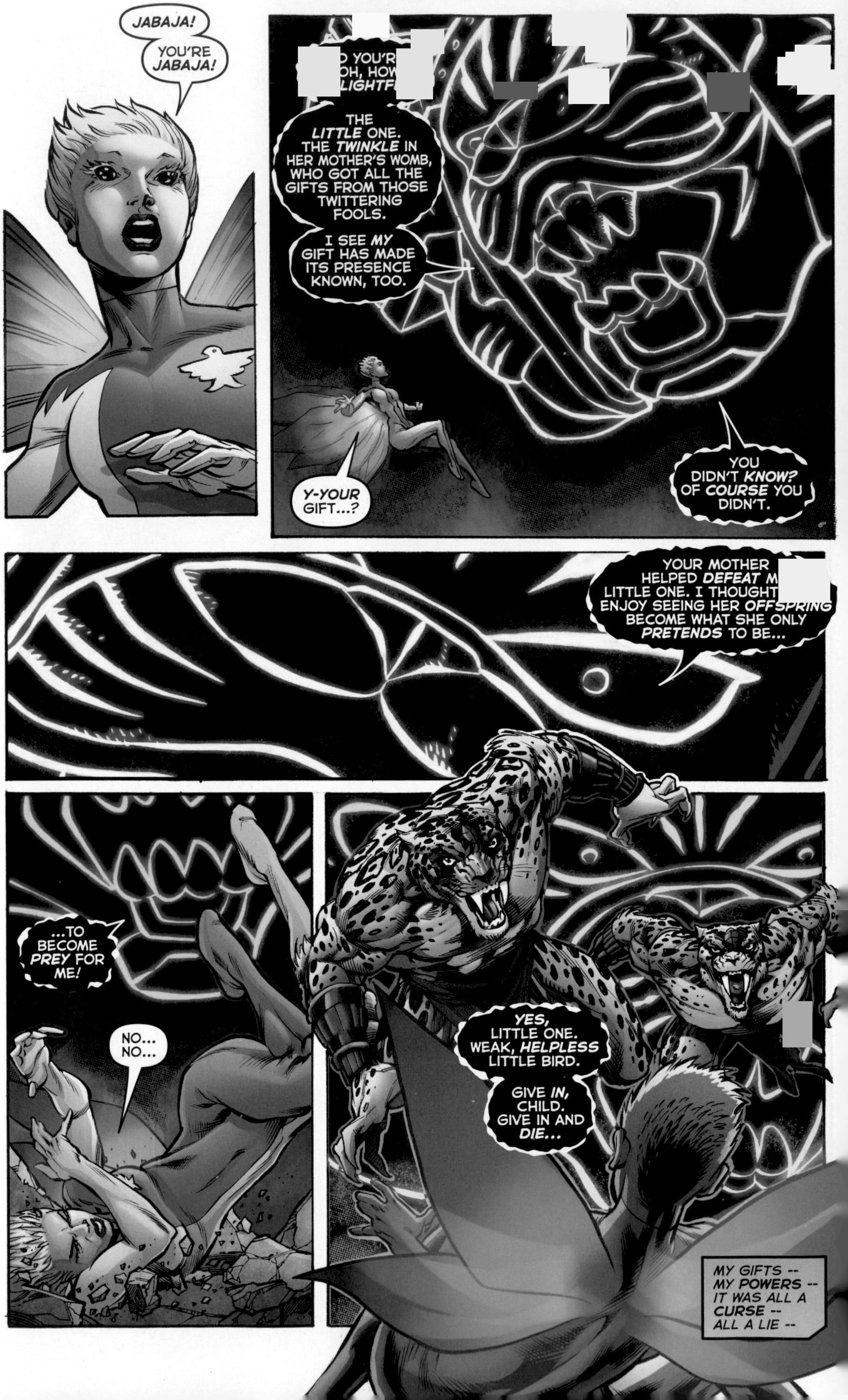

JABAJA!
YOU'RE JABAJA!
THE LITTLE ONE. THE TWINKLE IN HER MOTHER'S WOMB, WHO GOT ALL THE GIFTS FROM THOSE TWITTERING FOOLS.
I SEE MY GIFT HAS MADE ITS PRESENCE KNOWN, TOO.
Y-YOUR GIFT...?
YOU DIDN'T KNOW? OF COURSE YOU DIDN'T.
YOUR MOTHER HELPED DEFEAT M LITTLE ONE. I THOUGHT ENJOY SEEING HER OFFSPRING BECOME WHAT SHE ONLY PRETENDS TO BE...
...TO BECOME PREY FOR ME!
NO... NO...
YES, LITTLE ONE. WEAK, HELPLESS LITTLE BIRD.
GIVE IN, CHILD. GIVE IN AND DIE...
MY GIFTS -- MY POWERS -- IT WAS ALL A CURSE -- ALL A LIE --

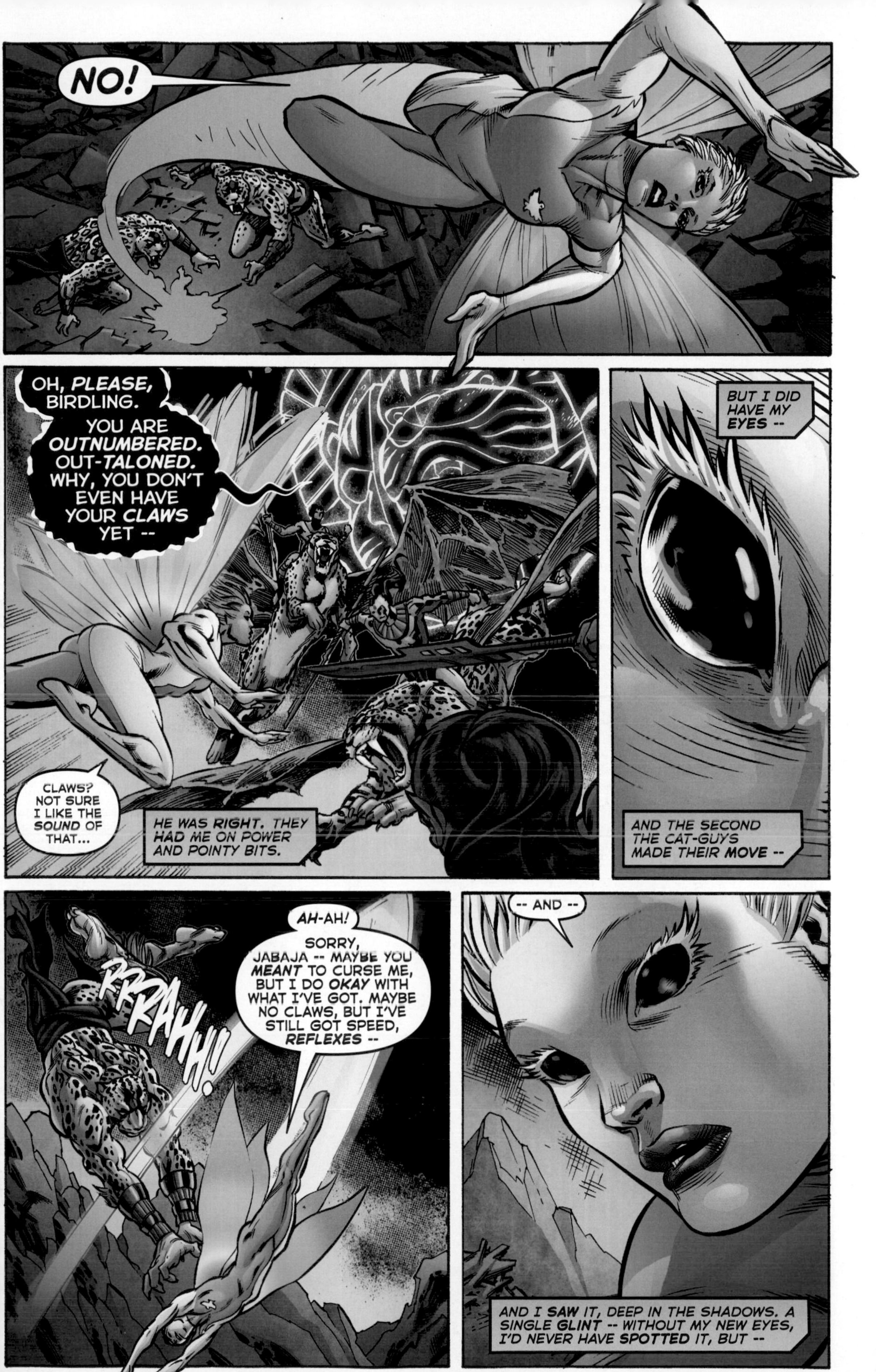
NO!
OH, PLEASE, BIRDLING.
YOU ARE OUTNUMBERED. OUT-TALONED. WHY, YOU DON'T EVEN HAVE YOUR CLAWS YET --
CLAWS? NOT SURE I LIKE THE SOUND OF THAT...
HE WAS RIGHT. THEY HAD ME ON POWER AND POINTY BITS.
BUT I DID HAVE MY EYES --
AND THE SECOND THE CAT-GUYS MADE THEIR MOVE --
RRRAHH!!
AH-AH!
SORRY, JABAJA -- MAYBE YOU MEANT TO CURSE ME, BUT I DO OKAY WITH WHAT I'VE GOT. MAYBE NO CLAWS, BUT I'VE STILL GOT SPEED, REFLEXES --
-- AND --
AND I SAW IT, DEEP IN THE SHADOWS. A SINGLE GLINT -- WITHOUT MY NEW EYES, I'D NEVER HAVE SPOTTED IT, BUT --

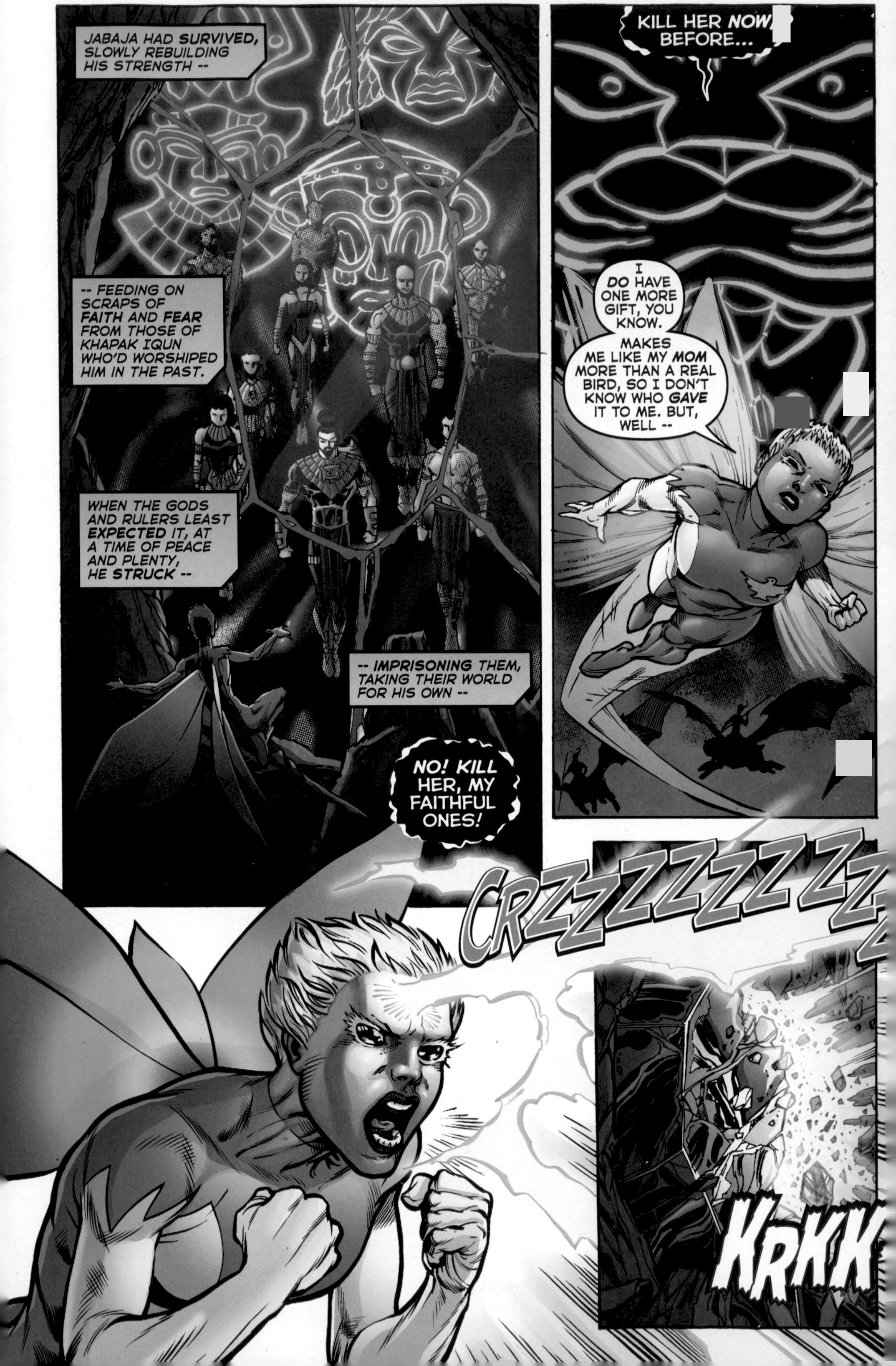
JABAJA HAD SURVIVED, SLOWLY REBUILDING HIS STRENGTH --
-- FEEDING ON SCRAPS OF FAITH AND FEAR FROM THOSE OF KHAPAK IQUN WHO'D WORSHIPED HIM IN THE PAST.
WHEN THE GODS AND RULERS LEAST EXPECTED IT, AT A TIME OF PEACE AND PLENTY, HE STRUCK --
-- IMPRISONING THEM, TAKING THEIR WORLD FOR HIS OWN --
KILL HER NOW! BEFORE...
I DO HAVE ONE MORE GIFT, YOU KNOW.
MAKES ME LIKE MY MOM MORE THAN A REAL BIRD, SO I DON'T KNOW WHO GAVE IT TO ME. BUT, WELL --
NO! KILL HER, MY FAITHFUL ONES!
CRZZZZZZZZ
KRKK

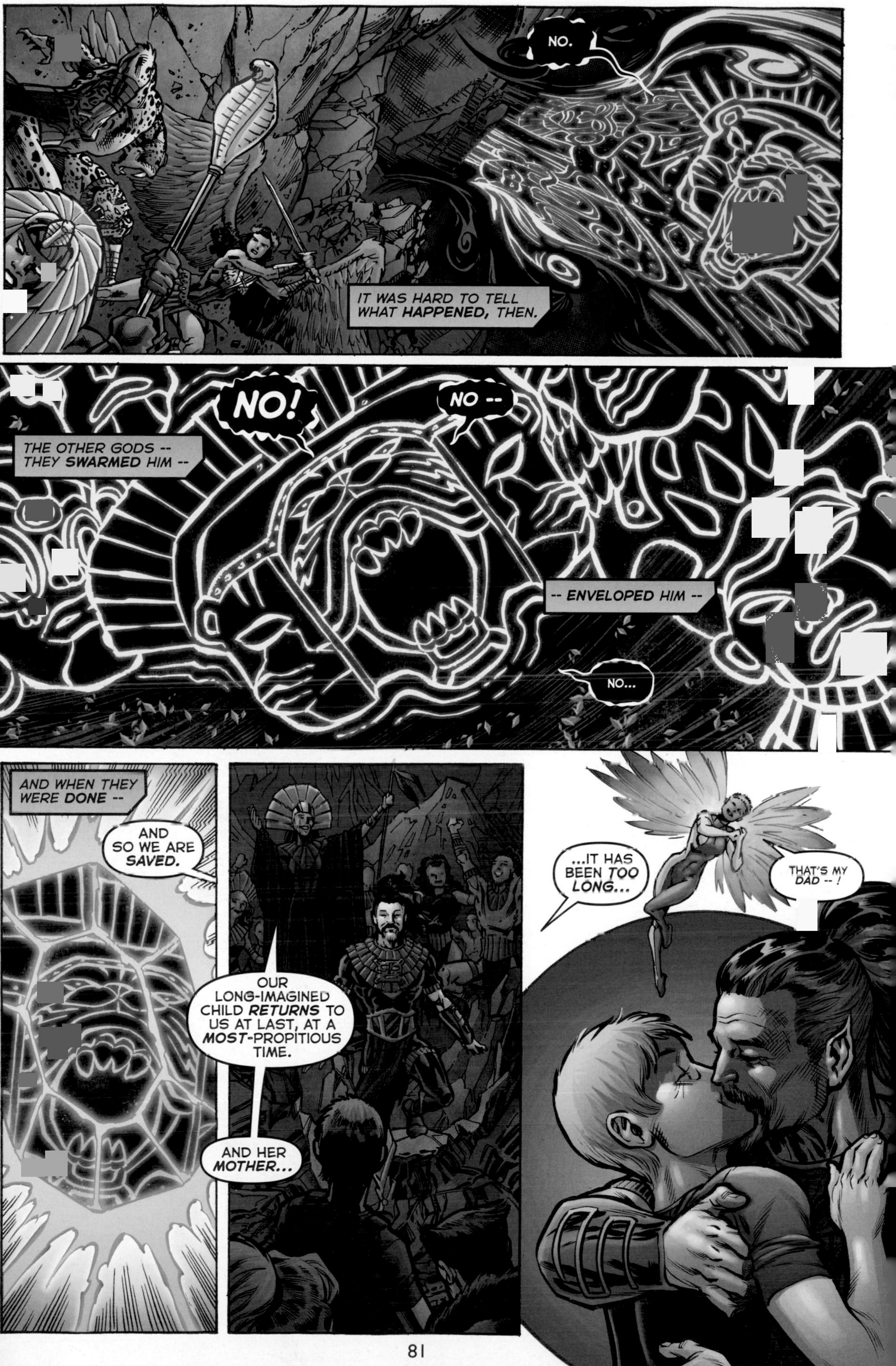
NO.
IT WAS HARD TO TELL WHAT *HAPPENED*, THEN.
THE OTHER GODS -- THEY *SWARMED* HIM --
NO!
NO --
-- *ENVELOPED* HIM --
NO...
AND WHEN THEY WERE *DONE* --
AND SO WE ARE *SAVED.*
OUR LONG-IMAGINED CHILD *RETURNS* TO US AT LAST, AT A *MOST*-PROPITIOUS TIME.
AND HER *MOTHER...*
...IT HAS BEEN *TOO LONG...*
THAT'S MY DAD -- !

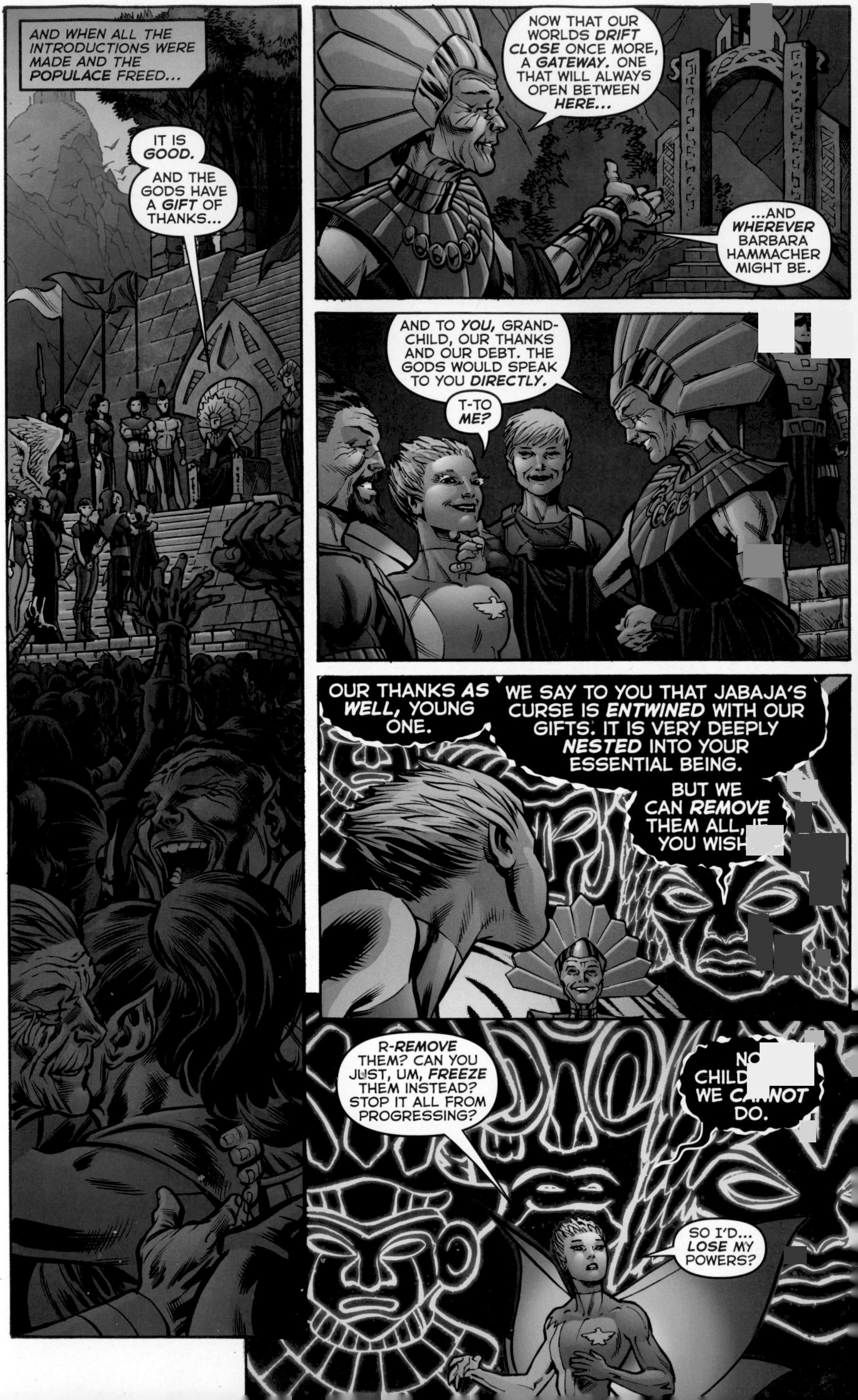

AND WHEN ALL THE INTRODUCTIONS WERE MADE AND THE POPULACE FREED...
IT IS GOOD.
AND THE GODS HAVE A GIFT OF THANKS...
NOW THAT OUR WORLDS DRIFT CLOSE ONCE MORE, A GATEWAY. ONE THAT WILL ALWAYS OPEN BETWEEN HERE...
...AND WHEREVER BARBARA HAMMACHER MIGHT BE.
AND TO YOU, GRAND-CHILD, OUR THANKS AND OUR DEBT. THE GODS WOULD SPEAK TO YOU DIRECTLY.
T-TO ME?
OUR THANKS AS WELL, YOUNG ONE.
WE SAY TO YOU THAT JABAJA'S CURSE IS ENTWINED WITH OUR GIFTS. IT IS VERY DEEPLY NESTED INTO YOUR ESSENTIAL BEING.
BUT WE CAN REMOVE THEM ALL, IF YOU WISH.
R-REMOVE THEM? CAN YOU JUST, UM, FREEZE THEM INSTEAD? STOP IT ALL FROM PROGRESSING?
NO CHILD WE CANNOT DO.
SO I'D... LOSE MY POWERS?

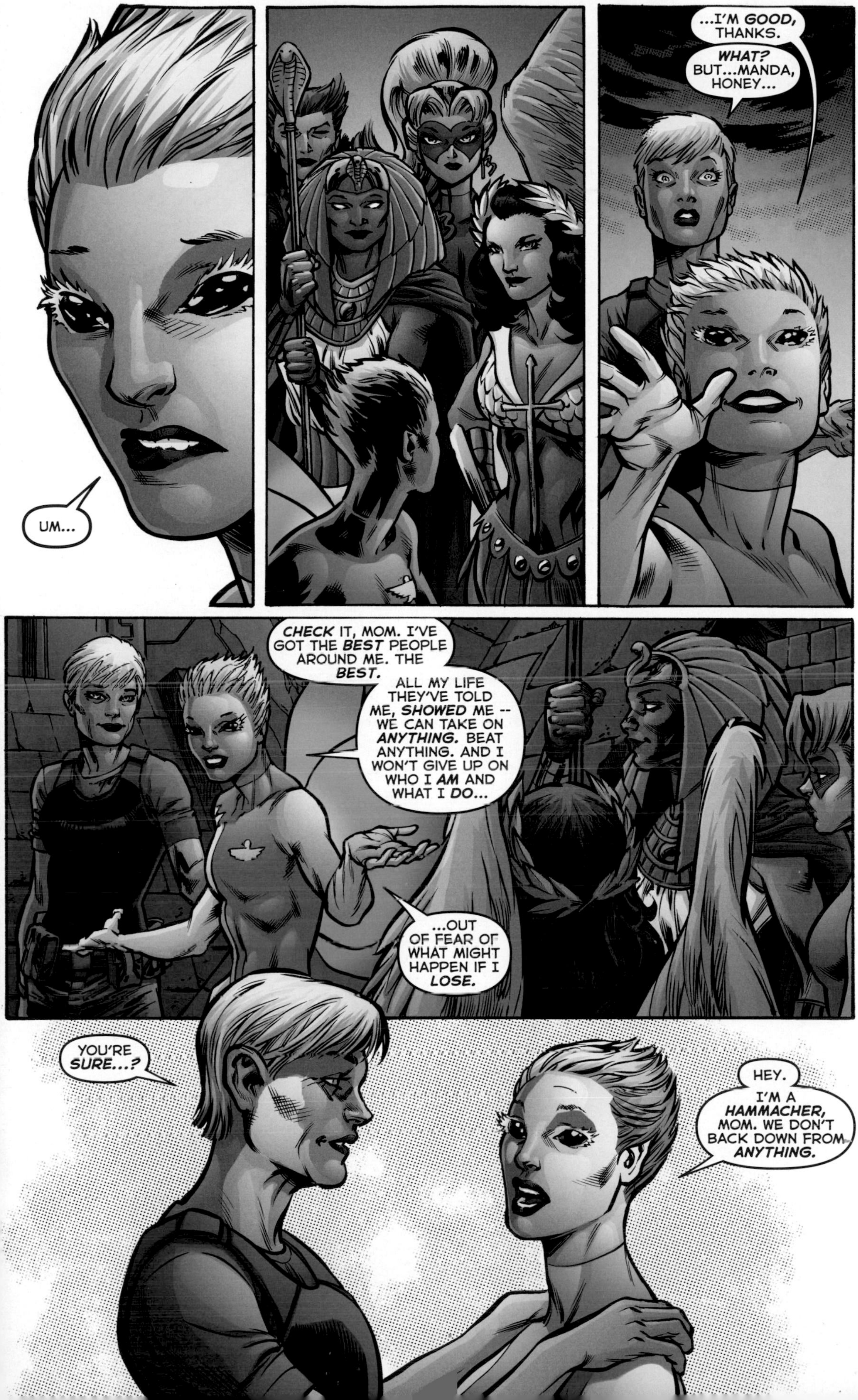
UM...
...I'M GOOD, THANKS.
WHAT? BUT...MANDA, HONEY...
CHECK IT, MOM. I'VE GOT THE BEST PEOPLE AROUND ME. THE BEST.
ALL MY LIFE THEY'VE TOLD ME, SHOWED ME -- WE CAN TAKE ON ANYTHING. BEAT ANYTHING. AND I WON'T GIVE UP ON WHO I AM AND WHAT I DO...
...OUT OF FEAR OF WHAT MIGHT HAPPEN IF I LOSE.
YOU'RE SURE...?
HEY.
I'M A HAMMACHER, MOM. WE DON'T BACK DOWN FROM ANYTHING.

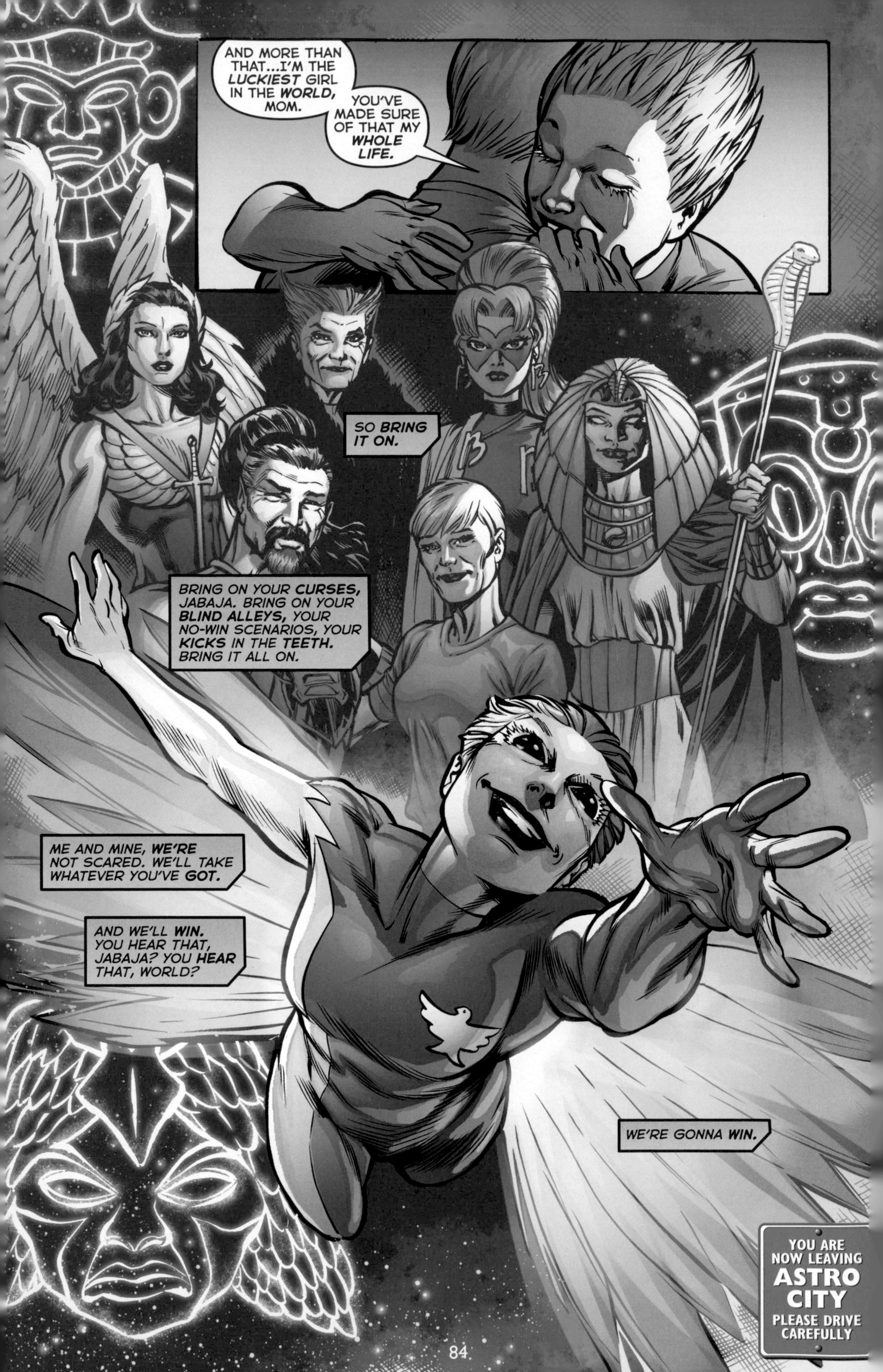
AND MORE THAN THAT...I'M THE LUCKIEST GIRL IN THE WORLD, MOM.
YOU'VE MADE SURE OF THAT MY WHOLE LIFE.
SO BRING IT ON.
BRING ON YOUR CURSES, JABAJA. BRING ON YOUR BLIND ALLEYS, YOUR NO-WIN SCENARIOS, YOUR KICKS IN THE TEETH. BRING IT ALL ON.
ME AND MINE, WE'RE NOT SCARED. WE'LL TAKE WHATEVER YOU'VE GOT.
AND WE'LL WIN. YOU HEAR THAT, JABAJA? YOU HEAR THAT, WORLD?
WE'RE GONNA WIN.
YOU ARE NOW LEAVING ASTRO CITY PLEASE DRIVE CAREFULLY

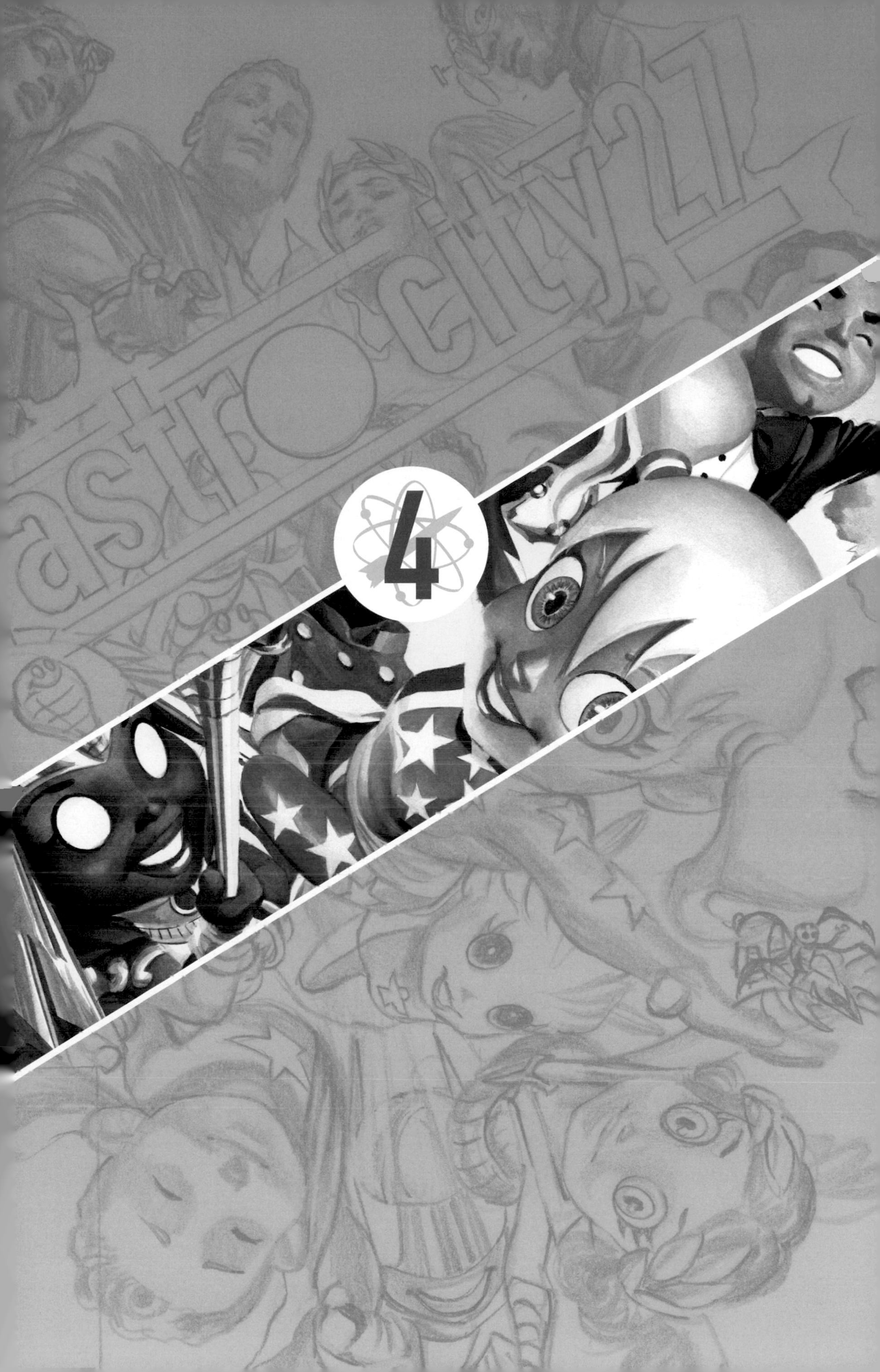
astro city
4

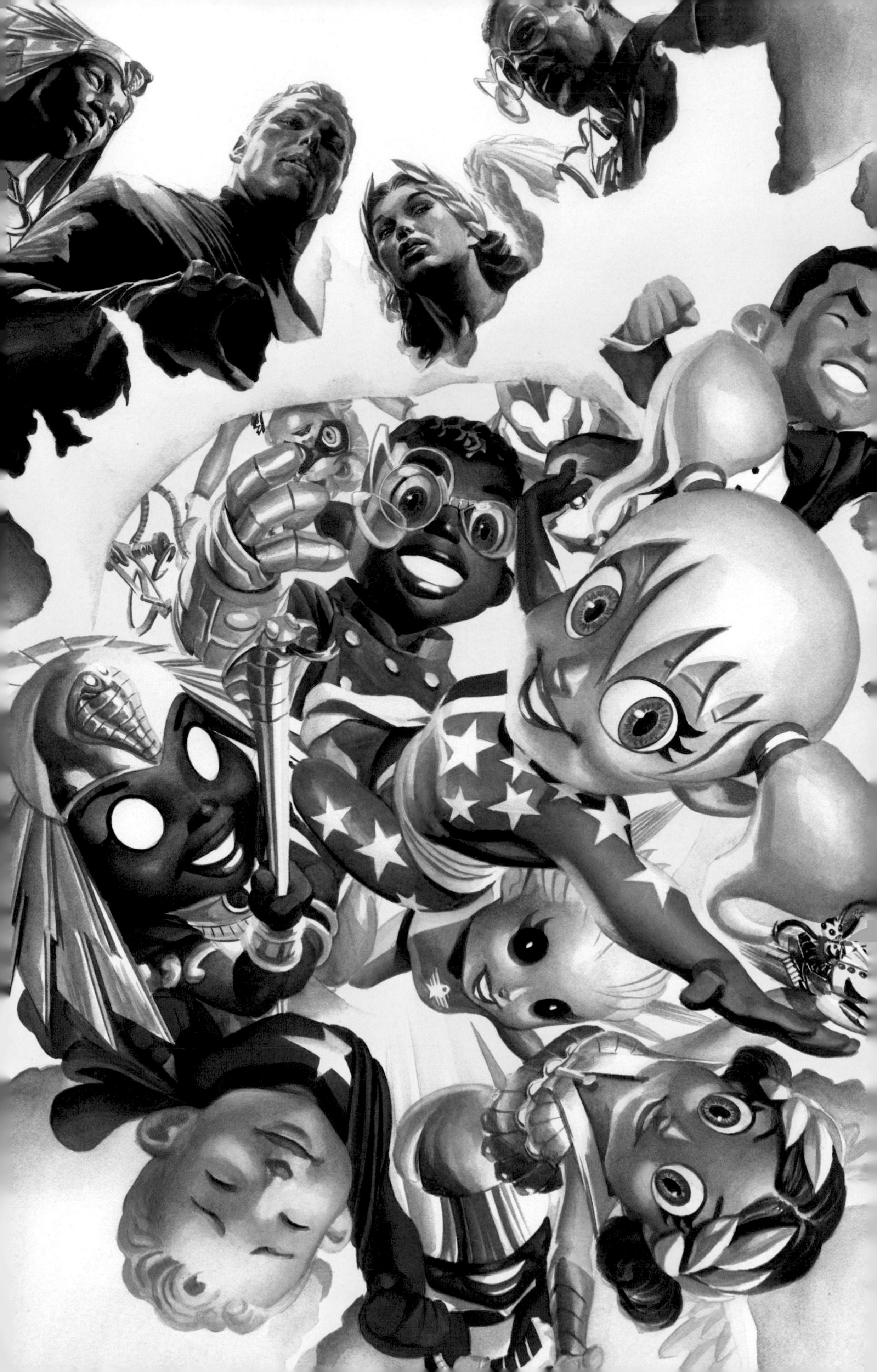

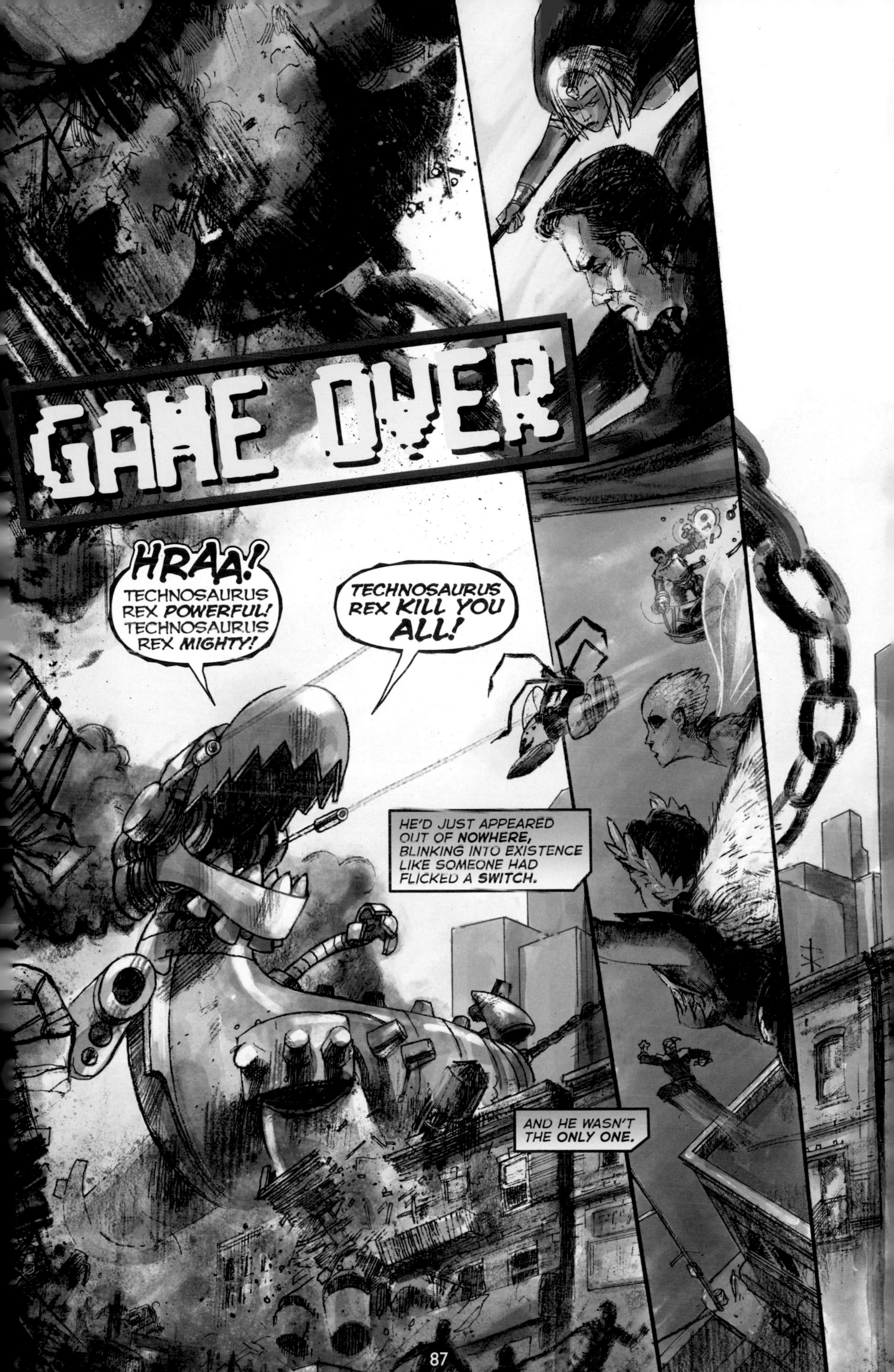
GAME OVER
HRAA! TECHNOSAURUS REX POWERFUL! TECHNOSAURUS REX MIGHTY!
TECHNOSAURUS REX KILL YOU ALL!
HE'D JUST APPEARED OUT OF NOWHERE, BLINKING INTO EXISTENCE LIKE SOMEONE HAD FLICKED A SWITCH.
AND HE WASN'T THE ONLY ONE.

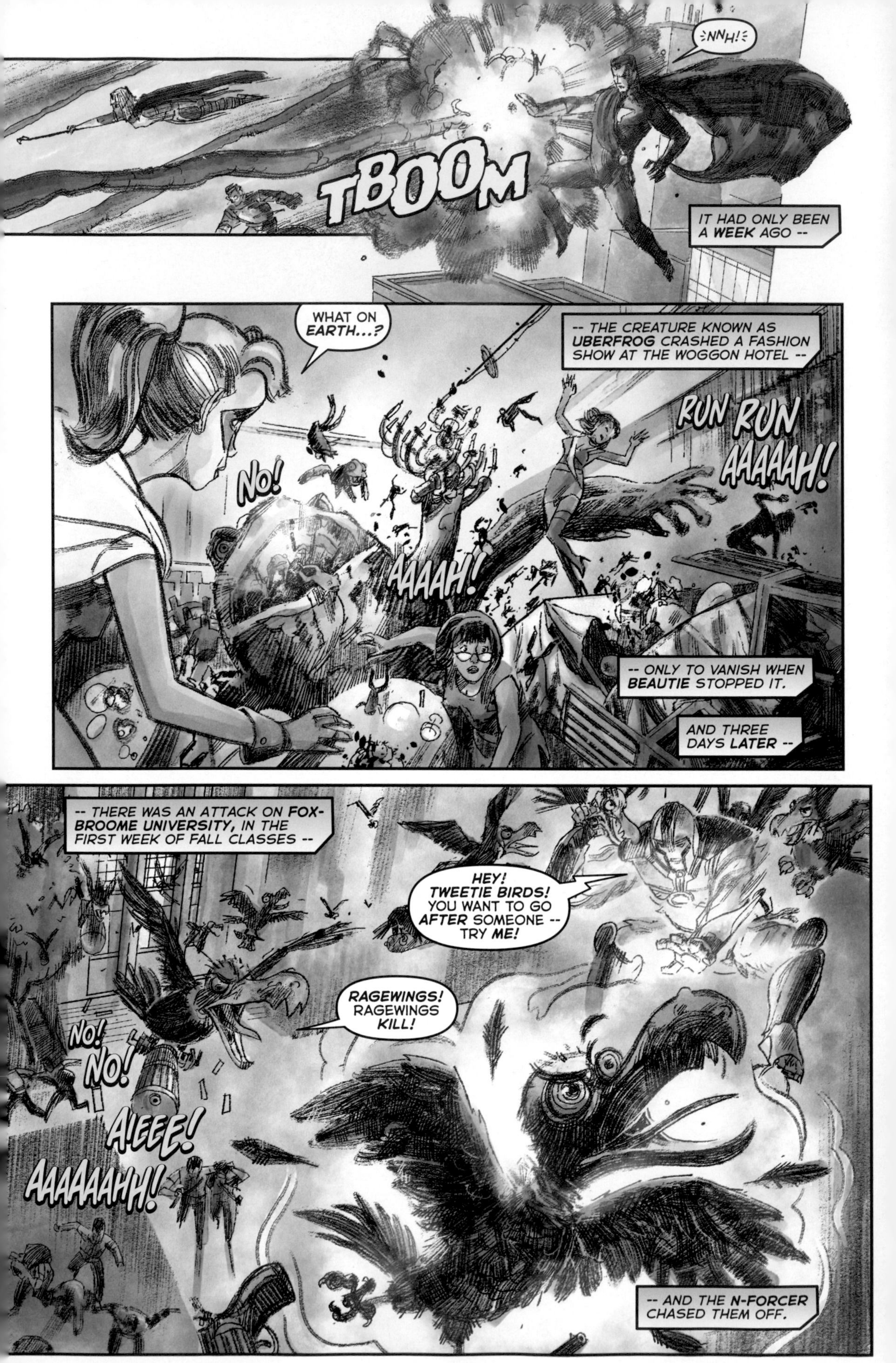
NNH!
TBOOM
IT HAD ONLY BEEN A WEEK AGO --
WHAT ON EARTH...?
-- THE CREATURE KNOWN AS UBERFROG CRASHED A FASHION SHOW AT THE WOGGON HOTEL --
RUN RUN
AAAAAH!
NO!
AAAAH!
-- ONLY TO VANISH WHEN BEAUTIE STOPPED IT.
AND THREE DAYS LATER --
-- THERE WAS AN ATTACK ON FOX-BROOME UNIVERSITY, IN THE FIRST WEEK OF FALL CLASSES --
HEY! TWEETIE BIRDS! YOU WANT TO GO AFTER SOMEONE -- TRY ME!
RAGEWINGS! RAGEWINGS KILL!
NO! NO!
AIEEE!
AAAAAAHH!
-- AND THE N-FORCER CHASED THEM OFF.

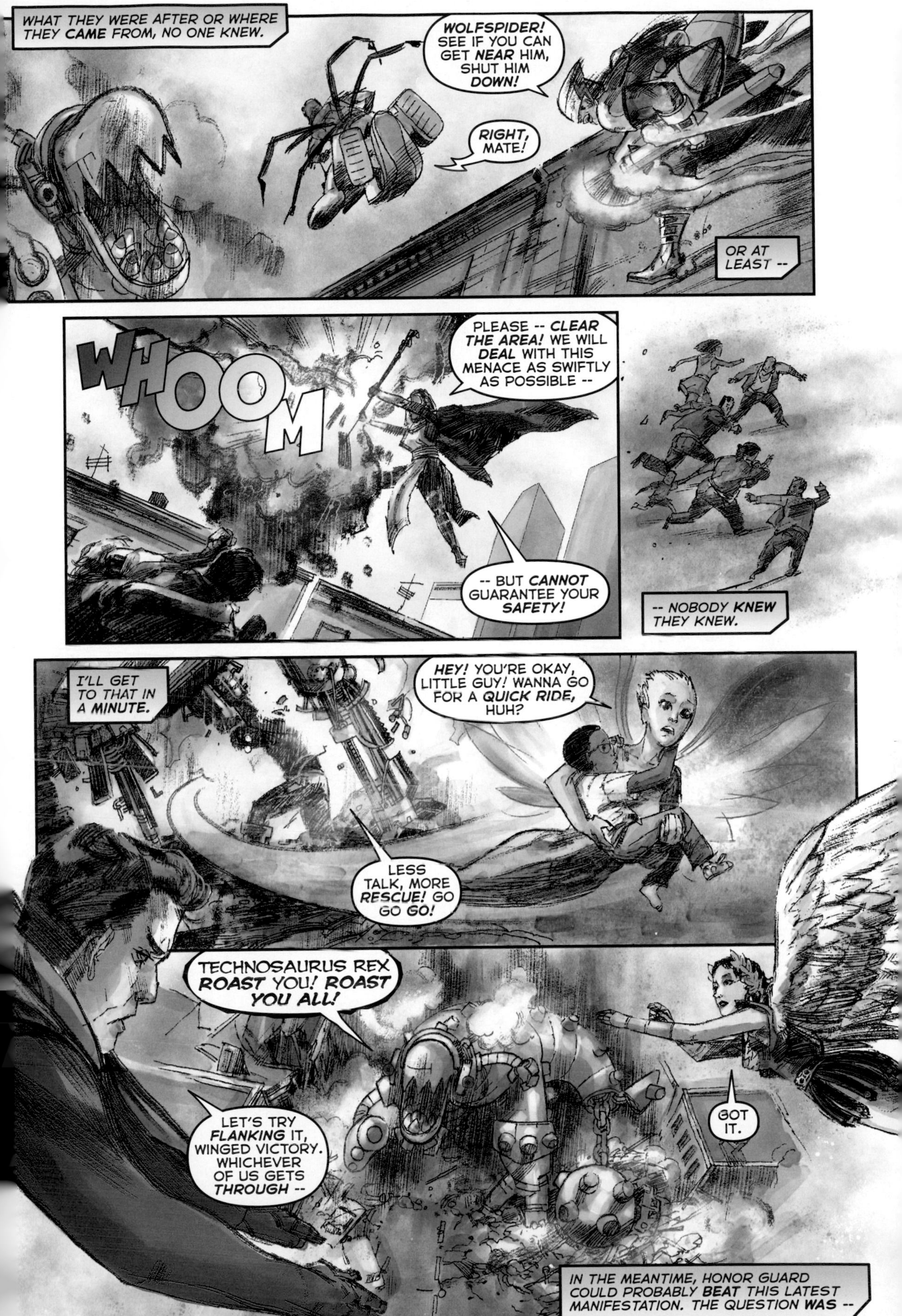
WHAT THEY WERE AFTER OR WHERE THEY CAME FROM, NO ONE KNEW.
WOLFSPIDER! SEE IF YOU CAN GET NEAR HIM, SHUT HIM DOWN!
RIGHT, MATE!
OR AT LEAST --
WHOOM
PLEASE -- CLEAR THE AREA! WE WILL DEAL WITH THIS MENACE AS SWIFTLY AS POSSIBLE --
-- BUT CANNOT GUARANTEE YOUR SAFETY!
-- NOBODY KNEW THEY KNEW.
I'LL GET TO THAT IN A MINUTE.
HEY! YOU'RE OKAY, LITTLE GUY! WANNA GO FOR A QUICK RIDE, HUH?
LESS TALK, MORE RESCUE! GO GO GO!
TECHNOSAURUS REX ROAST YOU! ROAST YOU ALL!
LET'S TRY FLANKING IT, WINGED VICTORY. WHICHEVER OF US GETS THROUGH --
GOT IT.
IN THE MEANTIME, HONOR GUARD COULD PROBABLY BEAT THIS LATEST MANIFESTATION. THE QUESTION WAS --

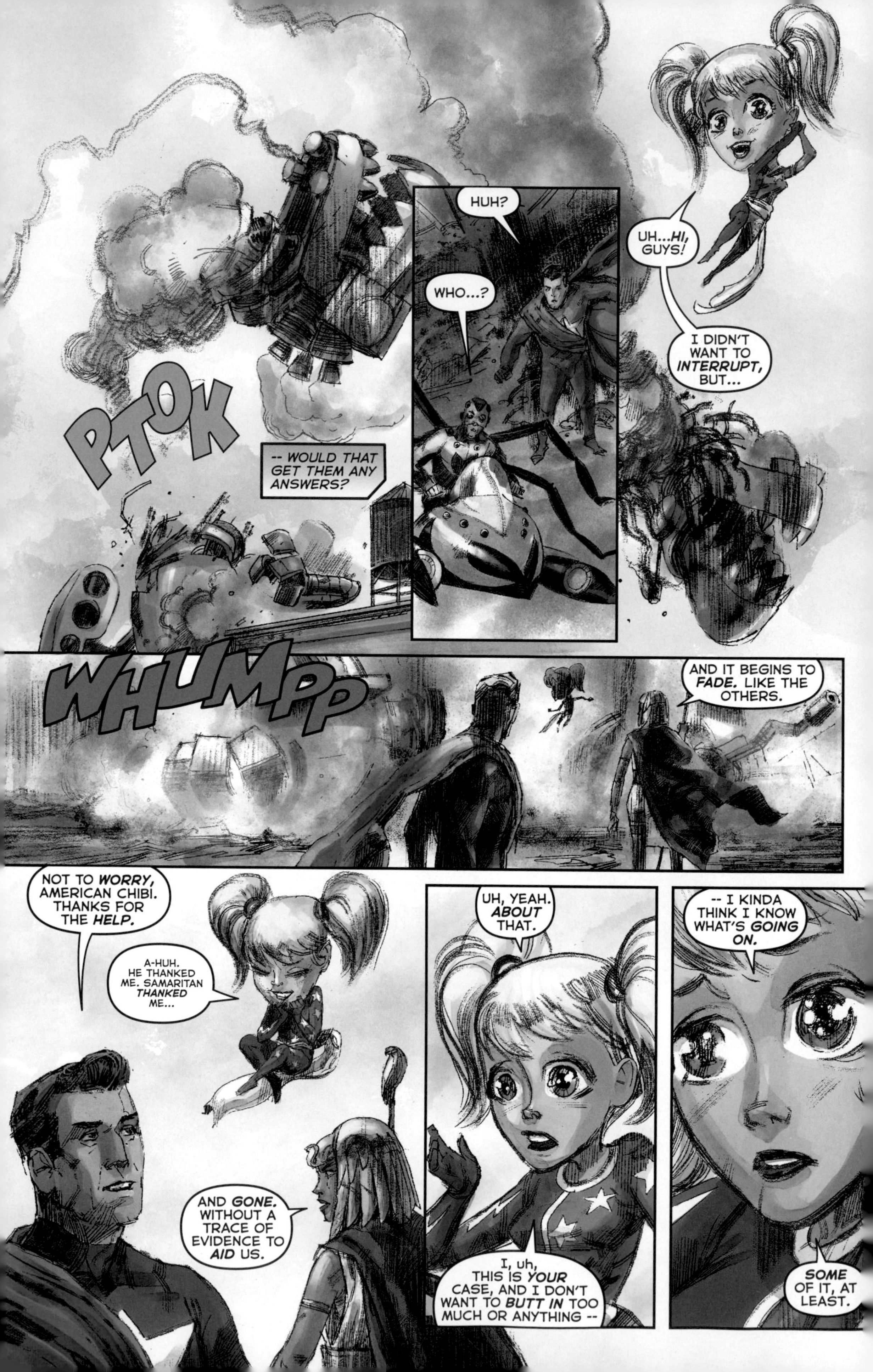
PTOK
-- WOULD THAT GET THEM ANY ANSWERS?
HUH?
WHO...?
UH...HI, GUYS!
I DIDN'T WANT TO INTERRUPT, BUT...
WHUMPP
AND IT BEGINS TO FADE. LIKE THE OTHERS.
NOT TO WORRY, AMERICAN CHIBI. THANKS FOR THE HELP.
A-HUH. HE THANKED ME. SAMARITAN THANKED ME...
AND GONE. WITHOUT A TRACE OF EVIDENCE TO AID US.
UH, YEAH. ABOUT THAT.
I, UH, THIS IS YOUR CASE, AND I DON'T WANT TO BUTT IN TOO MUCH OR ANYTHING --
-- I KINDA THINK I KNOW WHAT'S GOING ON.
SOME OF IT, AT LEAST.

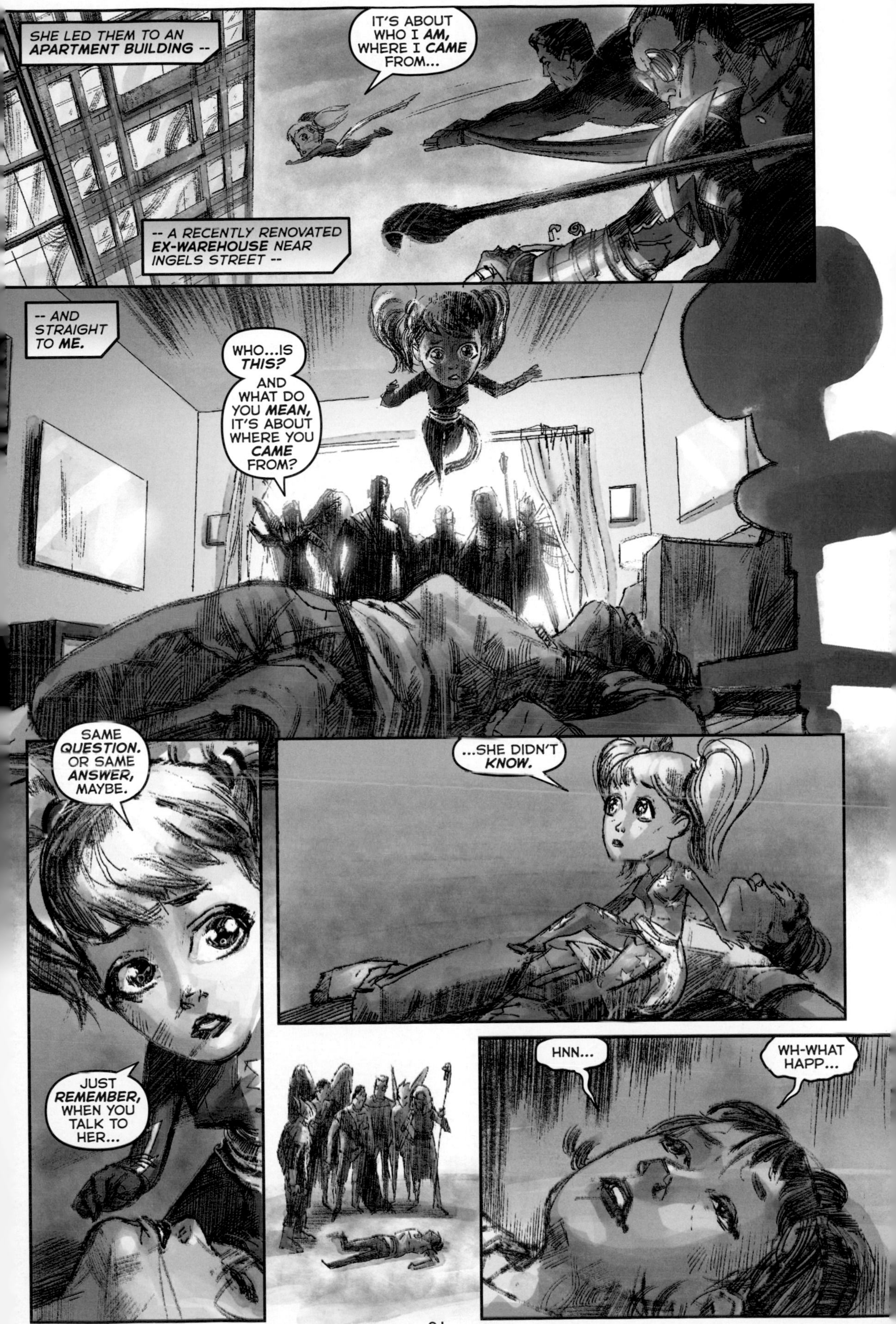
SHE LED THEM TO AN APARTMENT BUILDING --
IT'S ABOUT WHO I AM, WHERE I CAME FROM...
-- A RECENTLY RENOVATED EX-WAREHOUSE NEAR INGELS STREET --
-- AND STRAIGHT TO ME.
WHO...IS THIS? AND WHAT DO YOU MEAN, IT'S ABOUT WHERE YOU CAME FROM?
SAME QUESTION. OR SAME ANSWER, MAYBE.
...SHE DIDN'T KNOW.
JUST REMEMBER, WHEN YOU TALK TO HER...
HNN...
WH-WHAT HAPP...

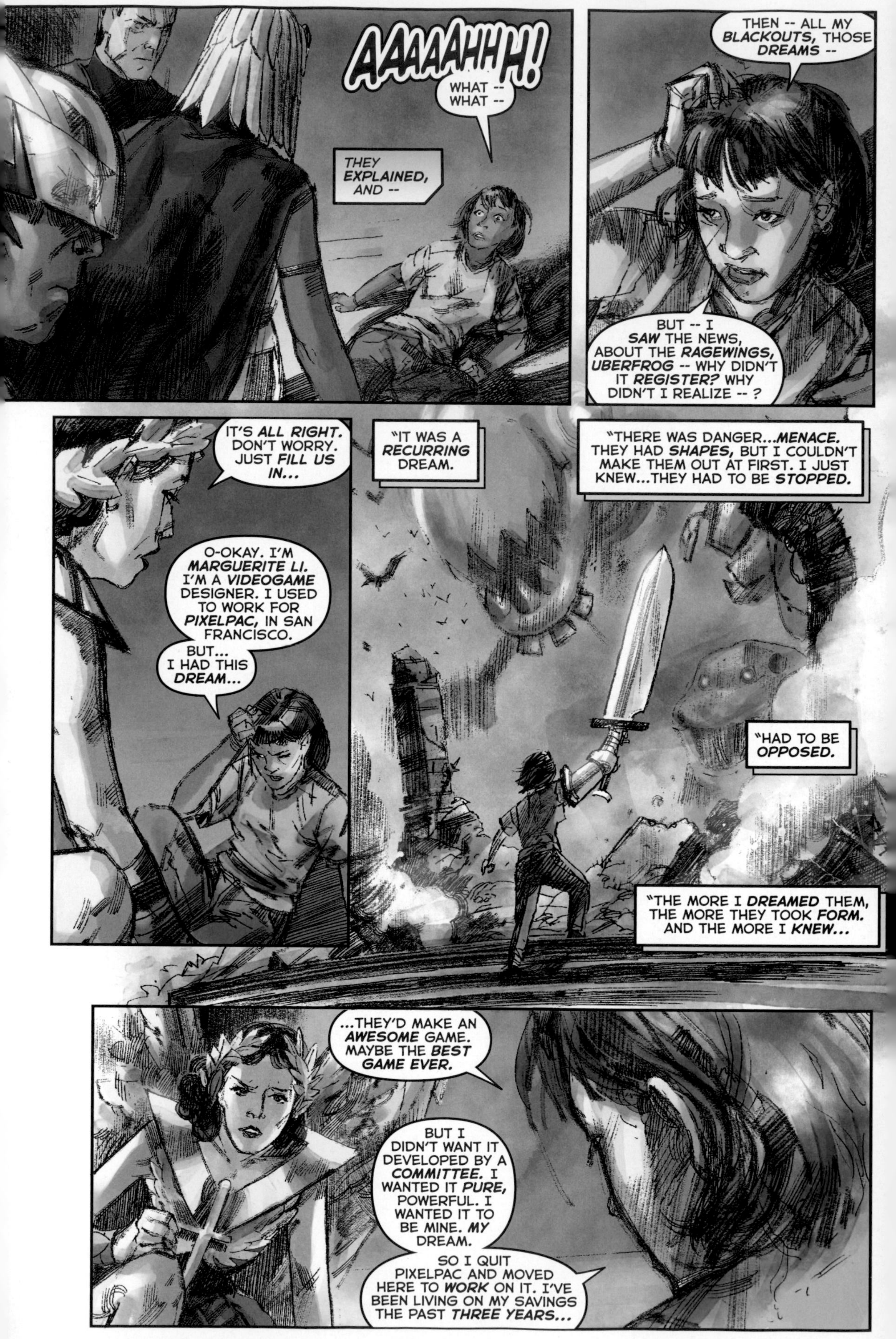
AAAAAHHH!
WHAT -- WHAT --
THEY EXPLAINED, AND --
THEN -- ALL MY BLACKOUTS, THOSE DREAMS --
BUT -- I SAW THE NEWS, ABOUT THE RAGEWINGS, UBERFROG -- WHY DIDN'T IT REGISTER? WHY DIDN'T I REALIZE -- ?
IT'S ALL RIGHT. DON'T WORRY. JUST FILL US IN...
O-OKAY. I'M MARGUERITE LI. I'M A VIDEOGAME DESIGNER. I USED TO WORK FOR PIXELPAC, IN SAN FRANCISCO.
BUT... I HAD THIS DREAM...
"IT WAS A RECURRING DREAM.
"THERE WAS DANGER...MENACE. THEY HAD SHAPES, BUT I COULDN'T MAKE THEM OUT AT FIRST. I JUST KNEW...THEY HAD TO BE STOPPED.
"HAD TO BE OPPOSED.
"THE MORE I DREAMED THEM, THE MORE THEY TOOK FORM. AND THE MORE I KNEW...
...THEY'D MAKE AN AWESOME GAME. MAYBE THE BEST GAME EVER.
BUT I DIDN'T WANT IT DEVELOPED BY A COMMITTEE. I WANTED IT PURE, POWERFUL. I WANTED IT TO BE MINE. MY DREAM.
SO I QUIT PIXELPAC AND MOVED HERE TO WORK ON IT. I'VE BEEN LIVING ON MY SAVINGS THE PAST THREE YEARS...

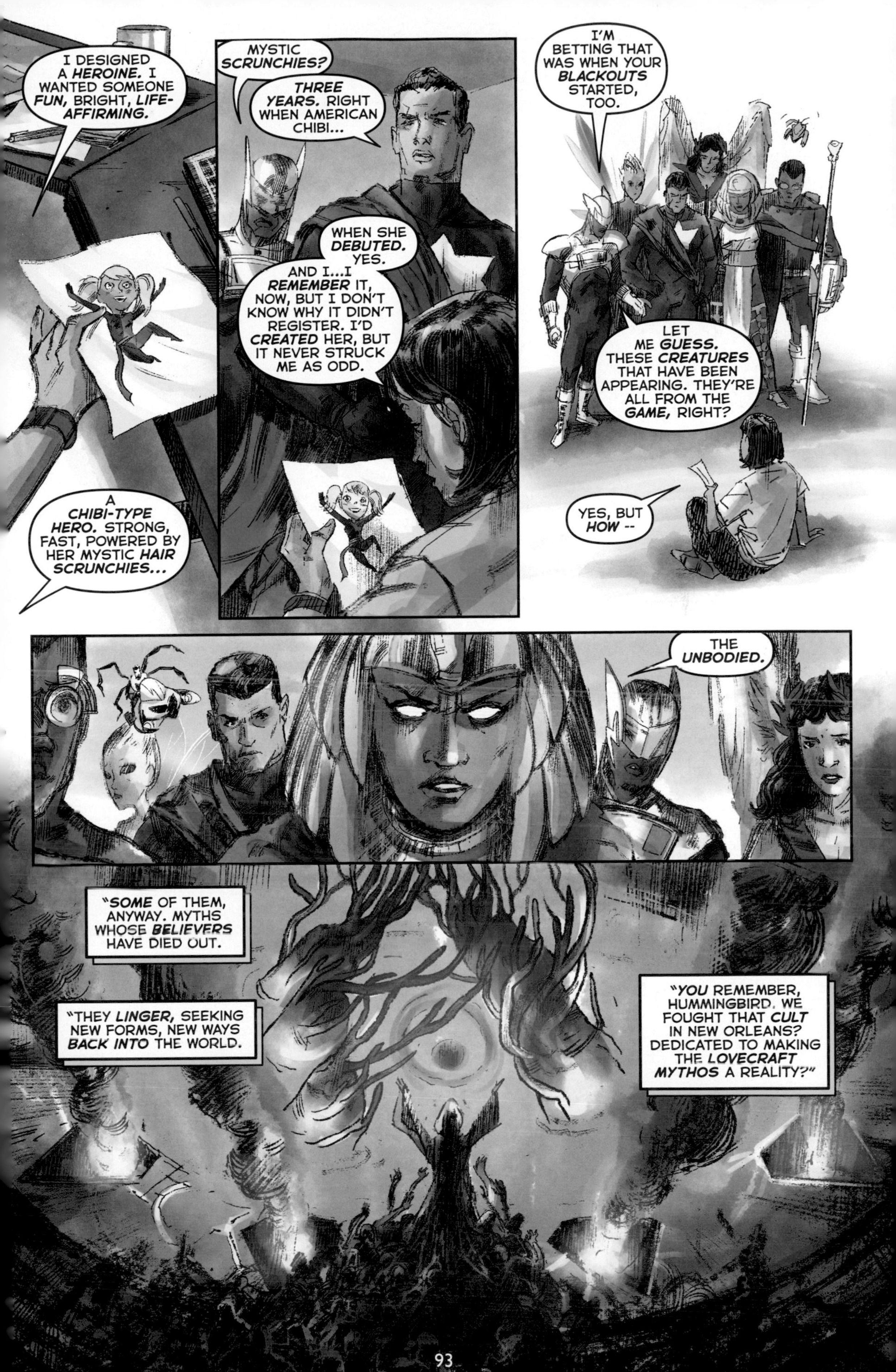
I DESIGNED A HEROINE. I WANTED SOMEONE FUN, BRIGHT, LIFE-AFFIRMING.
A CHIBI-TYPE HERO. STRONG, FAST, POWERED BY HER MYSTIC HAIR SCRUNCHIES...
MYSTIC SCRUNCHIES?
THREE YEARS. RIGHT WHEN AMERICAN CHIBI...
WHEN SHE DEBUTED. YES.
AND I...I REMEMBER IT, NOW, BUT I DON'T KNOW WHY IT DIDN'T REGISTER. I'D CREATED HER, BUT IT NEVER STRUCK ME AS ODD.
I'M BETTING THAT WAS WHEN YOUR BLACKOUTS STARTED, TOO.
LET ME GUESS. THESE CREATURES THAT HAVE BEEN APPEARING. THEY'RE ALL FROM THE GAME, RIGHT?
YES, BUT HOW --
THE UNBODIED.
"SOME OF THEM, ANYWAY. MYTHS WHOSE BELIEVERS HAVE DIED OUT.
"THEY LINGER, SEEKING NEW FORMS, NEW WAYS BACK INTO THE WORLD.
"YOU REMEMBER, HUMMINGBIRD. WE FOUGHT THAT CULT IN NEW ORLEANS? DEDICATED TO MAKING THE LOVECRAFT MYTHOS A REALITY?"

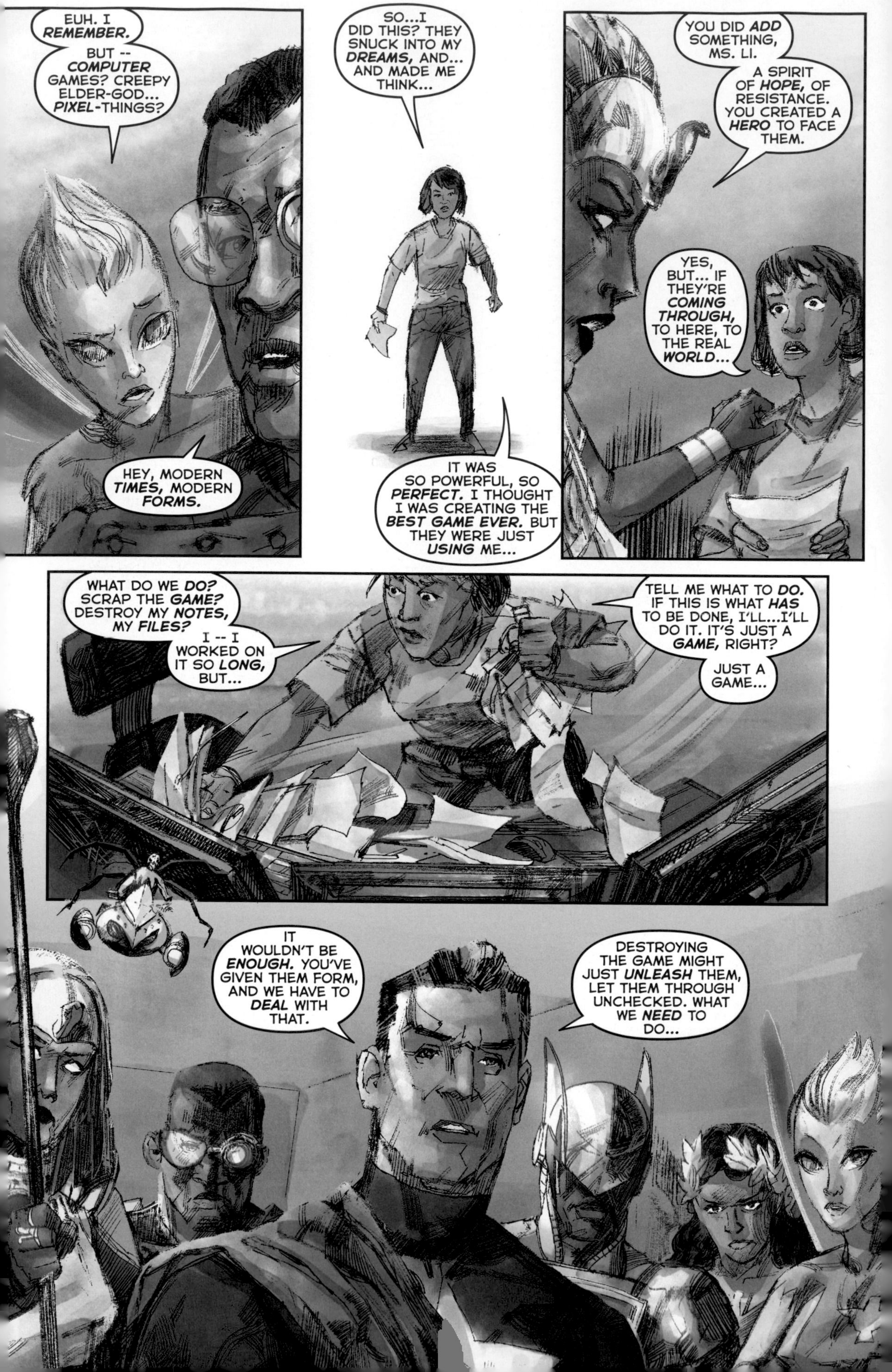
EUH. I REMEMBER.
BUT -- COMPUTER GAMES? CREEPY ELDER-GOD... PIXEL-THINGS?
HEY, MODERN TIMES, MODERN FORMS.
SO...I DID THIS? THEY SNUCK INTO MY DREAMS, AND... AND MADE ME THINK...
IT WAS SO POWERFUL, SO PERFECT. I THOUGHT I WAS CREATING THE BEST GAME EVER. BUT THEY WERE JUST USING ME...
YOU DID ADD SOMETHING, MS. LI.
A SPIRIT OF HOPE, OF RESISTANCE. YOU CREATED A HERO TO FACE THEM.
YES, BUT... IF THEY'RE COMING THROUGH, TO HERE, TO THE REAL WORLD...
WHAT DO WE DO? SCRAP THE GAME? DESTROY MY NOTES, MY FILES?
I -- I WORKED ON IT SO LONG, BUT...
TELL ME WHAT TO DO. IF THIS IS WHAT HAS TO BE DONE, I'LL...I'LL DO IT. IT'S JUST A GAME, RIGHT?
JUST A GAME...
IT WOULDN'T BE ENOUGH. YOU'VE GIVEN THEM FORM, AND WE HAVE TO DEAL WITH THAT.
DESTROYING THE GAME MIGHT JUST UNLEASH THEM, LET THEM THROUGH UNCHECKED. WHAT WE NEED TO DO...

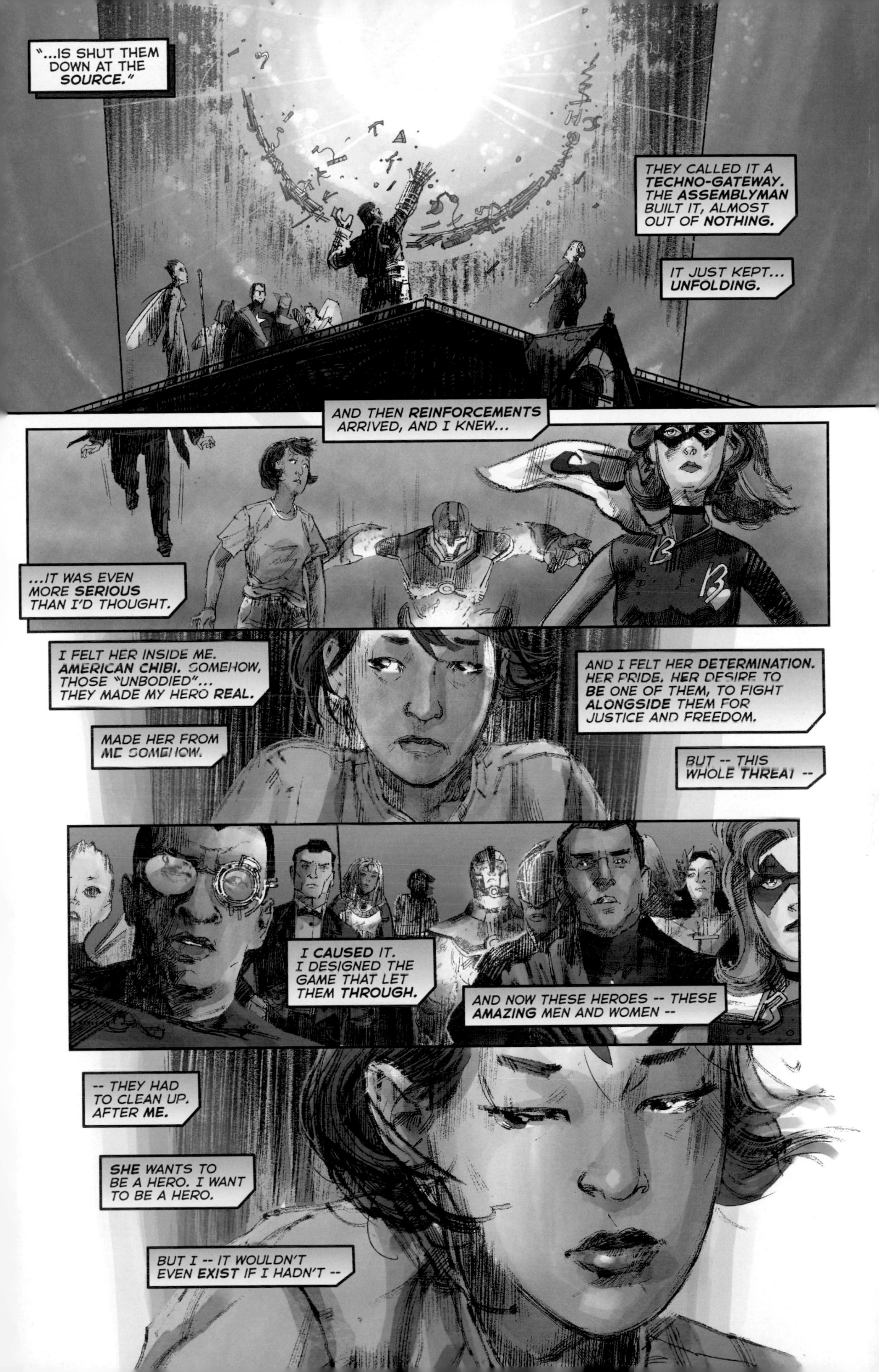
"...IS SHUT THEM DOWN AT THE SOURCE."
THEY CALLED IT A TECHNO-GATEWAY. THE ASSEMBLYMAN BUILT IT, ALMOST OUT OF NOTHING.
IT JUST KEPT... UNFOLDING.
AND THEN REINFORCEMENTS ARRIVED, AND I KNEW...
...IT WAS EVEN MORE SERIOUS THAN I'D THOUGHT.
I FELT HER INSIDE ME. AMERICAN CHIBI. SOMEHOW, THOSE "UNBODIED"... THEY MADE MY HERO REAL.
MADE HER FROM ME SOMEHOW.
AND I FELT HER DETERMINATION. HER PRIDE. HER DESIRE TO BE ONE OF THEM, TO FIGHT ALONGSIDE THEM FOR JUSTICE AND FREEDOM.
BUT -- THIS WHOLE THREAT --
I CAUSED IT. I DESIGNED THE GAME THAT LET THEM THROUGH.
AND NOW THESE HEROES -- THESE AMAZING MEN AND WOMEN --
-- THEY HAD TO CLEAN UP. AFTER ME.
SHE WANTS TO BE A HERO. I WANT TO BE A HERO.
BUT I -- IT WOULDN'T EVEN EXIST IF I HADN'T --

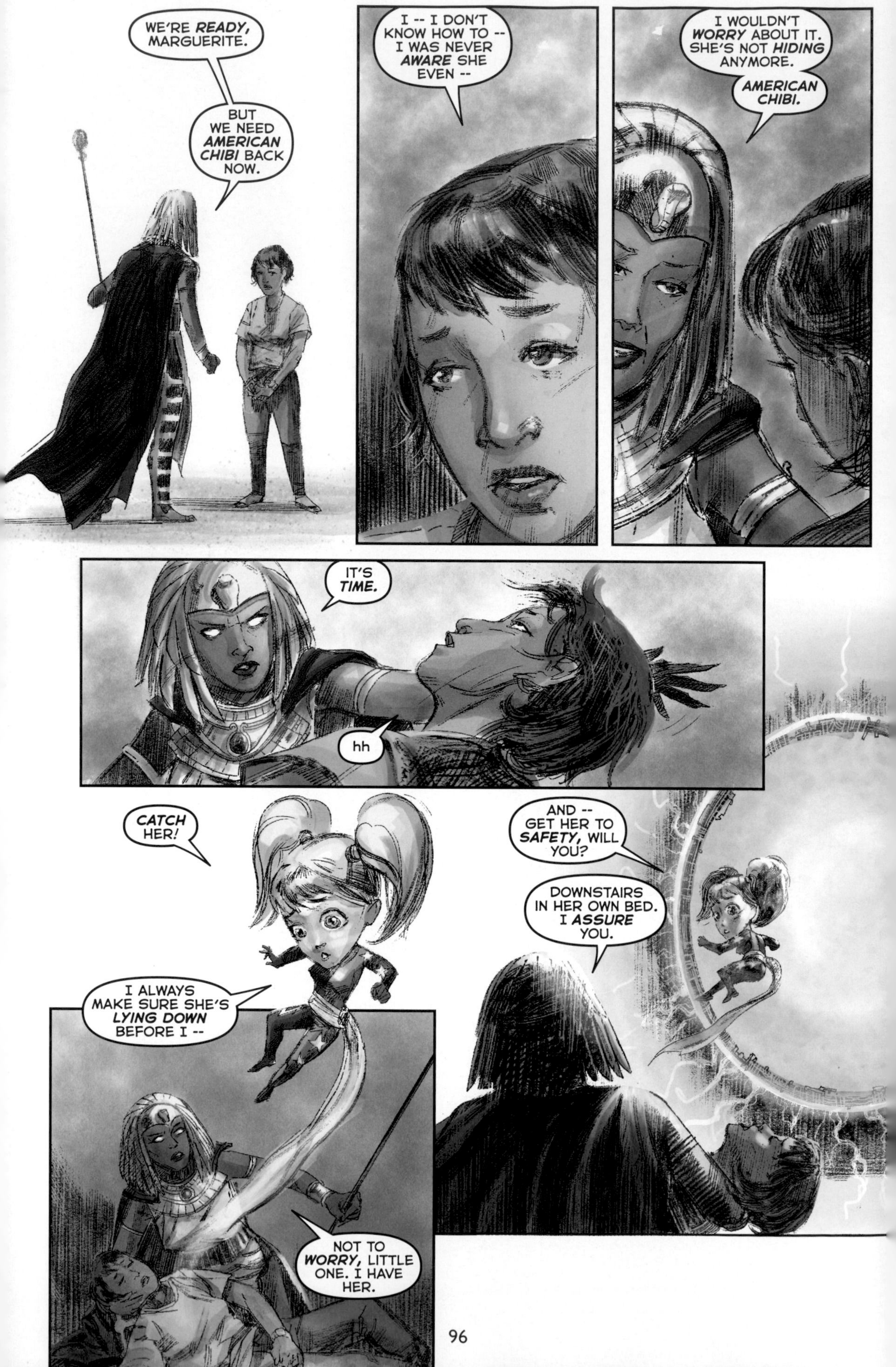
WE'RE READY, MARGUERITE.
BUT WE NEED AMERICAN CHIBI BACK NOW.
I -- I DON'T KNOW HOW TO -- I WAS NEVER AWARE SHE EVEN --
I WOULDN'T WORRY ABOUT IT. SHE'S NOT HIDING ANYMORE.
AMERICAN CHIBI.
IT'S TIME.
hh
CATCH HER!
AND -- GET HER TO SAFETY, WILL YOU?
DOWNSTAIRS IN HER OWN BED. I ASSURE YOU.
I ALWAYS MAKE SURE SHE'S LYING DOWN BEFORE I --
NOT TO WORRY, LITTLE ONE. I HAVE HER.

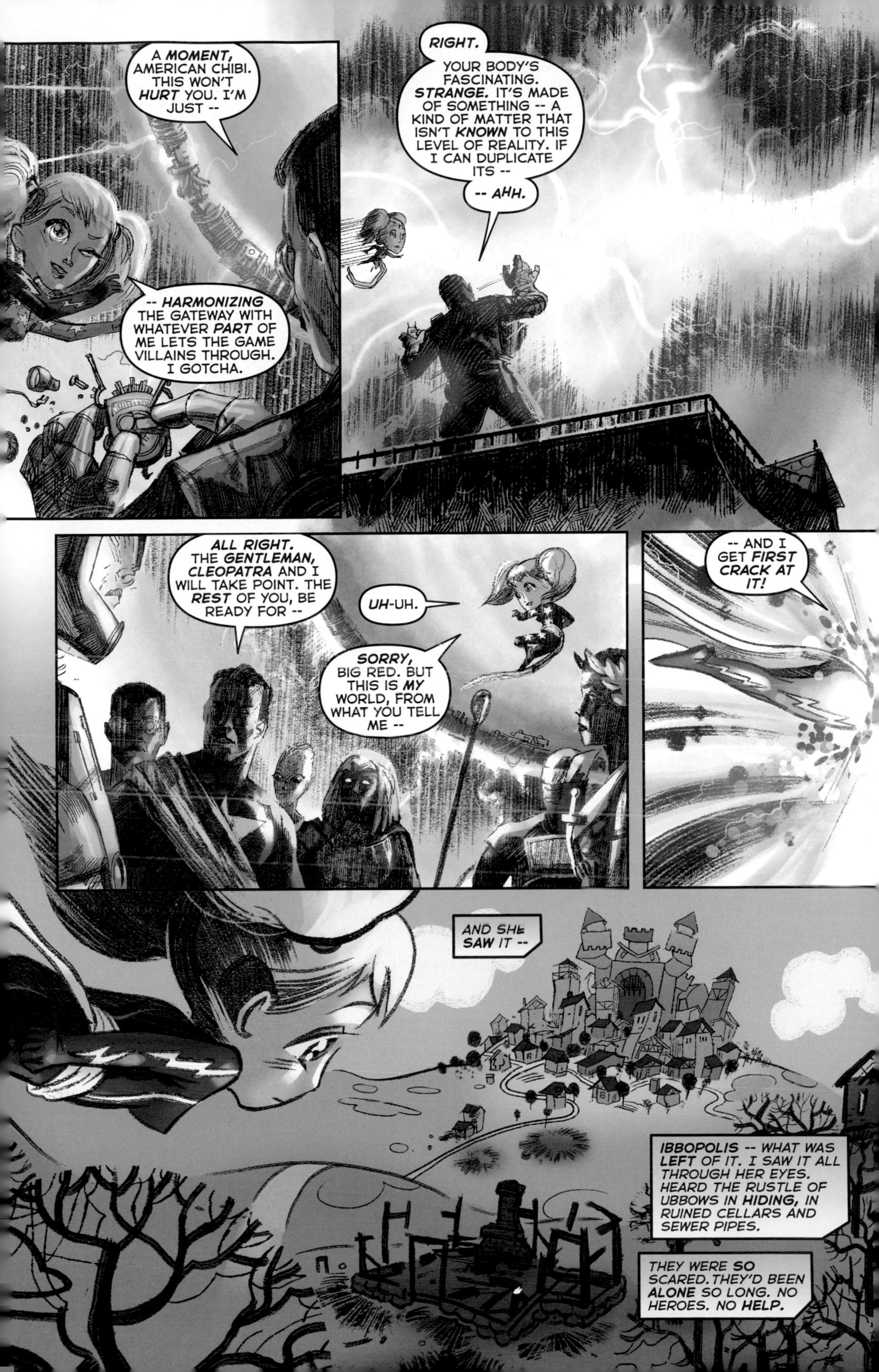
A MOMENT, AMERICAN CHIBI. THIS WON'T HURT YOU. I'M JUST --
-- HARMONIZING THE GATEWAY WITH WHATEVER PART OF ME LETS THE GAME VILLAINS THROUGH. I GOTCHA.
RIGHT.
YOUR BODY'S FASCINATING. STRANGE. IT'S MADE OF SOMETHING -- A KIND OF MATTER THAT ISN'T KNOWN TO THIS LEVEL OF REALITY. IF I CAN DUPLICATE ITS --
-- AHH.
ALL RIGHT. THE GENTLEMAN, CLEOPATRA AND I WILL TAKE POINT. THE REST OF YOU, BE READY FOR --
UH-UH.
SORRY, BIG RED. BUT THIS IS MY WORLD, FROM WHAT YOU TELL ME --
-- AND I GET FIRST CRACK AT IT!
AND SHE SAW IT --
IBBOPOLIS -- WHAT WAS LEFT OF IT. I SAW IT ALL THROUGH HER EYES. HEARD THE RUSTLE OF UBBOWS IN HIDING, IN RUINED CELLARS AND SEWER PIPES.
THEY WERE SO SCARED. THEY'D BEEN ALONE SO LONG. NO HEROES. NO HELP.

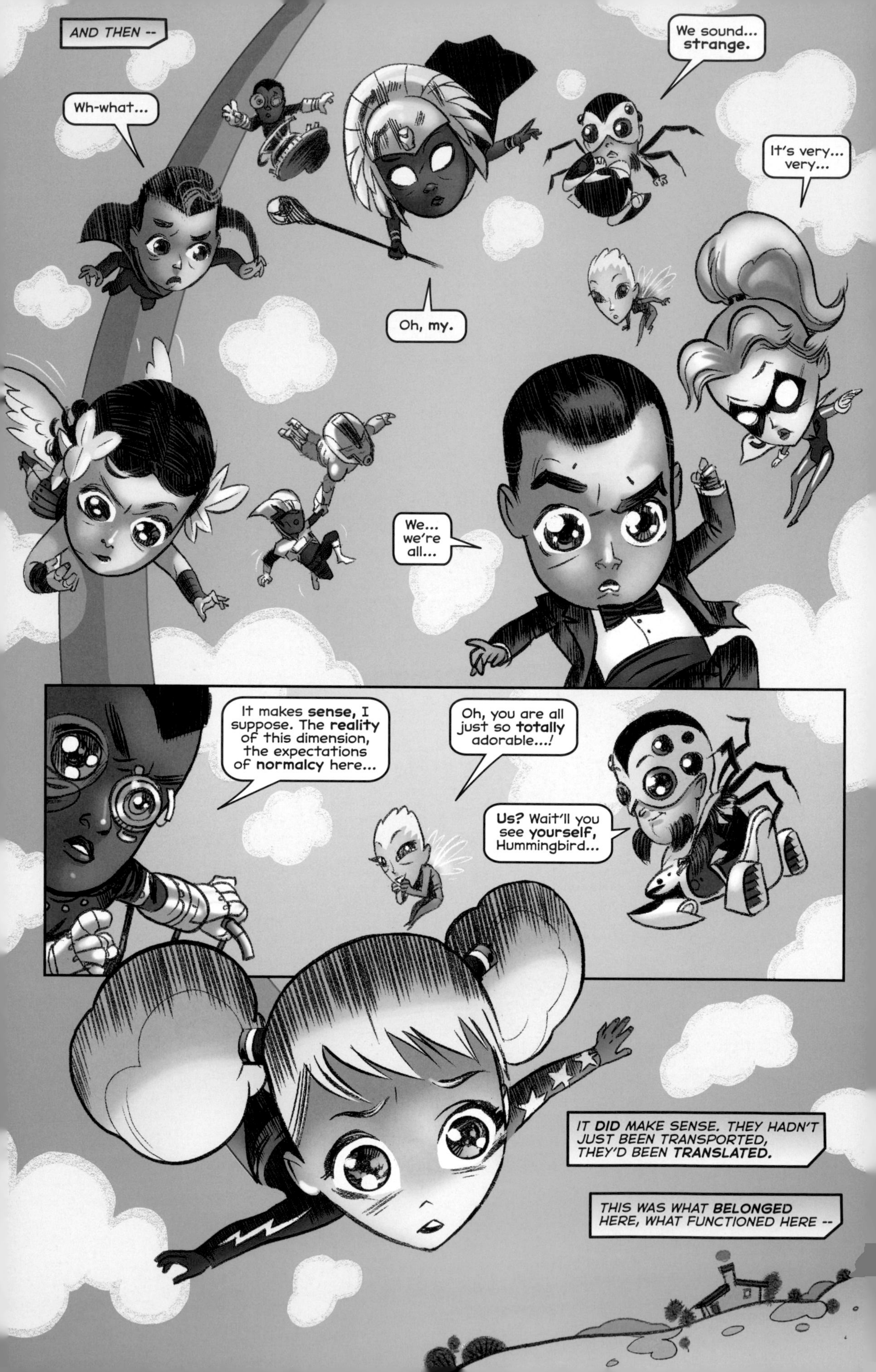
AND THEN --
Wh-what...
Oh, my.
We sound... strange.
It's very... very...
We... we're all...
It makes sense, I suppose. The reality of this dimension, the expectations of normalcy here...
Oh, you are all just so totally adorable...!
Us? Wait'll you see yourself, Hummingbird...
IT DID MAKE SENSE. THEY HADN'T JUST BEEN TRANSPORTED, THEY'D BEEN TRANSLATED.
THIS WAS WHAT BELONGED HERE, WHAT FUNCTIONED HERE --

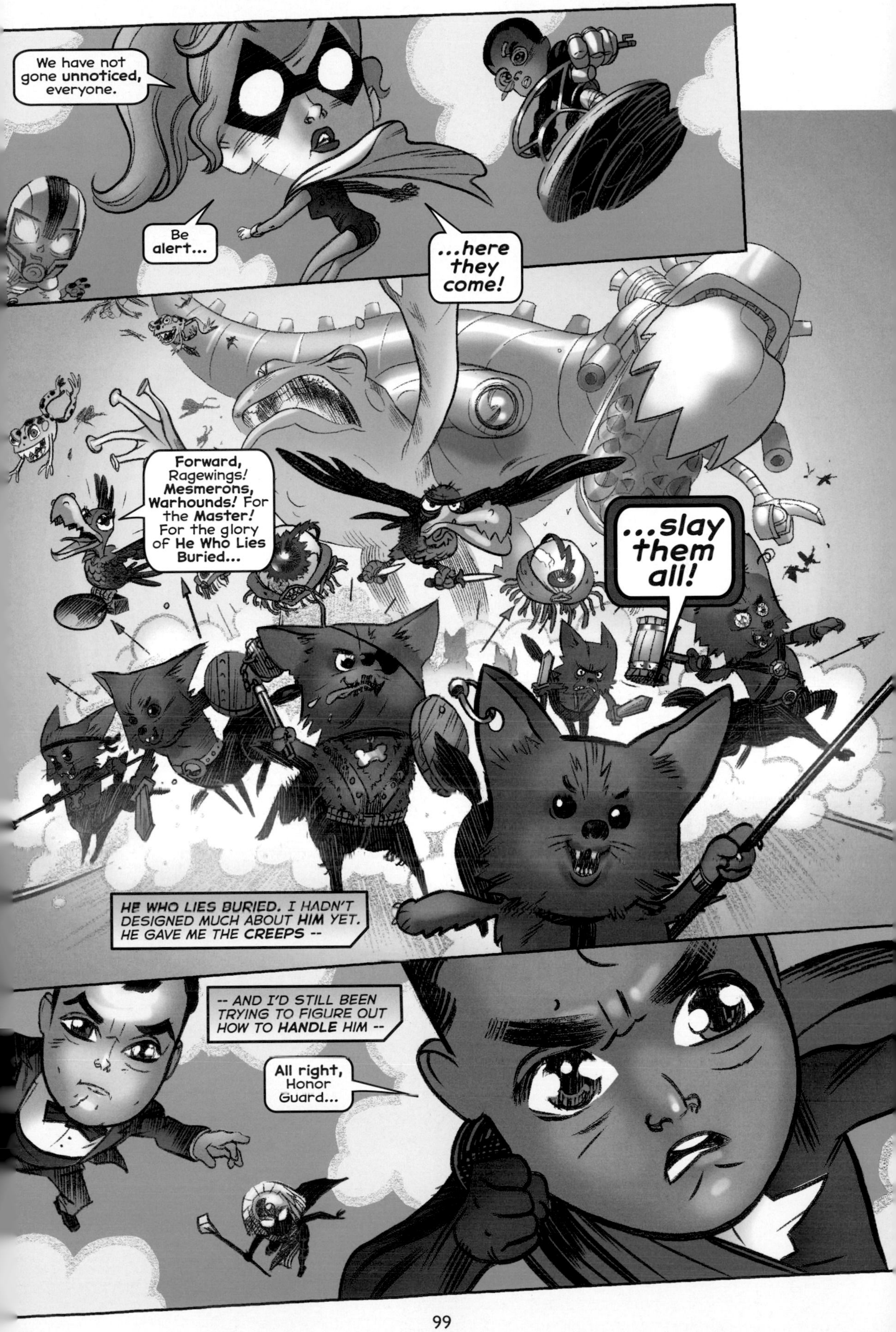
We have not gone **unnoticed**, everyone.
Be alert...
...here they come!
Forward, Ragewings! **Mesmerons, Warhounds!** For **the Master!** For the glory of **He Who Lies Buried...**
...slay them all!
*HE WHO LIES BURIED. I HADN'T DESIGNED MUCH ABOUT **HIM** YET. HE GAVE ME THE **CREEPS** --*
*-- AND I'D STILL BEEN TRYING TO FIGURE OUT HOW TO **HANDLE** HIM --*
All right, Honor Guard...

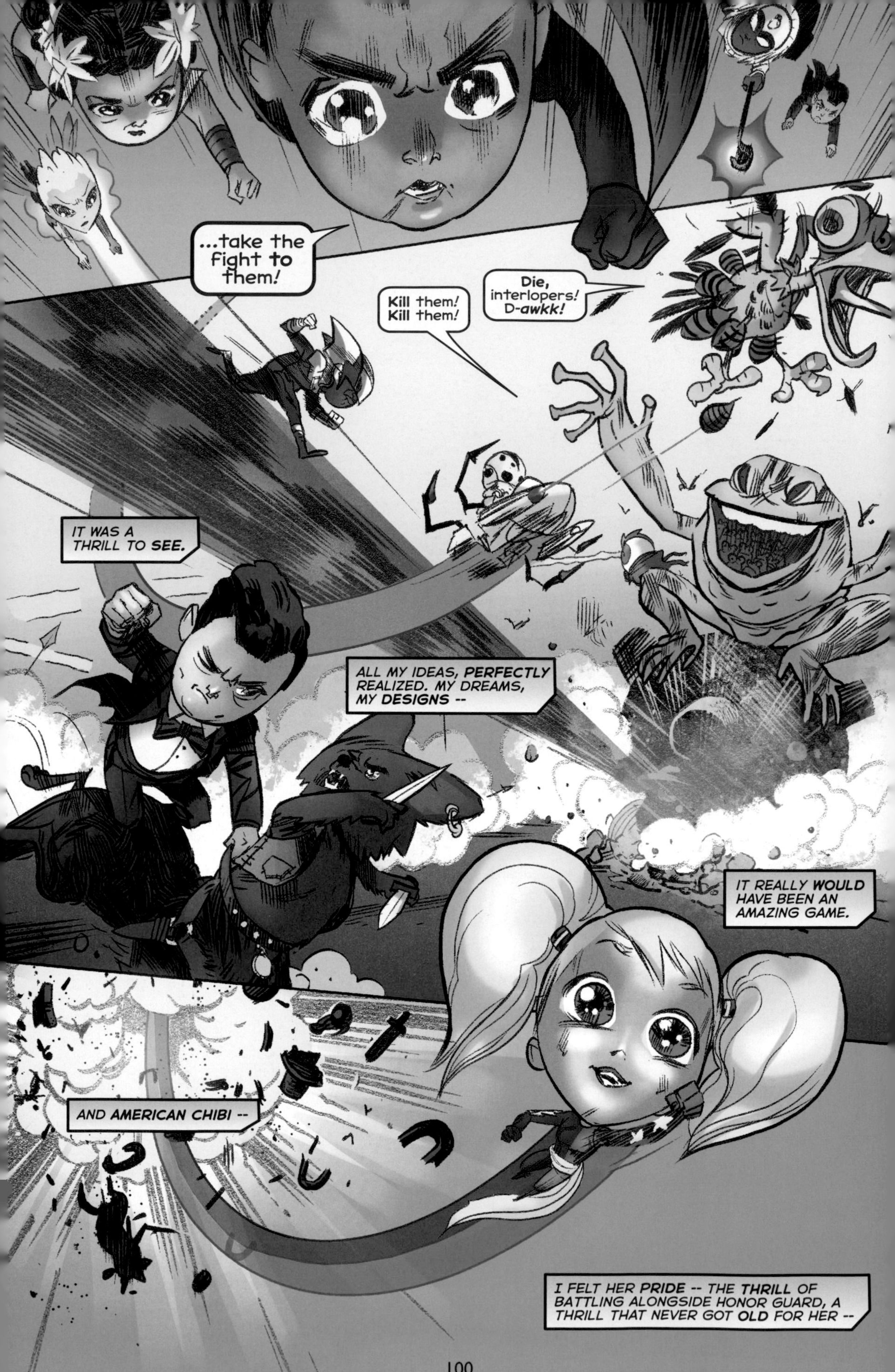
...take the fight to them!
Kill them! Kill them!
Die, interlopers! D-awkk!
IT WAS A THRILL TO SEE.
ALL MY IDEAS, PERFECTLY REALIZED. MY DREAMS, MY DESIGNS --
IT REALLY WOULD HAVE BEEN AN AMAZING GAME.
AND AMERICAN CHIBI --
I FELT HER PRIDE -- THE THRILL OF BATTLING ALONGSIDE HONOR GUARD, A THRILL THAT NEVER GOT OLD FOR HER --

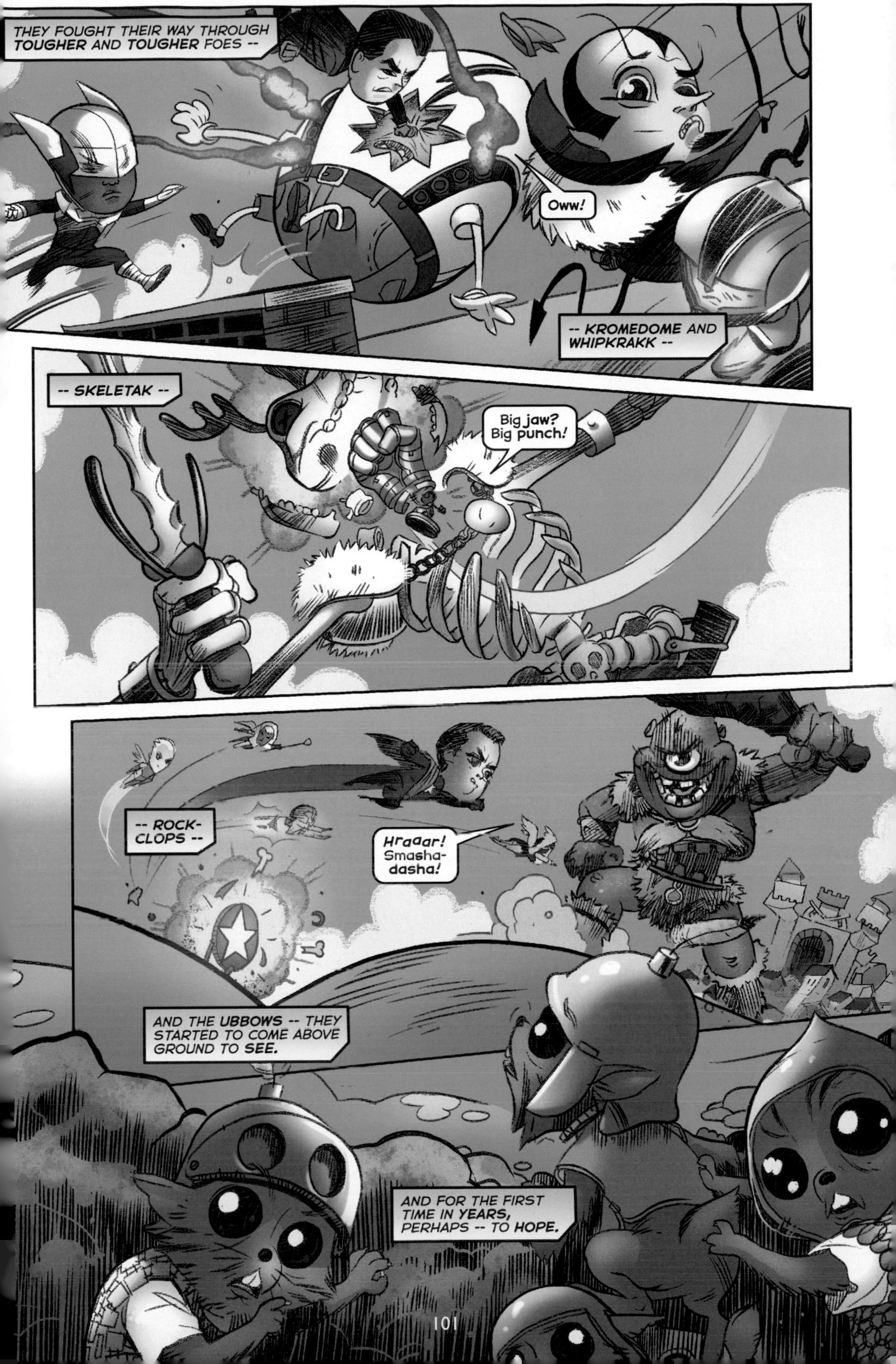
THEY FOUGHT THEIR WAY THROUGH TOUGHER AND TOUGHER FOES --
Oww!
-- KROMEDOME AND WHIPKRAKK --
-- SKELETAK --
Big jaw? Big punch!
-- ROCK-CLOPS --
Hraaar! Smasha-dasha!
AND THE UBBOWS -- THEY STARTED TO COME ABOVE GROUND TO SEE.
AND FOR THE FIRST TIME IN YEARS, PERHAPS -- TO HOPE.

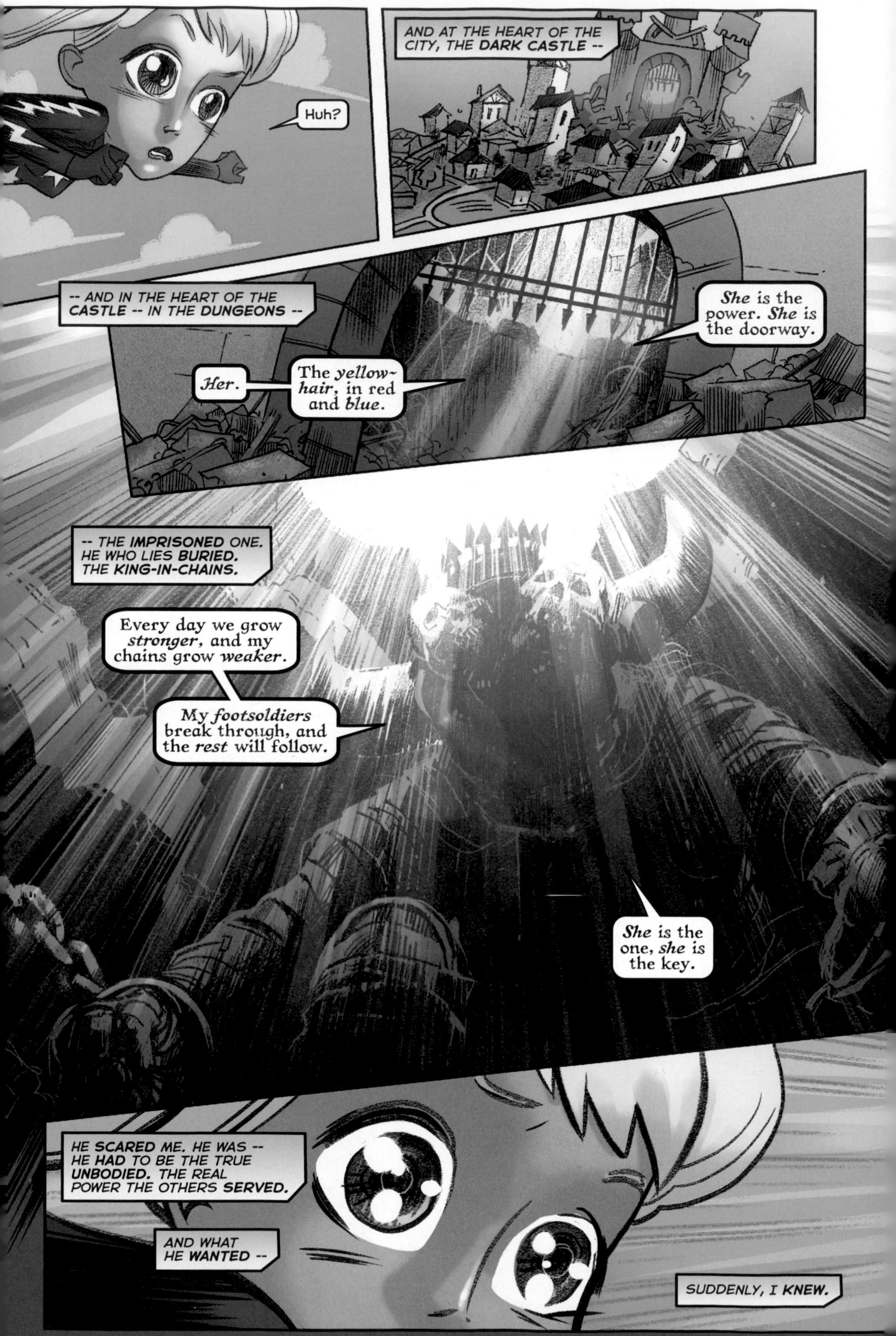
Huh?
AND AT THE HEART OF THE CITY, THE DARK CASTLE --
-- AND IN THE HEART OF THE CASTLE -- IN THE DUNGEONS --
She is the power. She is the doorway.
Her.
The yellow-hair, in red and blue.
-- THE IMPRISONED ONE. HE WHO LIES BURIED. THE KING-IN-CHAINS.
Every day we grow stronger, and my chains grow weaker.
My footsoldiers break through, and the rest will follow.
She is the one, she is the key.
HE SCARED ME. HE WAS -- HE HAD TO BE THE TRUE UNBODIED. THE REAL POWER THE OTHERS SERVED.
AND WHAT HE WANTED --
SUDDENLY, I KNEW.

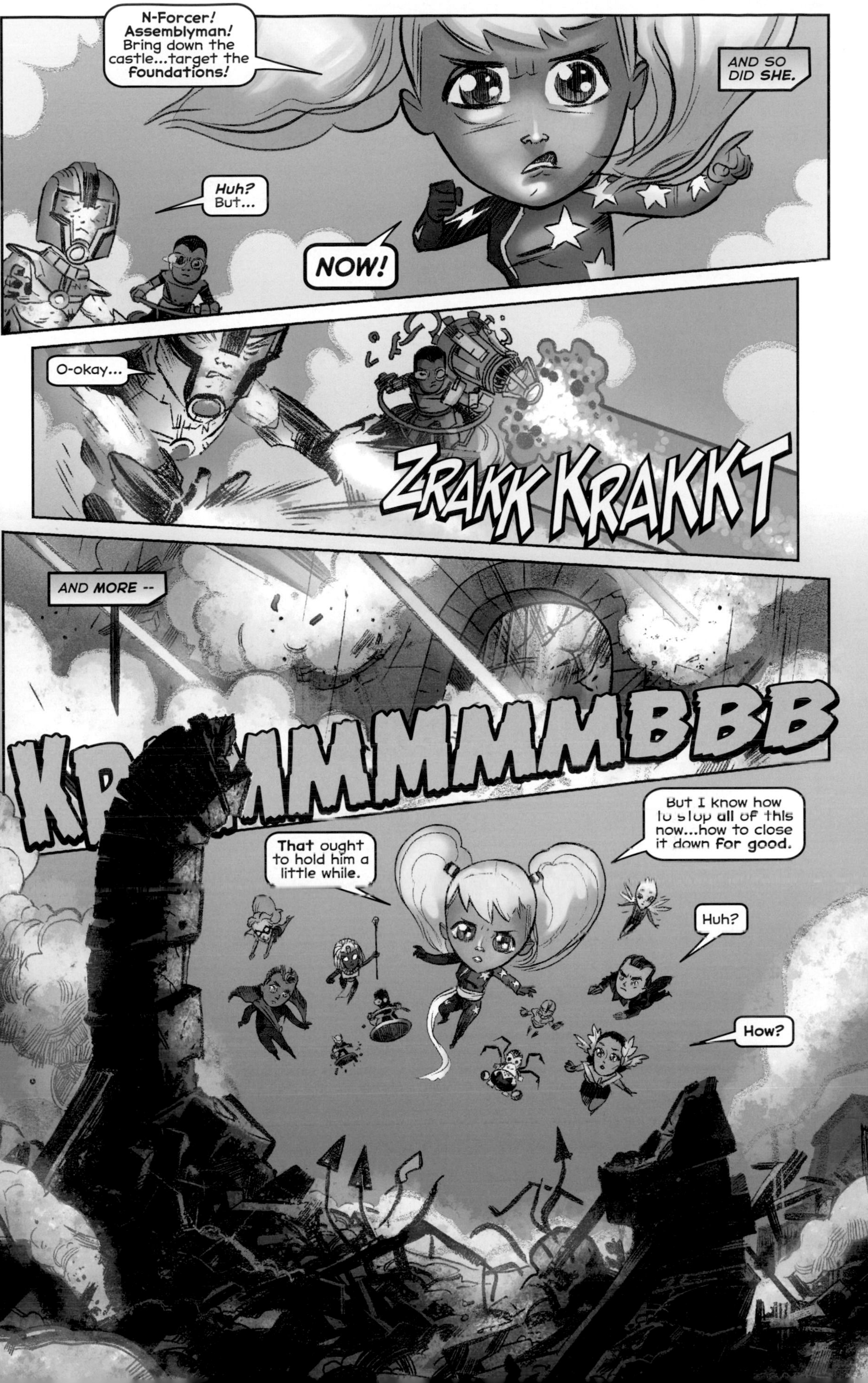
N-Forcer! Assemblyman! Bring down the castle...target the foundations!
AND SO DID SHE.
Huh? But...
NOW!
O-okay...
ZRAKK KRAKKT
AND MORE --
That ought to hold him a little while.
But I know how to stop all of this now...how to close it down for good.
Huh?
How?

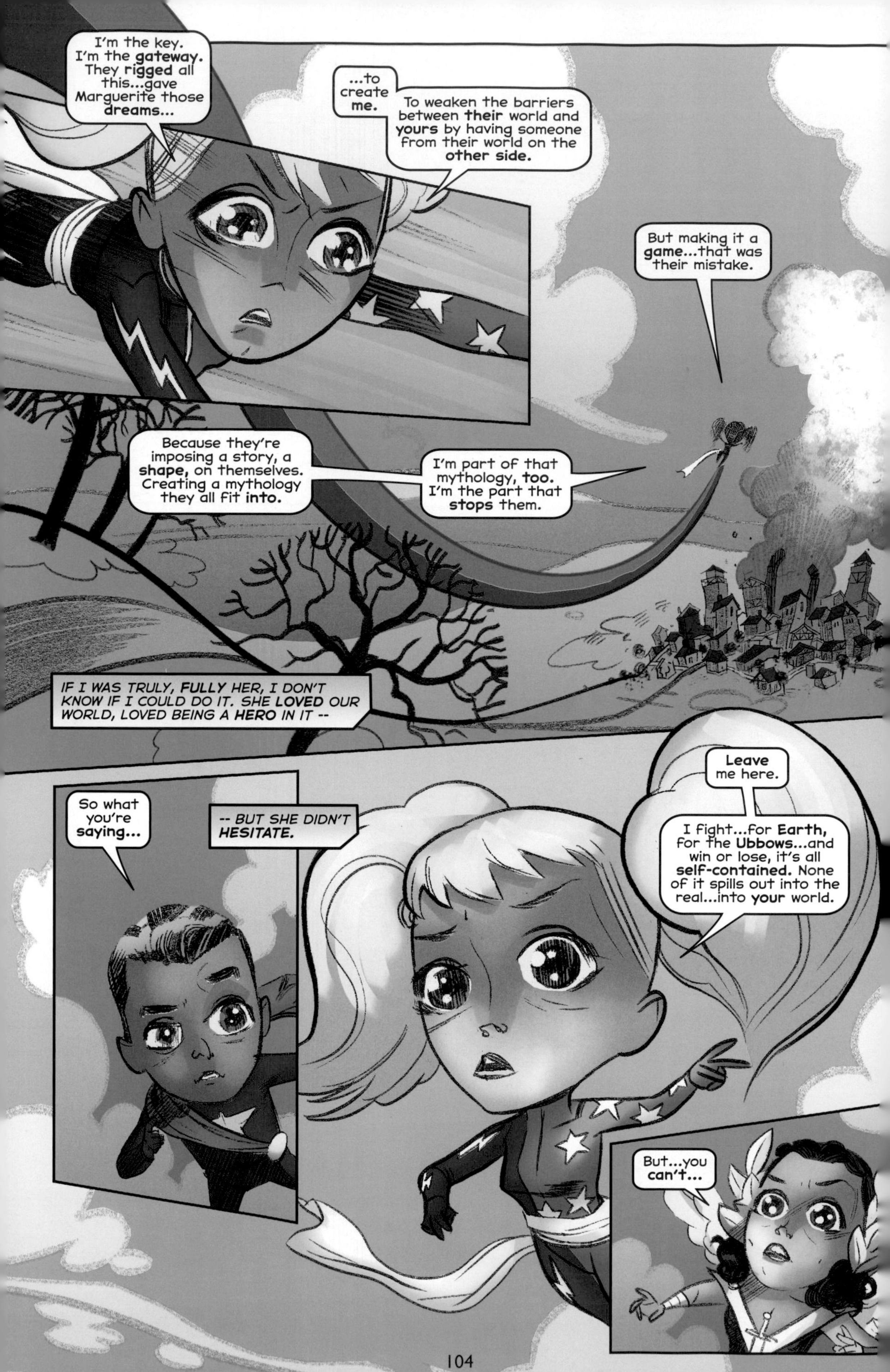

I'm the key. I'm the gateway. They rigged all this...gave Marguerite those dreams...
...to create me.
To weaken the barriers between their world and yours by having someone from their world on the other side.
But making it a game...that was their mistake.
Because they're imposing a story, a shape, on themselves. Creating a mythology they all fit into.
I'm part of that mythology, too. I'm the part that stops them.
IF I WAS TRULY, FULLY HER, I DON'T KNOW IF I COULD DO IT. SHE LOVED OUR WORLD, LOVED BEING A HERO IN IT --
So what you're saying...
-- BUT SHE DIDN'T HESITATE.
Leave me here.
I fight...for Earth, for the Ubbows...and win or lose, it's all self-contained. None of it spills out into the real...into your world.
But...you can't...

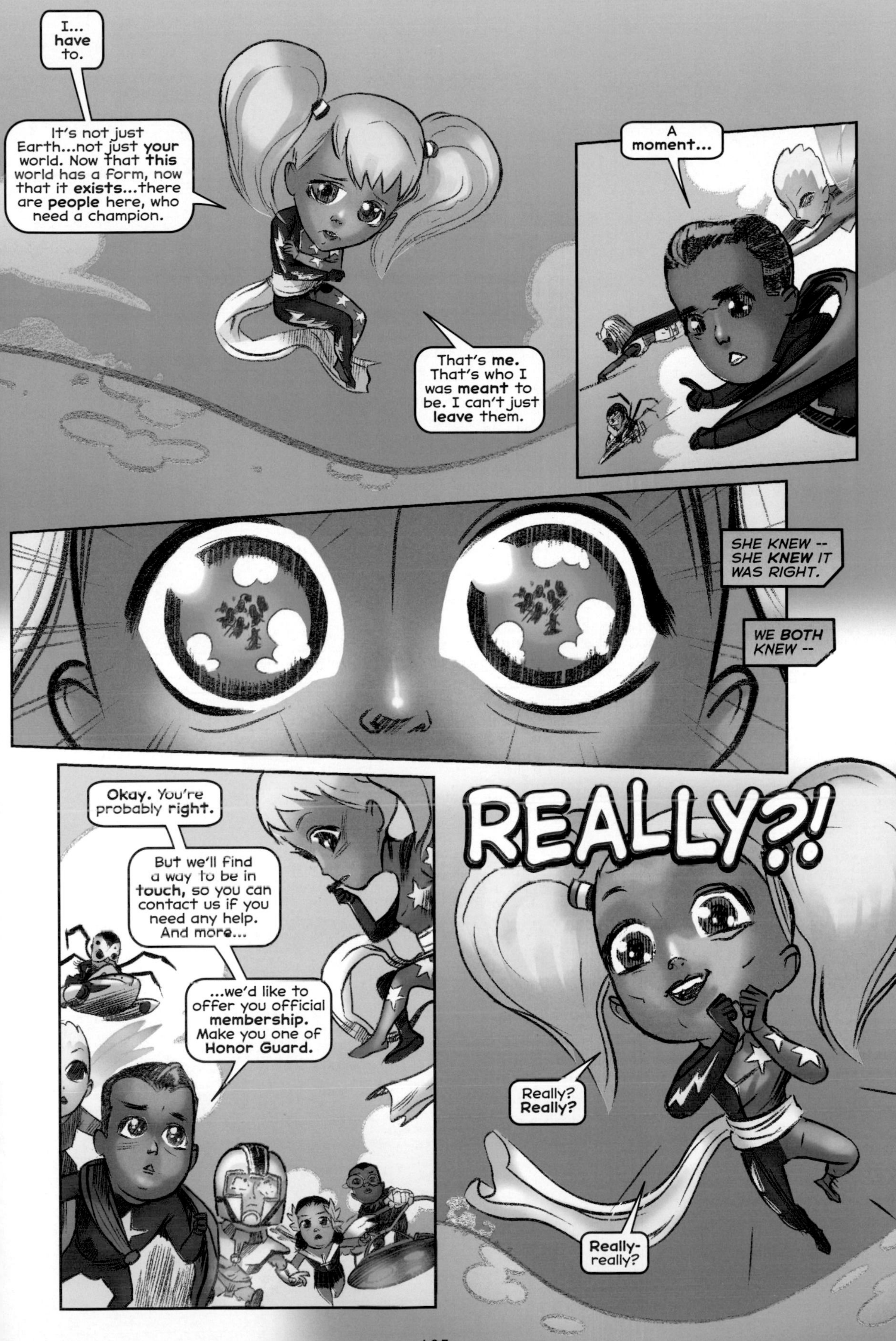
I... have to.
It's not just Earth...not just your world. Now that this world has a form, now that it exists...there are people here, who need a champion.
That's me. That's who I was meant to be. I can't just leave them.
A moment...
SHE KNEW -- SHE KNEW IT WAS RIGHT.
WE BOTH KNEW --
Okay. You're probably right.
But we'll find a way to be in touch, so you can contact us if you need any help. And more...
...we'd like to offer you official membership. Make you one of Honor Guard.
REALLY?!
Really? Really?
Really-really?

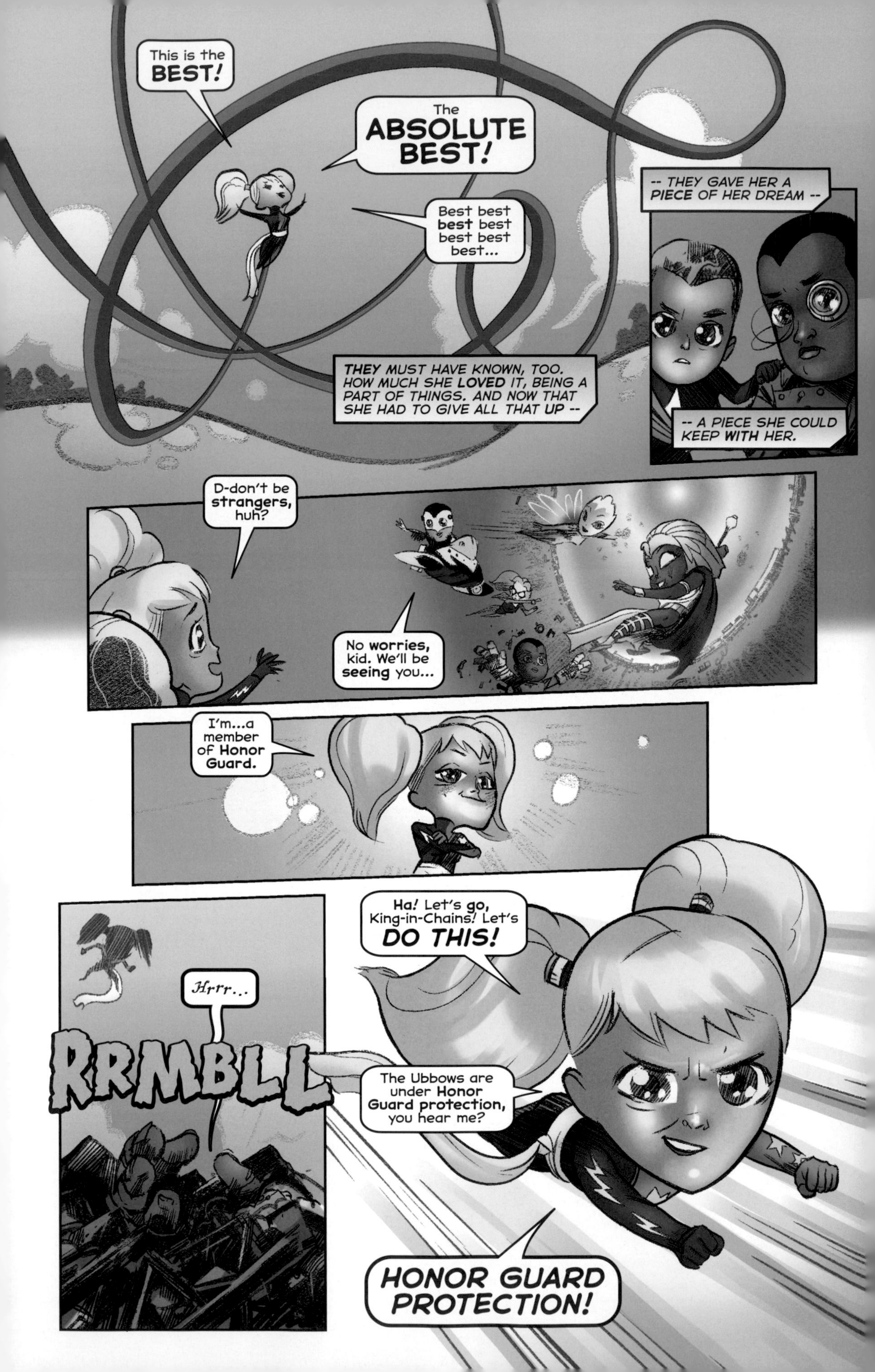
This is the BEST!
The ABSOLUTE BEST!
Best best best best best best best...
THEY MUST HAVE KNOWN, TOO. HOW MUCH SHE LOVED IT, BEING A PART OF THINGS. AND NOW THAT SHE HAD TO GIVE ALL THAT UP --
-- THEY GAVE HER A PIECE OF HER DREAM --
-- A PIECE SHE COULD KEEP WITH HER.
D-don't be strangers, huh?
No worries, kid. We'll be seeing you...
I'm...a member of Honor Guard.
Hrrr...
RRMBLL
Ha! Let's go, King-in-Chains! Let's DO THIS!
The Ubbows are under Honor Guard protection, you hear me?
HONOR GUARD PROTECTION!

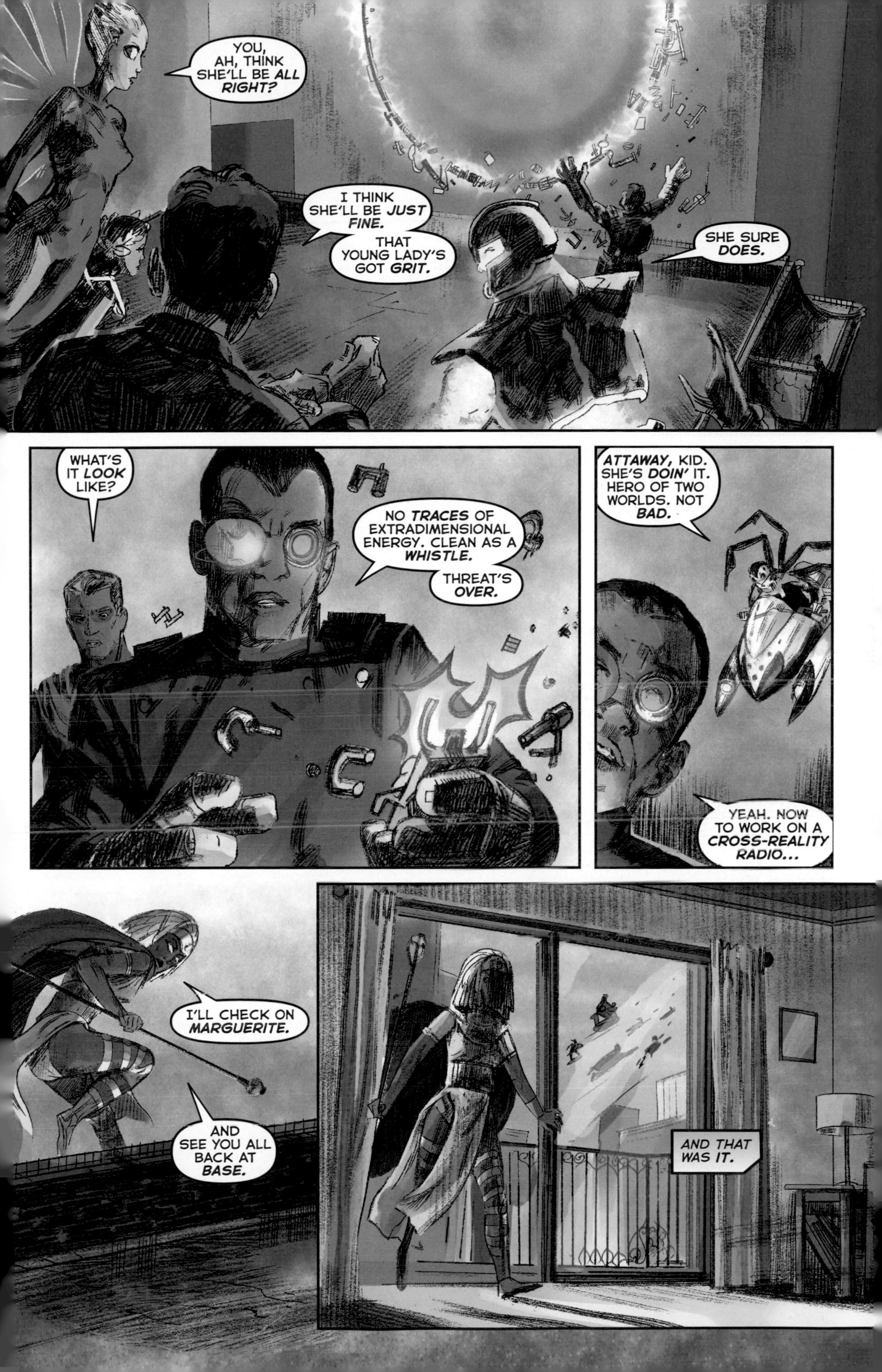
YOU, AH, THINK SHE'LL BE ALL RIGHT?
I THINK SHE'LL BE JUST FINE.
THAT YOUNG LADY'S GOT GRIT.
SHE SURE DOES.
WHAT'S IT LOOK LIKE?
NO TRACES OF EXTRADIMENSIONAL ENERGY. CLEAN AS A WHISTLE.
THREAT'S OVER.
ATTAWAY, KID. SHE'S DOIN' IT. HERO OF TWO WORLDS. NOT BAD.
YEAH. NOW TO WORK ON A CROSS-REALITY RADIO...
I'LL CHECK ON MARGUERITE.
AND SEE YOU ALL BACK AT BASE.
AND THAT WAS IT.

CLEOPATRA **TOLD** ME WHAT HAD HAPPENED.

SHE DIDN'T REALLY **NEED** TO. I'D SEEN IT. I'D EVEN **BEEN** THERE, A LITTLE.

BUT NOW --

-- I TRIED TO CONCENTRATE, TRIED TO **REACH** HER --

SHE WAS GONE. WE WEREN'T **LINKED** ANY MORE. SHE WAS ON HER **OWN**.

AND I --

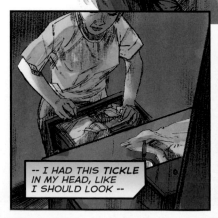

-- I HAD THIS **TICKLE** IN MY HEAD, LIKE I SHOULD LOOK --

WHAT?

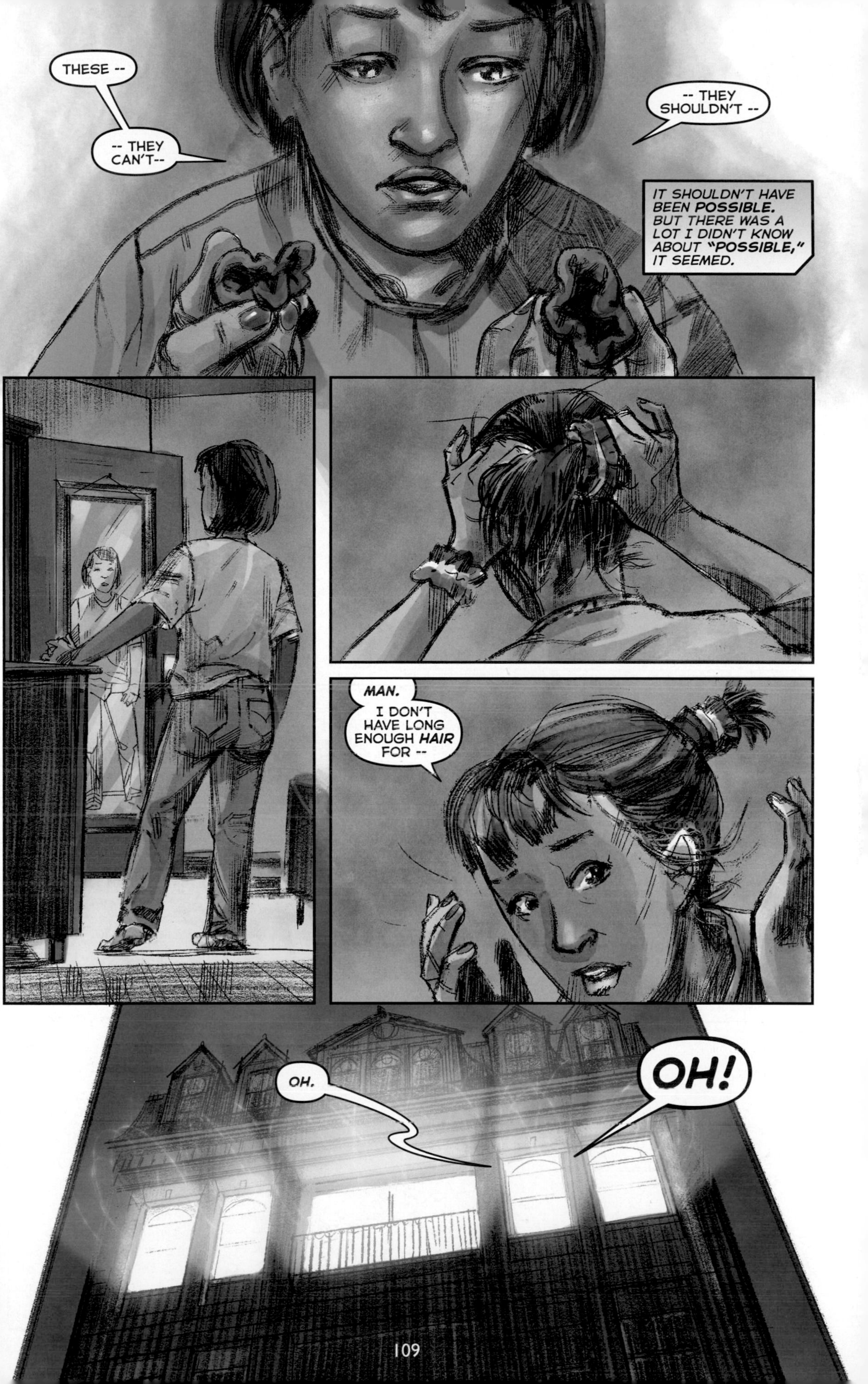
THESE --
-- THEY CAN'T--
-- THEY SHOULDN'T --
IT SHOULDN'T HAVE BEEN POSSIBLE. BUT THERE WAS A LOT I DIDN'T KNOW ABOUT "POSSIBLE," IT SEEMED.
MAN. I DON'T HAVE LONG ENOUGH HAIR FOR --
OH.
OH!

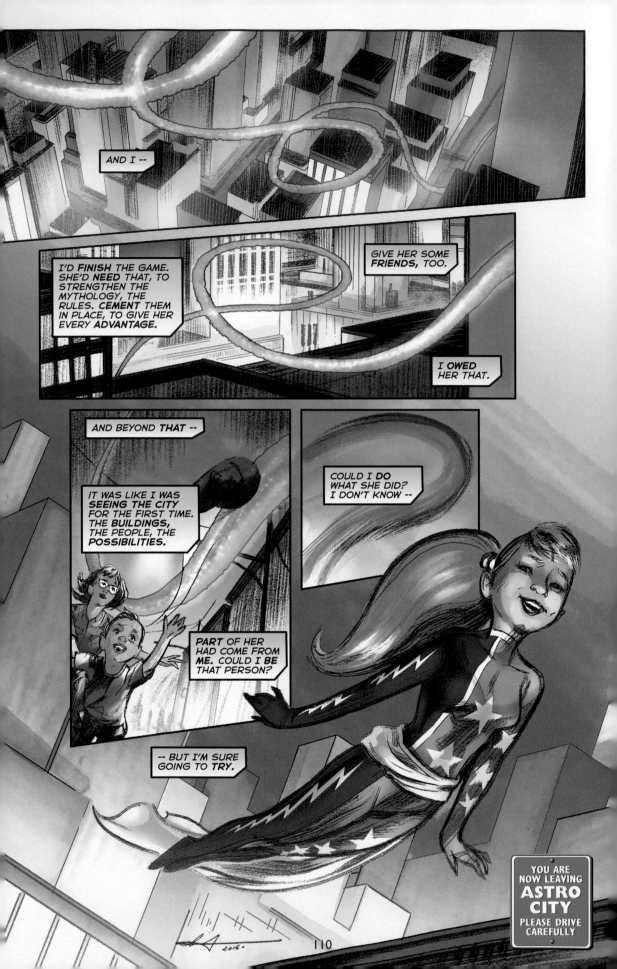

AND I --

I'D FINISH THE GAME. SHE'D NEED THAT, TO STRENGTHEN THE MYTHOLOGY, THE RULES. CEMENT THEM IN PLACE, TO GIVE HER EVERY ADVANTAGE.

GIVE HER SOME FRIENDS, TOO.

I OWED HER THAT.

AND BEYOND THAT --

IT WAS LIKE I WAS SEEING THE CITY FOR THE FIRST TIME. THE BUILDINGS, THE PEOPLE, THE POSSIBILITIES.

COULD I DO WHAT SHE DID? I DON'T KNOW --

PART OF HER HAD COME FROM ME. COULD I BE THAT PERSON?

-- BUT I'M SURE GOING TO TRY.

YOU ARE NOW LEAVING ASTRO CITY PLEASE DRIVE CAREFULLY

110

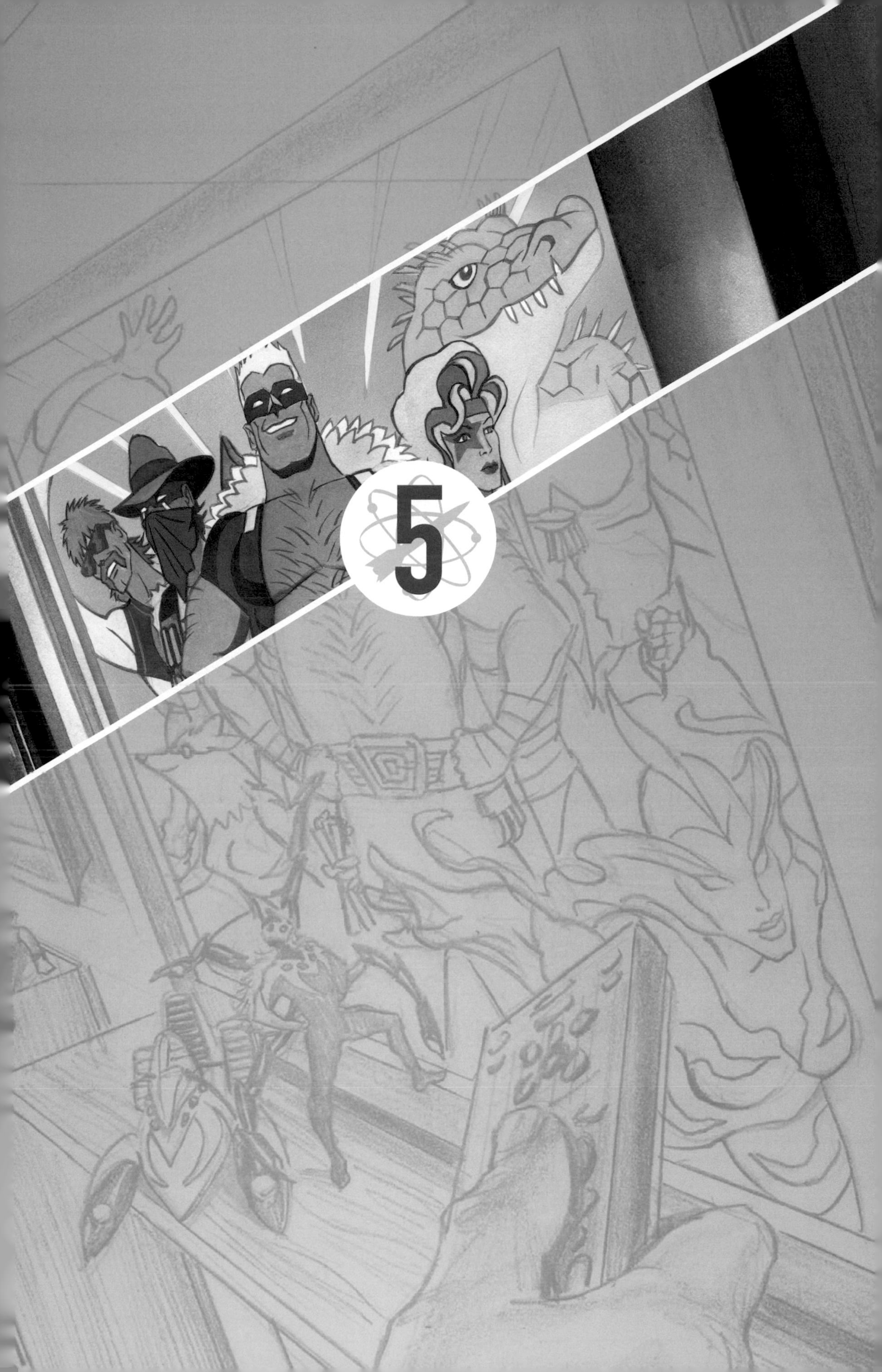
5

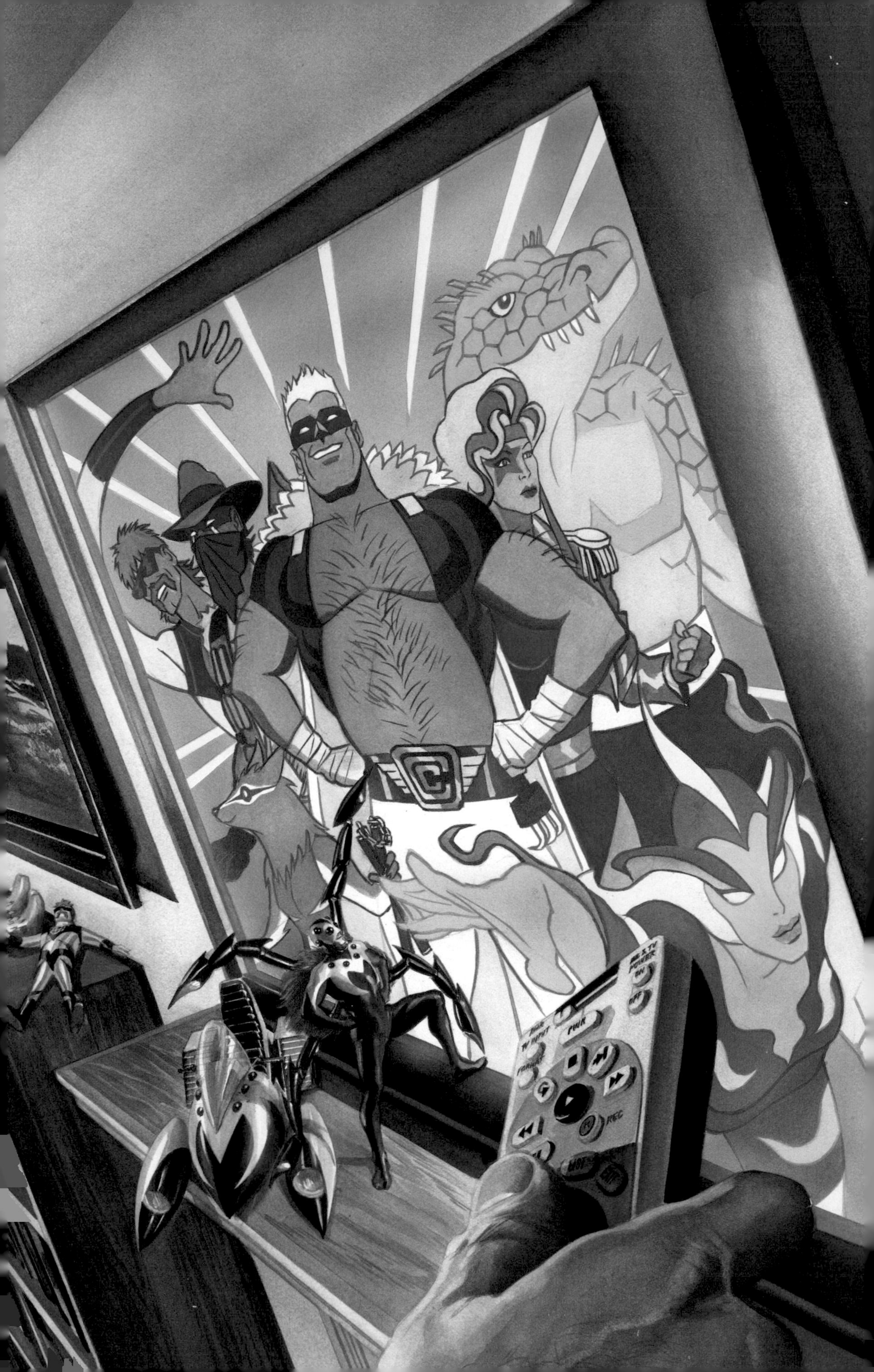
POWER
ON
OFF
TV INPUT
PWR
REC

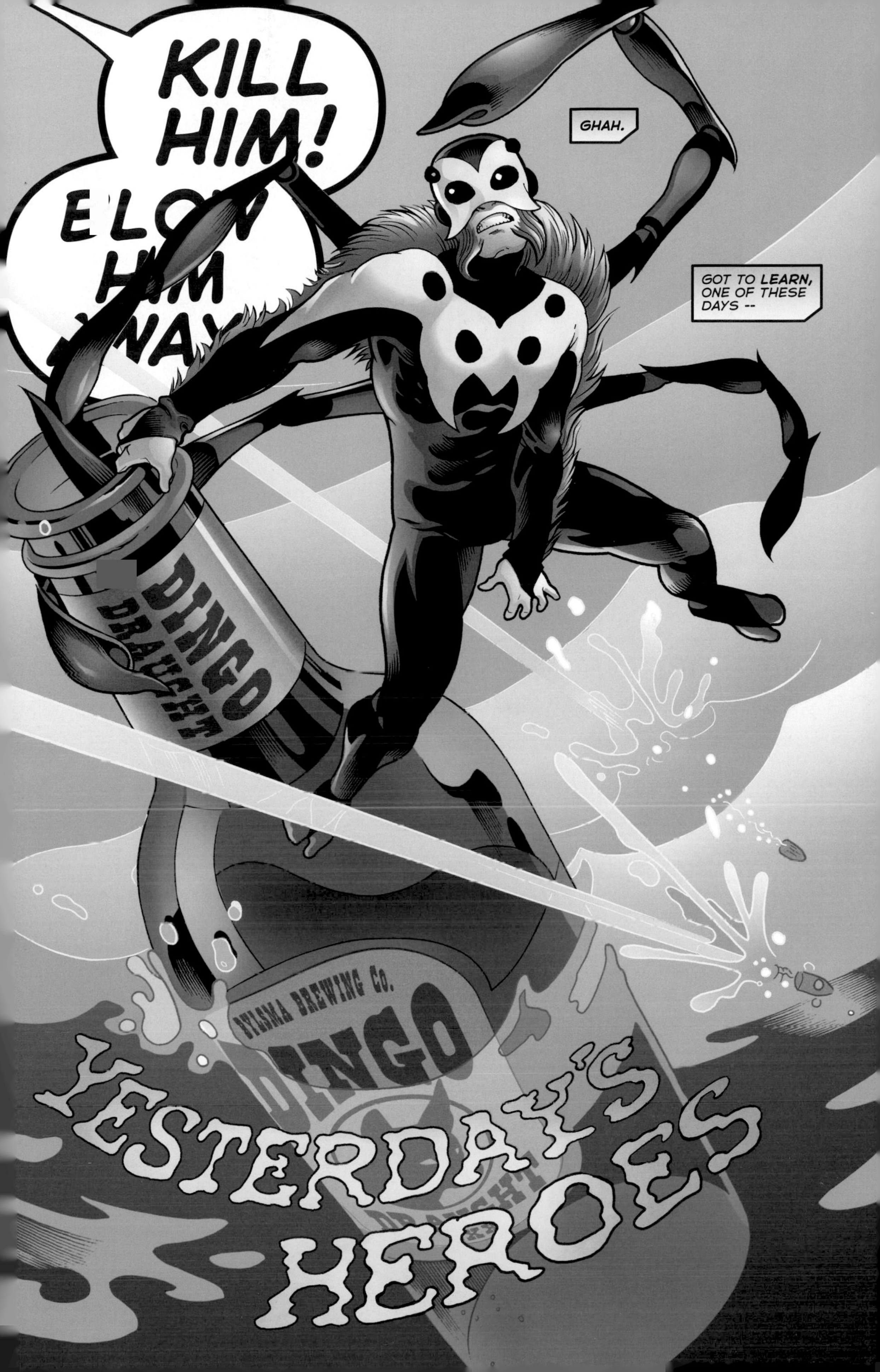
KILL HIM!
GHAH.
GOT TO LEARN, ONE OF THESE DAYS --
DINGO DRAUGHT
BYLSMA BREWING CO.
DINGO
YESTERDAY'S HEROES

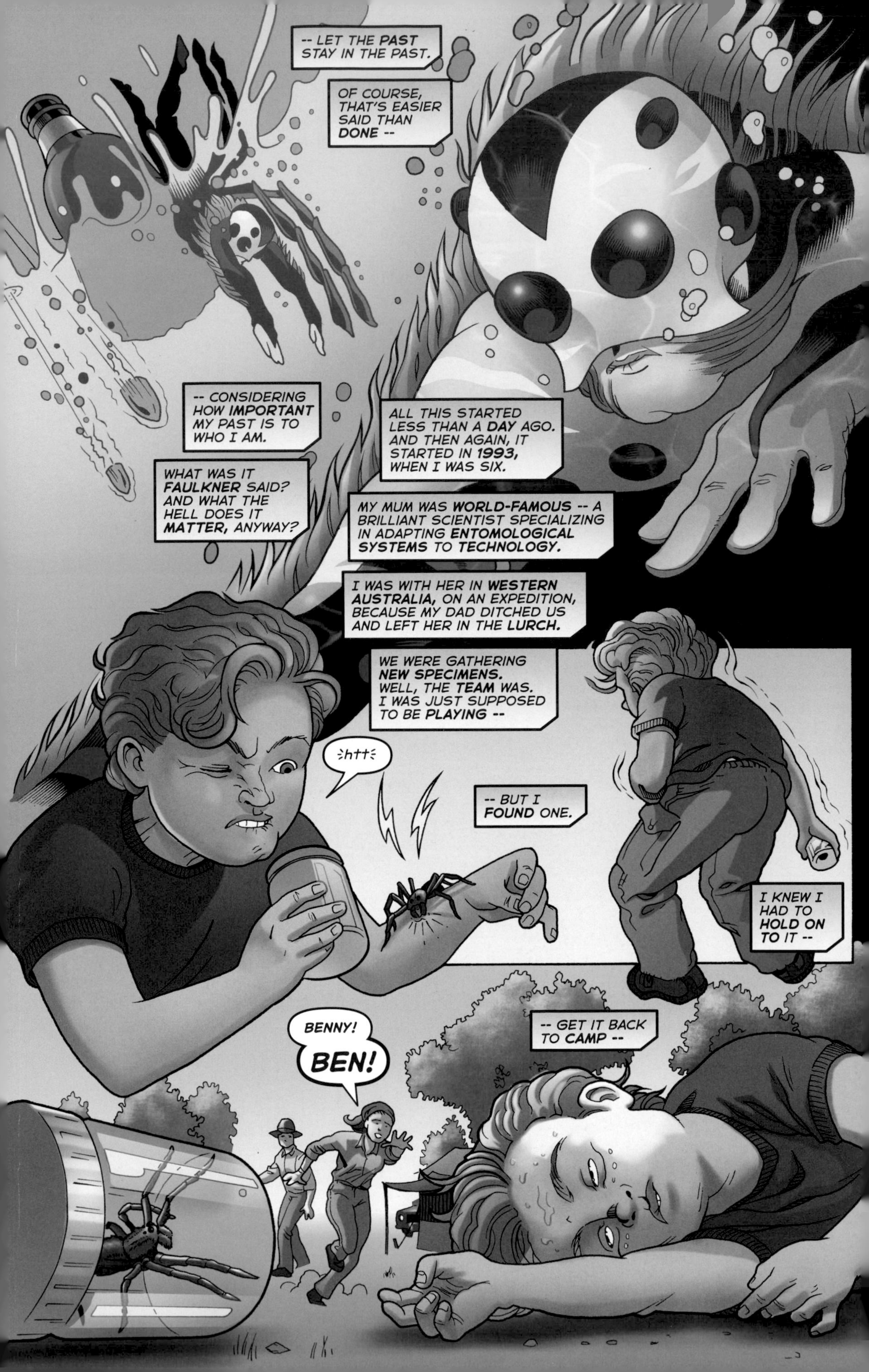
-- LET THE PAST STAY IN THE PAST.
OF COURSE, THAT'S EASIER SAID THAN DONE --
-- CONSIDERING HOW IMPORTANT MY PAST IS TO WHO I AM.
WHAT WAS IT FAULKNER SAID? AND WHAT THE HELL DOES IT MATTER, ANYWAY?
ALL THIS STARTED LESS THAN A DAY AGO. AND THEN AGAIN, IT STARTED IN 1993, WHEN I WAS SIX.
MY MUM WAS WORLD-FAMOUS -- A BRILLIANT SCIENTIST SPECIALIZING IN ADAPTING ENTOMOLOGICAL SYSTEMS TO TECHNOLOGY.
I WAS WITH HER IN WESTERN AUSTRALIA, ON AN EXPEDITION, BECAUSE MY DAD DITCHED US AND LEFT HER IN THE LURCH.
WE WERE GATHERING NEW SPECIMENS. WELL, THE TEAM WAS. I WAS JUST SUPPOSED TO BE PLAYING --
htt
-- BUT I FOUND ONE.
I KNEW I HAD TO HOLD ON TO IT --
-- GET IT BACK TO CAMP --
BENNY! BEN!

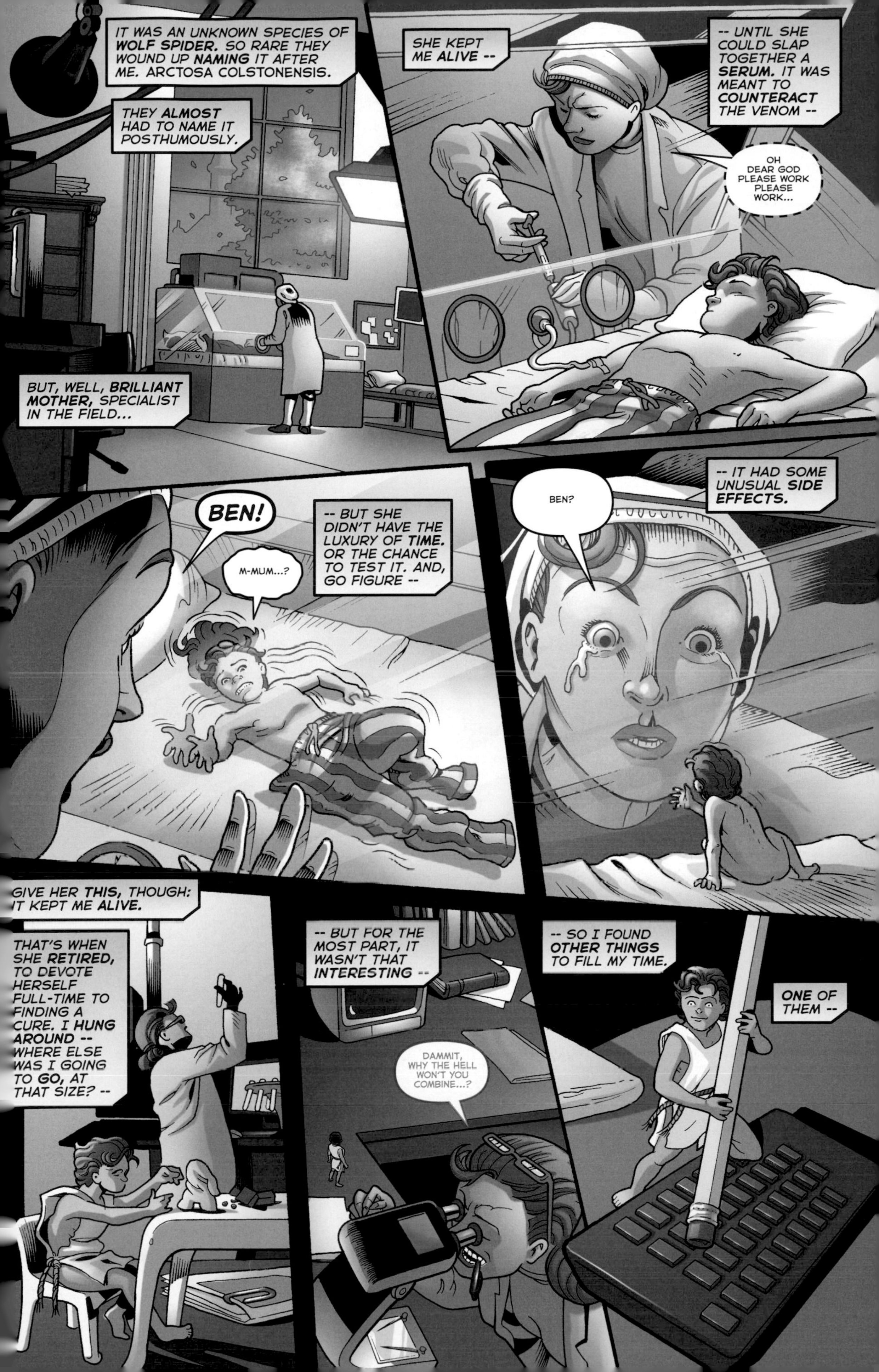
IT WAS AN UNKNOWN SPECIES OF WOLF SPIDER. SO RARE THEY WOUND UP NAMING IT AFTER ME. ARCTOSA COLSTONENSIS.
THEY ALMOST HAD TO NAME IT POSTHUMOUSLY.
BUT, WELL, BRILLIANT MOTHER, SPECIALIST IN THE FIELD...
SHE KEPT ME ALIVE --
-- UNTIL SHE COULD SLAP TOGETHER A SERUM. IT WAS MEANT TO COUNTERACT THE VENOM --
OH DEAR GOD PLEASE WORK PLEASE WORK...
BEN!
-- BUT SHE DIDN'T HAVE THE LUXURY OF TIME. OR THE CHANCE TO TEST IT. AND, GO FIGURE --
M-MUM...?
-- IT HAD SOME UNUSUAL SIDE EFFECTS.
BEN?
GIVE HER THIS, THOUGH: IT KEPT ME ALIVE.
THAT'S WHEN SHE RETIRED, TO DEVOTE HERSELF FULL-TIME TO FINDING A CURE. I HUNG AROUND -- WHERE ELSE WAS I GOING TO GO, AT THAT SIZE? --
-- BUT FOR THE MOST PART, IT WASN'T THAT INTERESTING --
DAMMIT, WHY THE HELL WON'T YOU COMBINE...?
-- SO I FOUND OTHER THINGS TO FILL MY TIME.
ONE OF THEM --

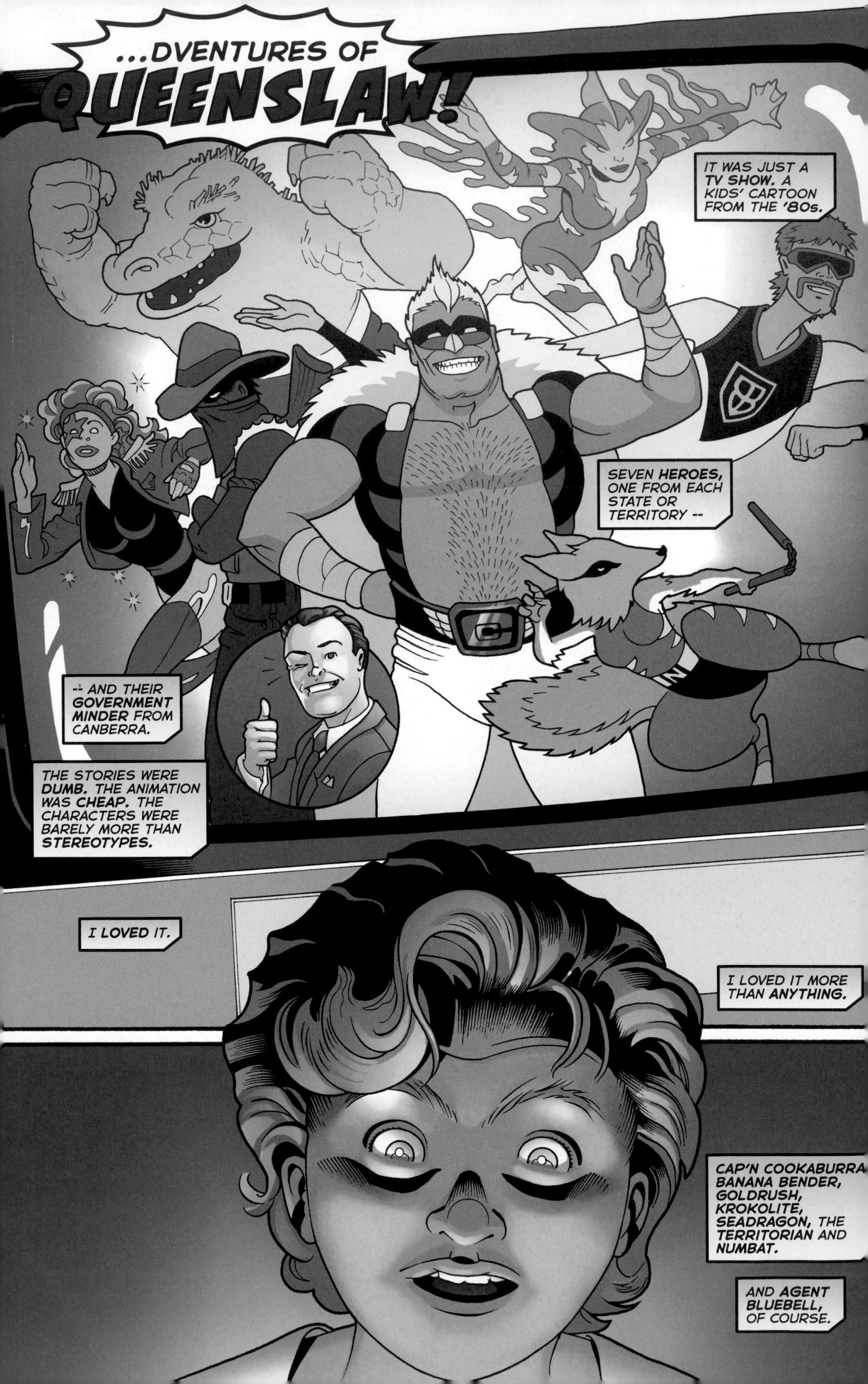
...DVENTURES OF
QUEENSLAW!
IT WAS JUST A TV SHOW. A KIDS' CARTOON FROM THE '80s.
SEVEN HEROES, ONE FROM EACH STATE OR TERRITORY --
-- AND THEIR GOVERNMENT MINDER FROM CANBERRA.
THE STORIES WERE DUMB. THE ANIMATION WAS CHEAP. THE CHARACTERS WERE BARELY MORE THAN STEREOTYPES.
I LOVED IT.
I LOVED IT MORE THAN ANYTHING.
CAP'N COOKABURRA, BANANA BENDER, GOLDRUSH, KROKOLITE, SEADRAGON, THE TERRITORIAN AND NUMBAT.
AND AGENT BLUEBELL, OF COURSE.

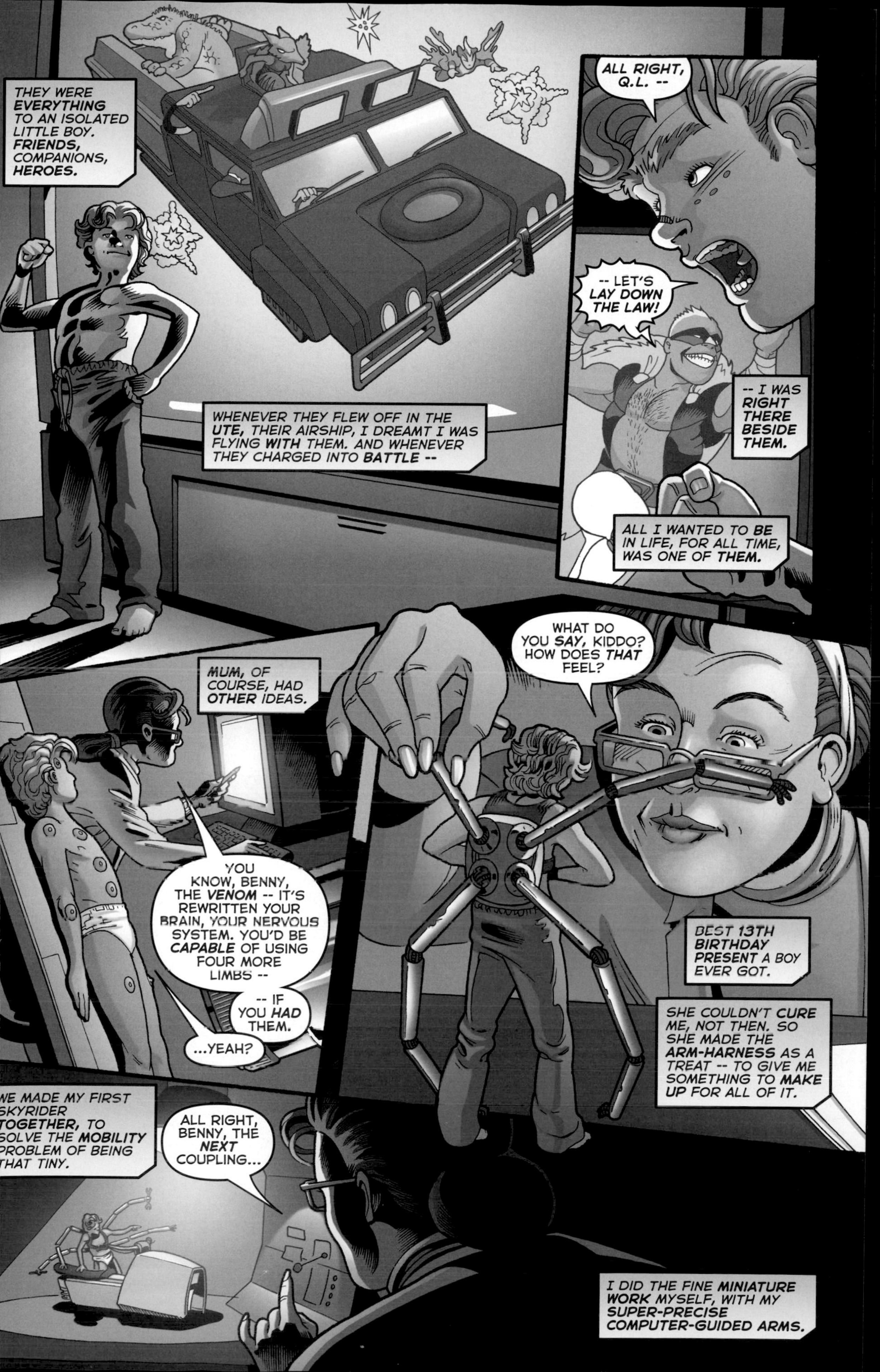
THEY WERE EVERYTHING TO AN ISOLATED LITTLE BOY. FRIENDS, COMPANIONS, HEROES.
WHENEVER THEY FLEW OFF IN THE UTE, THEIR AIRSHIP, I DREAMT I WAS FLYING WITH THEM. AND WHENEVER THEY CHARGED INTO BATTLE --
ALL RIGHT, Q.L. --
-- LET'S LAY DOWN THE LAW!
-- I WAS RIGHT THERE BESIDE THEM.
ALL I WANTED TO BE IN LIFE, FOR ALL TIME, WAS ONE OF THEM.
MUM, OF COURSE, HAD OTHER IDEAS.
YOU KNOW, BENNY, THE VENOM -- IT'S REWRITTEN YOUR BRAIN, YOUR NERVOUS SYSTEM. YOU'D BE CAPABLE OF USING FOUR MORE LIMBS --
-- IF YOU HAD THEM.
...YEAH?
WHAT DO YOU SAY, KIDDO? HOW DOES THAT FEEL?
BEST 13TH BIRTHDAY PRESENT A BOY EVER GOT.
SHE COULDN'T CURE ME, NOT THEN. SO SHE MADE THE ARM-HARNESS AS A TREAT -- TO GIVE ME SOMETHING TO MAKE UP FOR ALL OF IT.
WE MADE MY FIRST SKYRIDER TOGETHER, TO SOLVE THE MOBILITY PROBLEM OF BEING THAT TINY.
ALL RIGHT, BENNY, THE NEXT COUPLING...
I DID THE FINE MINIATURE WORK MYSELF, WITH MY SUPER-PRECISE COMPUTER-GUIDED ARMS.

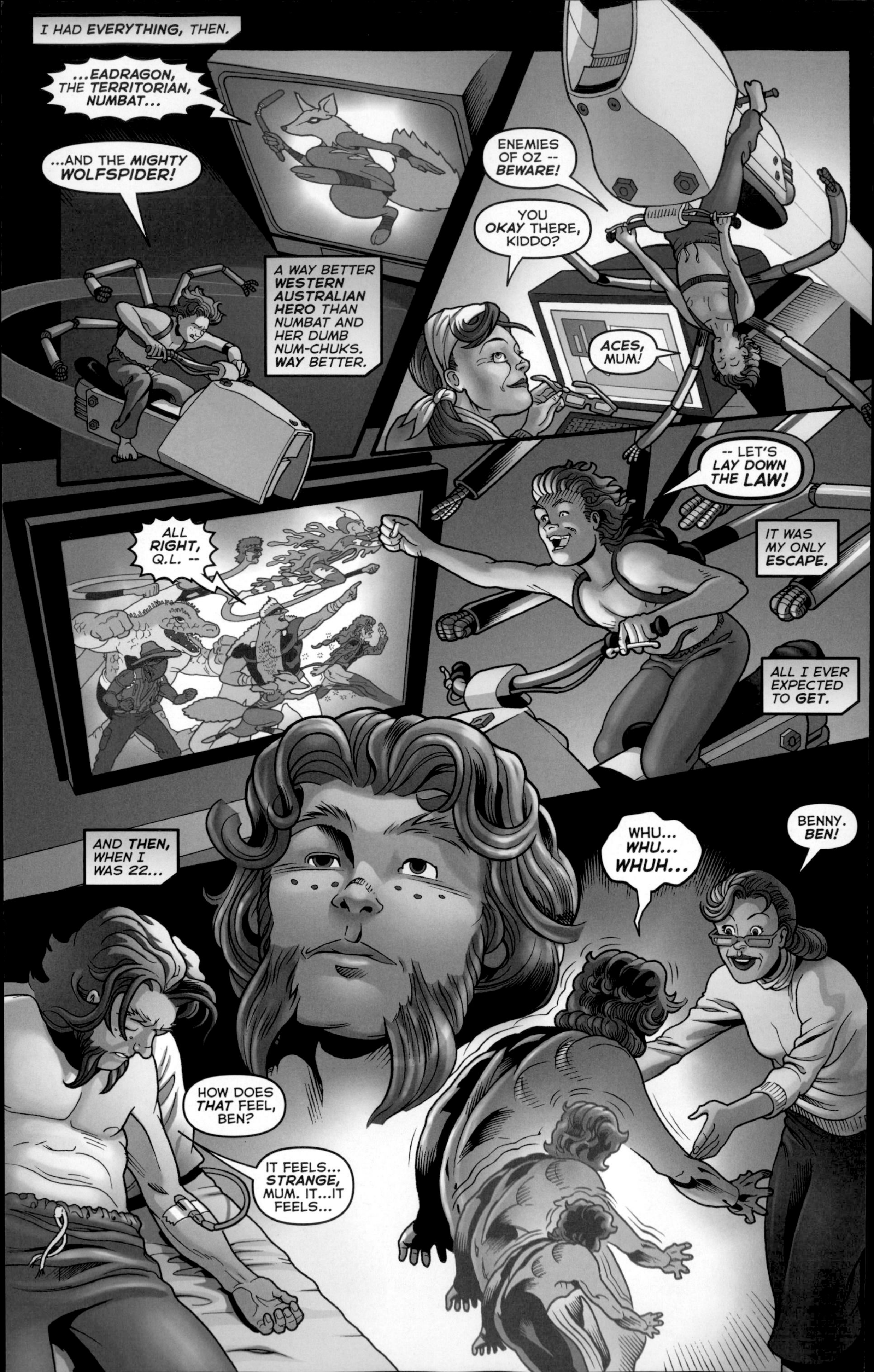
I HAD EVERYTHING, THEN.
...EADRAGON, THE TERRITORIAN, NUMBAT...
...AND THE MIGHTY WOLFSPIDER!
A WAY BETTER WESTERN AUSTRALIAN HERO THAN NUMBAT AND HER DUMB NUM-CHUKS. WAY BETTER.
ENEMIES OF OZ -- BEWARE!
YOU OKAY THERE, KIDDO?
ACES, MUM!
ALL RIGHT, Q.L. --
-- LET'S LAY DOWN THE LAW!
IT WAS MY ONLY ESCAPE.
ALL I EVER EXPECTED TO GET.
AND THEN, WHEN I WAS 22...
WHU... WHU... WHUH...
BENNY. BEN!
HOW DOES THAT FEEL, BEN?
IT FEELS... STRANGE, MUM. IT...IT FEELS...

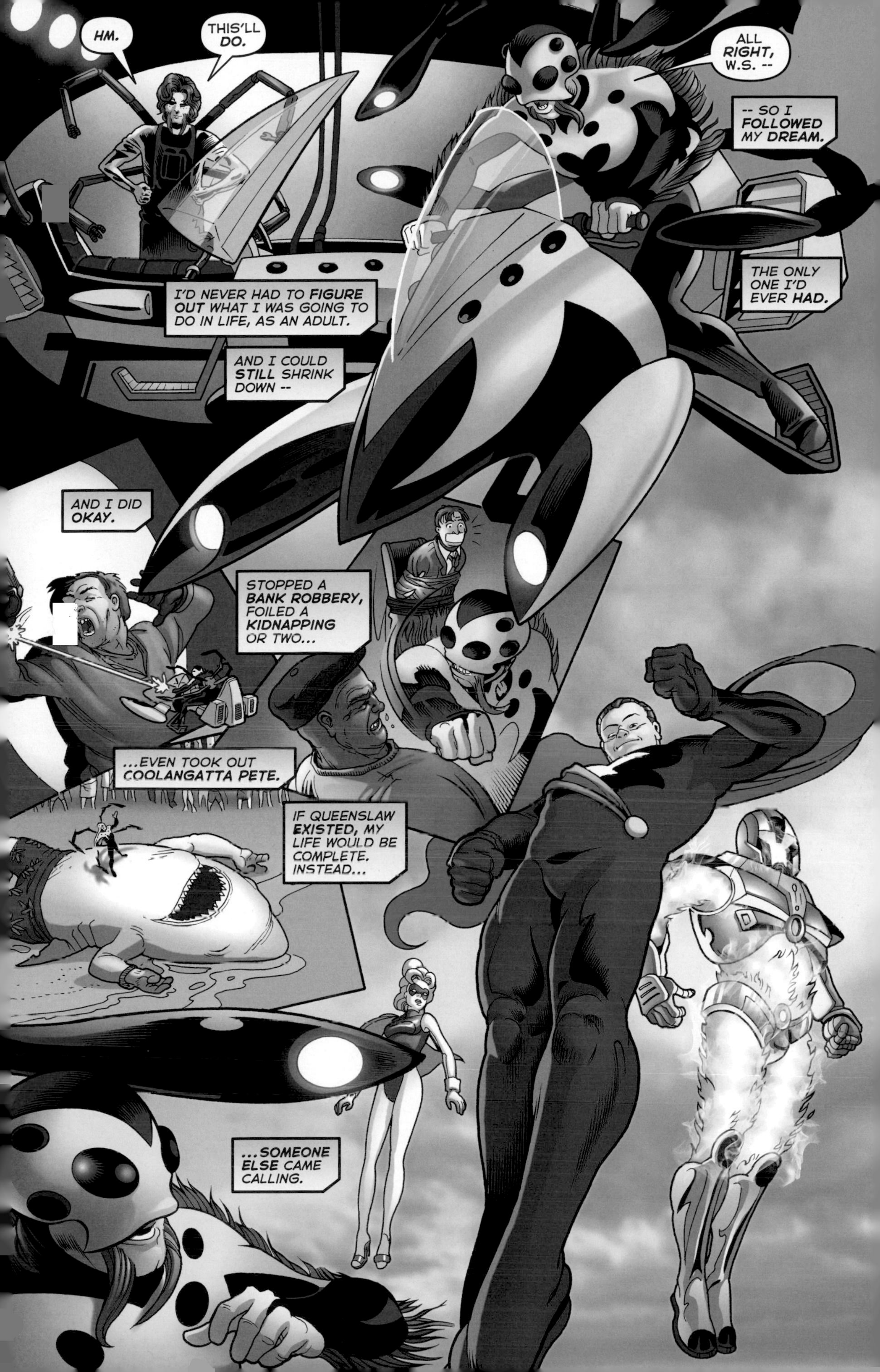
HM.
THIS'LL DO.
ALL RIGHT, W.S. --
-- SO I FOLLOWED MY DREAM.
THE ONLY ONE I'D EVER HAD.
I'D NEVER HAD TO FIGURE OUT WHAT I WAS GOING TO DO IN LIFE, AS AN ADULT.
AND I COULD STILL SHRINK DOWN --
AND I DID OKAY.
STOPPED A BANK ROBBERY, FOILED A KIDNAPPING OR TWO...
...EVEN TOOK OUT COOLANGATTA PETE.
IF QUEENSLAW EXISTED, MY LIFE WOULD BE COMPLETE. INSTEAD...
...SOMEONE ELSE CAME CALLING.

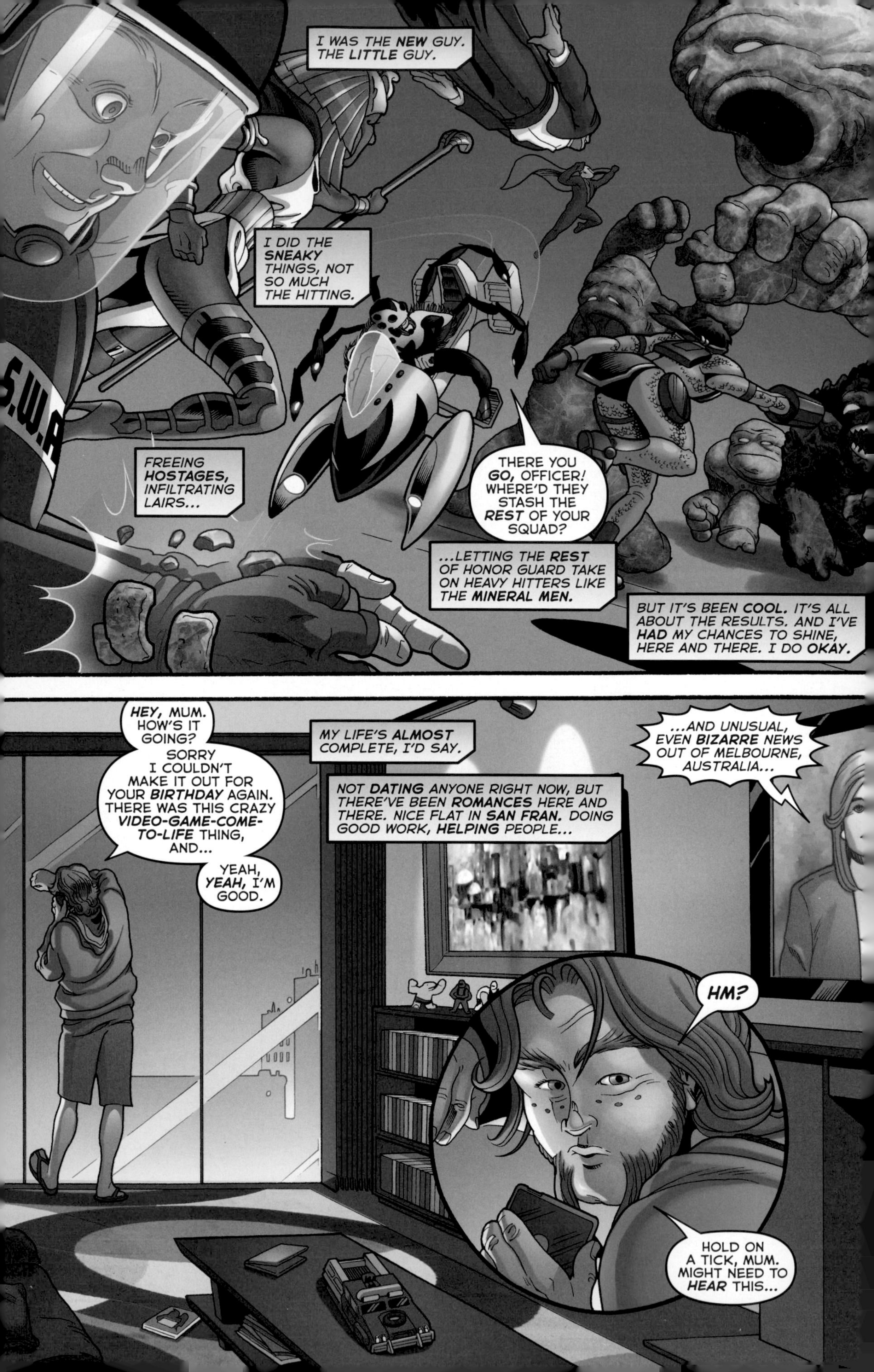
I WAS THE NEW GUY. THE LITTLE GUY.
I DID THE SNEAKY THINGS, NOT SO MUCH THE HITTING.
FREEING HOSTAGES, INFILTRATING LAIRS...
THERE YOU GO, OFFICER! WHERE'D THEY STASH THE REST OF YOUR SQUAD?
...LETTING THE REST OF HONOR GUARD TAKE ON HEAVY HITTERS LIKE THE MINERAL MEN.
BUT IT'S BEEN COOL. IT'S ALL ABOUT THE RESULTS. AND I'VE HAD MY CHANCES TO SHINE, HERE AND THERE. I DO OKAY.
HEY, MUM. HOW'S IT GOING?
SORRY I COULDN'T MAKE IT OUT FOR YOUR BIRTHDAY AGAIN. THERE WAS THIS CRAZY VIDEO-GAME-COME-TO-LIFE THING, AND...
YEAH, YEAH, I'M GOOD.
MY LIFE'S ALMOST COMPLETE, I'D SAY.
NOT DATING ANYONE RIGHT NOW, BUT THERE'VE BEEN ROMANCES HERE AND THERE. NICE FLAT IN SAN FRAN. DOING GOOD WORK, HELPING PEOPLE...
...AND UNUSUAL, EVEN BIZARRE NEWS OUT OF MELBOURNE, AUSTRALIA...
HM?
HOLD ON A TICK, MUM. MIGHT NEED TO HEAR THIS...

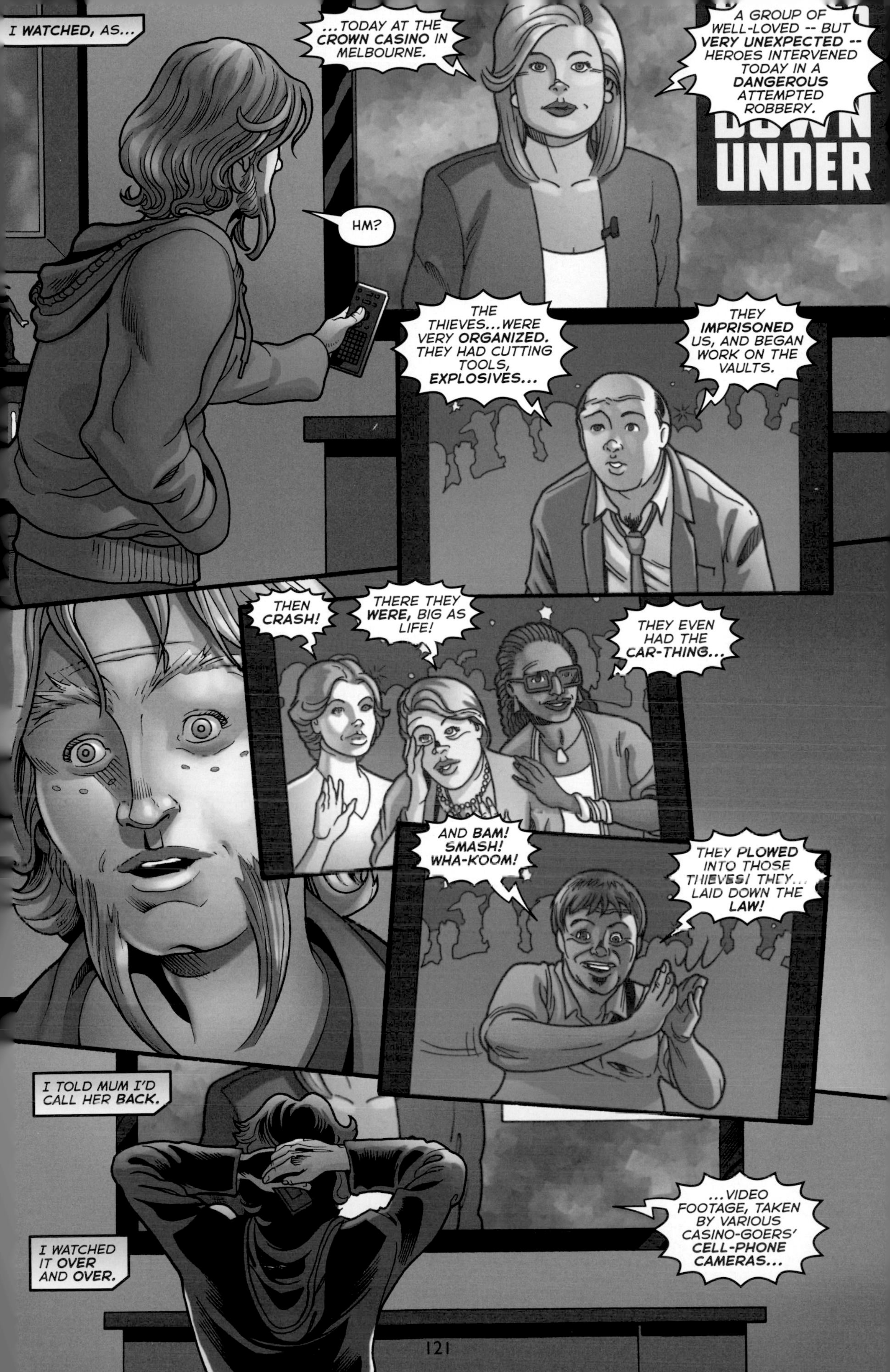
I WATCHED, AS...
...TODAY AT THE CROWN CASINO IN MELBOURNE.
A GROUP OF WELL-LOVED -- BUT VERY UNEXPECTED -- HEROES INTERVENED TODAY IN A DANGEROUS ATTEMPTED ROBBERY.
UNDER
HM?
THE THIEVES...WERE VERY ORGANIZED. THEY HAD CUTTING TOOLS, EXPLOSIVES...
THEY IMPRISONED US, AND BEGAN WORK ON THE VAULTS.
THEN CRASH!
THERE THEY WERE, BIG AS LIFE!
THEY EVEN HAD THE CAR-THING...
AND BAM! SMASH! WHA-KOOM!
THEY PLOWED INTO THOSE THIEVES! THEY... LAID DOWN THE LAW!
I TOLD MUM I'D CALL HER BACK.
I WATCHED IT OVER AND OVER.
...VIDEO FOOTAGE, TAKEN BY VARIOUS CASINO-GOERS' CELL-PHONE CAMERAS...

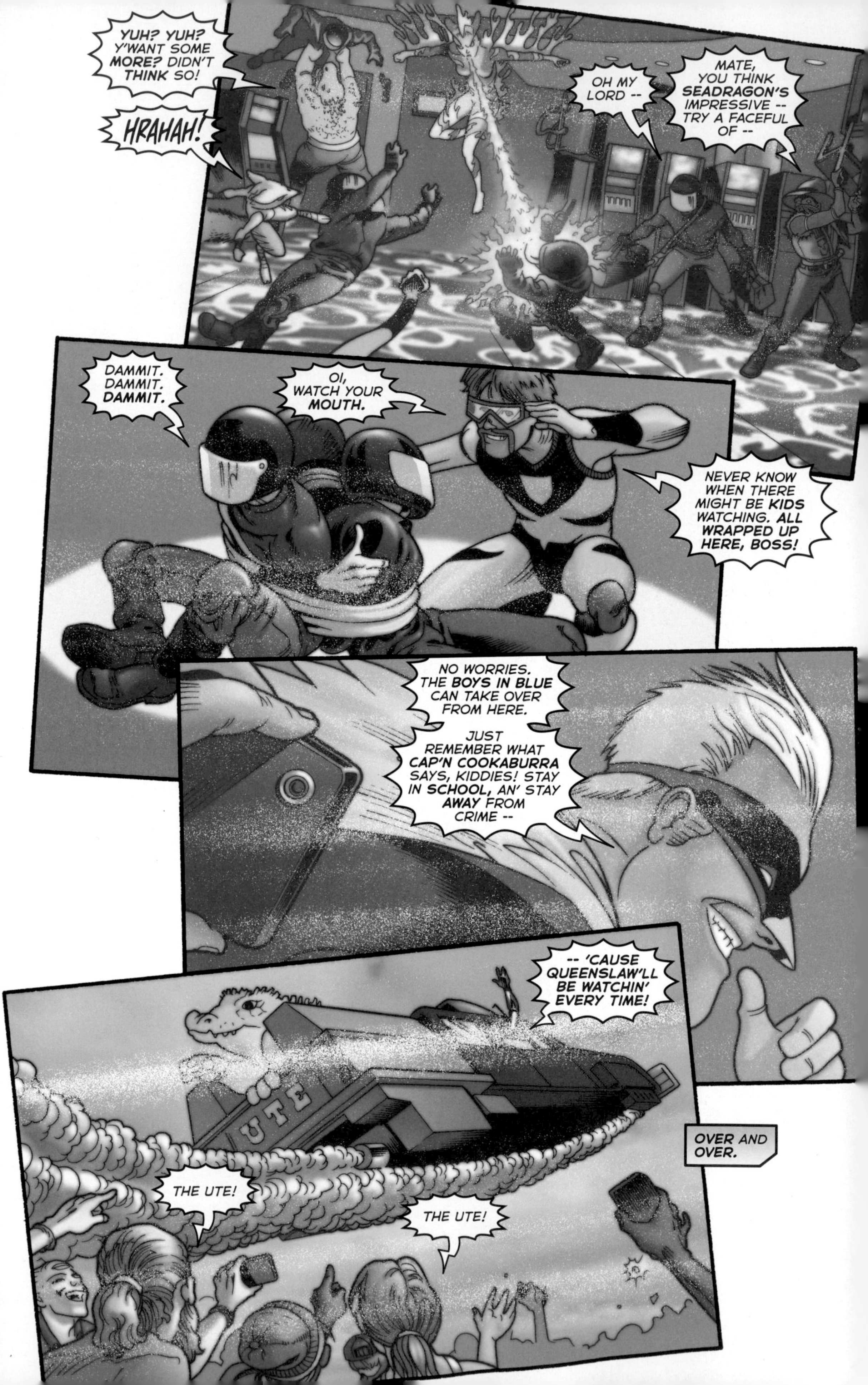
YUH? YUH? Y'WANT SOME MORE? DIDN'T THINK SO!
HRAHAH!
OH MY LORD --
MATE, YOU THINK SEADRAGON'S IMPRESSIVE -- TRY A FACEFUL OF --
DAMMIT. DAMMIT. DAMMIT.
OI, WATCH YOUR MOUTH.
NEVER KNOW WHEN THERE MIGHT BE KIDS WATCHING. ALL WRAPPED UP HERE, BOSS!
NO WORRIES. THE BOYS IN BLUE CAN TAKE OVER FROM HERE.
JUST REMEMBER WHAT CAP'N COOKABURRA SAYS, KIDDIES! STAY IN SCHOOL, AN' STAY AWAY FROM CRIME --
-- 'CAUSE QUEENSLAW'LL BE WATCHIN' EVERY TIME!
UTE
OVER AND OVER.
THE UTE!
THE UTE!

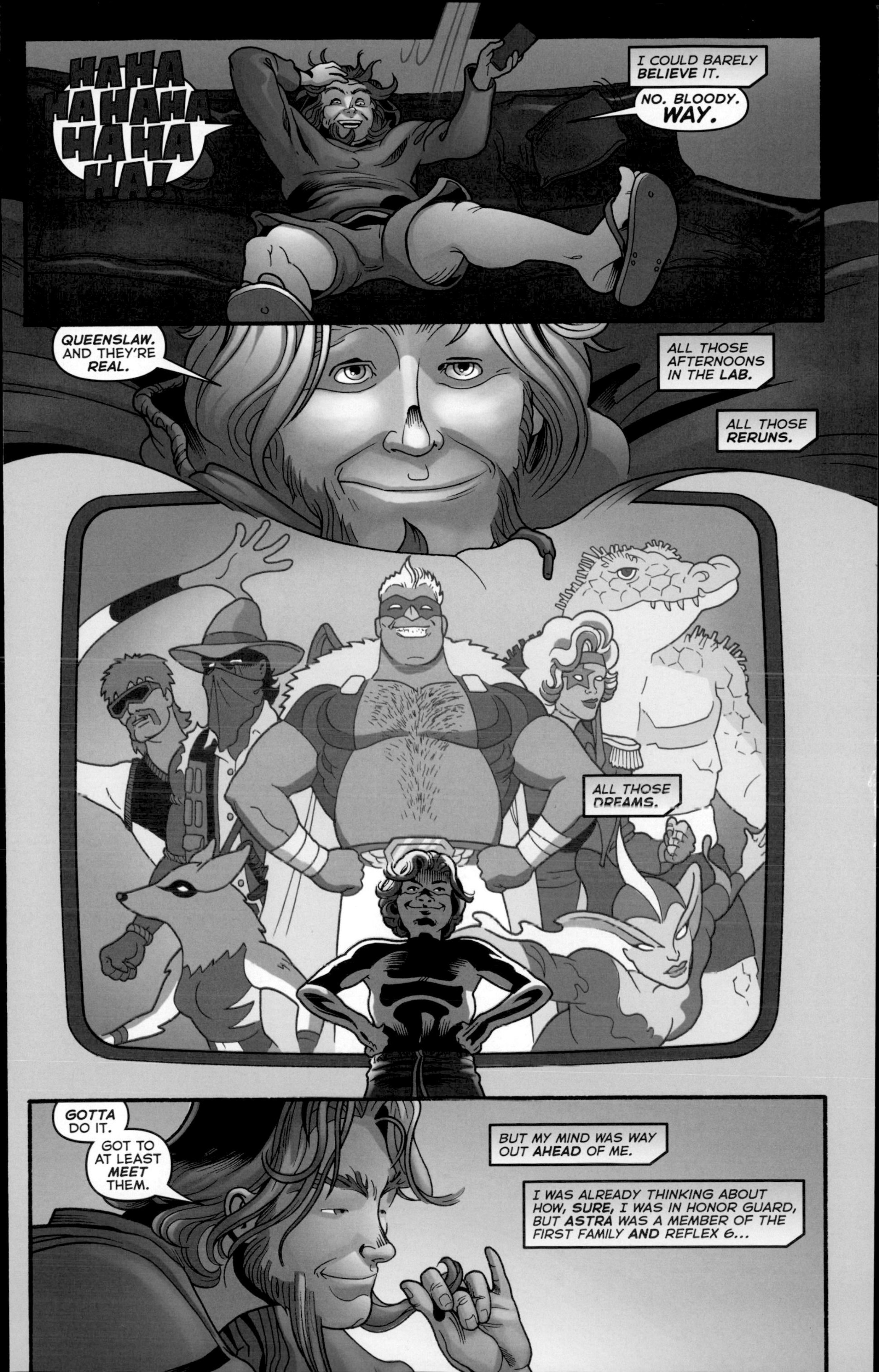
HAHA HAHAHA HAHA HA!
I COULD BARELY BELIEVE IT.
NO. BLOODY. WAY.
QUEENSLAW. AND THEY'RE REAL.
ALL THOSE AFTERNOONS IN THE LAB.
ALL THOSE RERUNS.
ALL THOSE DREAMS.
GOTTA DO IT.
GOT TO AT LEAST MEET THEM.
BUT MY MIND WAS WAY OUT AHEAD OF ME.
I WAS ALREADY THINKING ABOUT HOW, SURE, I WAS IN HONOR GUARD, BUT ASTRA WAS A MEMBER OF THE FIRST FAMILY AND REFLEX 6...

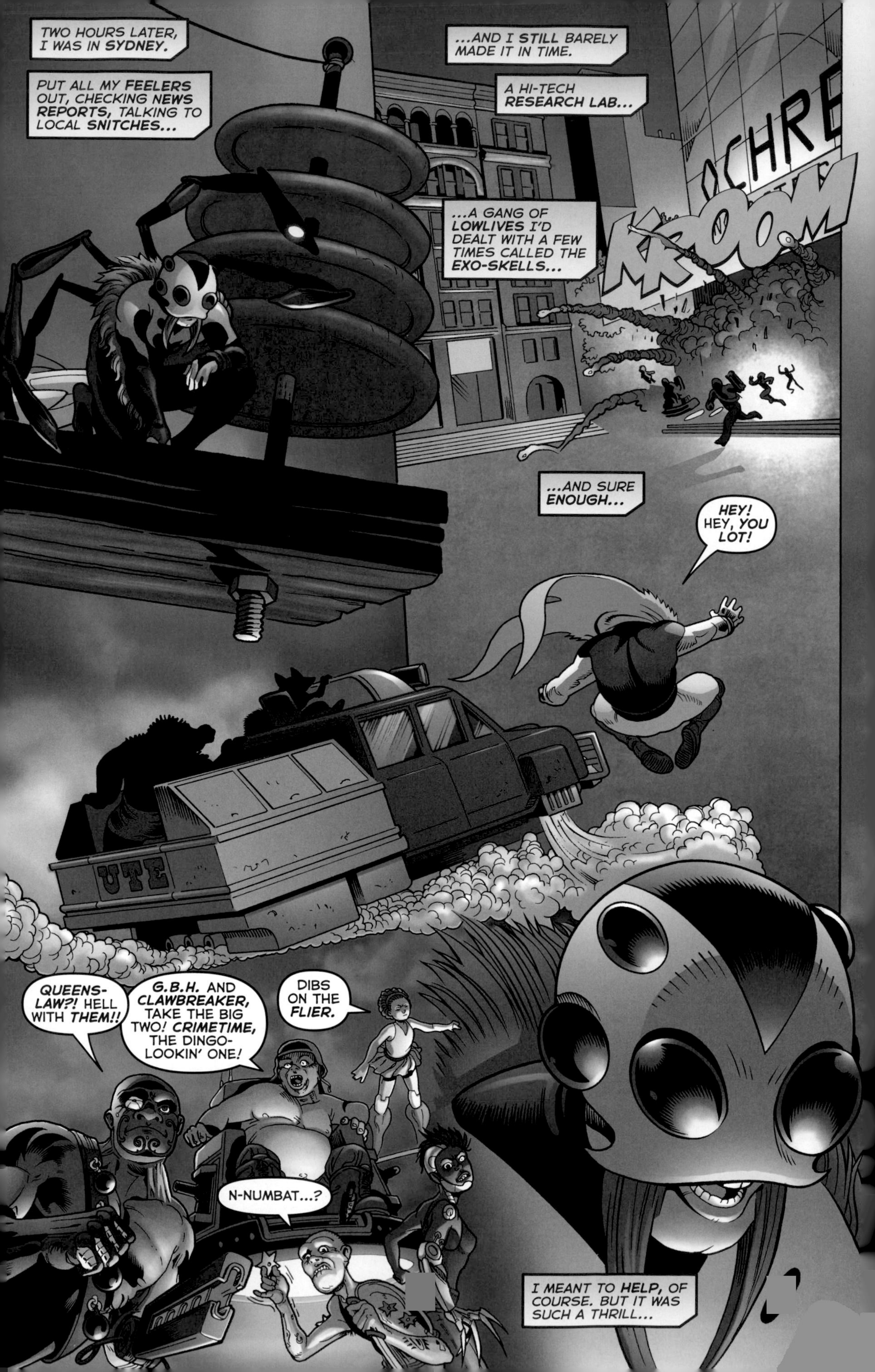
TWO HOURS LATER, I WAS IN SYDNEY.
PUT ALL MY FEELERS OUT, CHECKING NEWS REPORTS, TALKING TO LOCAL SNITCHES...
...AND I STILL BARELY MADE IT IN TIME.
A HI-TECH RESEARCH LAB...
...A GANG OF LOWLIVES I'D DEALT WITH A FEW TIMES CALLED THE EXO-SKELLS...
OCHRE
KROOOM
...AND SURE ENOUGH...
HEY! HEY, YOU LOT!
UTE
QUEENS-LAW?! HELL WITH THEM!!
G.B.H. AND CLAWBREAKER, TAKE THE BIG TWO! CRIMETIME, THE DINGO-LOOKIN' ONE!
DIBS ON THE FLIER.
N-NUMBAT...?
I MEANT TO HELP, OF COURSE. BUT IT WAS SUCH A THRILL...

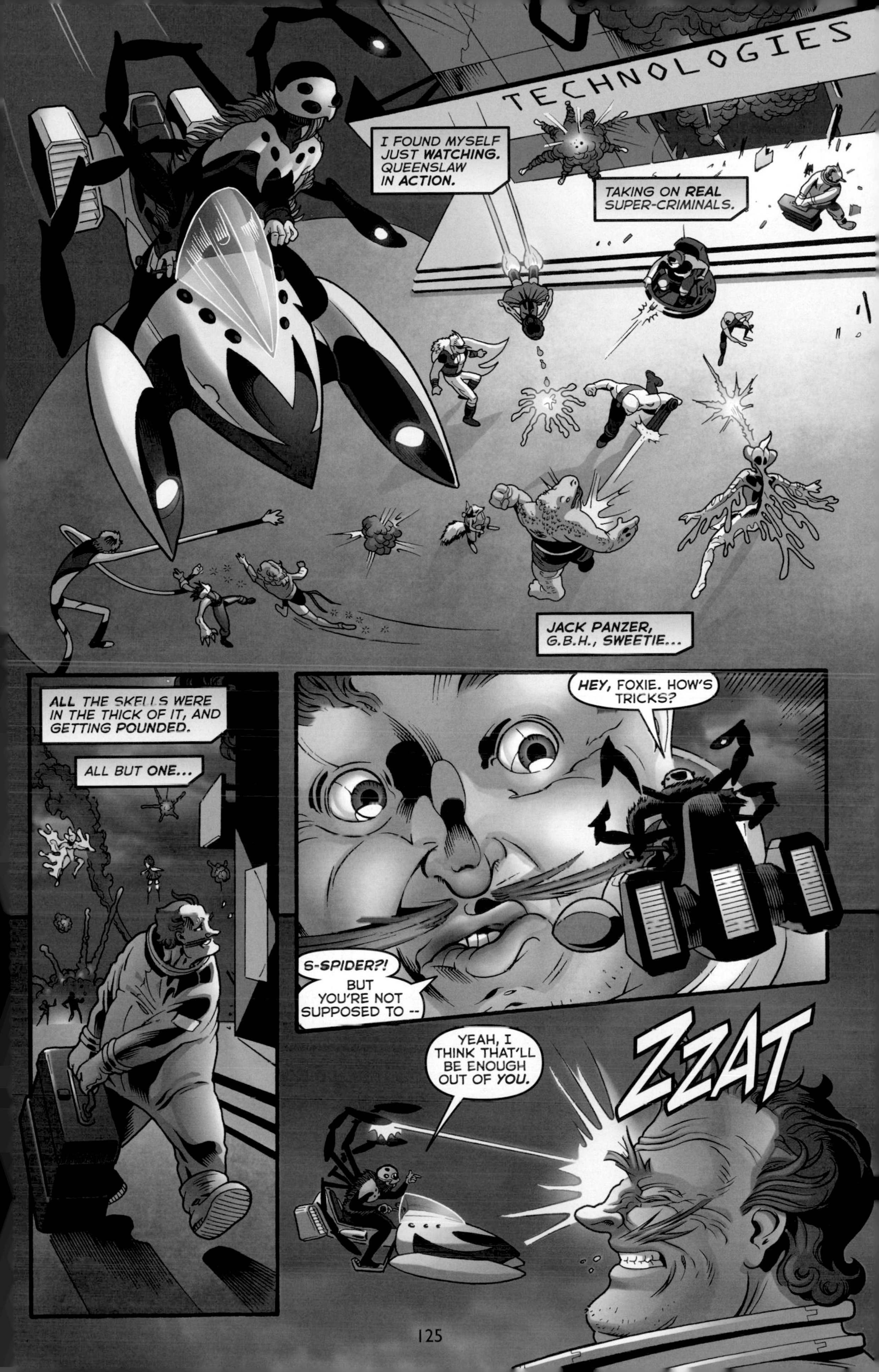
TECHNOLOGIES
I FOUND MYSELF JUST WATCHING. QUEENSLAW IN ACTION.
TAKING ON REAL SUPER-CRIMINALS.
JACK PANZER, G.B.H., SWEETIE...
ALL THE SKELLS WERE IN THE THICK OF IT, AND GETTING POUNDED.
ALL BUT ONE...
HEY, FOXIE. HOW'S TRICKS?
S-SPIDER?! BUT YOU'RE NOT SUPPOSED TO --
YEAH, I THINK THAT'LL BE ENOUGH OUT OF YOU.
ZZAT

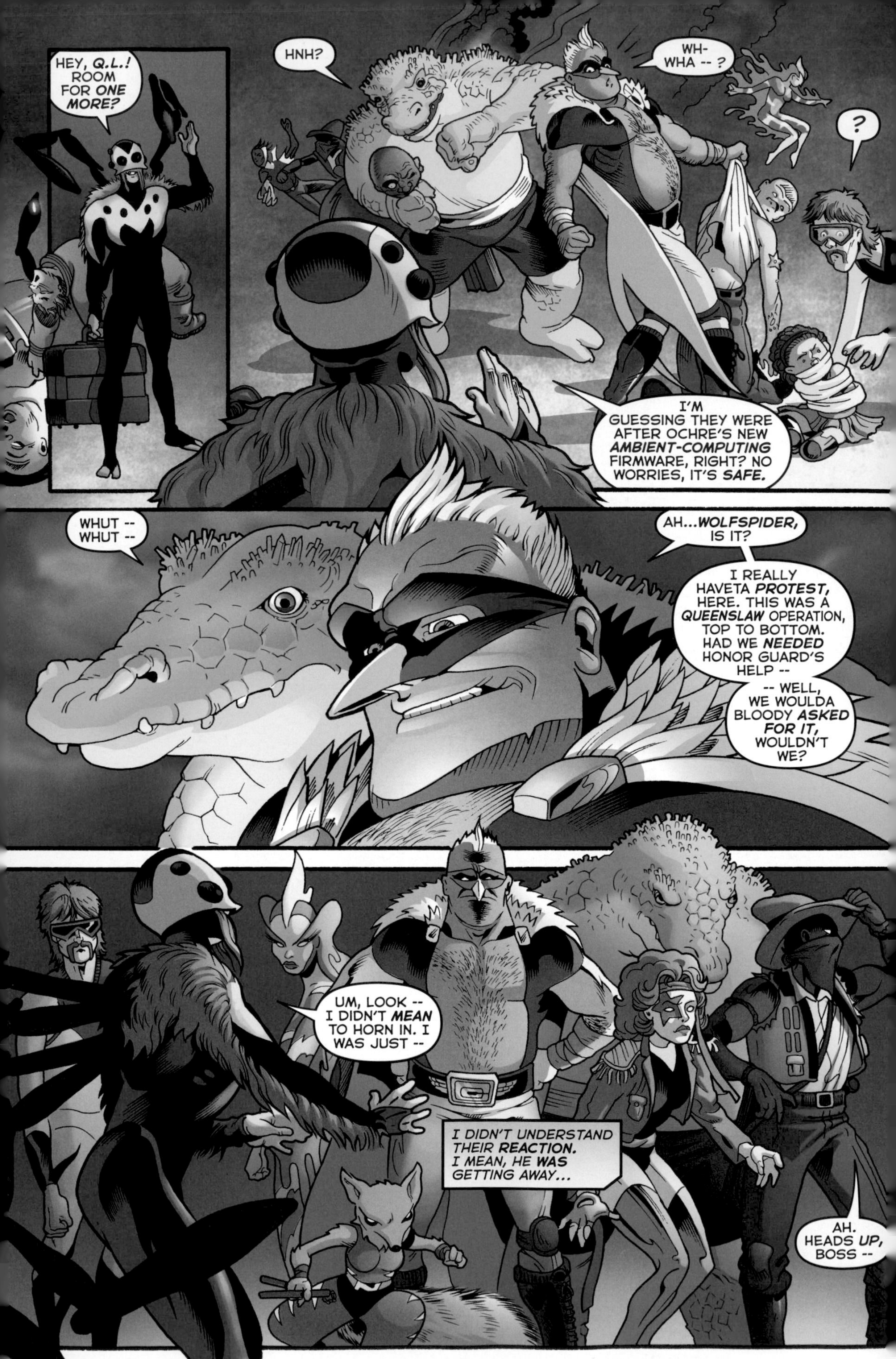
HEY, Q.L.! ROOM FOR ONE MORE?
HNH?
WH- WHA -- ?
?
I'M GUESSING THEY WERE AFTER OCHRE'S NEW AMBIENT-COMPUTING FIRMWARE, RIGHT? NO WORRIES, IT'S SAFE.
WHUT -- WHUT --
AH...WOLFSPIDER, IS IT?
I REALLY HAVETA PROTEST, HERE. THIS WAS A QUEENSLAW OPERATION, TOP TO BOTTOM. HAD WE NEEDED HONOR GUARD'S HELP --
-- WELL, WE WOULDA BLOODY ASKED FOR IT, WOULDN'T WE?
UM, LOOK -- I DIDN'T MEAN TO HORN IN. I WAS JUST --
I DIDN'T UNDERSTAND THEIR REACTION. I MEAN, HE WAS GETTING AWAY...
AH. HEADS UP, BOSS --

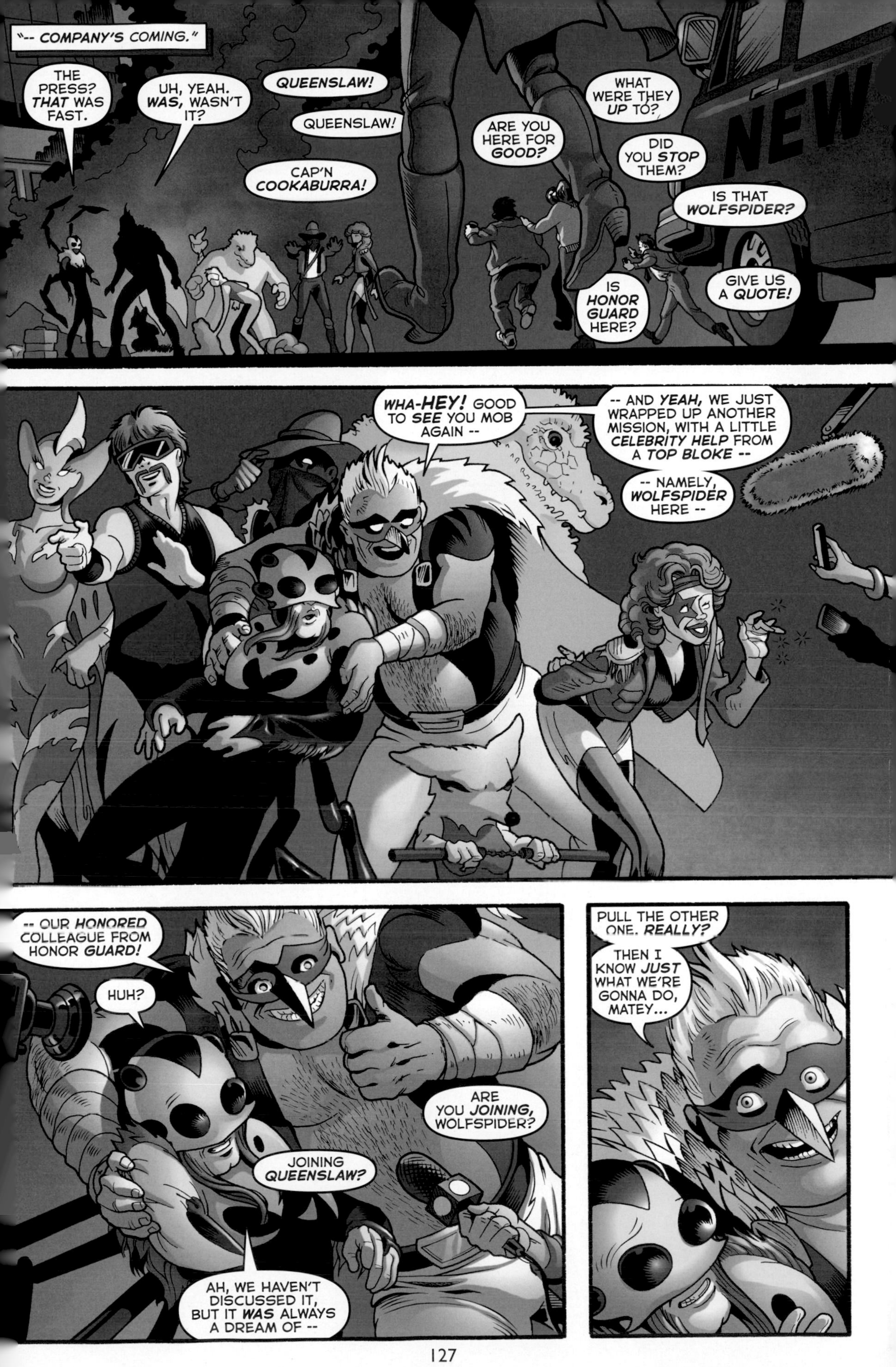
"-- COMPANY'S COMING."
THE PRESS? THAT WAS FAST.
UH, YEAH. WAS, WASN'T IT?
QUEENSLAW!
QUEENSLAW!
CAP'N COOKABURRA!
ARE YOU HERE FOR GOOD?
WHAT WERE THEY UP TO?
DID YOU STOP THEM?
IS THAT WOLFSPIDER?
IS HONOR GUARD HERE?
GIVE US A QUOTE!
WHA-HEY! GOOD TO SEE YOU MOB AGAIN --
-- AND YEAH, WE JUST WRAPPED UP ANOTHER MISSION, WITH A LITTLE CELEBRITY HELP FROM A TOP BLOKE --
-- NAMELY, WOLFSPIDER HERE --
-- OUR HONORED COLLEAGUE FROM HONOR GUARD!
HUH?
ARE YOU JOINING, WOLFSPIDER?
JOINING QUEENSLAW?
AH, WE HAVEN'T DISCUSSED IT, BUT IT WAS ALWAYS A DREAM OF --
PULL THE OTHER ONE. REALLY?
THEN I KNOW JUST WHAT WE'RE GONNA DO, MATEY...

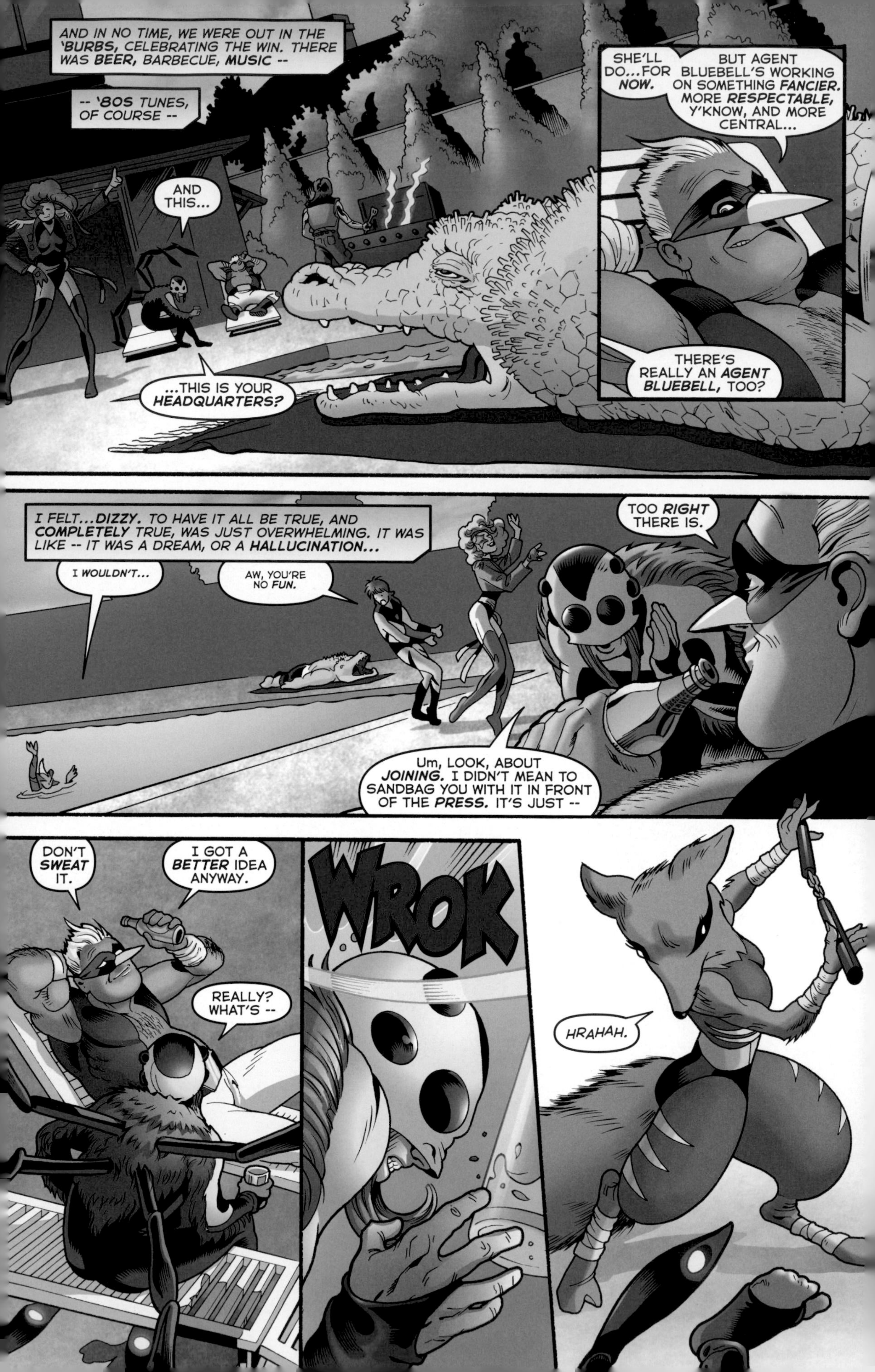
AND IN NO TIME, WE WERE OUT IN THE 'BURBS, CELEBRATING THE WIN. THERE WAS BEER, BARBECUE, MUSIC --
-- '80S TUNES, OF COURSE --
AND THIS...
...THIS IS YOUR HEADQUARTERS?
SHE'LL DO...FOR NOW.
BUT AGENT BLUEBELL'S WORKING ON SOMETHING FANCIER. MORE RESPECTABLE, Y'KNOW, AND MORE CENTRAL...
THERE'S REALLY AN AGENT BLUEBELL, TOO?
I FELT...DIZZY. TO HAVE IT ALL BE TRUE, AND COMPLETELY TRUE, WAS JUST OVERWHELMING. IT WAS LIKE -- IT WAS A DREAM, OR A HALLUCINATION...
I WOULDN'T...
AW, YOU'RE NO FUN.
TOO RIGHT THERE IS.
Um, LOOK, ABOUT JOINING. I DIDN'T MEAN TO SANDBAG YOU WITH IT IN FRONT OF THE PRESS. IT'S JUST --
DON'T SWEAT IT.
I GOT A BETTER IDEA ANYWAY.
REALLY? WHAT'S --
WROK
HRAHAH.

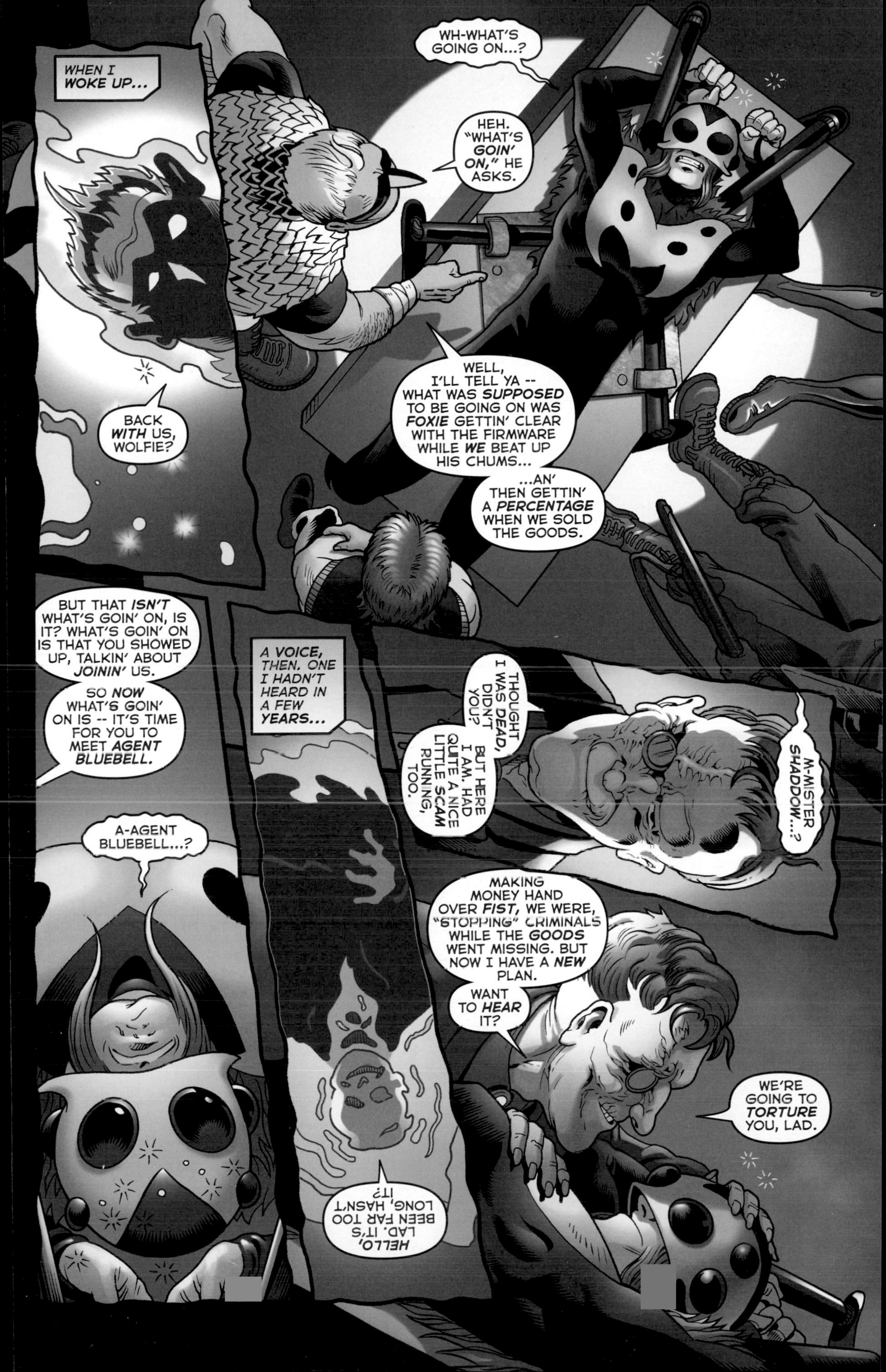

WHEN I WOKE UP...
WH-WHAT'S GOING ON...?
HEH. "WHAT'S GOIN' ON," HE ASKS.
BACK WITH US, WOLFIE?
WELL, I'LL TELL YA -- WHAT WAS SUPPOSED TO BE GOING ON WAS FOXIE GETTIN' CLEAR WITH THE FIRMWARE WHILE WE BEAT UP HIS CHUMS...
...AN' THEN GETTIN' A PERCENTAGE WHEN WE SOLD THE GOODS.
BUT THAT ISN'T WHAT'S GOIN' ON, IS IT? WHAT'S GOIN' ON IS THAT YOU SHOWED UP, TALKIN' ABOUT JOININ' US.
SO NOW WHAT'S GOIN' ON IS -- IT'S TIME FOR YOU TO MEET AGENT BLUEBELL.
A-AGENT BLUEBELL...?
A VOICE, THEN. ONE I HADN'T HEARD IN A FEW YEARS...
HELLO, LAD. IT'S BEEN FAR TOO LONG, HASN'T IT?
M-MISTER SHADDOW...?
THOUGHT I WAS DEAD, DIDN'T YOU?
BUT HERE I AM. HAD QUITE A NICE LITTLE SCAM RUNNING, TOO.
MAKING MONEY HAND OVER FIST, WE WERE, "STOPPING" CRIMINALS WHILE THE GOODS WENT MISSING. BUT NOW I HAVE A NEW PLAN.
WANT TO HEAR IT?
WE'RE GOING TO TORTURE YOU, LAD.

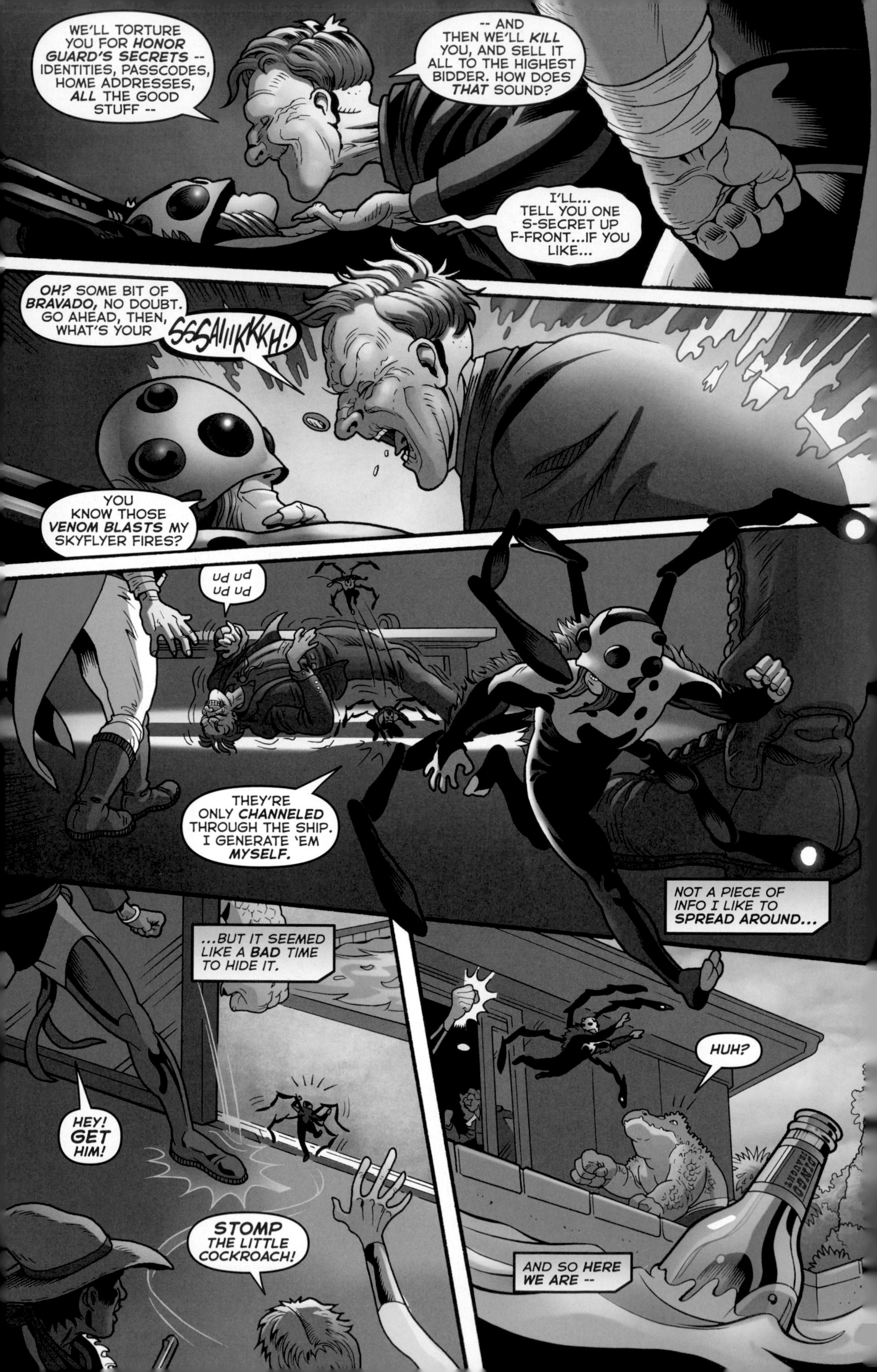
WE'LL TORTURE YOU FOR HONOR GUARD'S SECRETS -- IDENTITIES, PASSCODES, HOME ADDRESSES, ALL THE GOOD STUFF --
-- AND THEN WE'LL KILL YOU, AND SELL IT ALL TO THE HIGHEST BIDDER. HOW DOES THAT SOUND?
I'LL... TELL YOU ONE S-SECRET UP F-FRONT...IF YOU LIKE...
OH? SOME BIT OF BRAVADO, NO DOUBT. GO AHEAD, THEN, WHAT'S YOUR
SSSAIIIKKKH!
YOU KNOW THOSE VENOM BLASTS MY SKYFLYER FIRES?
ud ud
ud ud
THEY'RE ONLY CHANNELED THROUGH THE SHIP. I GENERATE 'EM MYSELF.
NOT A PIECE OF INFO I LIKE TO SPREAD AROUND...
...BUT IT SEEMED LIKE A BAD TIME TO HIDE IT.
HEY! GET HIM!
STOMP THE LITTLE COCKROACH!
HUH?
AND SO HERE WE ARE --

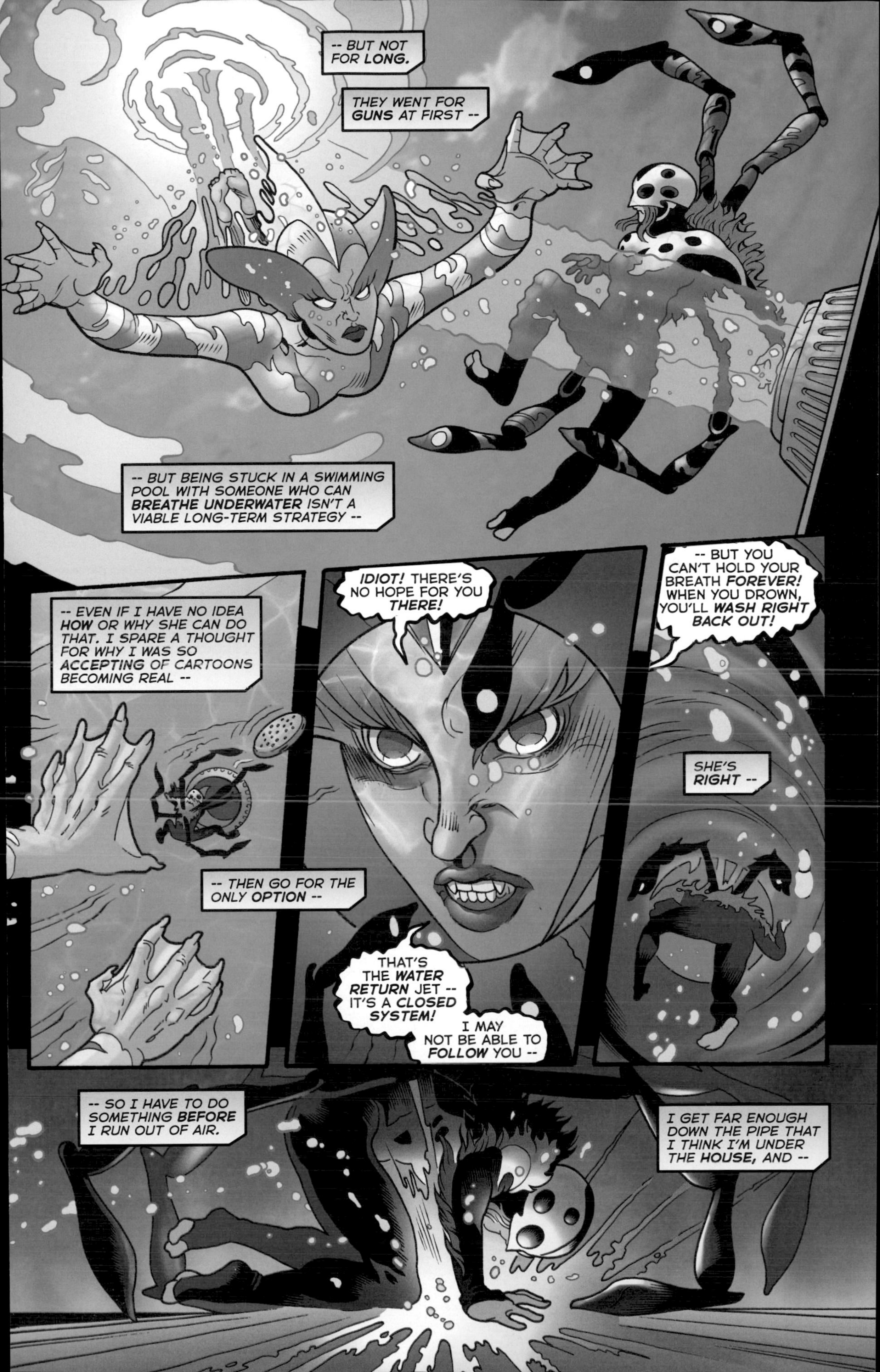
-- BUT NOT FOR LONG.
THEY WENT FOR GUNS AT FIRST --
-- BUT BEING STUCK IN A SWIMMING POOL WITH SOMEONE WHO CAN BREATHE UNDERWATER ISN'T A VIABLE LONG-TERM STRATEGY --
-- EVEN IF I HAVE NO IDEA HOW OR WHY SHE CAN DO THAT. I SPARE A THOUGHT FOR WHY I WAS SO ACCEPTING OF CARTOONS BECOMING REAL --
-- THEN GO FOR THE ONLY OPTION --
IDIOT! THERE'S NO HOPE FOR YOU THERE!
THAT'S THE WATER RETURN JET -- IT'S A CLOSED SYSTEM!
I MAY NOT BE ABLE TO FOLLOW YOU --
-- BUT YOU CAN'T HOLD YOUR BREATH FOREVER! WHEN YOU DROWN, YOU'LL WASH RIGHT BACK OUT!
SHE'S RIGHT --
-- SO I HAVE TO DO SOMETHING BEFORE I RUN OUT OF AIR.
I GET FAR ENOUGH DOWN THE PIPE THAT I THINK I'M UNDER THE HOUSE, AND --

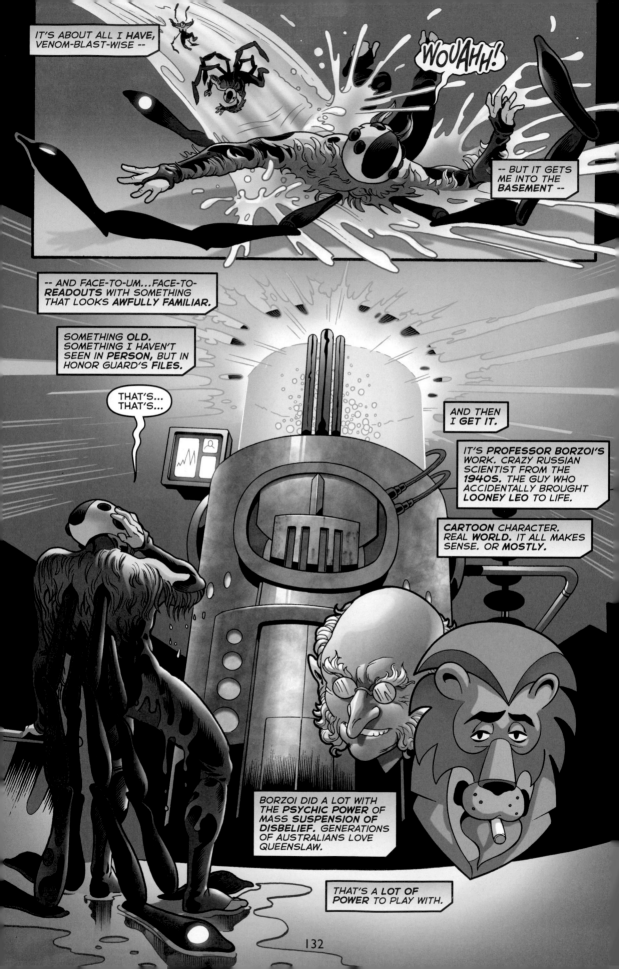

IT'S ABOUT ALL I *HAVE*, VENOM-BLAST-WISE --

WOUAHH!

-- BUT IT GETS ME INTO THE **BASEMENT** --

-- AND FACE-TO-UM...FACE-TO-**READOUTS** WITH SOMETHING THAT LOOKS *AWFULLY* FAMILIAR.

SOMETHING **OLD**. SOMETHING I *HAVEN'T* SEEN IN **PERSON**, BUT IN HONOR GUARD'S FILES.

THAT'S... THAT'S...

AND THEN I GET IT.

IT'S **PROFESSOR BORZOI'S** WORK. CRAZY RUSSIAN SCIENTIST FROM THE **1940s**. THE GUY WHO ACCIDENTALLY BROUGHT **LOONEY LEO** TO LIFE.

CARTOON CHARACTER. REAL **WORLD**. IT ALL MAKES SENSE. OR **MOSTLY**.

BORZOI DID A LOT WITH THE *PSYCHIC POWER* OF **MASS SUSPENSION OF DISBELIEF**. GENERATIONS OF AUSTRALIANS LOVE QUEENSLAW.

THAT'S A *LOT* OF POWER TO PLAY WITH.

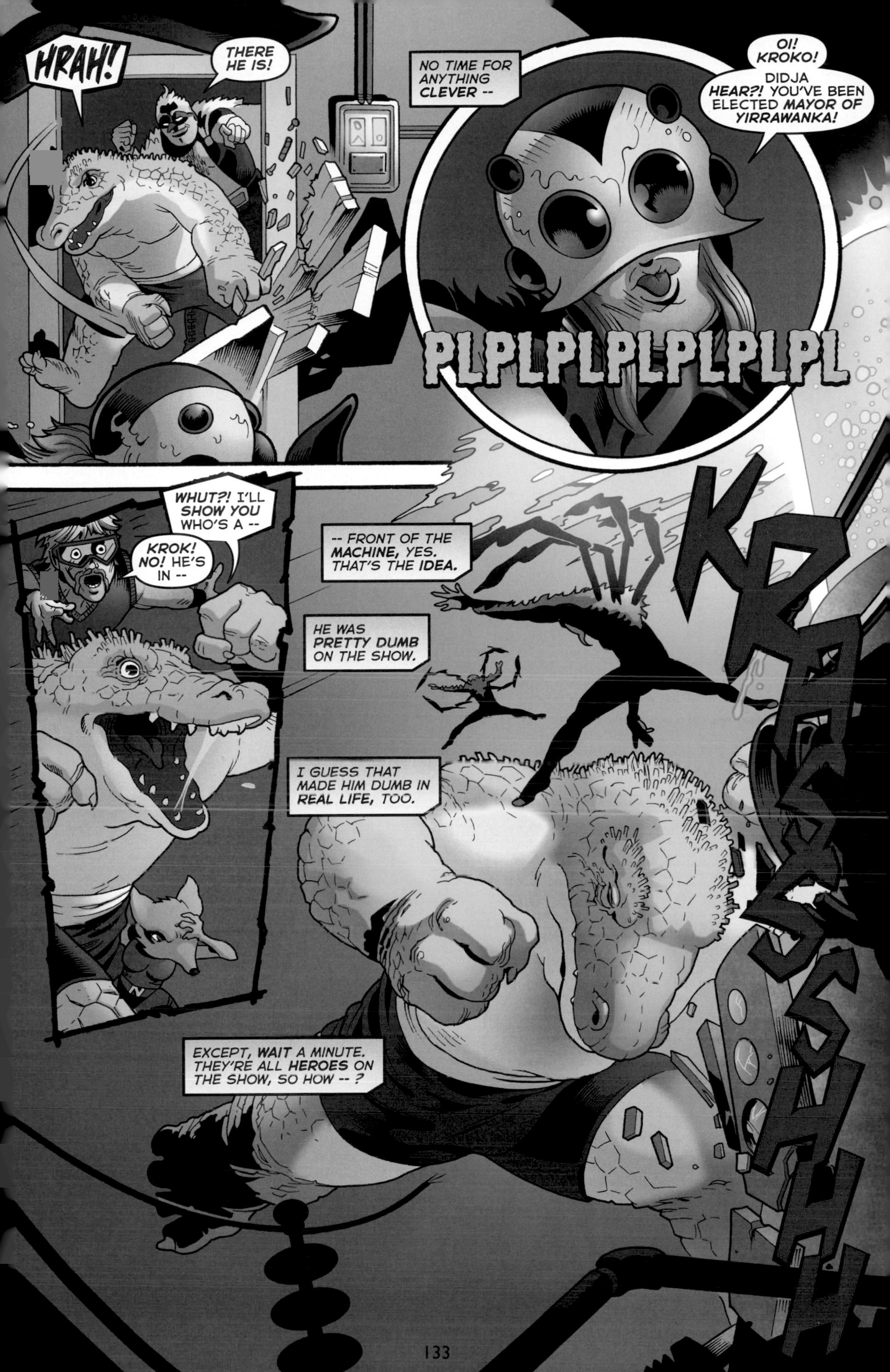
HRAH!
THERE HE IS!
NO TIME FOR ANYTHING CLEVER --
OI! KROKO! DIDJA HEAR?! YOU'VE BEEN ELECTED MAYOR OF YIRRAWANKA!
PLPLPLPLPLPLPLPL
WHUT?! I'LL SHOW YOU WHO'S A --
KROK! NO! HE'S IN --
-- FRONT OF THE MACHINE, YES. THAT'S THE IDEA.
HE WAS PRETTY DUMB ON THE SHOW.
I GUESS THAT MADE HIM DUMB IN REAL LIFE, TOO.
EXCEPT, WAIT A MINUTE. THEY'RE ALL HEROES ON THE SHOW, SO HOW -- ?
KRASSSHH

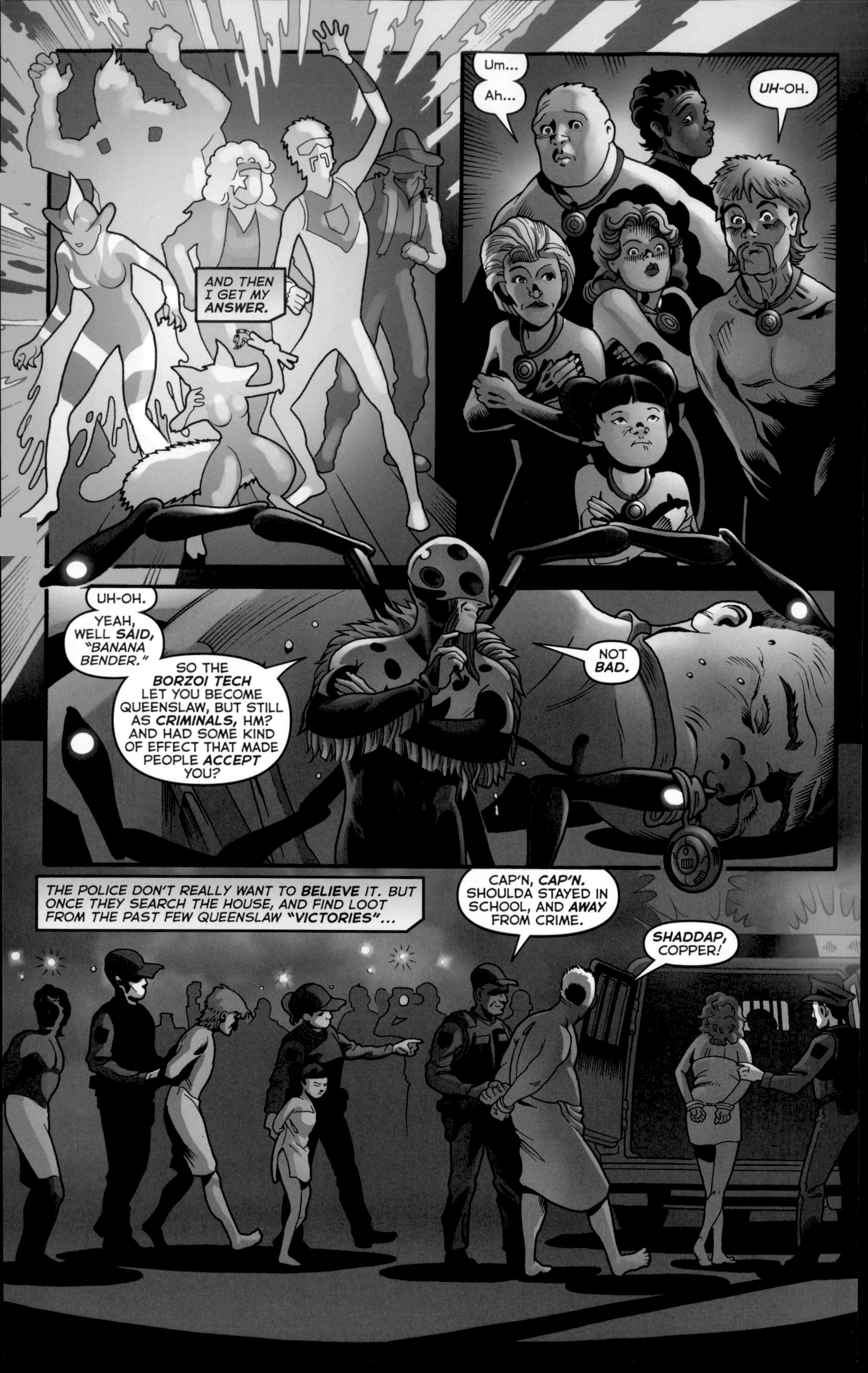
AND THEN I GET MY ANSWER.
Um...
Ah...
UH-OH.
UH-OH.
YEAH, WELL SAID, "BANANA BENDER."
SO THE BORZOI TECH LET YOU BECOME QUEENSLAW, BUT STILL AS CRIMINALS, HM? AND HAD SOME KIND OF EFFECT THAT MADE PEOPLE ACCEPT YOU?
NOT BAD.
THE POLICE DON'T REALLY WANT TO BELIEVE IT. BUT ONCE THEY SEARCH THE HOUSE, AND FIND LOOT FROM THE PAST FEW QUEENSLAW "VICTORIES"...
CAP'N, CAP'N. SHOULDA STAYED IN SCHOOL, AND AWAY FROM CRIME.
SHADDAP, COPPER!

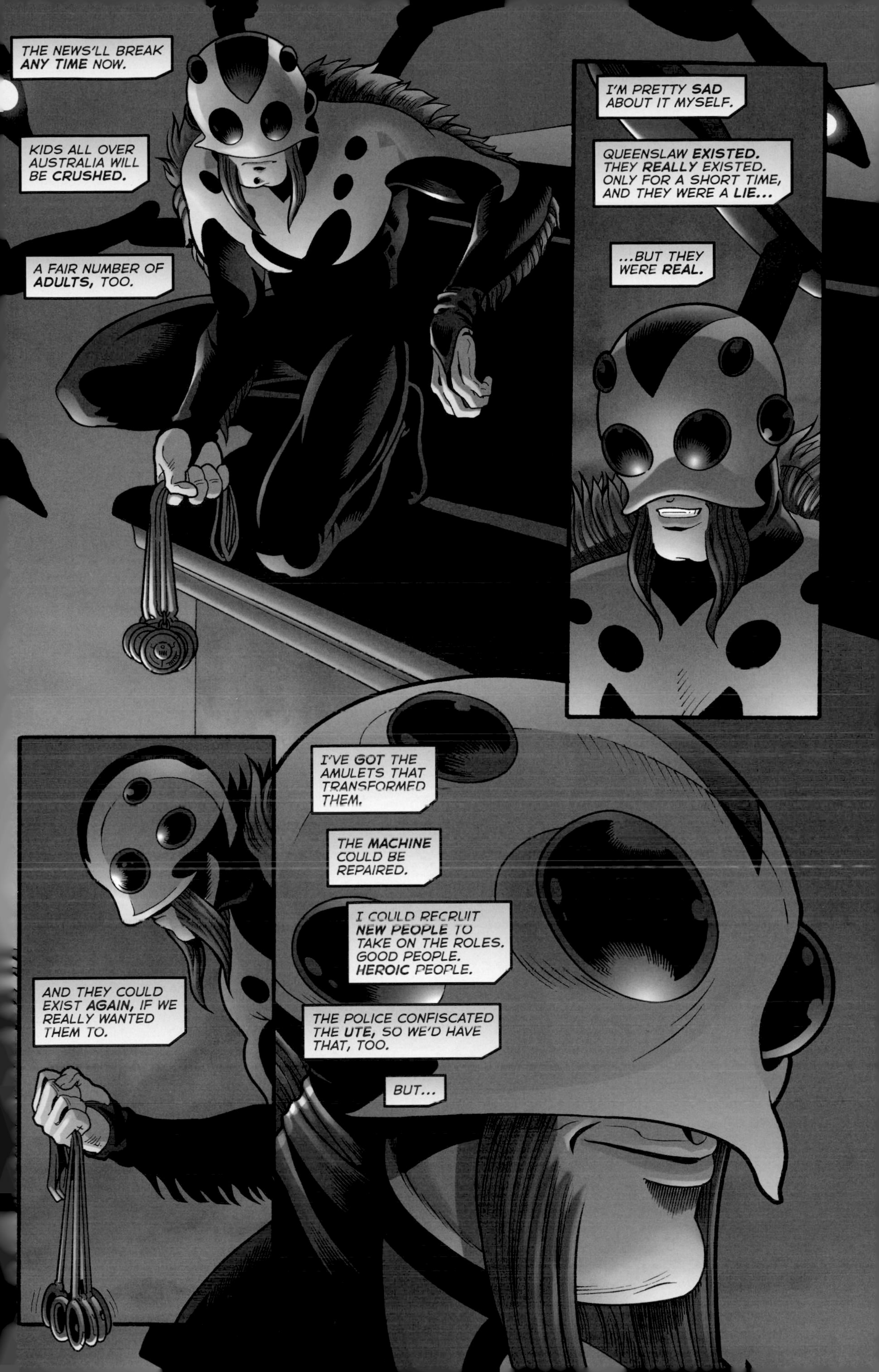
THE NEWS'LL BREAK ANY TIME NOW.
KIDS ALL OVER AUSTRALIA WILL BE CRUSHED.
A FAIR NUMBER OF ADULTS, TOO.
I'M PRETTY SAD ABOUT IT MYSELF.
QUEENSLAW EXISTED. THEY REALLY EXISTED. ONLY FOR A SHORT TIME, AND THEY WERE A LIE...
...BUT THEY WERE REAL.
AND THEY COULD EXIST AGAIN, IF WE REALLY WANTED THEM TO.
I'VE GOT THE AMULETS THAT TRANSFORMED THEM.
THE MACHINE COULD BE REPAIRED.
I COULD RECRUIT NEW PEOPLE TO TAKE ON THE ROLES. GOOD PEOPLE. HEROIC PEOPLE.
THE POLICE CONFISCATED THE UTE, SO WE'D HAVE THAT, TOO.
BUT...

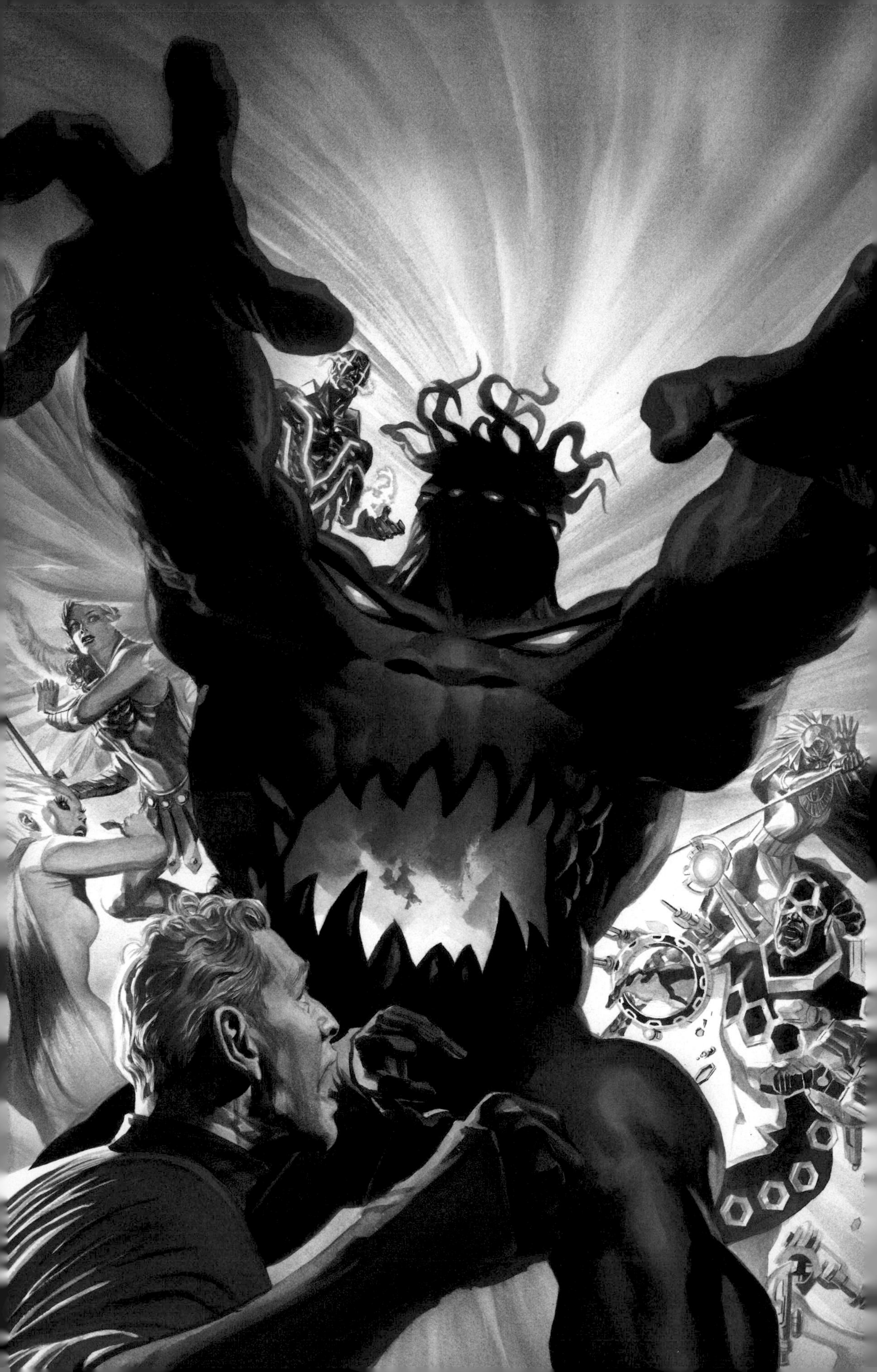

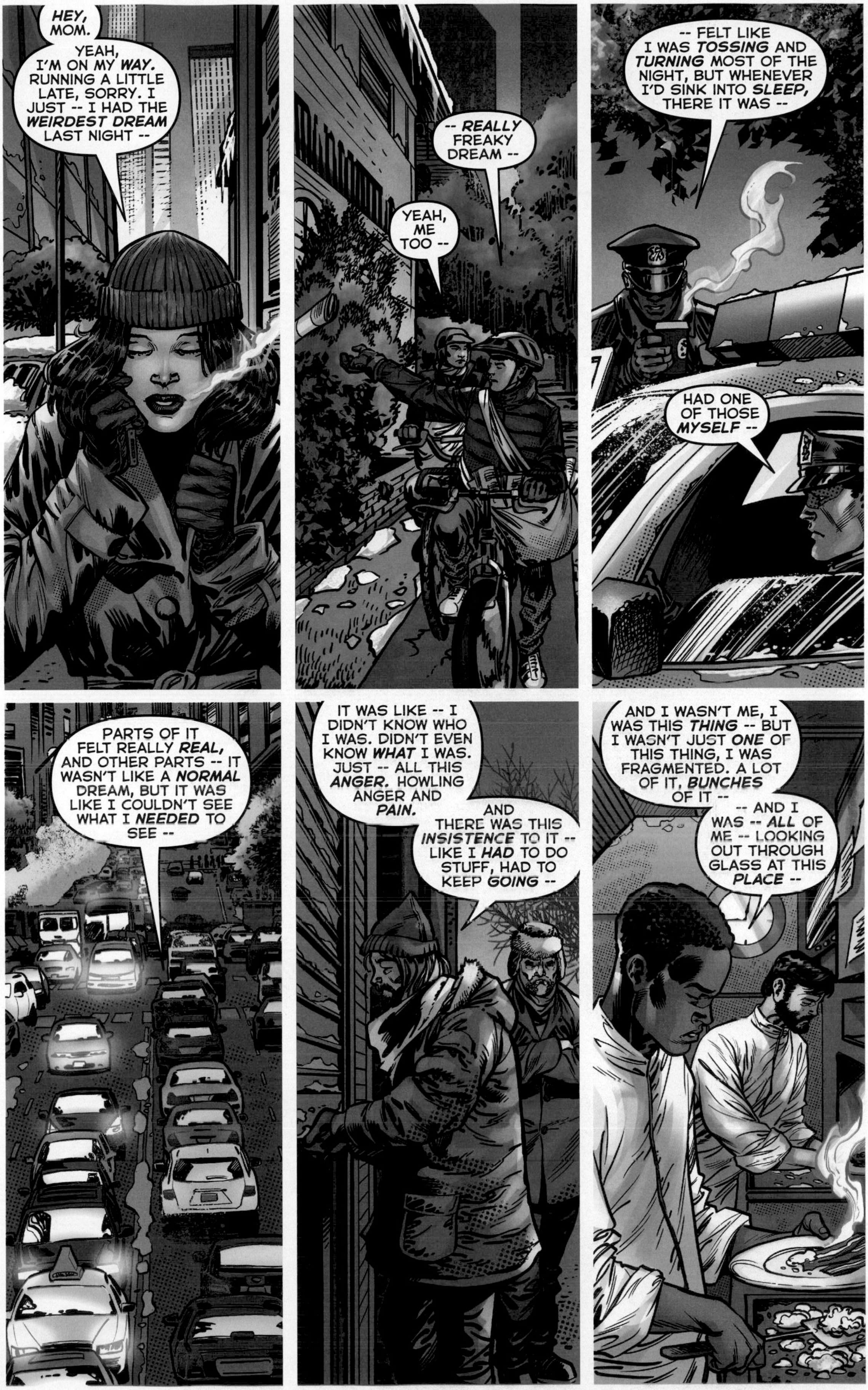
HEY, MOM.
YEAH, I'M ON MY WAY. RUNNING A LITTLE LATE, SORRY. I JUST -- I HAD THE WEIRDEST DREAM LAST NIGHT --
-- REALLY FREAKY DREAM --
YEAH, ME TOO --
-- FELT LIKE I WAS TOSSING AND TURNING MOST OF THE NIGHT, BUT WHENEVER I'D SINK INTO SLEEP, THERE IT WAS --
HAD ONE OF THOSE MYSELF --
PARTS OF IT FELT REALLY REAL, AND OTHER PARTS -- IT WASN'T LIKE A NORMAL DREAM, BUT IT WAS LIKE I COULDN'T SEE WHAT I NEEDED TO SEE --
IT WAS LIKE -- I DIDN'T KNOW WHO I WAS. DIDN'T EVEN KNOW WHAT I WAS. JUST -- ALL THIS ANGER. HOWLING ANGER AND PAIN.
AND THERE WAS THIS INSISTENCE TO IT -- LIKE I HAD TO DO STUFF, HAD TO KEEP GOING --
AND I WASN'T ME, I WAS THIS THING -- BUT I WASN'T JUST ONE OF THIS THING, I WAS FRAGMENTED. A LOT OF IT, BUNCHES OF IT --
-- AND I WAS -- ALL OF ME -- LOOKING OUT THROUGH GLASS AT THIS PLACE --

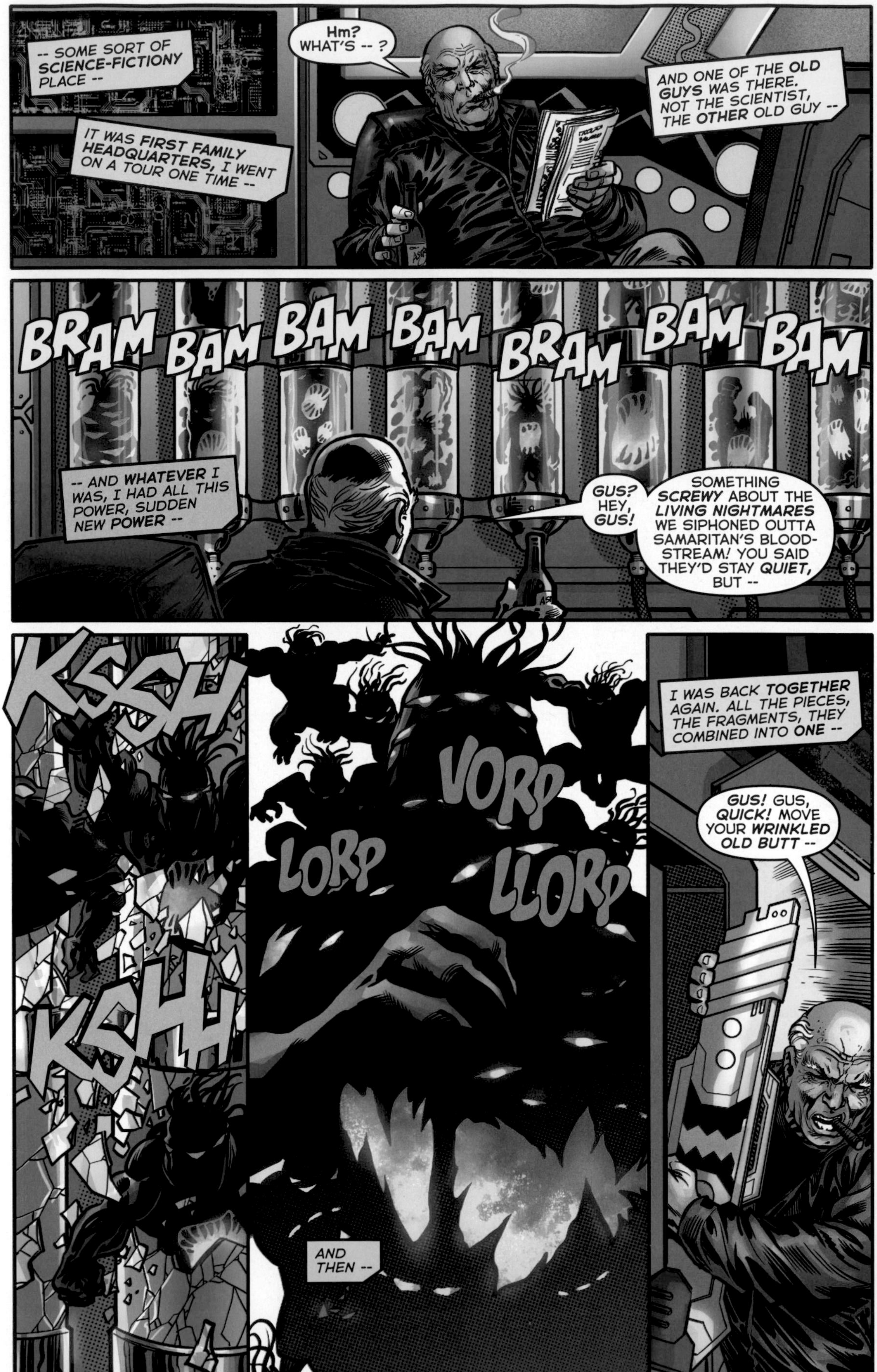
-- SOME SORT OF SCIENCE-FICTIONY PLACE --
IT WAS FIRST FAMILY HEADQUARTERS, I WENT ON A TOUR ONE TIME --
Hm? WHAT'S -- ?
AND ONE OF THE OLD GUYS WAS THERE. NOT THE SCIENTIST, THE OTHER OLD GUY --
BRAM BAM BAM BAM BRAM BAM BAM
-- AND WHATEVER I WAS, I HAD ALL THIS POWER, SUDDEN NEW POWER --
GUS? HEY, GUS!
SOMETHING SCREWY ABOUT THE LIVING NIGHTMARES WE SIPHONED OUTTA SAMARITAN'S BLOOD-STREAM! YOU SAID THEY'D STAY QUIET, BUT --
KSSH
KSHH
VORP
LORP
LLORP
AND THEN --
I WAS BACK TOGETHER AGAIN. ALL THE PIECES, THE FRAGMENTS, THEY COMBINED INTO ONE --
GUS! GUS, QUICK! MOVE YOUR WRINKLED OLD BUTT --

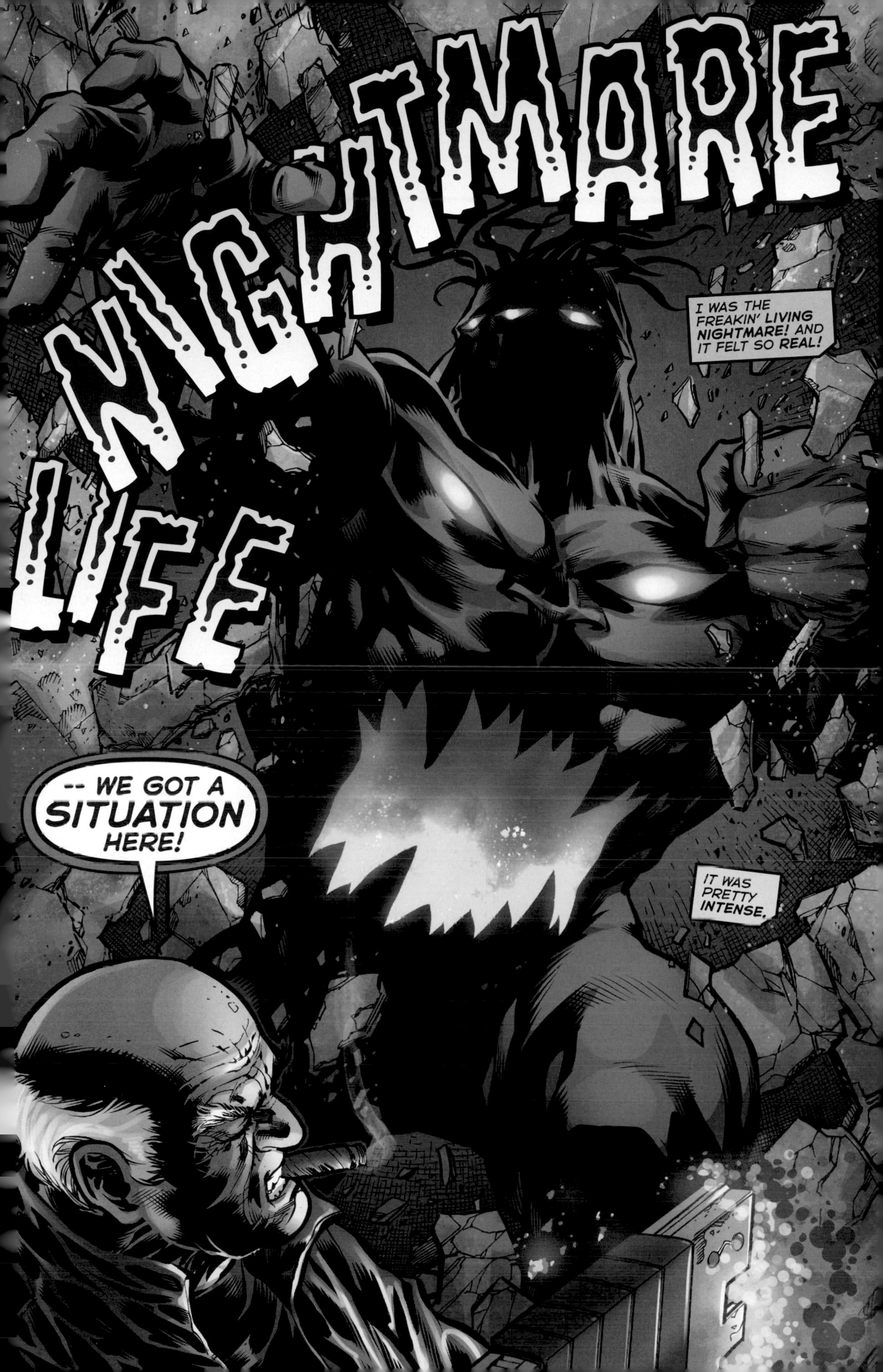

NIGHTMARE LIFE
I WAS THE FREAKIN' LIVING NIGHTMARE! AND IT FELT SO REAL!
-- WE GOT A SITUATION HERE!
IT WAS PRETTY INTENSE.

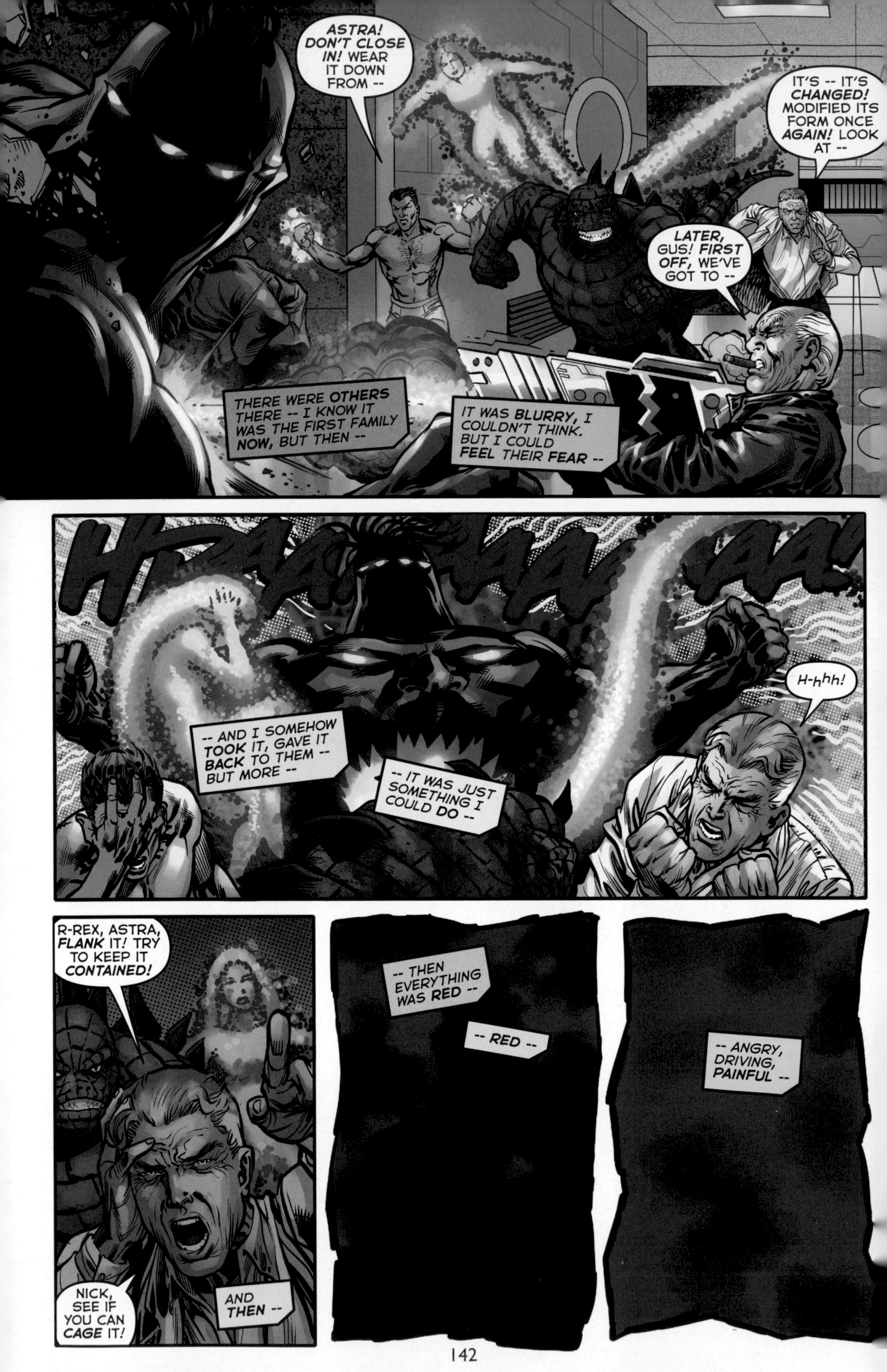
ASTRA! DON'T CLOSE IN! WEAR IT DOWN FROM --
IT'S -- IT'S CHANGED! MODIFIED ITS FORM ONCE AGAIN! LOOK AT --
LATER, GUS! FIRST OFF, WE'VE GOT TO --
THERE WERE OTHERS THERE -- I KNOW IT WAS THE FIRST FAMILY NOW, BUT THEN --
IT WAS BLURRY, I COULDN'T THINK. BUT I COULD FEEL THEIR FEAR --
H-hhh!
-- AND I SOMEHOW TOOK IT, GAVE IT BACK TO THEM -- BUT MORE --
-- IT WAS JUST SOMETHING I COULD DO --
R-REX, ASTRA, FLANK IT! TRY TO KEEP IT CONTAINED!
NICK, SEE IF YOU CAN CAGE IT!
AND THEN --
-- THEN EVERYTHING WAS RED --
-- RED --
-- ANGRY, DRIVING, PAINFUL --

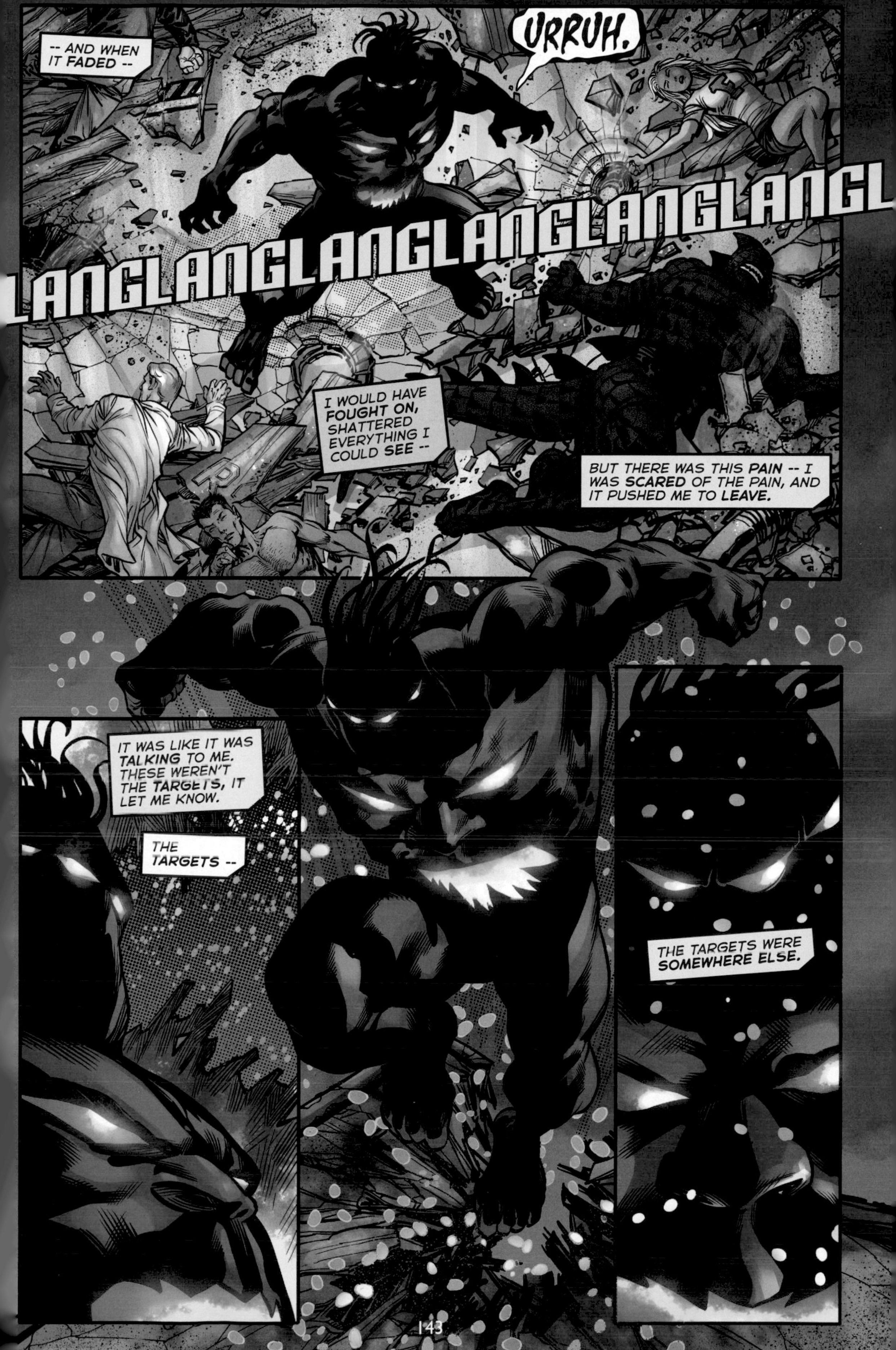
-- AND WHEN IT FADED --
URRUH.
LANGLANGLANGLANGLANGLANGL
I WOULD HAVE FOUGHT ON, SHATTERED EVERYTHING I COULD SEE --
BUT THERE WAS THIS PAIN -- I WAS SCARED OF THE PAIN, AND IT PUSHED ME TO LEAVE.
IT WAS LIKE IT WAS TALKING TO ME. THESE WEREN'T THE TARGETS, IT LET ME KNOW.
THE TARGETS --
THE TARGETS WERE SOMEWHERE ELSE.

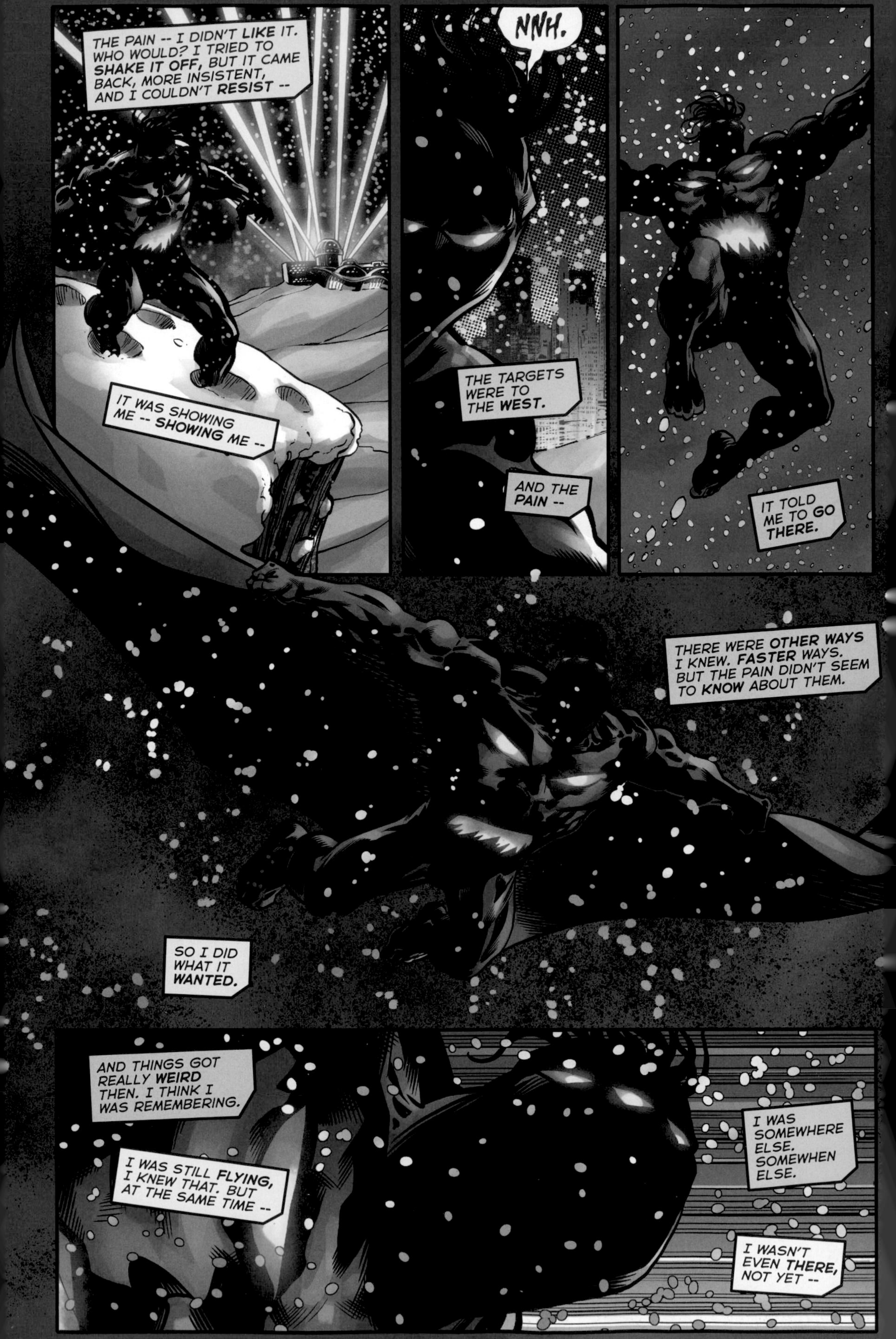
THE PAIN -- I DIDN'T LIKE IT. WHO WOULD? I TRIED TO SHAKE IT OFF, BUT IT CAME BACK, MORE INSISTENT, AND I COULDN'T RESIST --
IT WAS SHOWING ME -- SHOWING ME --
NNH.
THE TARGETS WERE TO THE WEST.
AND THE PAIN --
IT TOLD ME TO GO THERE.
THERE WERE OTHER WAYS I KNEW. FASTER WAYS. BUT THE PAIN DIDN'T SEEM TO KNOW ABOUT THEM.
SO I DID WHAT IT WANTED.
AND THINGS GOT REALLY WEIRD THEN. I THINK I WAS REMEMBERING.
I WAS STILL FLYING, I KNEW THAT. BUT AT THE SAME TIME --
I WAS SOMEWHERE ELSE. SOMEWHEN ELSE.
I WASN'T EVEN THERE, NOT YET --

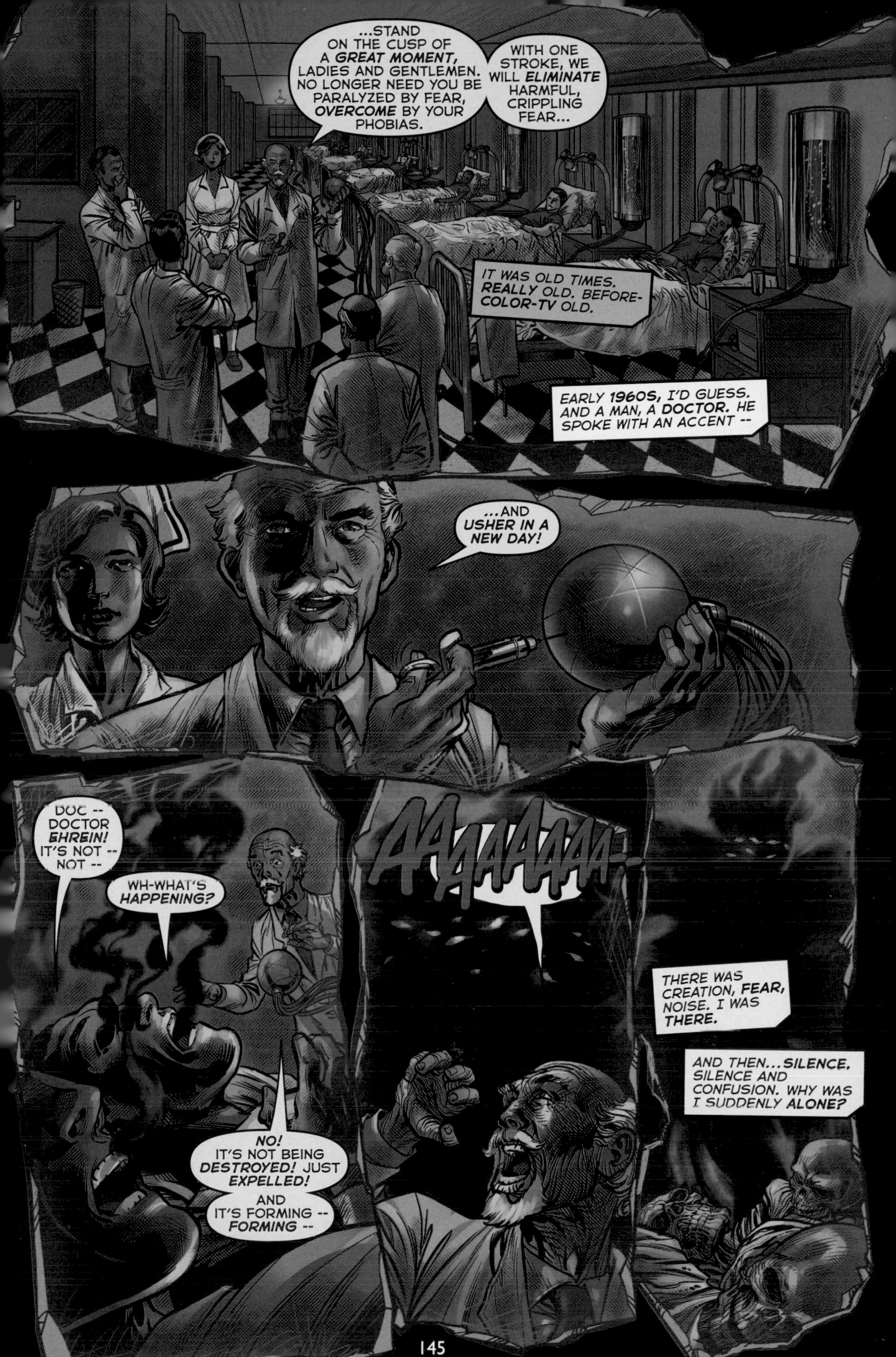
...STAND ON THE CUSP OF A GREAT MOMENT, LADIES AND GENTLEMEN. NO LONGER NEED YOU BE PARALYZED BY FEAR, OVERCOME BY YOUR PHOBIAS.
WITH ONE STROKE, WE WILL ELIMINATE HARMFUL, CRIPPLING FEAR...
IT WAS OLD TIMES. REALLY OLD. BEFORE-COLOR-TV OLD.
EARLY 1960S, I'D GUESS. AND A MAN, A DOCTOR. HE SPOKE WITH AN ACCENT --
...AND USHER IN A NEW DAY!
DOC -- DOCTOR EHREIN! IT'S NOT -- NOT --
WH-WHAT'S HAPPENING?
NO! IT'S NOT BEING DESTROYED! JUST EXPELLED!
AND IT'S FORMING -- FORMING --
AAAAAAAAA--
THERE WAS CREATION, FEAR, NOISE. I WAS THERE.
AND THEN...SILENCE. SILENCE AND CONFUSION. WHY WAS I SUDDENLY ALONE?

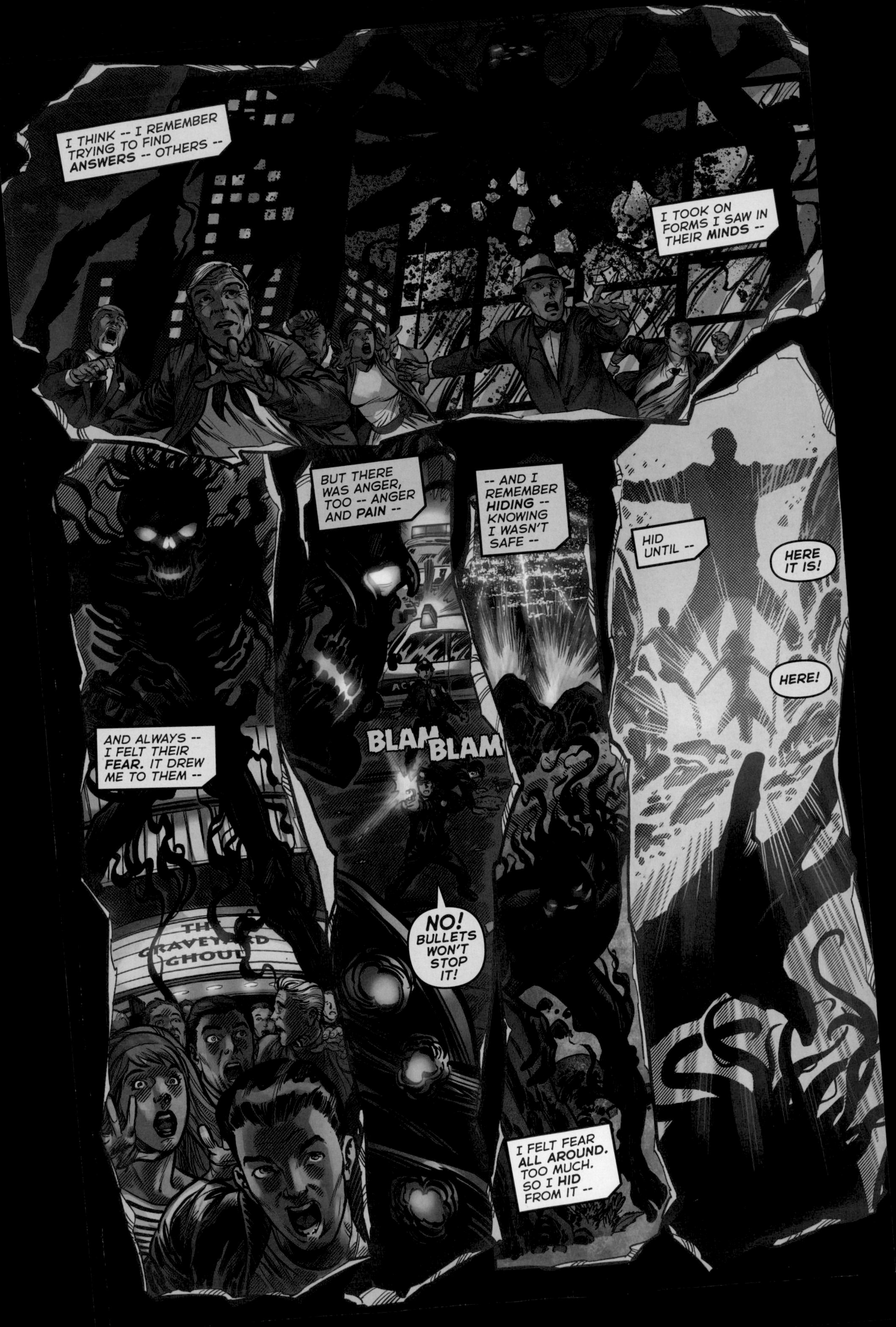
I THINK -- I REMEMBER TRYING TO FIND ANSWERS -- OTHERS --
I TOOK ON FORMS I SAW IN THEIR MINDS --
AND ALWAYS -- I FELT THEIR FEAR. IT DREW ME TO THEM --
THE GRAVEYARD GHOUL
BUT THERE WAS ANGER, TOO -- ANGER AND PAIN --
BLAM BLAM
NO! BULLETS WON'T STOP IT!
-- AND I REMEMBER HIDING -- KNOWING I WASN'T SAFE --
I FELT FEAR ALL AROUND. TOO MUCH. SO I HID FROM IT --
HID UNTIL --
HERE IT IS!
HERE!

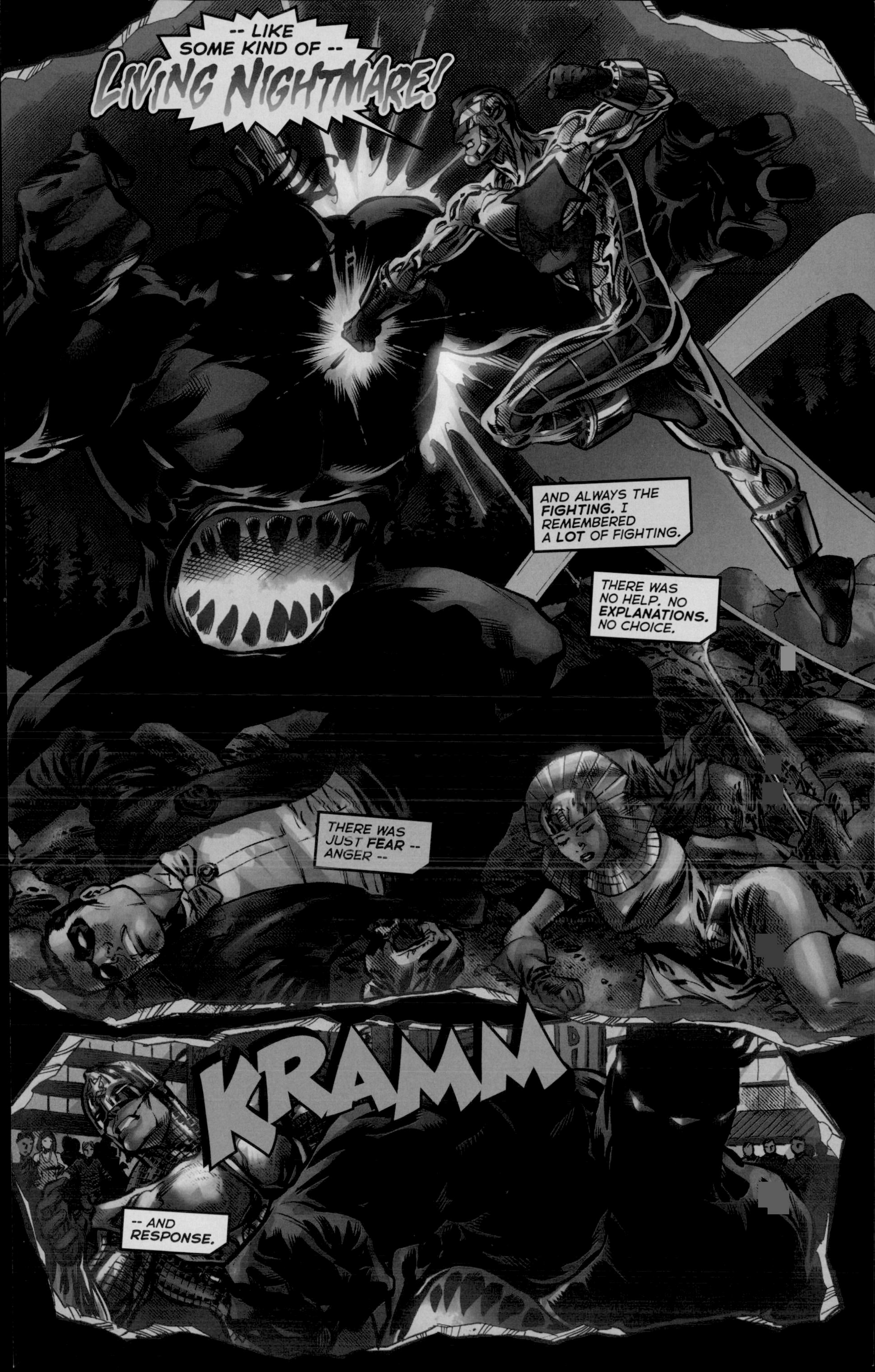
-- LIKE SOME KIND OF --
LIVING NIGHTMARE!
AND ALWAYS THE FIGHTING. I REMEMBERED A LOT OF FIGHTING.
THERE WAS NO HELP. NO EXPLANATIONS. NO CHOICE.
THERE WAS JUST FEAR -- ANGER --
KRAMM
-- AND RESPONSE.

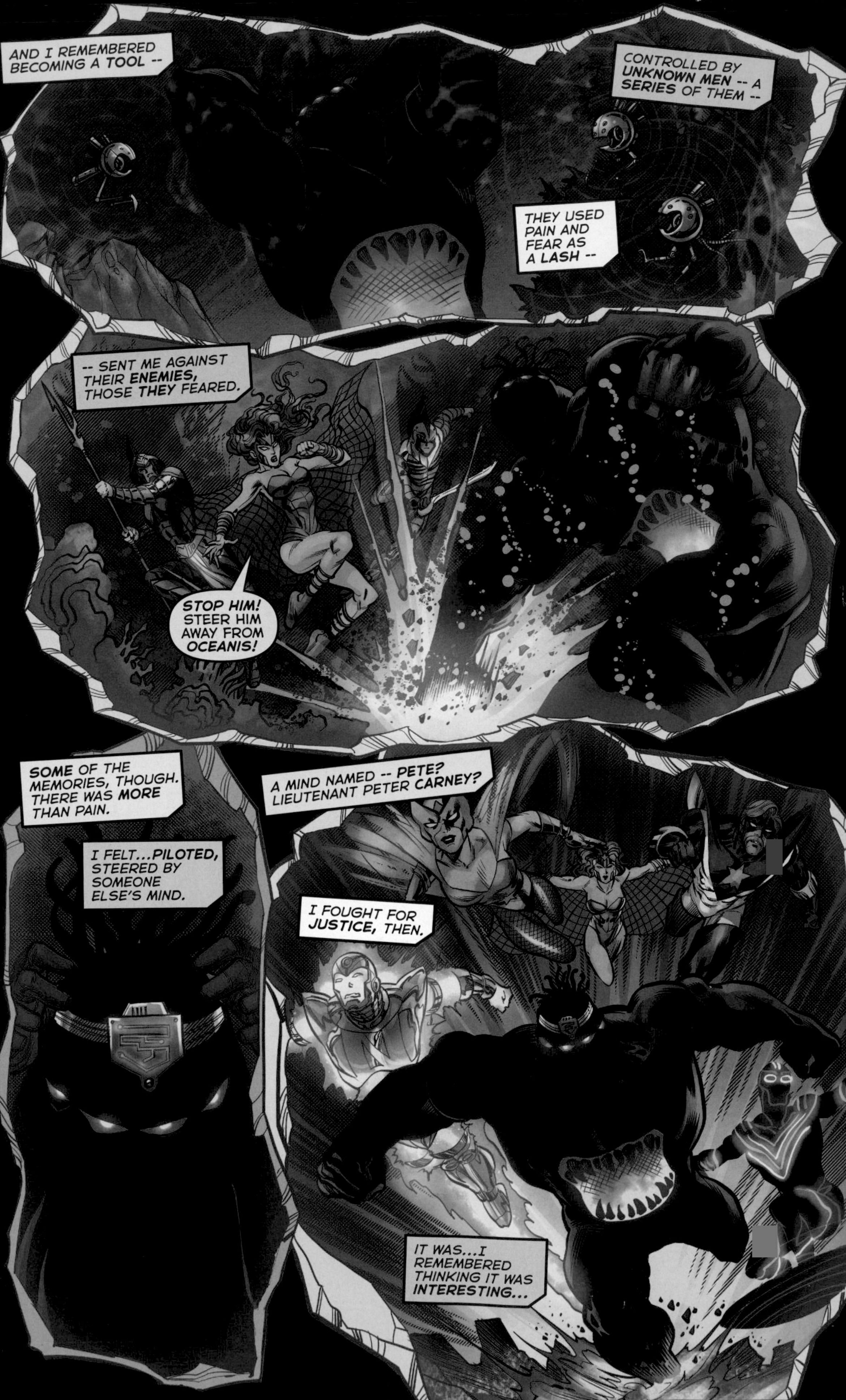
AND I REMEMBERED BECOMING A TOOL --
CONTROLLED BY UNKNOWN MEN -- A SERIES OF THEM --
THEY USED PAIN AND FEAR AS A LASH --
-- SENT ME AGAINST THEIR ENEMIES, THOSE THEY FEARED.
STOP HIM! STEER HIM AWAY FROM OCEANIS!
SOME OF THE MEMORIES, THOUGH. THERE WAS MORE THAN PAIN.
I FELT...PILOTED, STEERED BY SOMEONE ELSE'S MIND.
A MIND NAMED -- PETE? LIEUTENANT PETER CARNEY?
I FOUGHT FOR JUSTICE, THEN.
IT WAS...I REMEMBERED THINKING IT WAS INTERESTING...

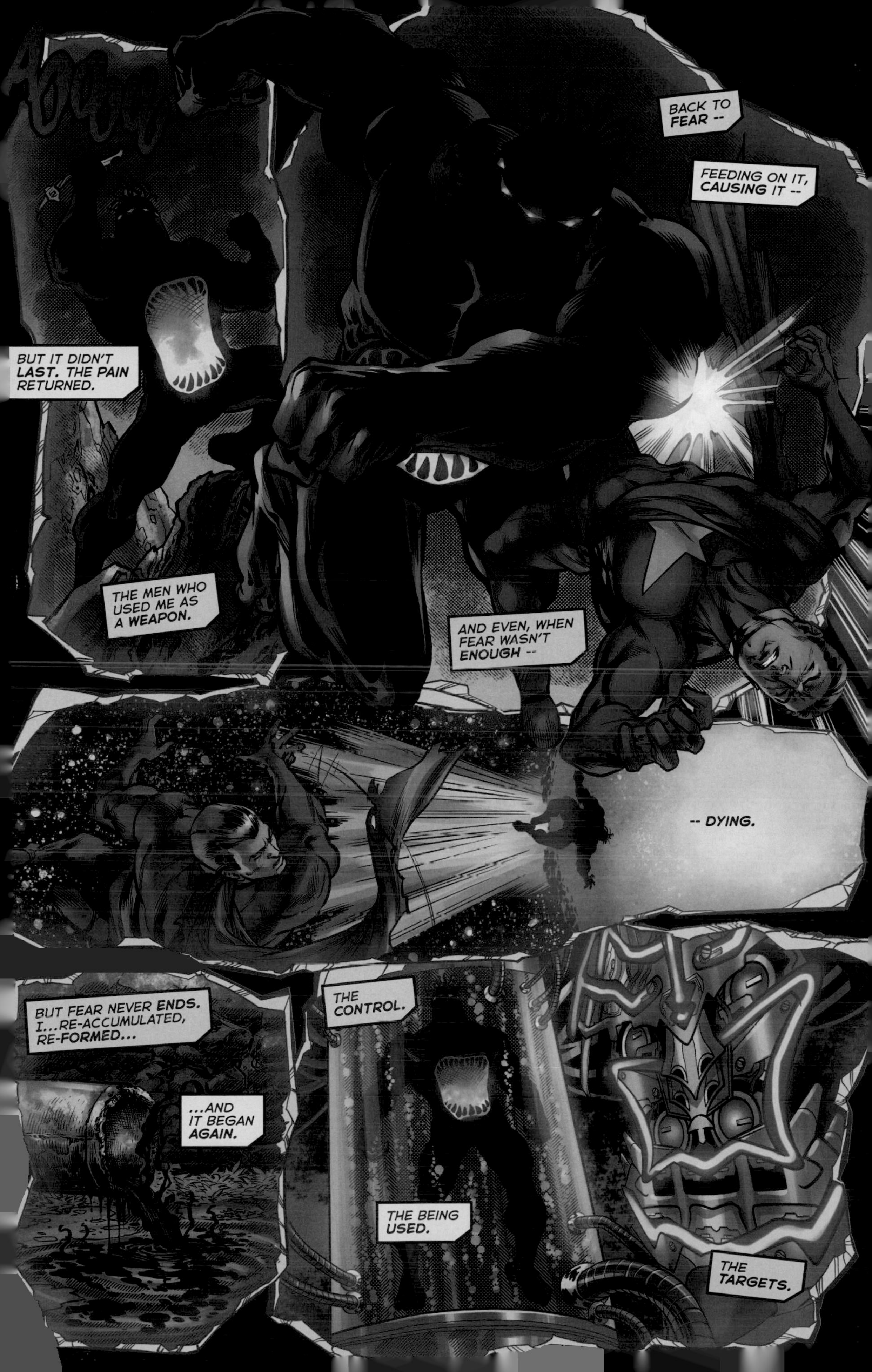
BACK TO FEAR --
FEEDING ON IT, CAUSING IT --
BUT IT DIDN'T LAST. THE PAIN RETURNED.
THE MEN WHO USED ME AS A WEAPON.
AND EVEN, WHEN FEAR WASN'T ENOUGH --
-- DYING.
BUT FEAR NEVER ENDS. I...RE-ACCUMULATED, RE-FORMED...
...AND IT BEGAN AGAIN.
THE CONTROL.
THE BEING USED.
THE TARGETS.

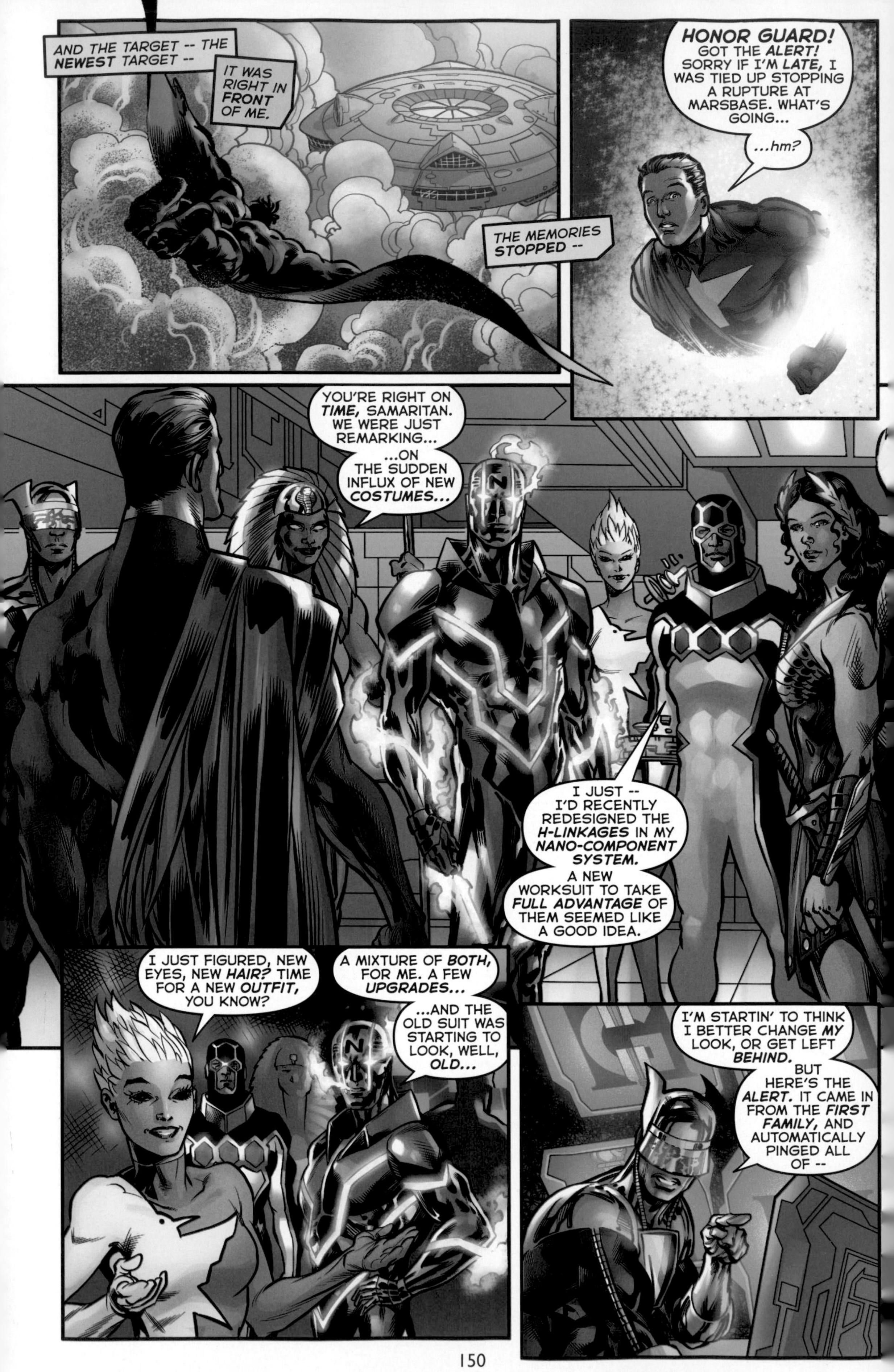
AND THE TARGET -- THE NEWEST TARGET --
IT WAS RIGHT IN FRONT OF ME.
THE MEMORIES STOPPED --
HONOR GUARD! GOT THE ALERT! SORRY IF I'M LATE, I WAS TIED UP STOPPING A RUPTURE AT MARSBASE. WHAT'S GOING...
...hm?
YOU'RE RIGHT ON TIME, SAMARITAN. WE WERE JUST REMARKING...
...ON THE SUDDEN INFLUX OF NEW COSTUMES...
I JUST -- I'D RECENTLY REDESIGNED THE H-LINKAGES IN MY NANO-COMPONENT SYSTEM.
A NEW WORKSUIT TO TAKE FULL ADVANTAGE OF THEM SEEMED LIKE A GOOD IDEA.
I JUST FIGURED, NEW EYES, NEW HAIR? TIME FOR A NEW OUTFIT, YOU KNOW?
A MIXTURE OF BOTH, FOR ME. A FEW UPGRADES...
...AND THE OLD SUIT WAS STARTING TO LOOK, WELL, OLD...
I'M STARTIN' TO THINK I BETTER CHANGE MY LOOK, OR GET LEFT BEHIND.
BUT HERE'S THE ALERT. IT CAME IN FROM THE FIRST FAMILY, AND AUTOMATICALLY PINGED ALL OF --

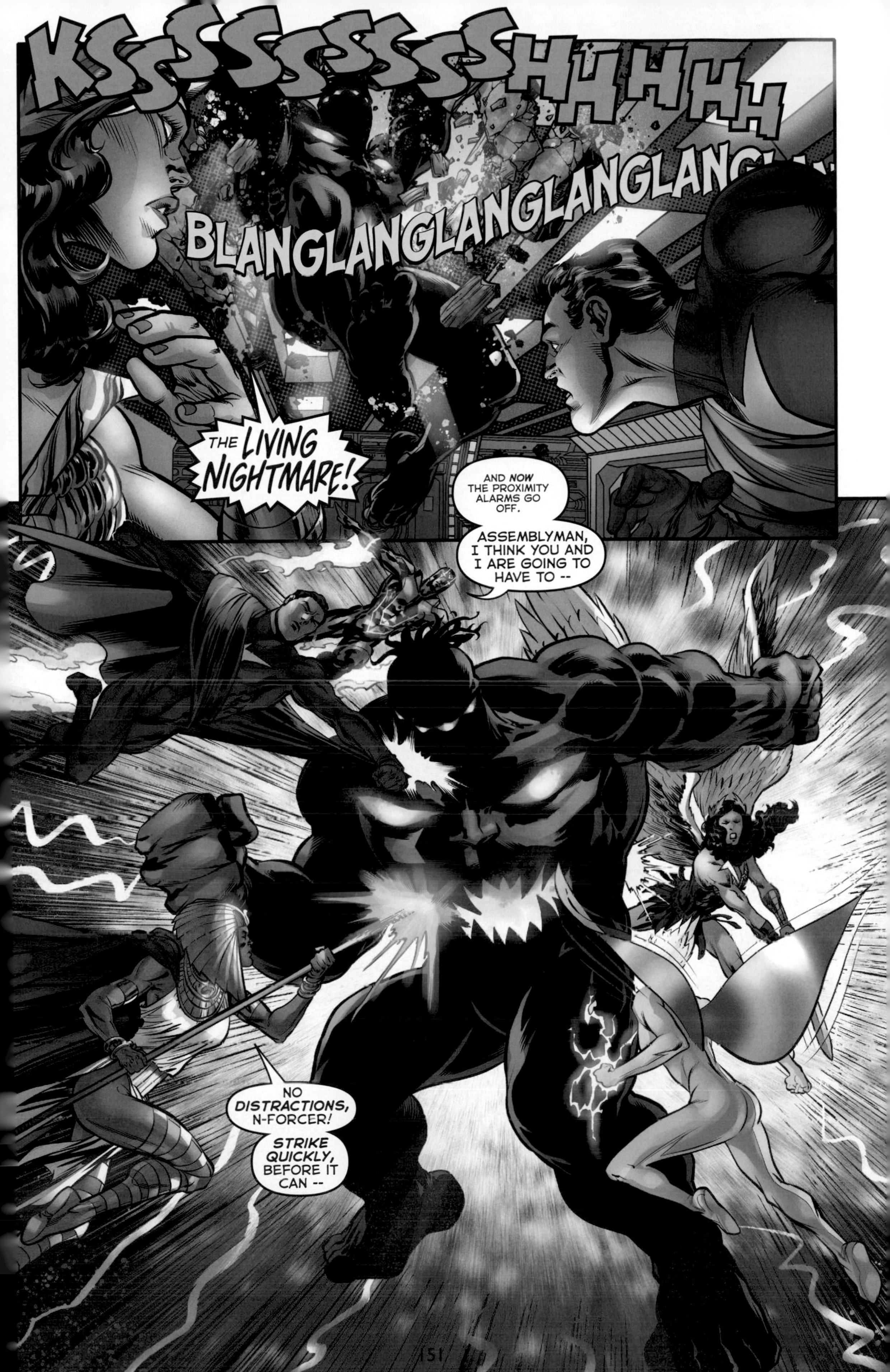
KSSSSSSSSHHHHH
BLANGLANGLANGLANGLANGLAN
THE LIVING NIGHTMARE!
AND NOW THE PROXIMITY ALARMS GO OFF.
ASSEMBLYMAN, I THINK YOU AND I ARE GOING TO HAVE TO --
NO DISTRACTIONS, N-FORCER!
STRIKE QUICKLY, BEFORE IT CAN --

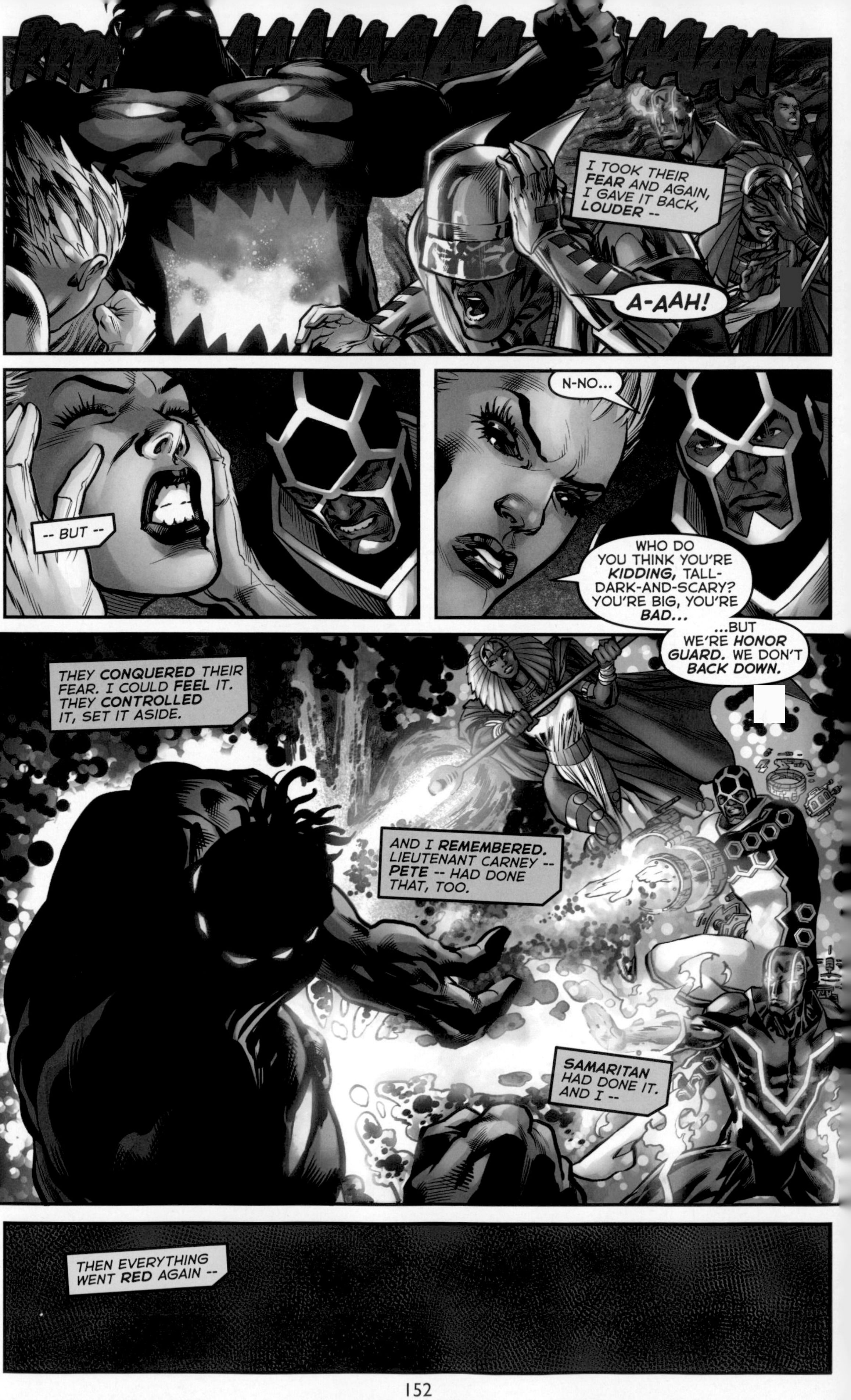

I TOOK THEIR FEAR AND AGAIN, I GAVE IT BACK, LOUDER --
A-AAH!
-- BUT --
N-NO...
WHO DO YOU THINK YOU'RE KIDDING, TALL-DARK-AND-SCARY? YOU'RE BIG, YOU'RE BAD...
...BUT WE'RE HONOR GUARD. WE DON'T BACK DOWN.
THEY CONQUERED THEIR FEAR. I COULD FEEL IT. THEY CONTROLLED IT, SET IT ASIDE.
AND I REMEMBERED. LIEUTENANT CARNEY -- PETE -- HAD DONE THAT, TOO.
SAMARITAN HAD DONE IT. AND I --
THEN EVERYTHING WENT RED AGAIN --

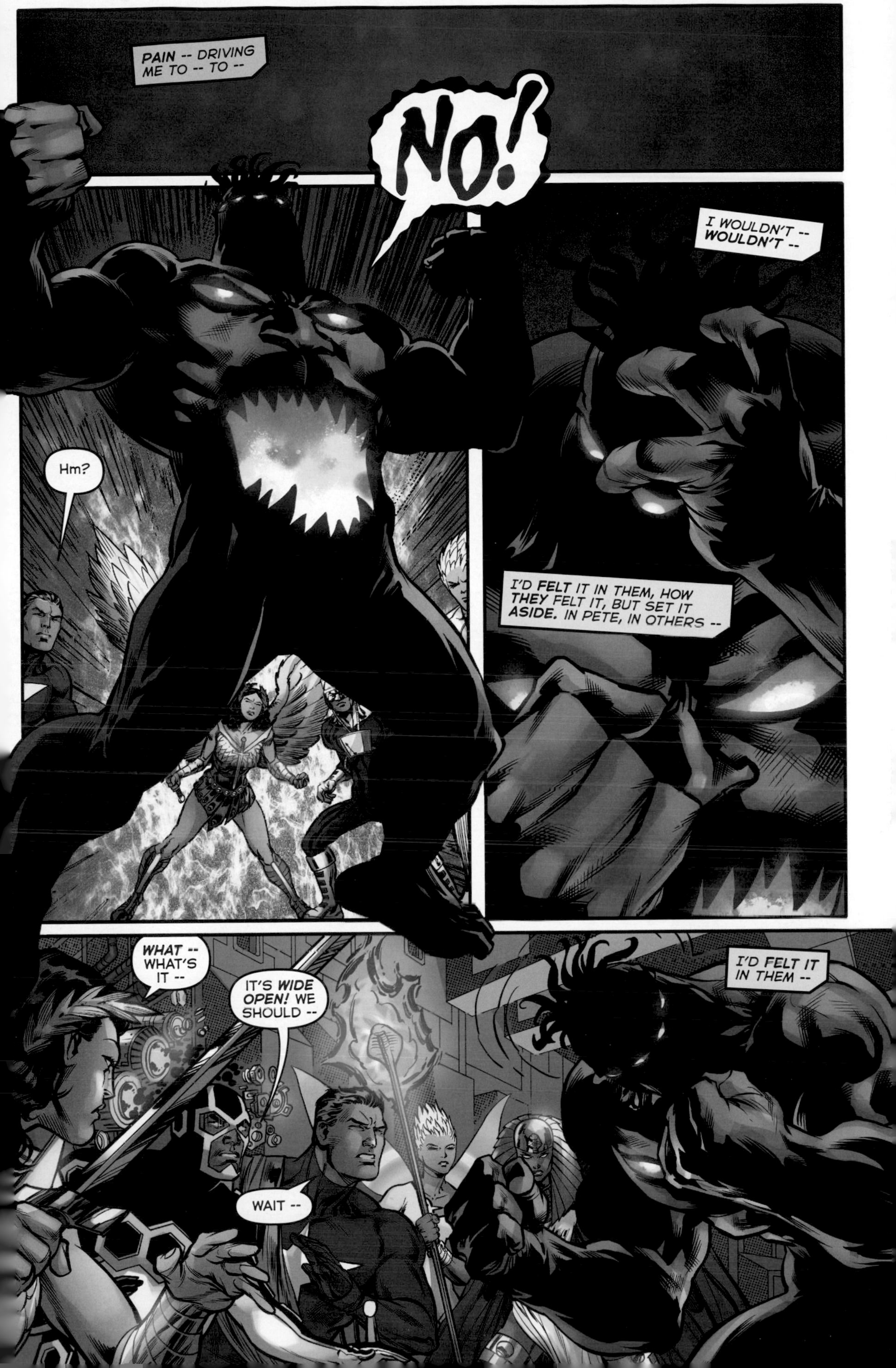
PAIN -- DRIVING ME TO -- TO --
NO!
I WOULDN'T -- WOULDN'T --
Hm?
I'D FELT IT IN THEM, HOW THEY FELT IT, BUT SET IT ASIDE. IN PETE, IN OTHERS --
WHAT -- WHAT'S IT --
IT'S WIDE OPEN! WE SHOULD --
I'D FELT IT IN THEM --
WAIT --

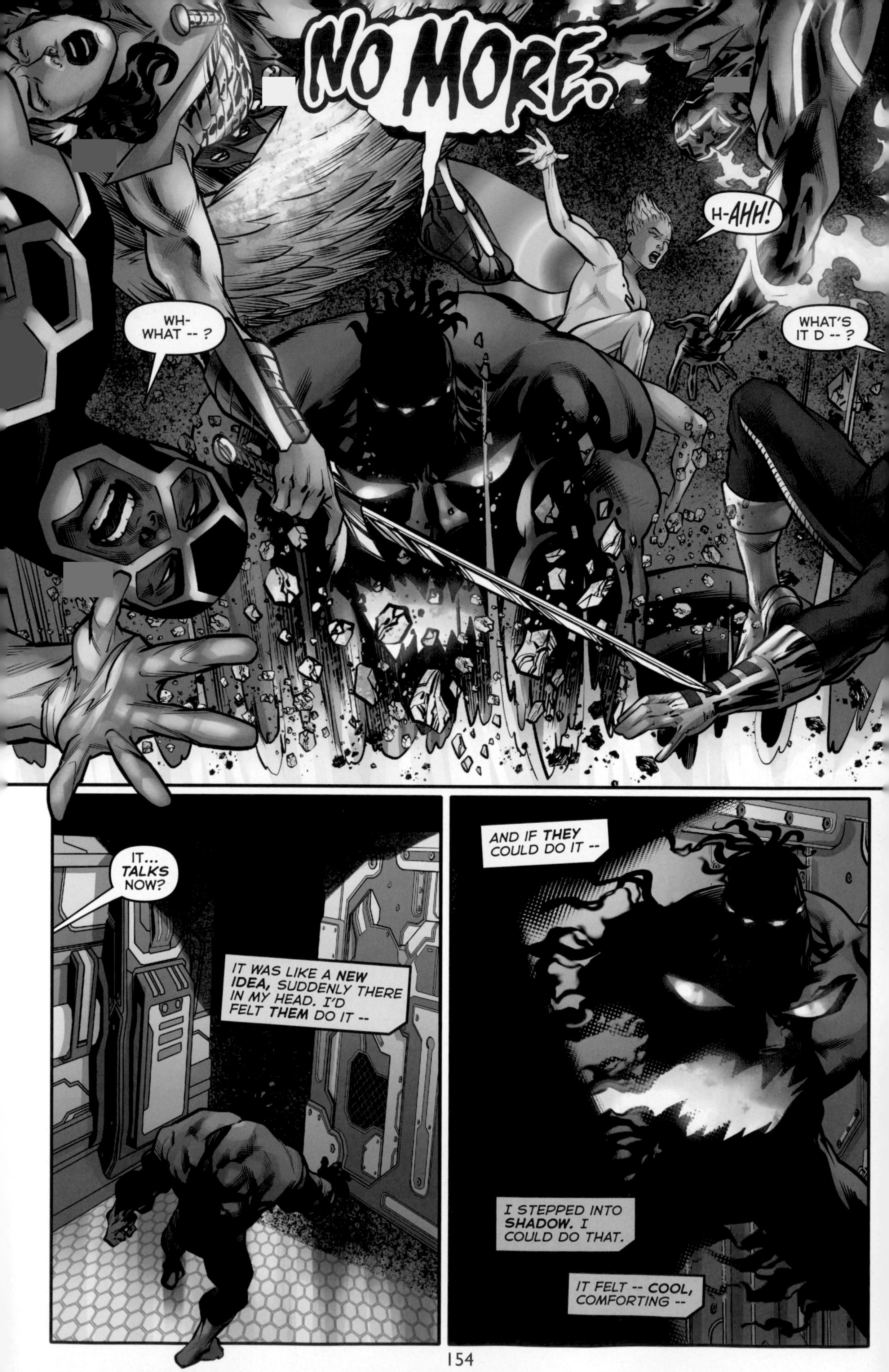
NO MORE.
H-AHH!
WH- WHAT -- ?
WHAT'S IT D -- ?
IT... TALKS NOW?
IT WAS LIKE A NEW IDEA, SUDDENLY THERE IN MY HEAD. I'D FELT THEM DO IT --
AND IF THEY COULD DO IT --
I STEPPED INTO SHADOW. I COULD DO THAT.
IT FELT -- COOL, COMFORTING --

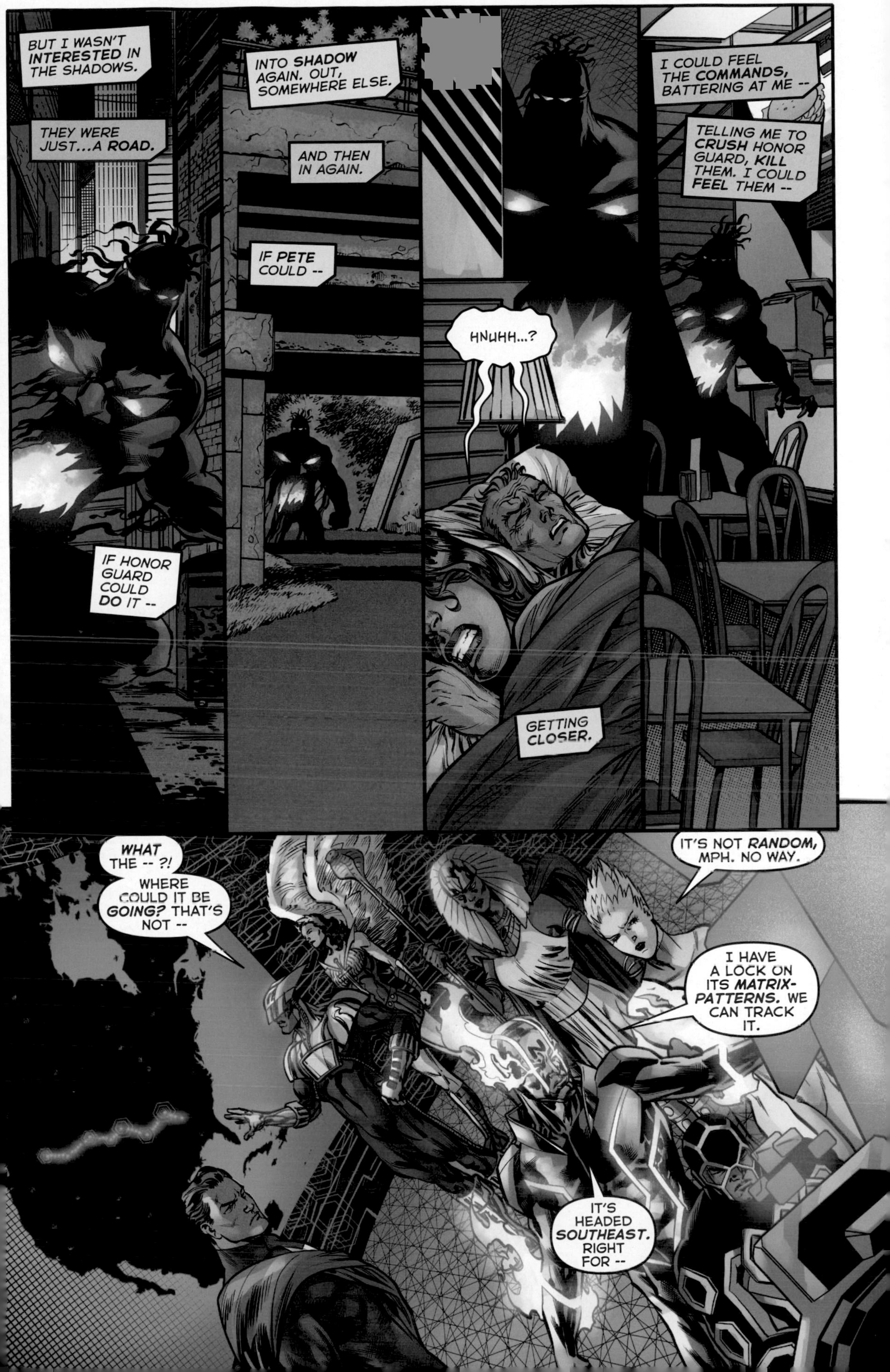
BUT I WASN'T INTERESTED IN THE SHADOWS.
THEY WERE JUST...A ROAD.
IF HONOR GUARD COULD DO IT --
INTO SHADOW AGAIN. OUT, SOMEWHERE ELSE.
AND THEN IN AGAIN.
IF PETE COULD --
HNUHH...?
GETTING CLOSER.
I COULD FEEL THE COMMANDS, BATTERING AT ME --
TELLING ME TO CRUSH HONOR GUARD, KILL THEM. I COULD FEEL THEM --
WHAT THE -- ?!
WHERE COULD IT BE GOING? THAT'S NOT --
IT'S NOT RANDOM, MPH. NO WAY.
I HAVE A LOCK ON ITS MATRIX-PATTERNS. WE CAN TRACK IT.
IT'S HEADED SOUTHEAST. RIGHT FOR --

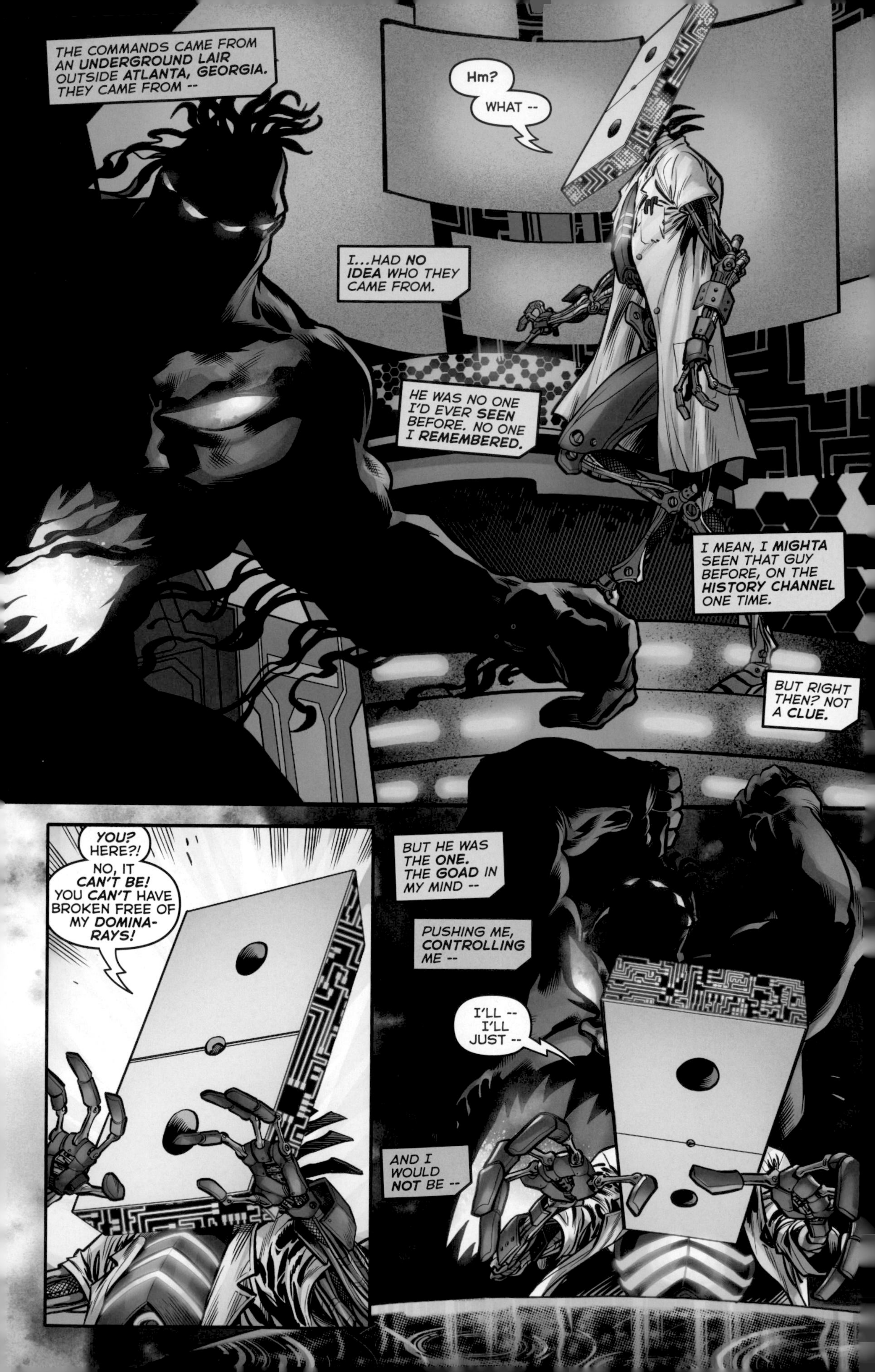

THE COMMANDS CAME FROM AN UNDERGROUND LAIR OUTSIDE ATLANTA, GEORGIA. THEY CAME FROM --
Hm?
WHAT --
I...HAD NO IDEA WHO THEY CAME FROM.
HE WAS NO ONE I'D EVER SEEN BEFORE. NO ONE I REMEMBERED.
I MEAN, I MIGHTA SEEN THAT GUY BEFORE, ON THE HISTORY CHANNEL ONE TIME.
BUT RIGHT THEN? NOT A CLUE.
YOU? HERE?! NO, IT CAN'T BE! YOU CAN'T HAVE BROKEN FREE OF MY DOMINA-RAYS!
BUT HE WAS THE ONE. THE GOAD IN MY MIND --
PUSHING ME, CONTROLLING ME --
I'LL -- I'LL JUST --
AND I WOULD NOT BE --

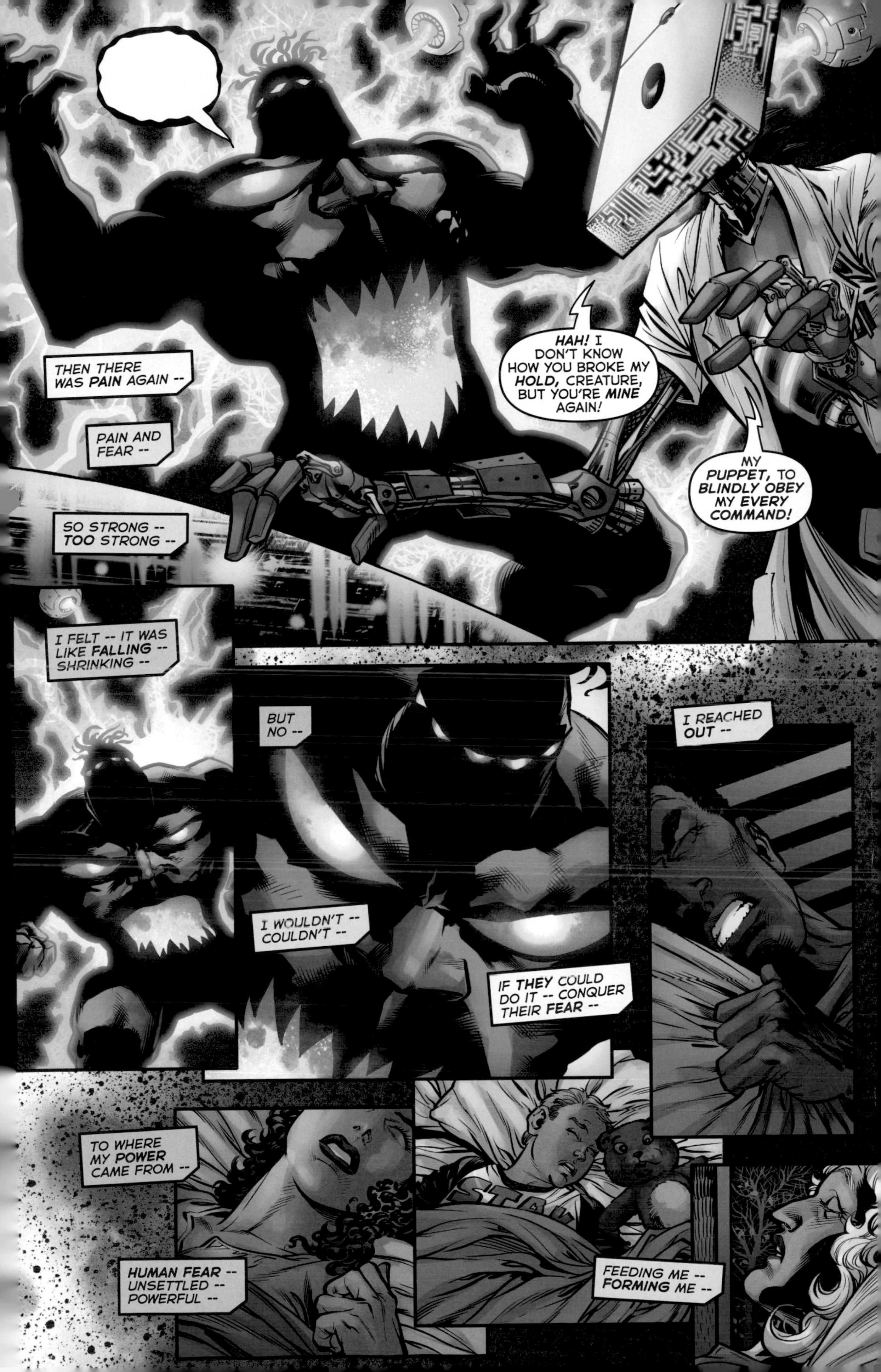

THEN THERE WAS PAIN AGAIN --
PAIN AND FEAR --
HAH! I DON'T KNOW HOW YOU BROKE MY HOLD, CREATURE, BUT YOU'RE MINE AGAIN!
MY PUPPET, TO BLINDLY OBEY MY EVERY COMMAND!
SO STRONG -- TOO STRONG --
I FELT -- IT WAS LIKE FALLING -- SHRINKING --
BUT NO --
I WOULDN'T -- COULDN'T --
IF THEY COULD DO IT -- CONQUER THEIR FEAR --
I REACHED OUT --
TO WHERE MY POWER CAME FROM --
HUMAN FEAR -- UNSETTLED -- POWERFUL --
FEEDING ME -- FORMING ME --

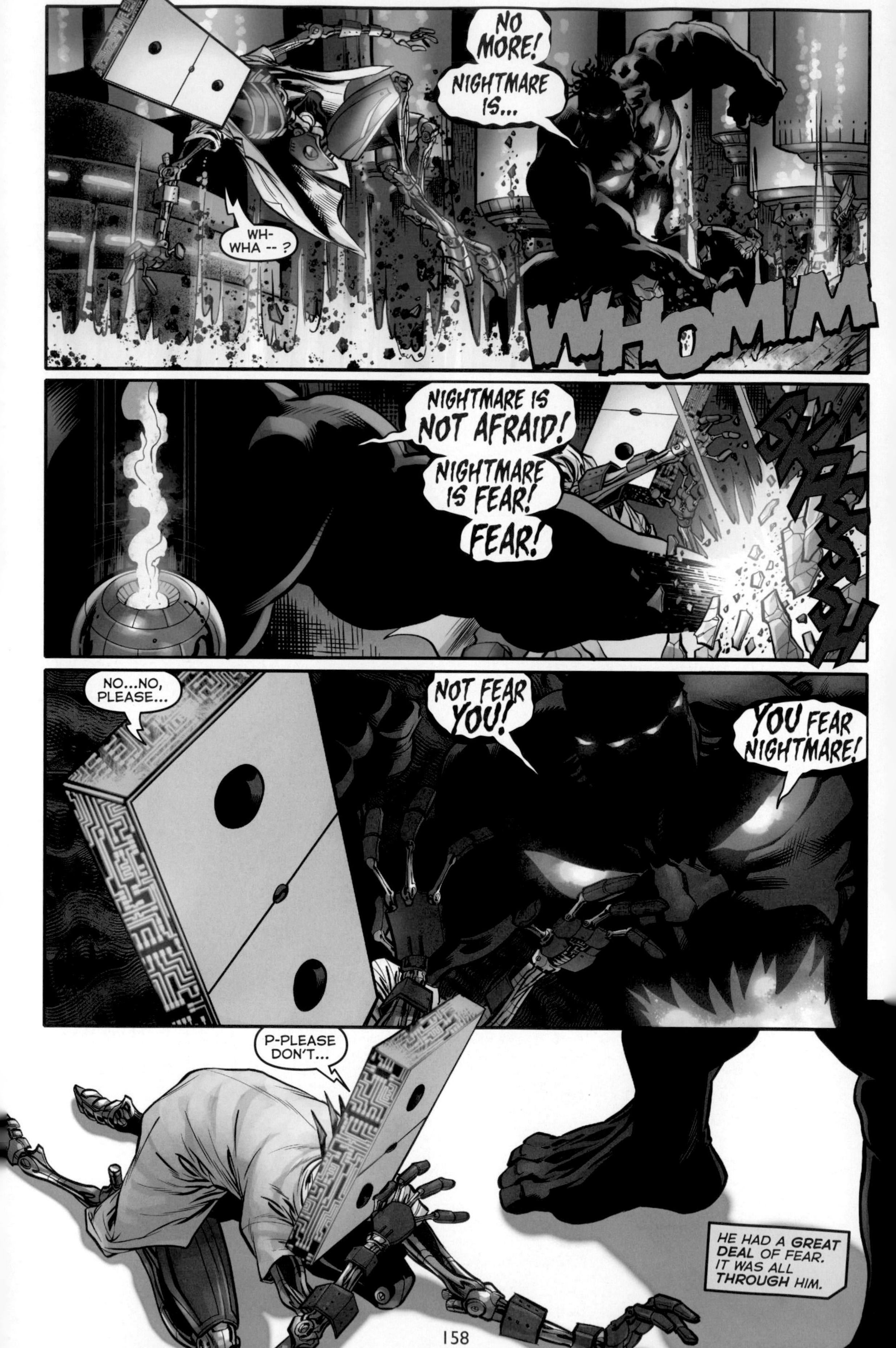
NO MORE! NIGHTMARE IS...
WH- WHA -- ?
WHOMM
NIGHTMARE IS NOT AFRAID!
NIGHTMARE IS FEAR!
FEAR!
NO...NO, PLEASE...
NOT FEAR YOU!
YOU FEAR NIGHTMARE!
P-PLEASE DON'T...
HE HAD A GREAT DEAL OF FEAR. IT WAS ALL THROUGH HIM.

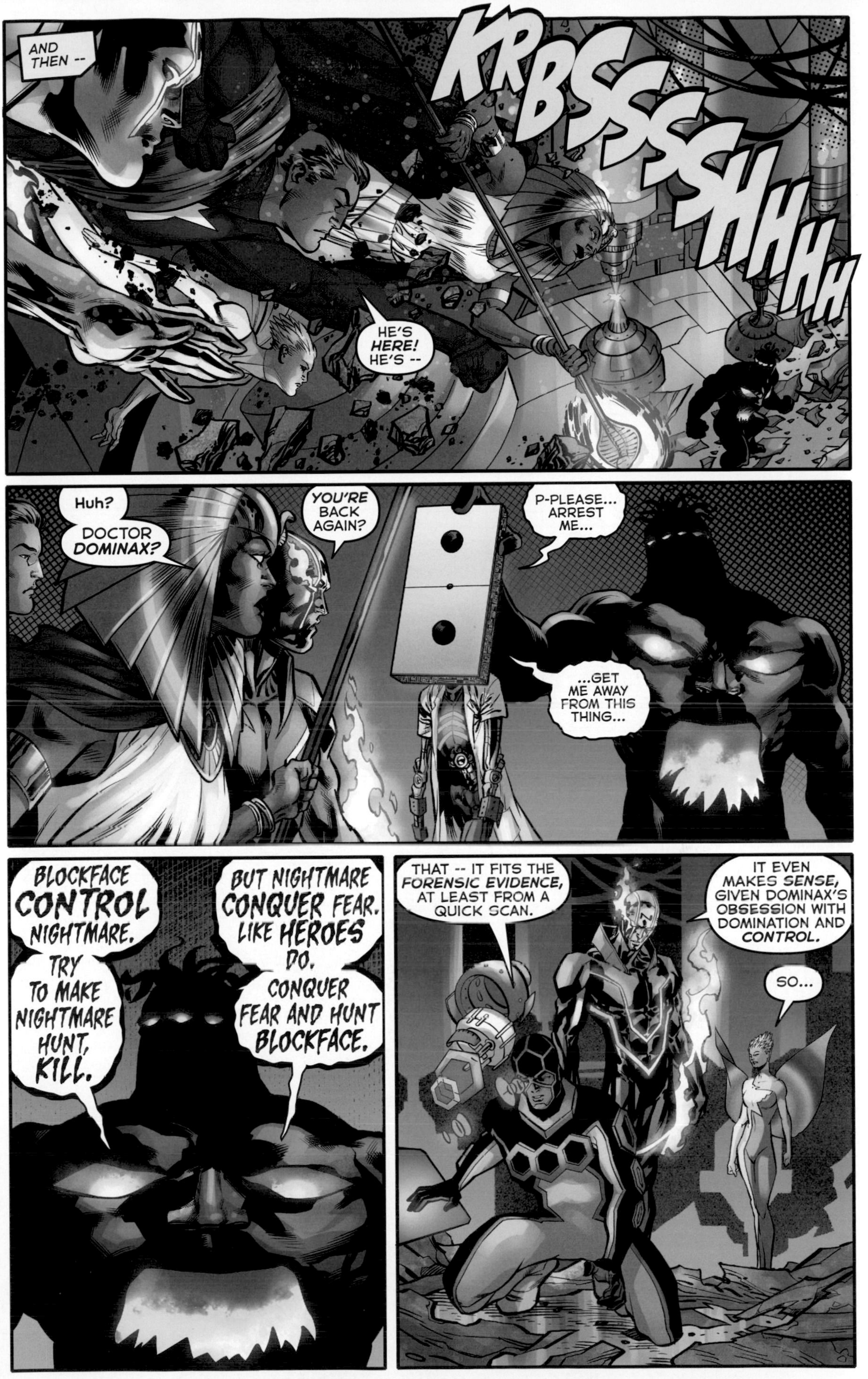
AND THEN --
KRBSSSSHHHHH
HE'S HERE! HE'S --
Huh? DOCTOR DOMINAX?
YOU'RE BACK AGAIN?
P-PLEASE... ARREST ME...
...GET ME AWAY FROM THIS THING...
BLOCKFACE CONTROL NIGHTMARE.
TRY TO MAKE NIGHTMARE HUNT, KILL.
BUT NIGHTMARE CONQUER FEAR. LIKE HEROES DO.
CONQUER FEAR AND HUNT BLOCKFACE.
THAT -- IT FITS THE FORENSIC EVIDENCE, AT LEAST FROM A QUICK SCAN.
IT EVEN MAKES SENSE, GIVEN DOMINAX'S OBSESSION WITH DOMINATION AND CONTROL.
SO...

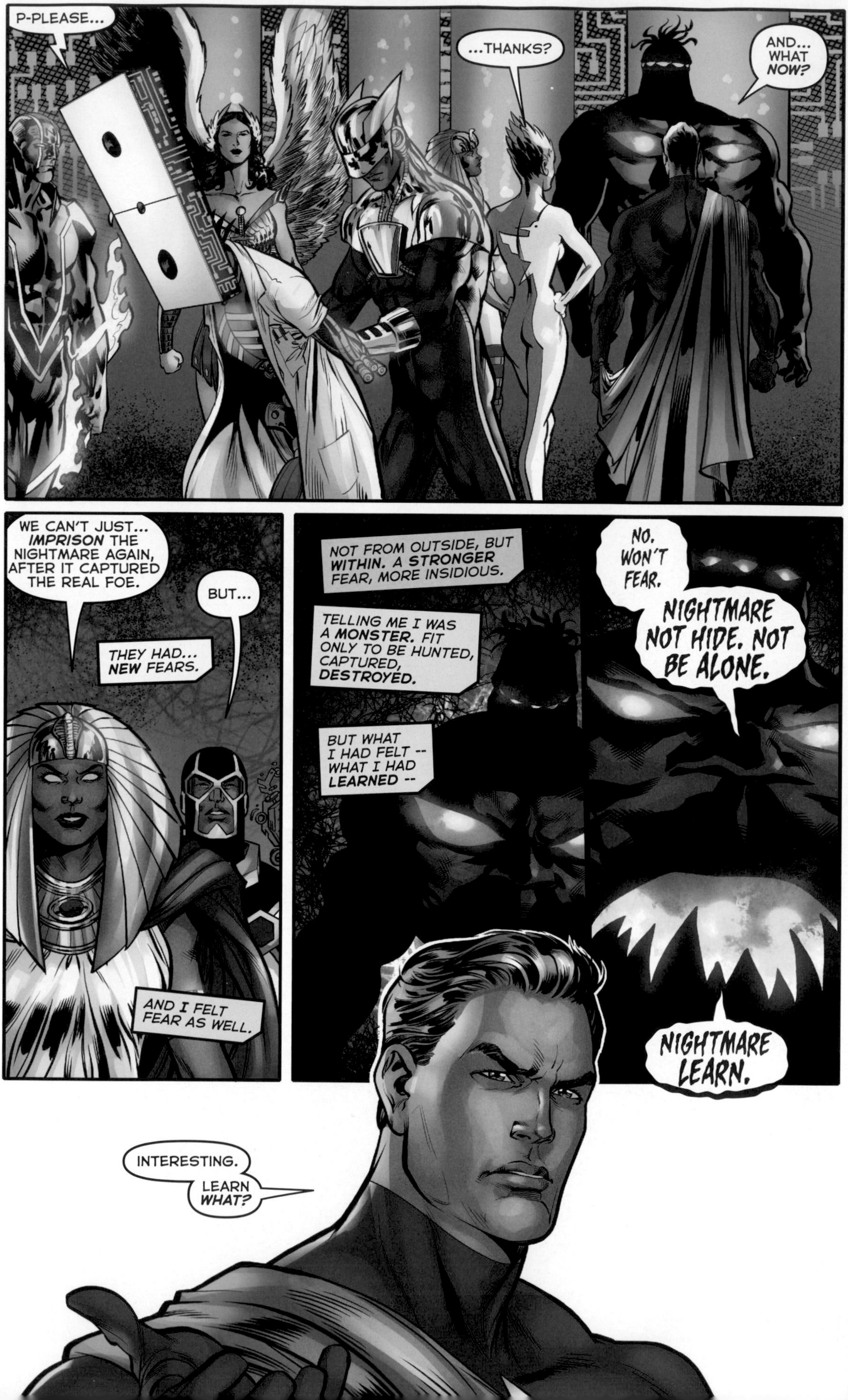
P-PLEASE...
...THANKS?
AND... WHAT NOW?
WE CAN'T JUST... IMPRISON THE NIGHTMARE AGAIN, AFTER IT CAPTURED THE REAL FOE.
BUT...
THEY HAD... NEW FEARS.
AND I FELT FEAR AS WELL.
NOT FROM OUTSIDE, BUT WITHIN. A STRONGER FEAR, MORE INSIDIOUS.
TELLING ME I WAS A MONSTER. FIT ONLY TO BE HUNTED, CAPTURED, DESTROYED.
BUT WHAT I HAD FELT -- WHAT I HAD LEARNED --
NO. WON'T FEAR.
NIGHTMARE NOT HIDE. NOT BE ALONE.
NIGHTMARE LEARN.
INTERESTING.
LEARN WHAT?

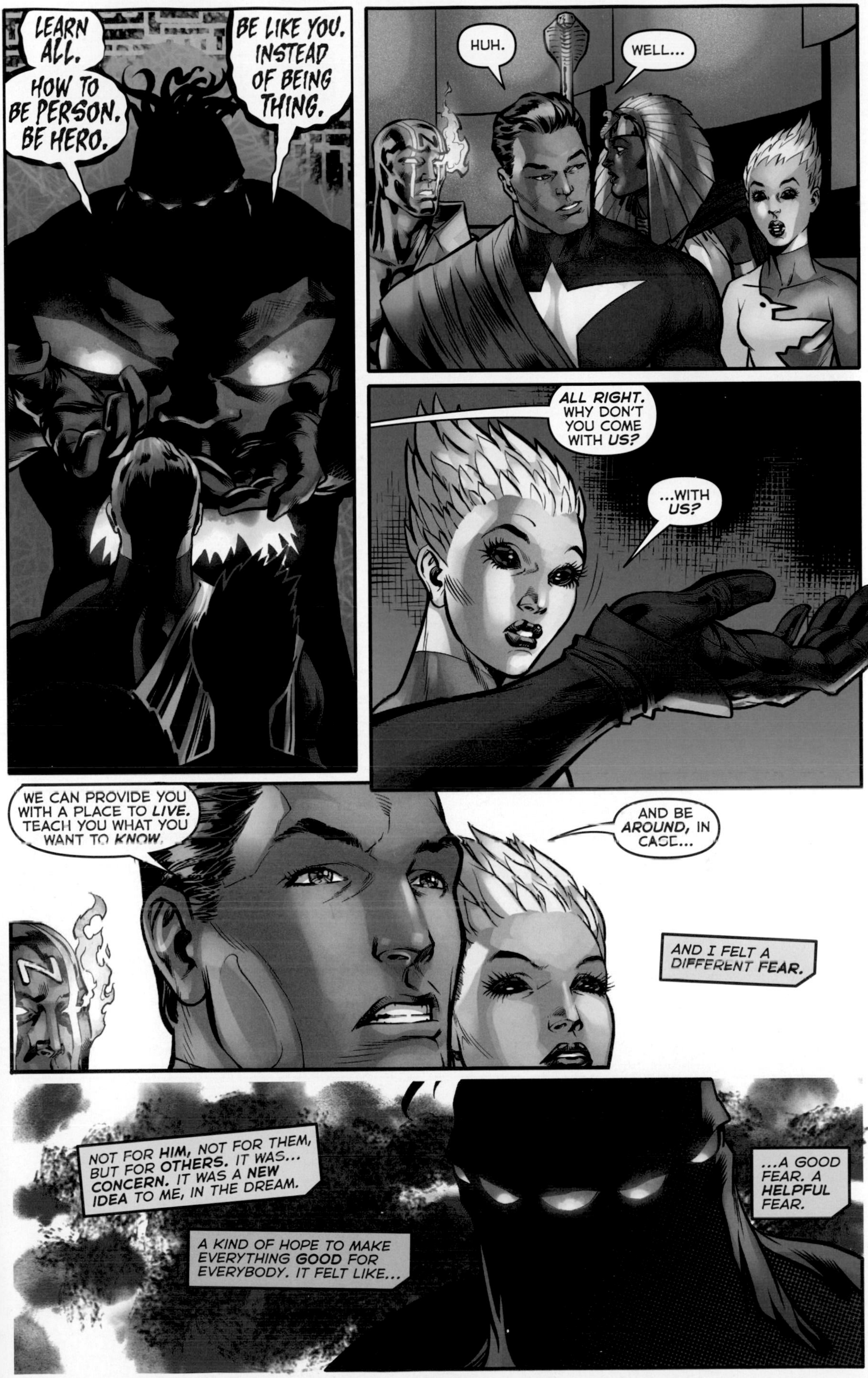
LEARN ALL. HOW TO BE PERSON. BE HERO.
BE LIKE YOU. INSTEAD OF BEING THING.
HUH.
WELL...
ALL RIGHT. WHY DON'T YOU COME WITH US?
...WITH US?
WE CAN PROVIDE YOU WITH A PLACE TO LIVE. TEACH YOU WHAT YOU WANT TO KNOW.
AND BE AROUND, IN CASE...
AND I FELT A DIFFERENT FEAR.
NOT FOR HIM, NOT FOR THEM, BUT FOR OTHERS. IT WAS... CONCERN. IT WAS A NEW IDEA TO ME, IN THE DREAM.
A KIND OF HOPE TO MAKE EVERYTHING GOOD FOR EVERYBODY. IT FELT LIKE...
...A GOOD FEAR. A HELPFUL FEAR.

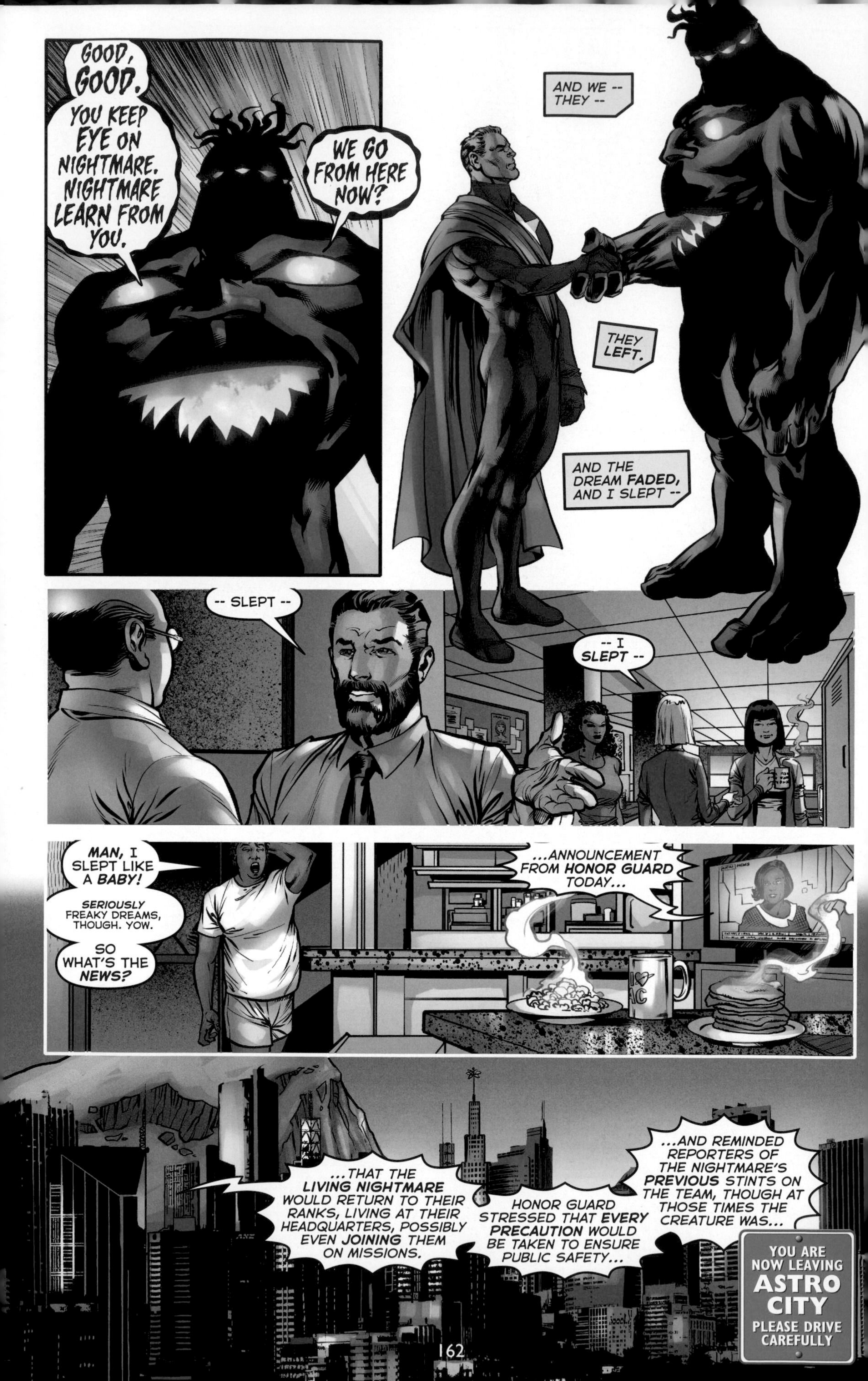
GOOD, GOOD.
YOU KEEP EYE ON NIGHTMARE. NIGHTMARE LEARN FROM YOU.
WE GO FROM HERE NOW?
AND WE -- THEY --
THEY LEFT.
AND THE DREAM FADED, AND I SLEPT --
-- SLEPT --
-- I SLEPT --
MAN, I SLEPT LIKE A BABY!
SERIOUSLY FREAKY DREAMS, THOUGH. YOW.
SO WHAT'S THE NEWS?
...ANNOUNCEMENT FROM HONOR GUARD TODAY...
...THAT THE LIVING NIGHTMARE WOULD RETURN TO THEIR RANKS, LIVING AT THEIR HEADQUARTERS, POSSIBLY EVEN JOINING THEM ON MISSIONS.
HONOR GUARD STRESSED THAT EVERY PRECAUTION WOULD BE TAKEN TO ENSURE PUBLIC SAFETY...
...AND REMINDED REPORTERS OF THE NIGHTMARE'S PREVIOUS STINTS ON THE TEAM, THOUGH AT THOSE TIMES THE CREATURE WAS...
YOU ARE NOW LEAVING ASTRO CITY PLEASE DRIVE CAREFULLY

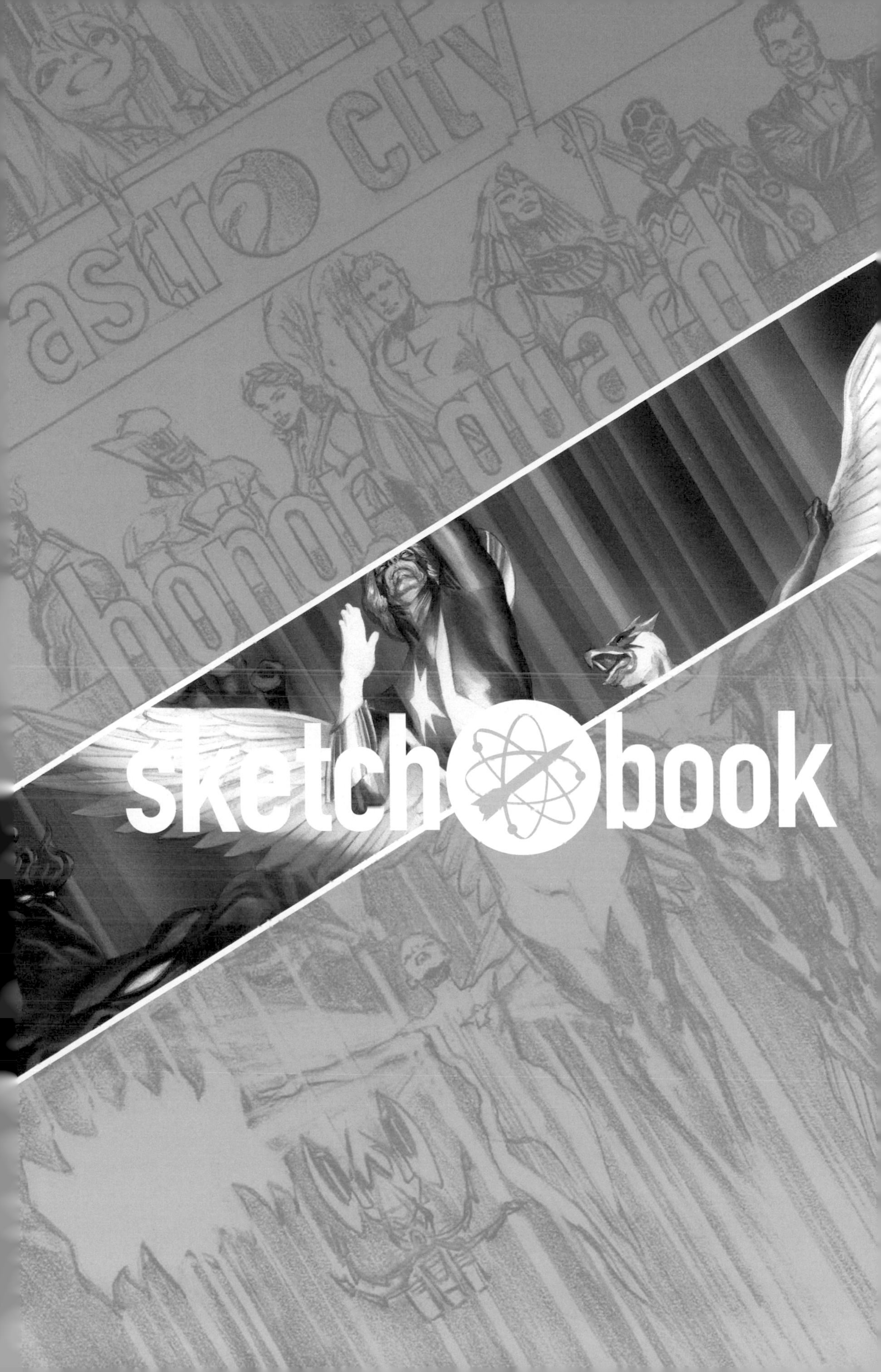
astro city
sketchbook

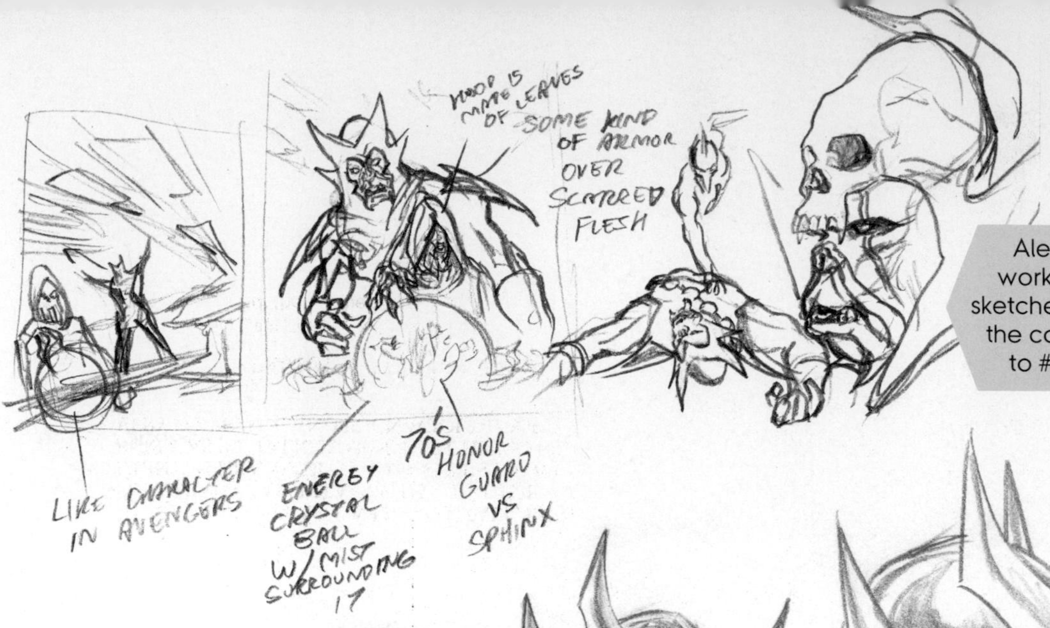
HOOP IS MADE OF LEAVES
SOME KIND OF ARMOR OVER SCARRED FLESH
LIKE CHARACTER IN AVENGERS
ENERGY CRYSTAL BALL W/ MIST SURROUNDING 17
70's HONOR GUARD VS SPHINX

Alex's working sketches for the cover to #17.

For Krigari Ironhand, we needed a look that could go through "evolutions" as Krigari himself did—from desperate, naked survivor to barbarian reaver to the ruler of a worlds-spanning empire and commander of a star fleet.

krigari

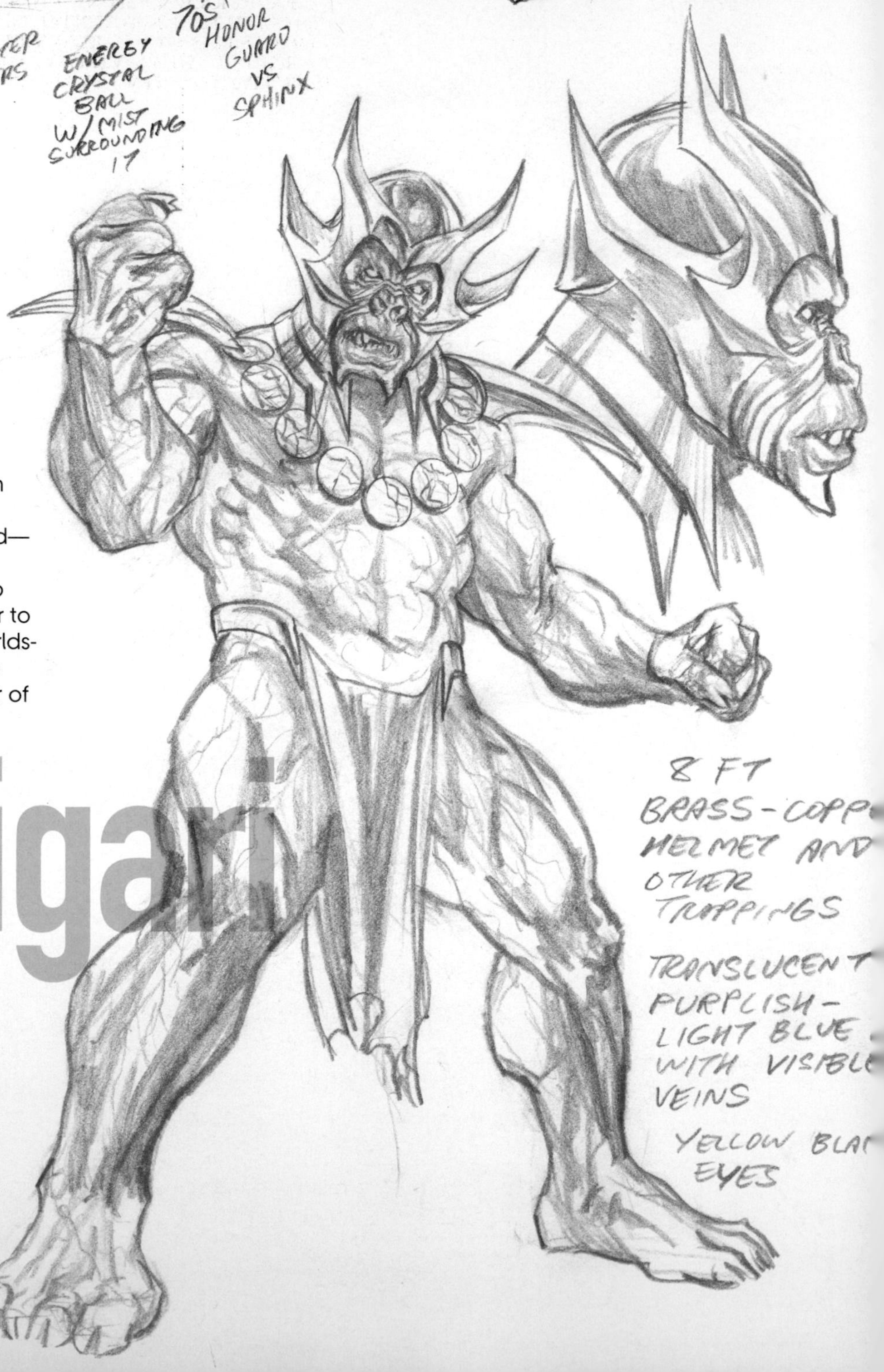
8 FT
BRASS-COPP
HELMET AND
OTHER
TRAPPINGS
TRANSLUCENT
PURPLISH-
LIGHT BLUE
WITH VISIBL
VEINS
YELLOW BLA
EYES

Alex started, roughly, with an ape-like figure, and built a versatile design that Tom Grummett, the penciler of #17, could ring changes on as needed.

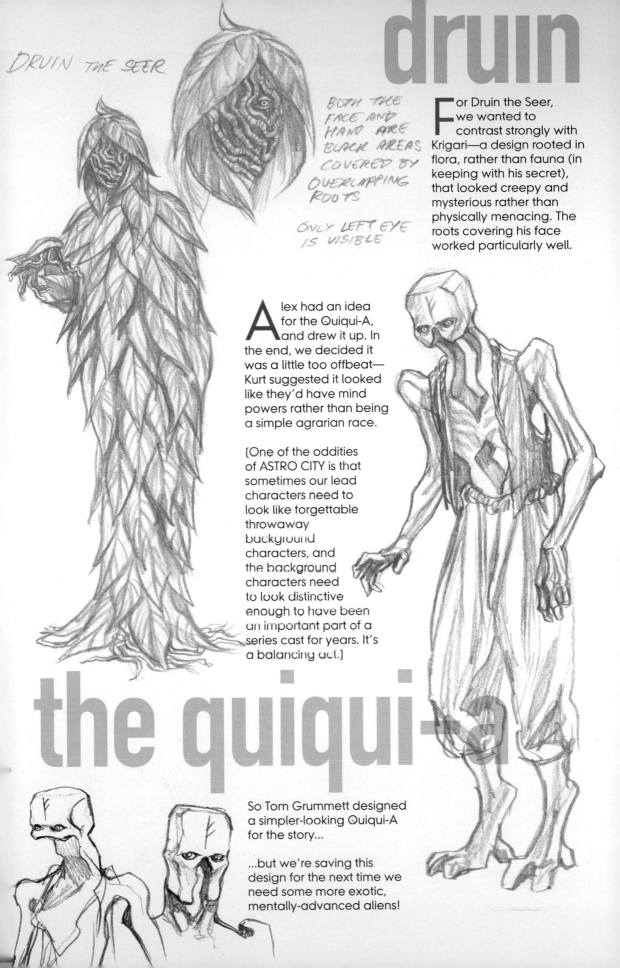

druin

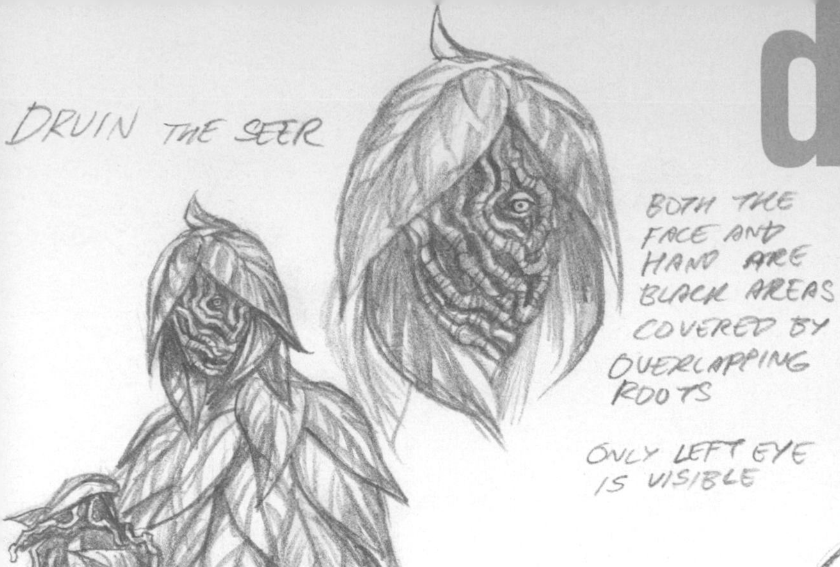
DRUIN THE SEER
BOTH THE FACE AND HAND ARE BLACK AREAS COVERED BY OVERLAPPING ROOTS
ONLY LEFT EYE IS VISIBLE

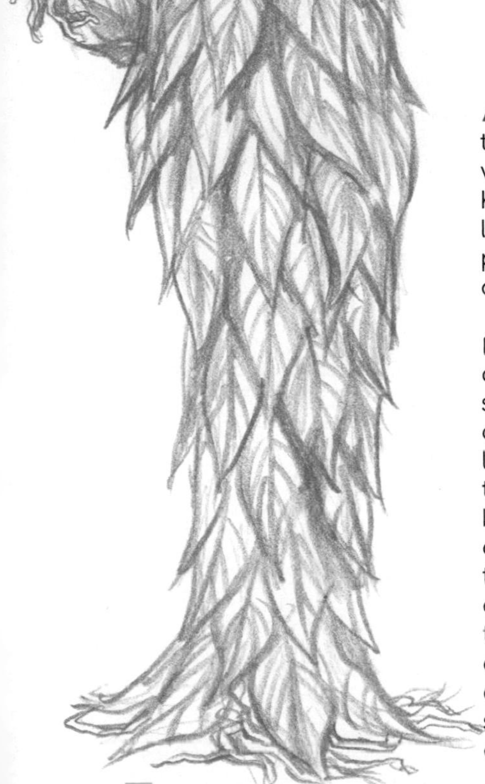

For Druin the Seer, we wanted to contrast strongly with Krigari—a design rooted in flora, rather than fauna (in keeping with his secret), that looked creepy and mysterious rather than physically menacing. The roots covering his face worked particularly well.

Alex had an idea for the Quiqui-A, and drew it up. In the end, we decided it was a little too offbeat—Kurt suggested it looked like they'd have mind powers rather than being a simple agrarian race.

(One of the oddities of ASTRO CITY is that sometimes our lead characters need to look like forgettable throwaway background characters, and the background characters need to look distinctive enough to have been an important part of a series cast for years. It's a balancing act.)

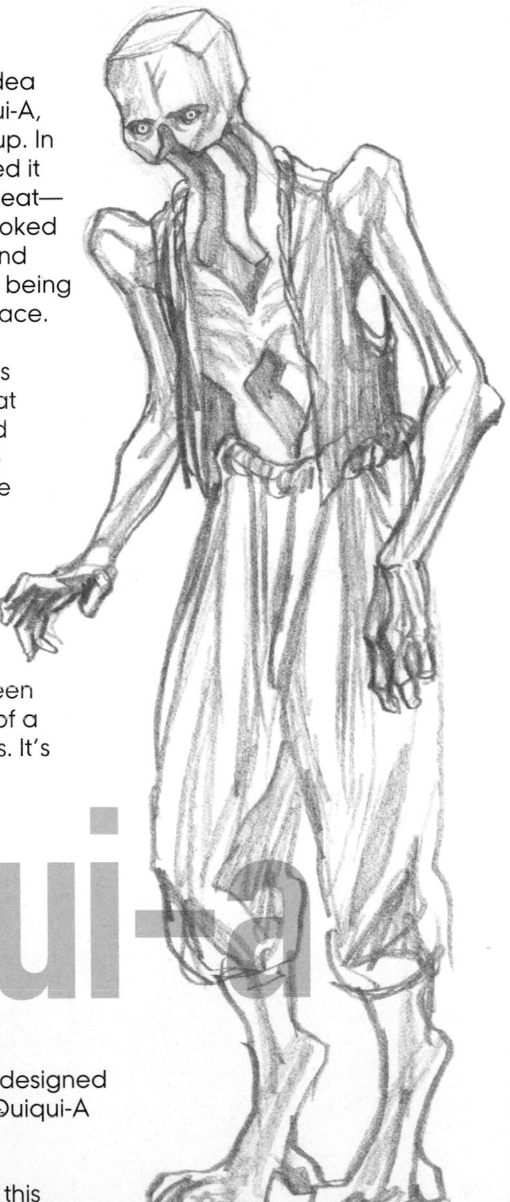

the quiqui-a

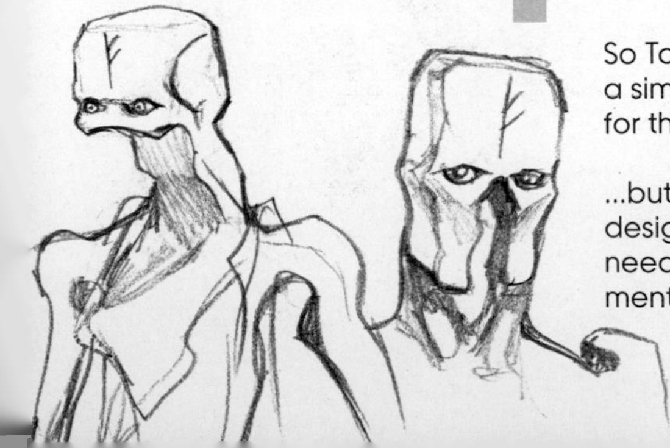

So Tom Grummett designed a simpler-looking Quiqui-A for the story...

...but we're saving this design for the next time we need some more exotic, mentally-advanced aliens!

Our interstellar hero, Starfighter, had looked slick and cosmic in his 1970s-era appearances, but now we needed him to look and feel old and weathered, like an aging gunfighter...

SONS OF ANARCHY LOOK

DUE ON THE 15th!

WIZENED OLD WIZARD VERSION OF SQURAMO PONY TAIL SAM NEILL

SHE'S OLDER TOO 52

BANSOOM BACKGROUND FLYING CREATURES VEGETATION

Starfighter

For the next generation of Starfighters, Kurt gave Jesús Merino rough descriptions, and Jesús worked magic with them.

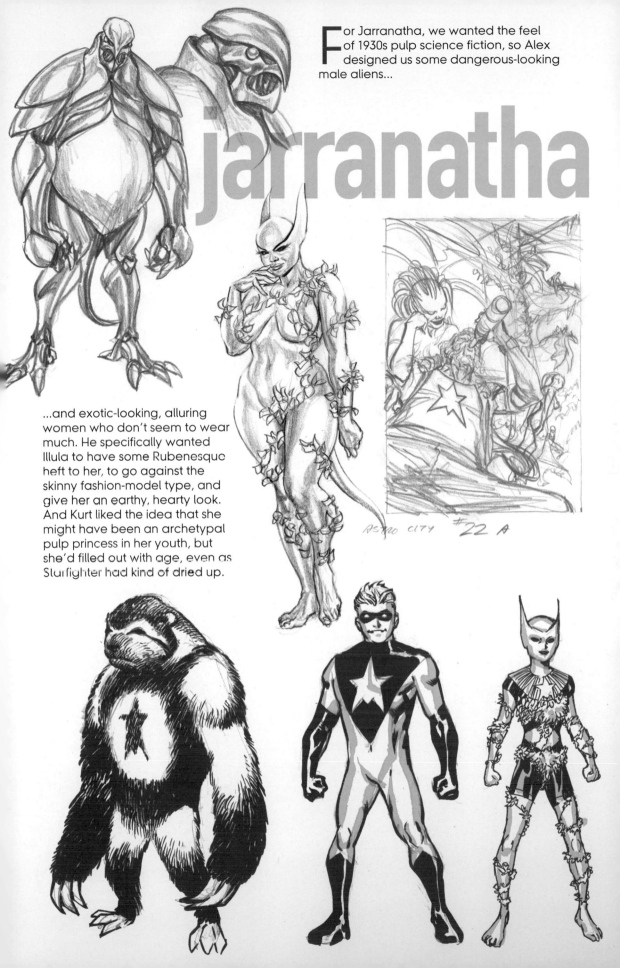

For Jarranatha, we wanted the feel of 1930s pulp science fiction, so Alex designed us some dangerous-looking male aliens...

jarranatha

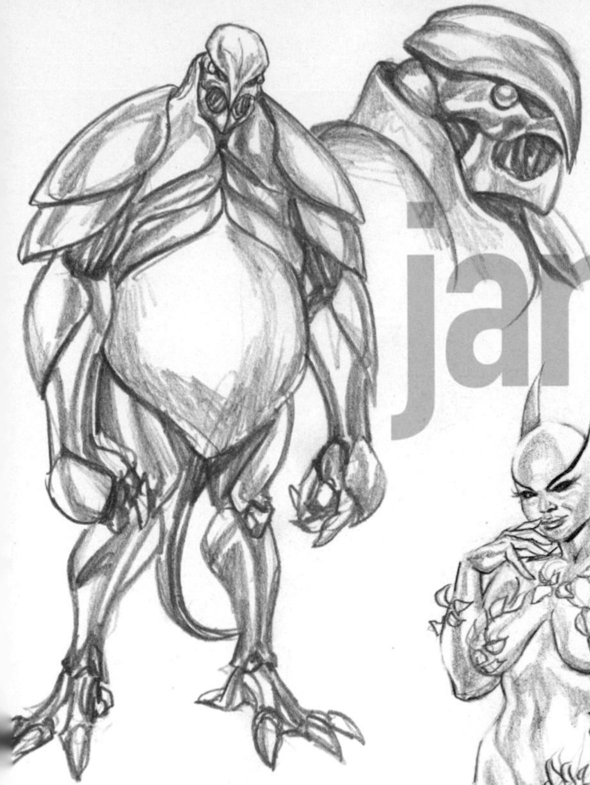

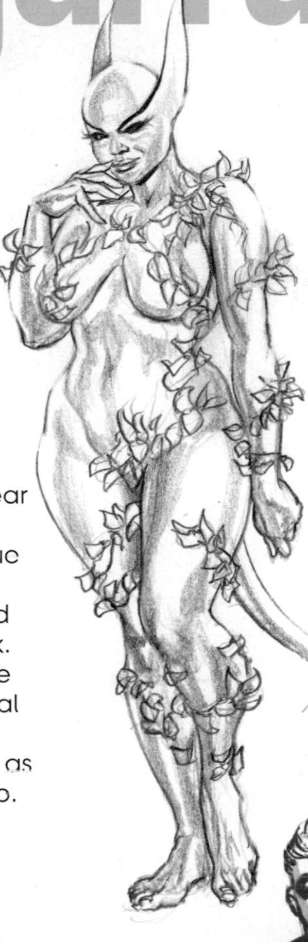

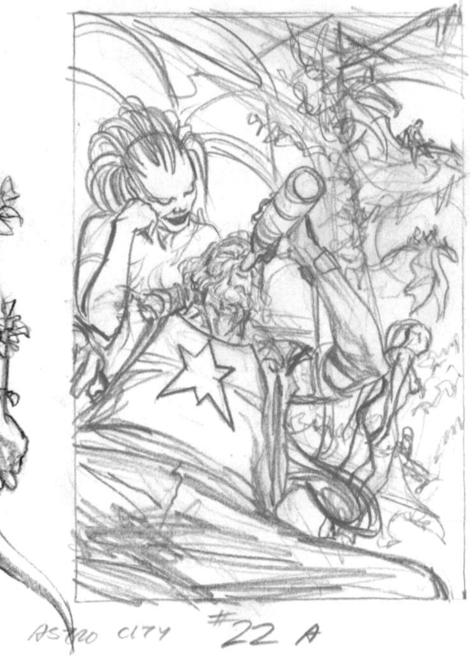
ASTRO CITY #22 A

...and exotic-looking, alluring women who don't seem to wear much. He specifically wanted Illula to have some Rubenesque heft to her, to go against the skinny fashion-model type, and give her an earthy, hearty look. And Kurt liked the idea that she might have been an archetypal pulp princess in her youth, but she'd filled out with age, even as Starfighter had kind of dried up.

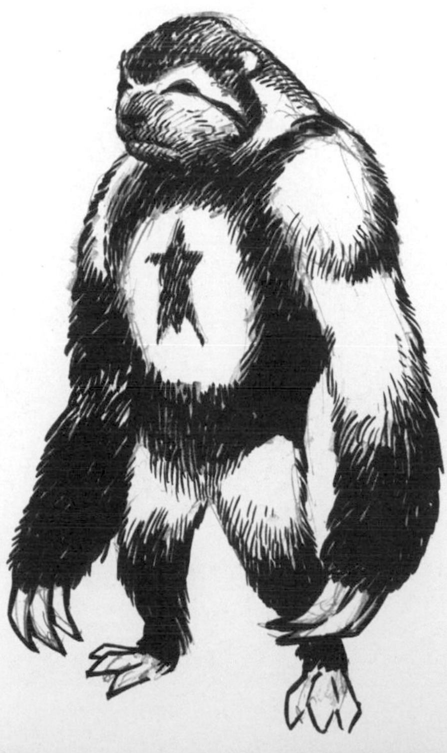

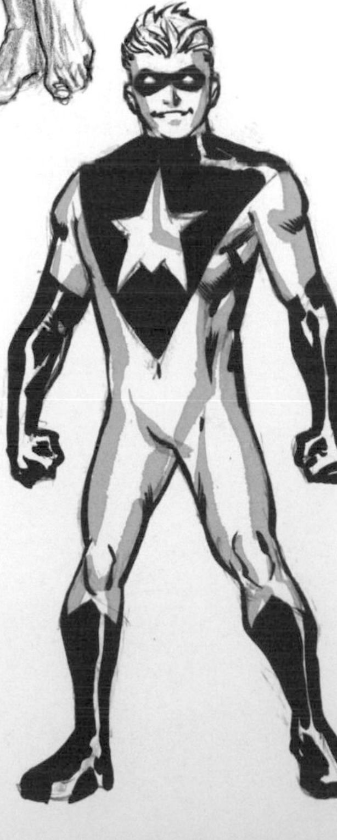

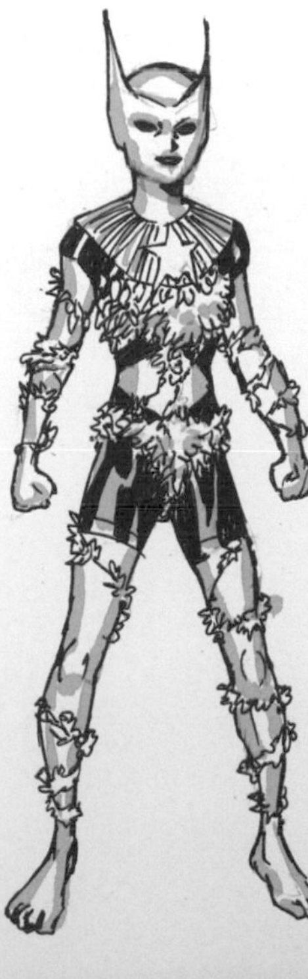

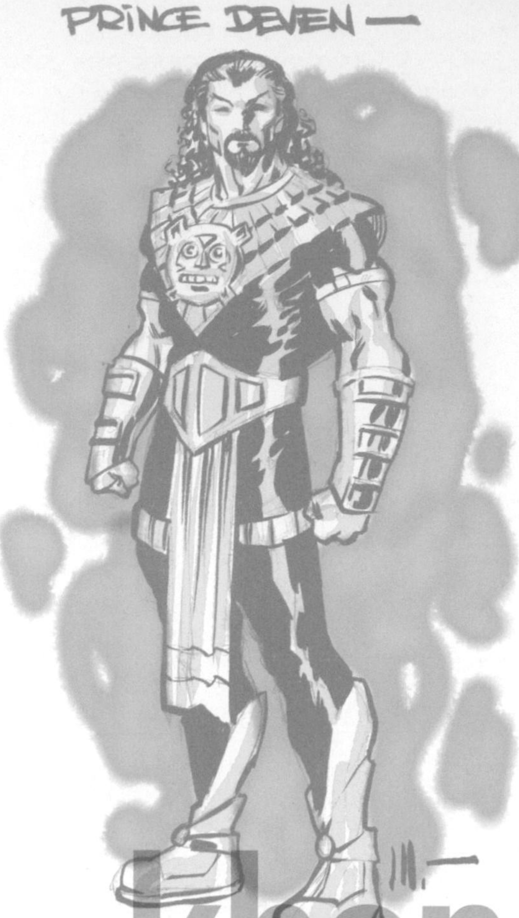
PRINCE DEVEN —

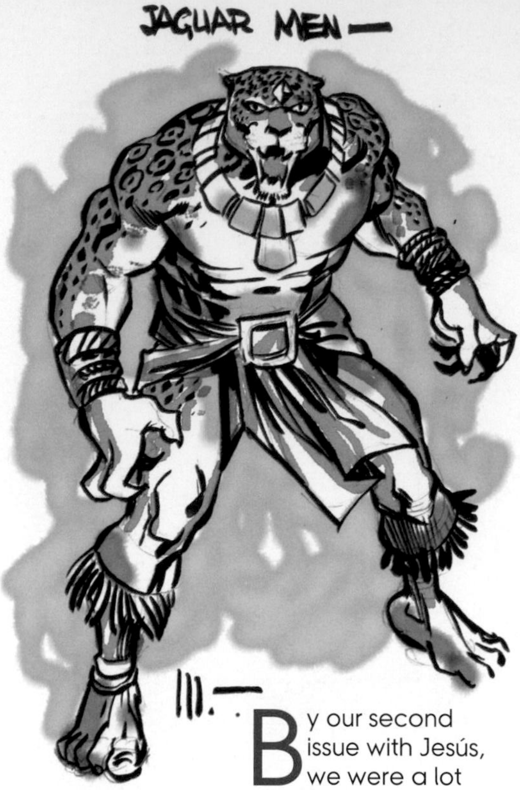
JAGUAR MEN —

By our second issue with Jesús, we were a lot more comfortable throwing character design work at him.

khapak iqun

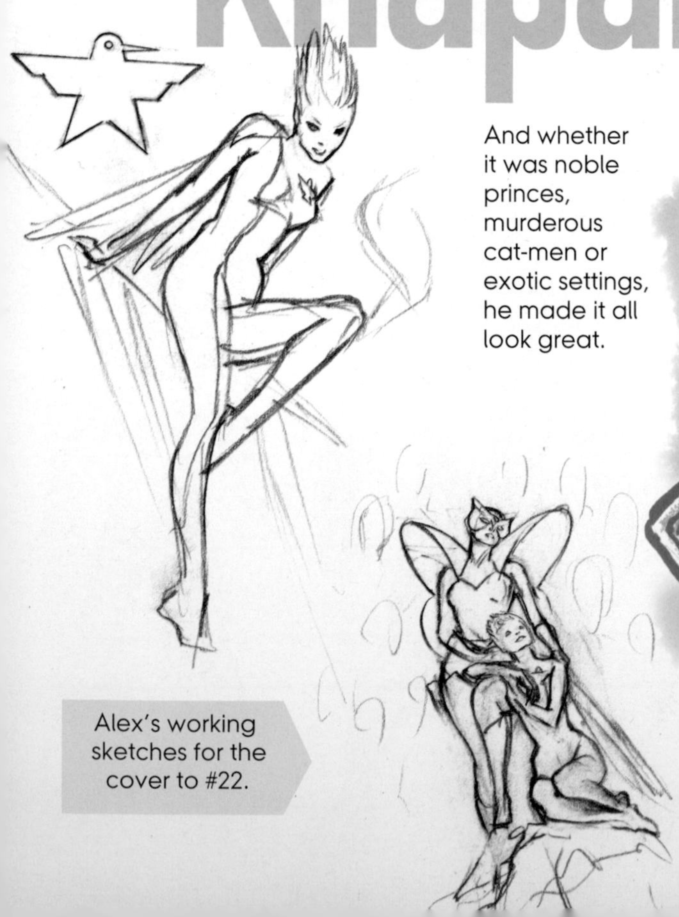

And whether it was noble princes, murderous cat-men or exotic settings, he made it all look great.

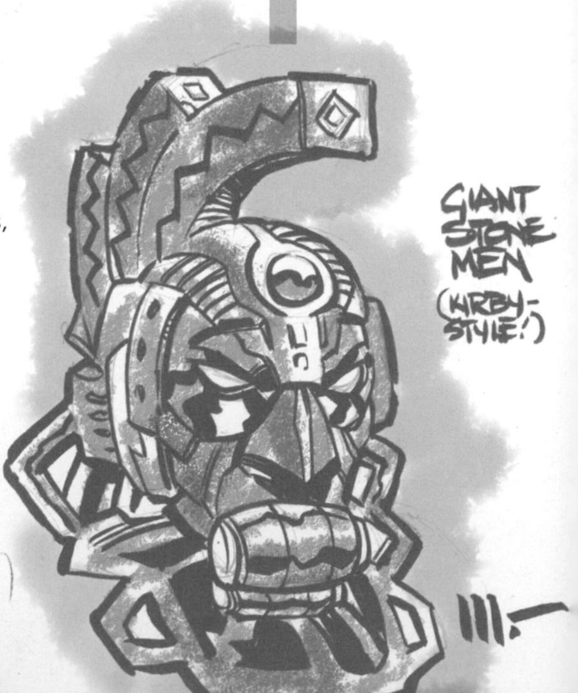
GIANT STONE MEN
(KIRBY-STYLE!)

Alex's working sketches for the cover to #22.

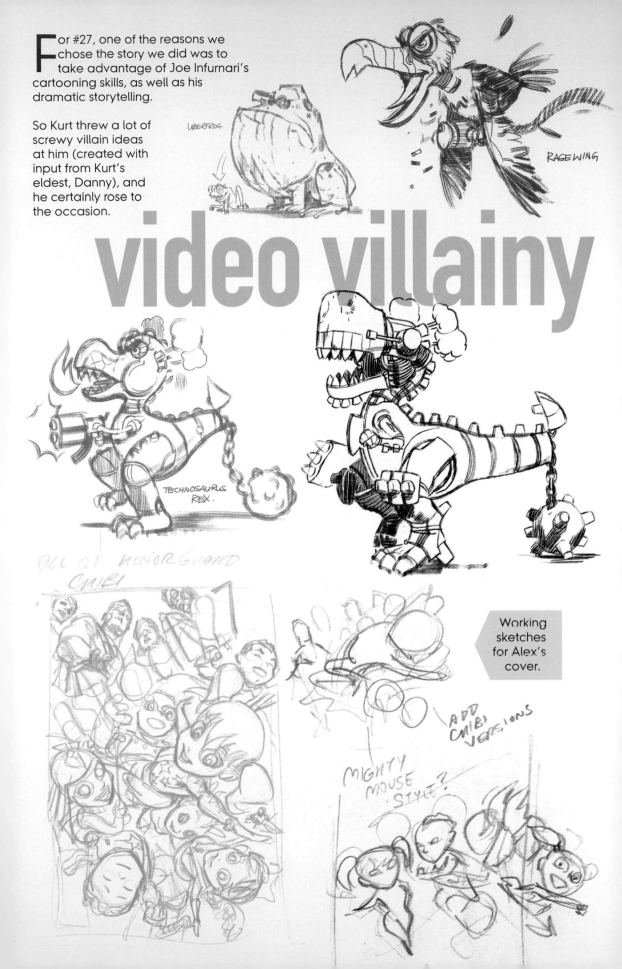

For #27, one of the reasons we chose the story we did was to take advantage of Joe Infurnari's cartooning skills, as well as his dramatic storytelling.

So Kurt threw a lot of screwy villain ideas at him (created with input from Kurt's eldest, Danny), and he certainly rose to the occasion.

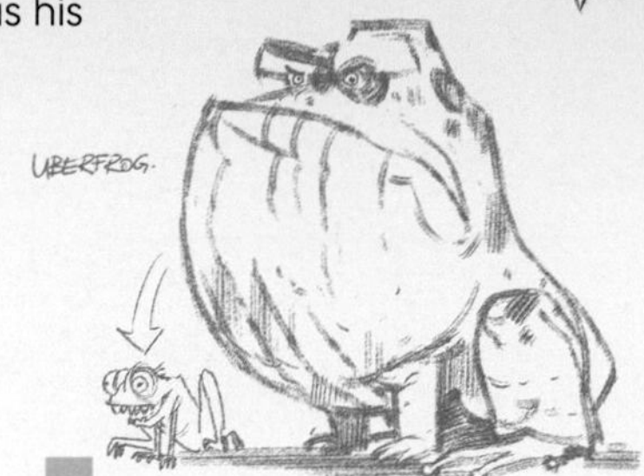
UBERFROG.

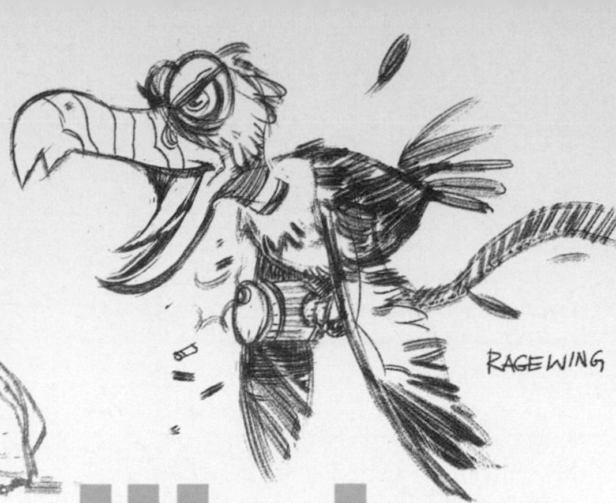
RAGEWING

video villainy

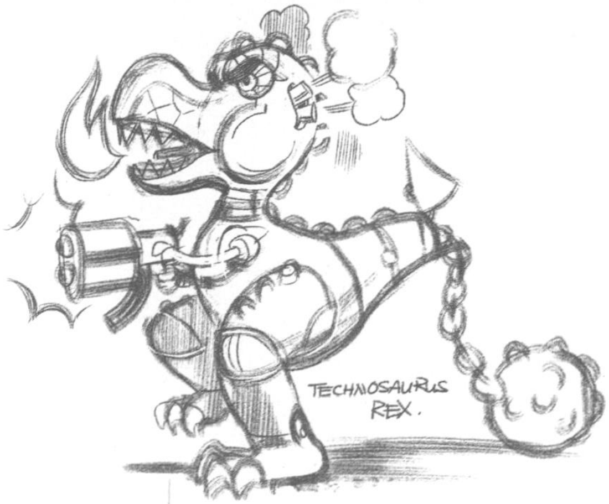
TECHNOSAURUS REX.

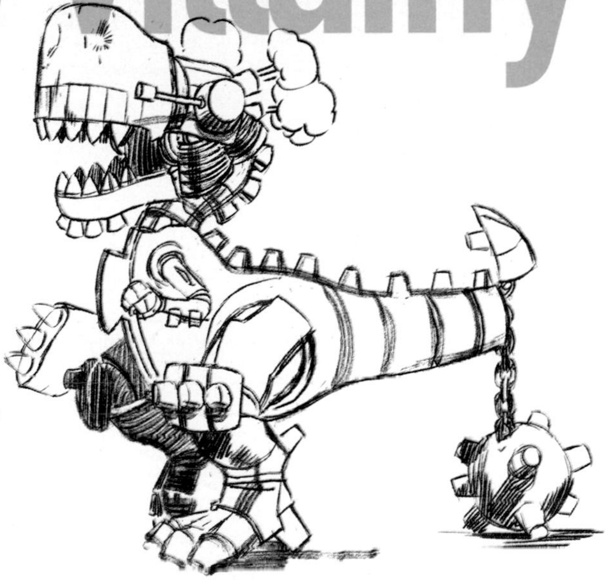

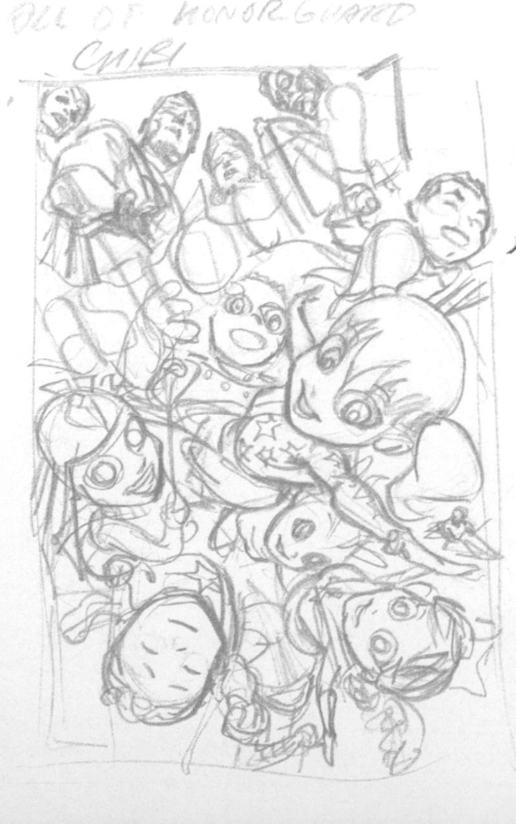
HONOR GUARD
CHIBI

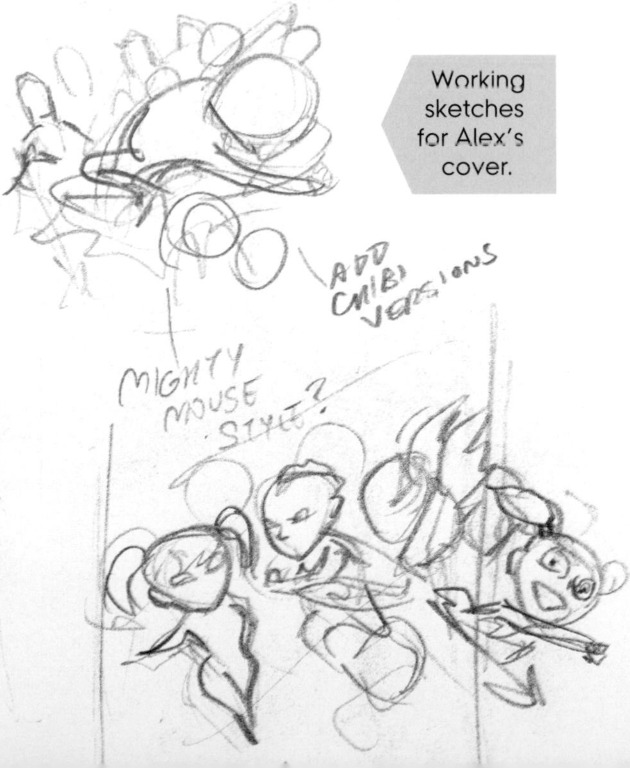
ADD CHIBI VERSIONS
MIGHTY MOUSE STYLE?

Working sketches for Alex's cover.

Issue #28 was designed for Australian artist Gary Chaloner's particular skills, as well. We asked him to design an entire 1980s cartoon superteam, one that was deliberately cheesy and built on cultural stereotypes, but still appealing. Not an easy job.

Kurt and Gary spent days Skyping or e-mailing, figuring out characters who could feel like Australian clichés about Australia, rather than American clichés about Australia. A key difference!

Cap'n Cookaburra, the team leader, is a perfect example. Technically built on two shallow touchpoints—Captain James Cook and a kookaburra—the hero of New South Wales is actually designed as a professional wrestler gone to seed. Cheerful, relaxed, expansive.

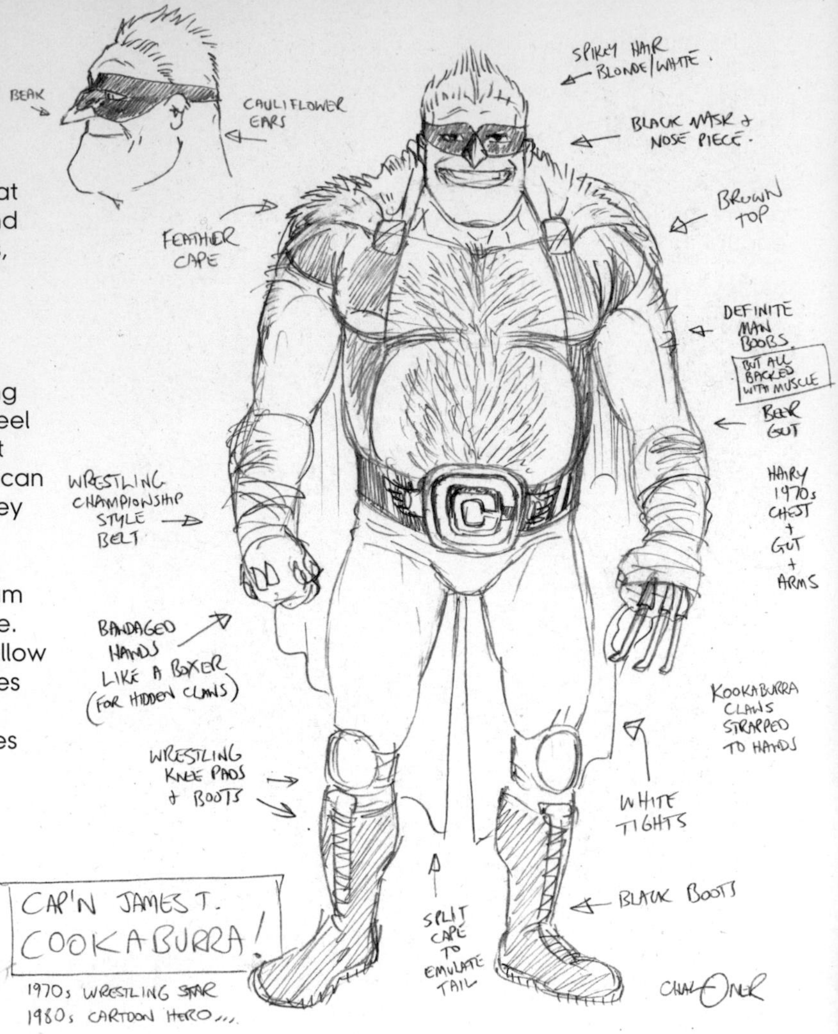
BEAK
CAULIFLOWER EARS
SPIKY HAIR BLONDE/WHITE.
BLACK MASK + NOSE PIECE.
BROWN TOP
FEATHER CAPE
DEFINITE MAN BOOBS.
BUT ALL BACKED WITH MUSCLE
BEER GUT
HAIRY 1970s CHEST + GUT + ARMS
WRESTLING CHAMPIONSHIP STYLE BELT
BANDAGED HANDS LIKE A BOXER (FOR HIDDEN CLAWS)
KOOKABURRA CLAWS STRAPPED TO HANDS
WRESTLING KNEE PADS + BOOTS
WHITE TIGHTS
BLACK BOOTS
SPLIT CAPE TO EMULATE TAIL
CAP'N JAMES T. COOKABURRA!
1970s WRESTLING STAR
1980s CARTOON HERO....
CHALONER

Alex's group "lunchbox art" shot, based on Gary's designs.

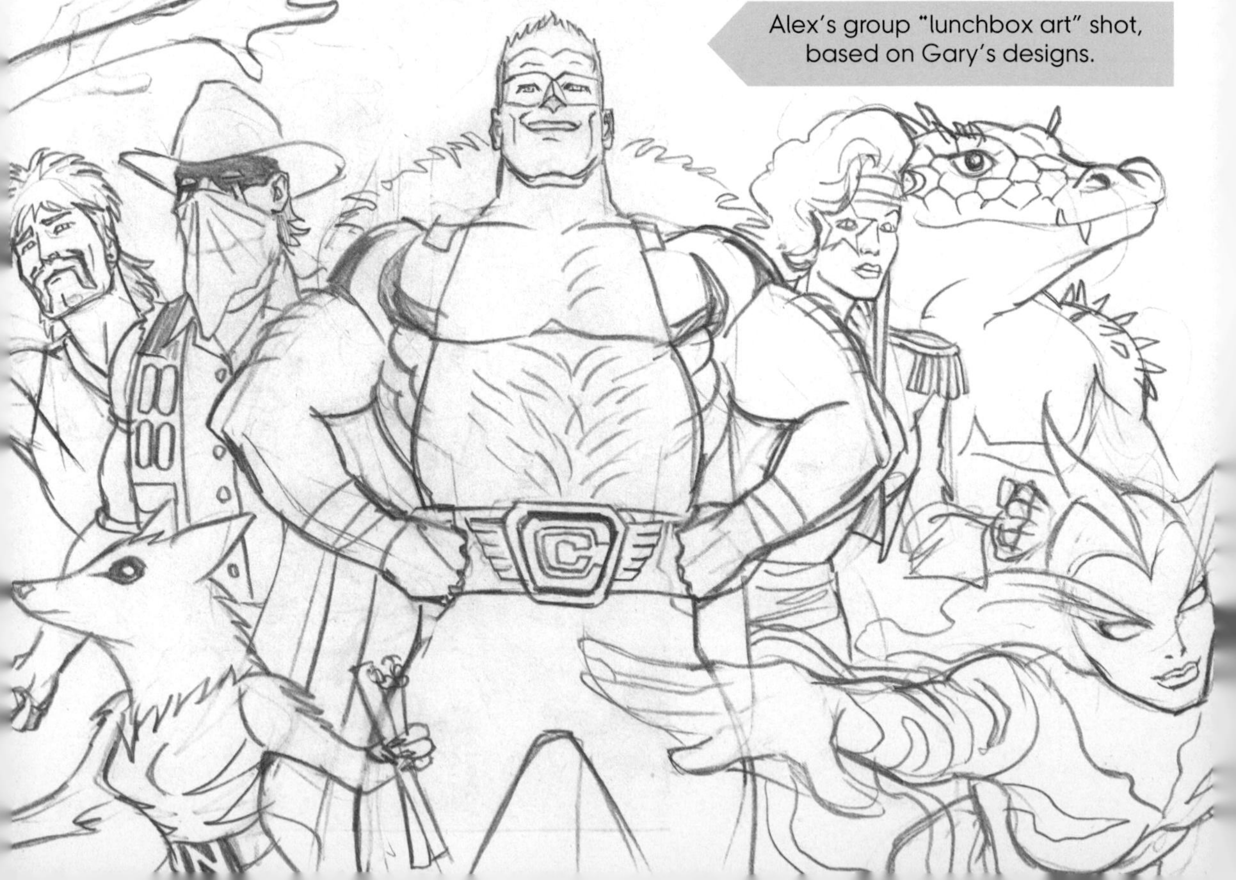

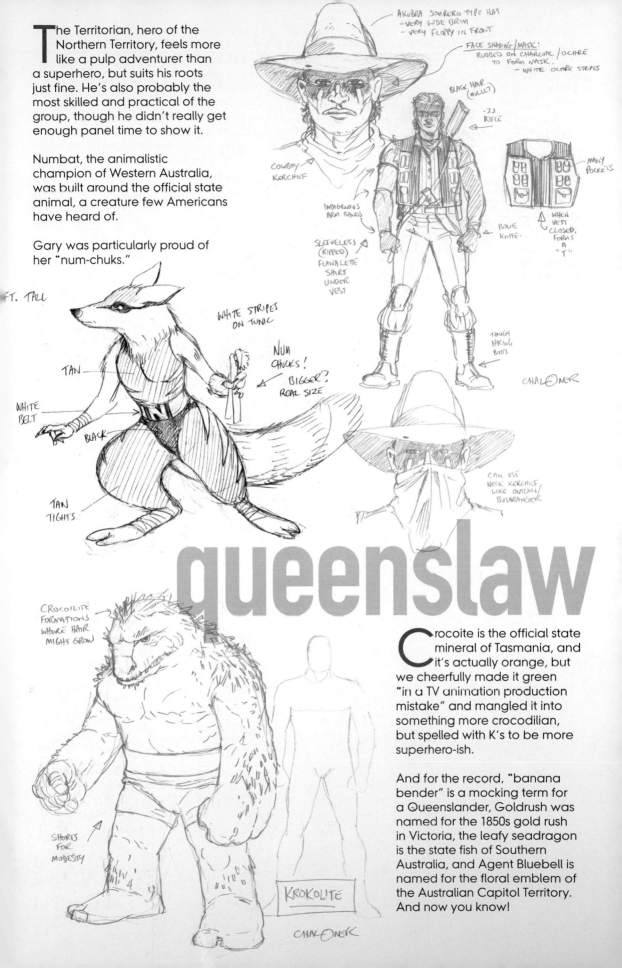

The Territorian, hero of the Northern Territory, feels more like a pulp adventurer than a superhero, but suits his roots just fine. He's also probably the most skilled and practical of the group, though he didn't really get enough panel time to show it.

Numbat, the animalistic champion of Western Australia, was built around the official state animal, a creature few Americans have heard of.

Gary was particularly proud of her "num-chuks."

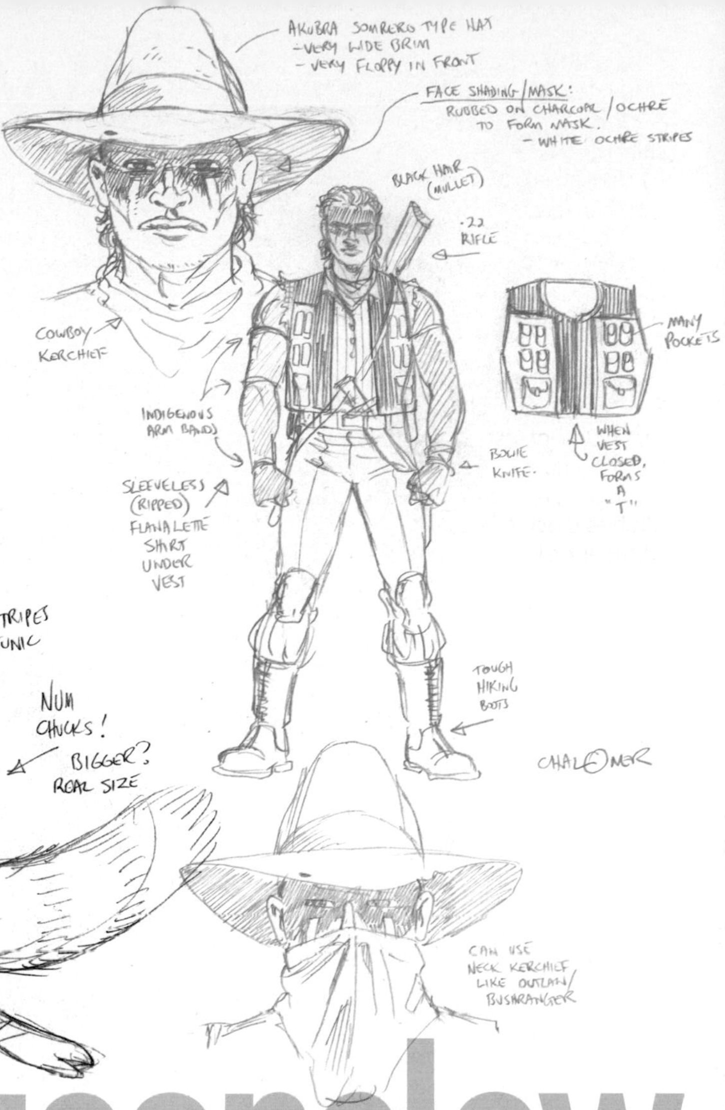
AKUBRA SOMBRERO TYPE HAT
- VERY WIDE BRIM
- VERY FLOPPY IN FRONT
FACE SHADING/MASK:
RUBBED ON CHARCOAL/OCHRE TO FORM MASK.
- WHITE OCHRE STRIPES
BLACK HAIR (MULLET)
.22 RIFLE
MANY POCKETS
COWBOY KERCHIEF
INDIGENOUS ARM BANDS
BOWIE KNIFE
WHEN VEST CLOSED, FORMS A "T"
SLEEVELESS (RIPPED) FLANNALETTE SHIRT UNDER VEST
TOUGH HIKING BOOTS
CHALONER
CAN USE NECK KERCHIEF LIKE OUTLAW/ BUSHRANGER

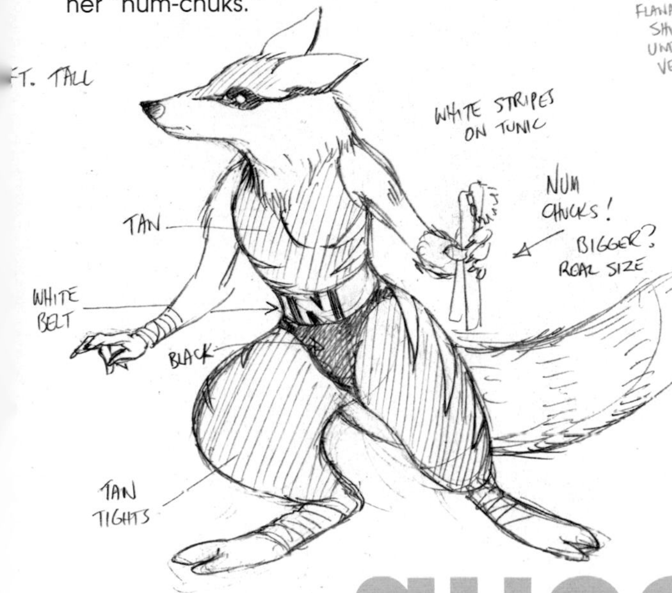
FT. TALL
WHITE STRIPES ON TUNIC
NUM CHUCKS!
BIGGER? REAL SIZE
TAN
WHITE BELT
BLACK
TAN TIGHTS

queenslaw

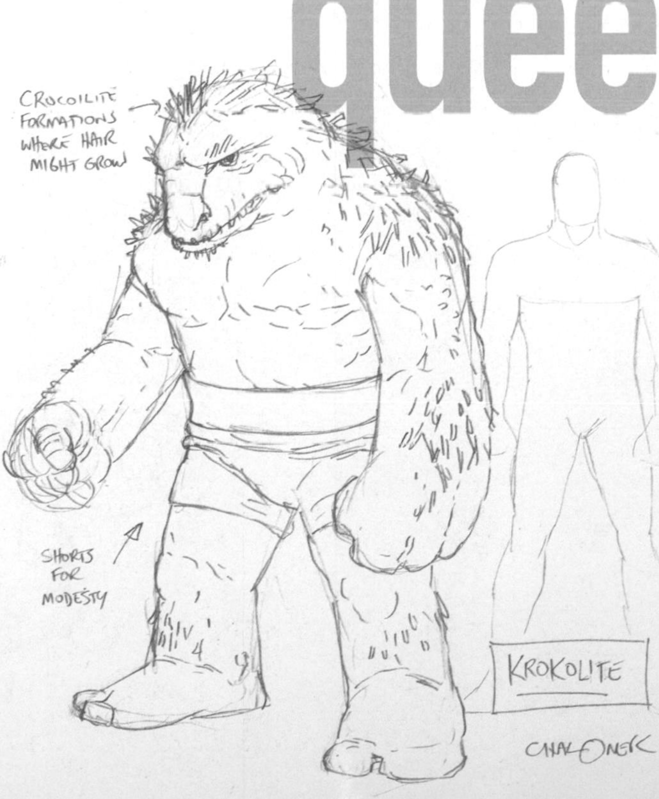
CROCOILITE FORMATIONS WHERE HAIR MIGHT GROW
SHORTS FOR MODESTY
KROKOLITE
CHALONER

Crocoite is the official state mineral of Tasmania, and it's actually orange, but we cheerfully made it green "in a TV animation production mistake" and mangled it into something more crocodilian, but spelled with K's to be more superhero-ish.

And for the record, "banana bender" is a mocking term for a Queenslander, Goldrush was named for the 1850s gold rush in Victoria, the leafy seadragon is the state fish of Southern Australia, and Agent Bluebell is named for the floral emblem of the Australian Capitol Territory. And now you know!

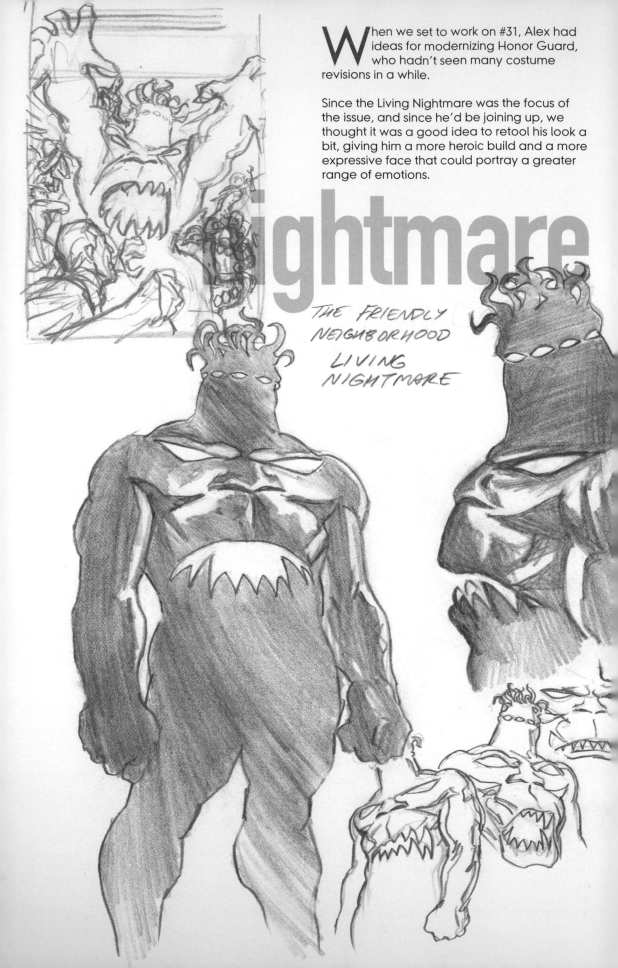

When we set to work on #31, Alex had ideas for modernizing Honor Guard, who hadn't seen many costume revisions in a while.

Since the Living Nightmare was the focus of the issue, and since he'd be joining up, we thought it was a good idea to retool his look a bit, giving him a more heroic build and a more expressive face that could portray a greater range of emotions.

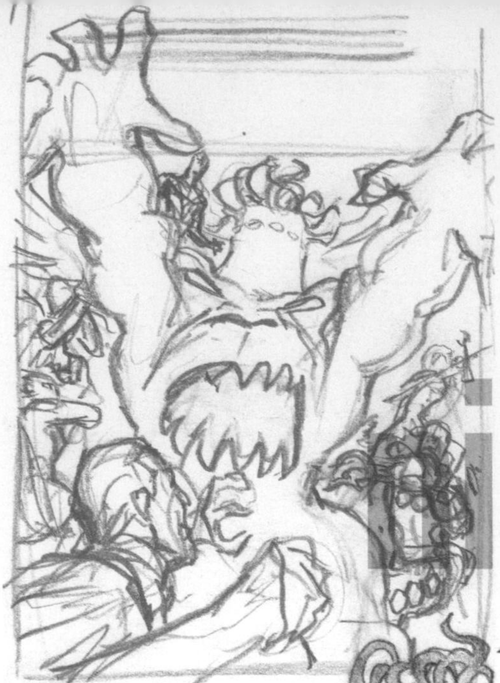

ightmare

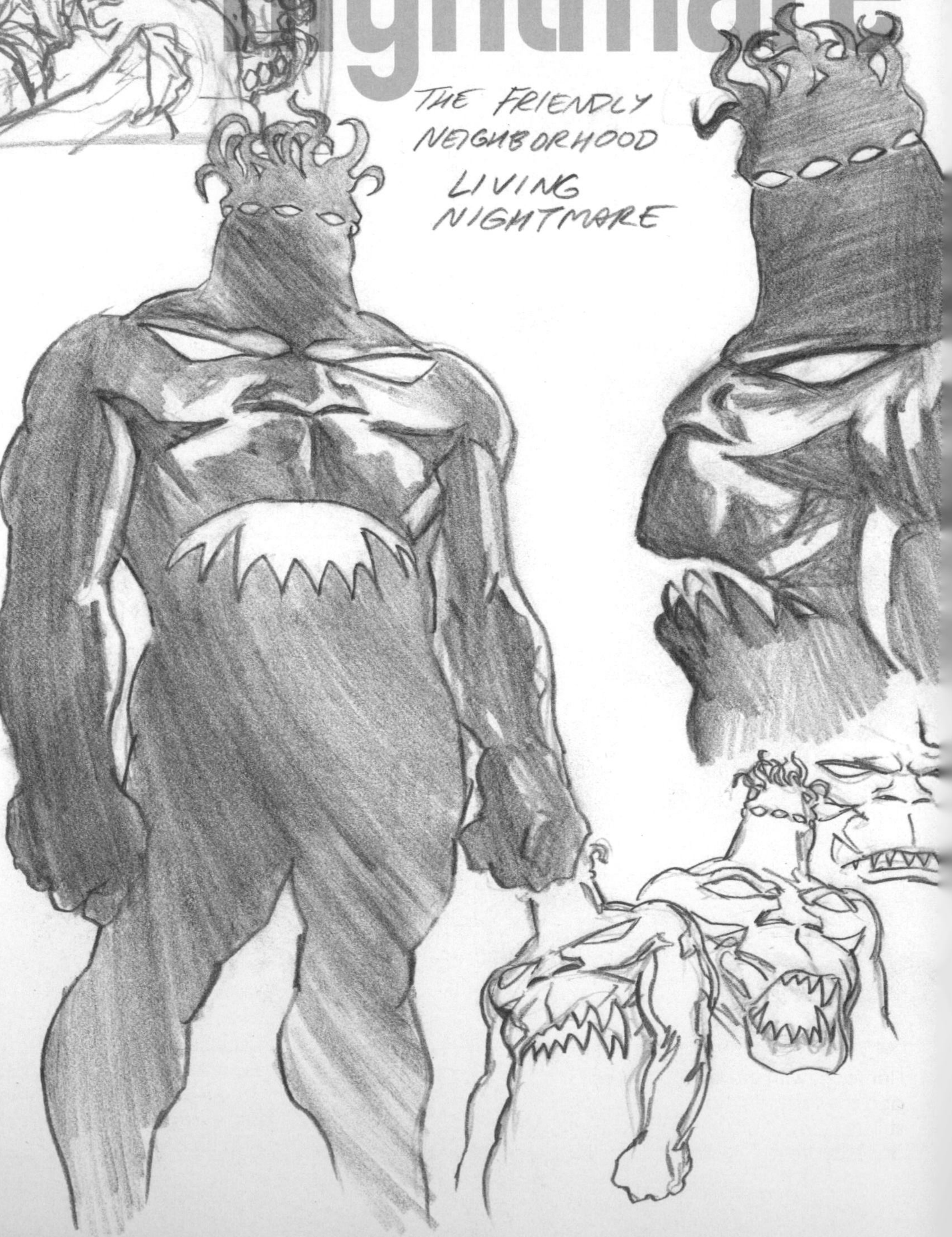
THE FRIENDLY
NEIGHBORHOOD
LIVING
NIGHTMARE

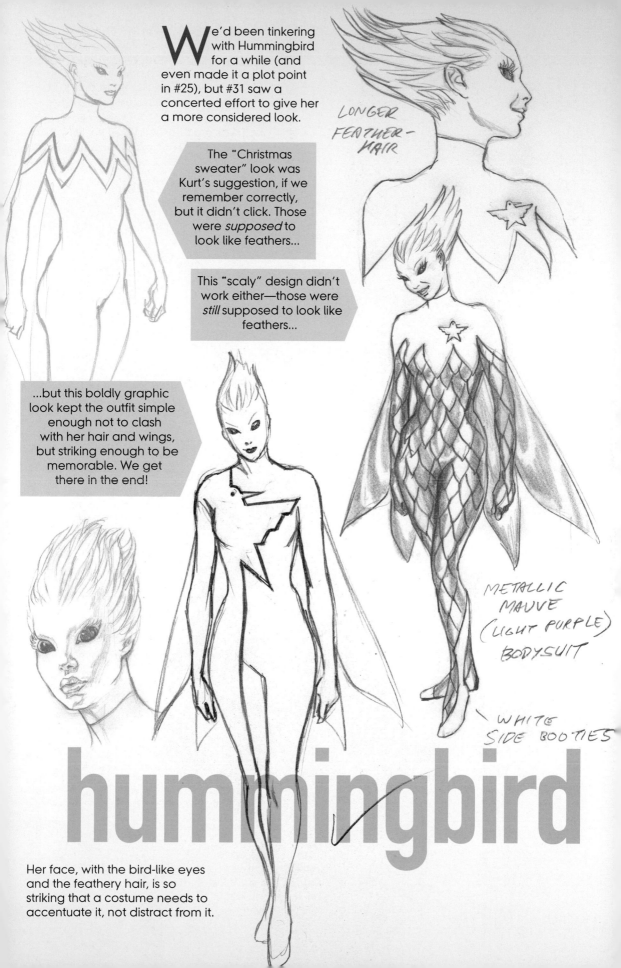

We'd been tinkering with Hummingbird for a while (and even made it a plot point in #25), but #31 saw a concerted effort to give her a more considered look.

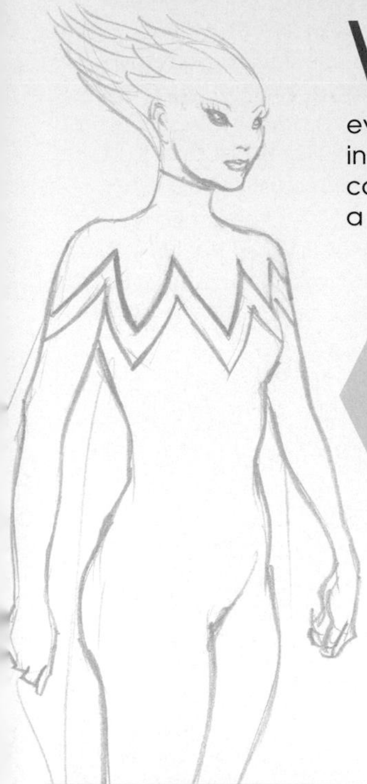

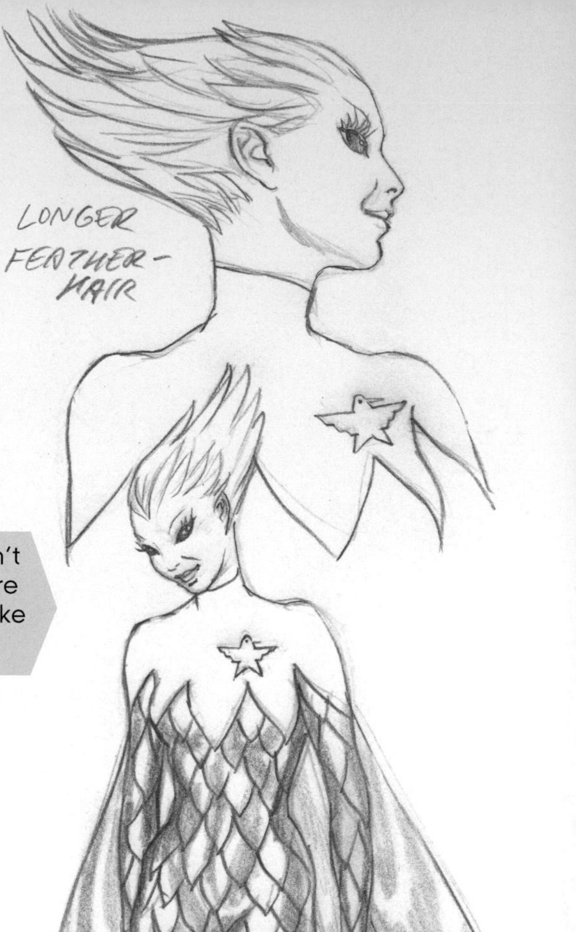
LONGER
FEATHER-
HAIR
METALLIC
MAUVE
(LIGHT PURPLE)
BODYSUIT
WHITE
SIDE BOOTIES

The "Christmas sweater" look was Kurt's suggestion, if we remember correctly, but it didn't click. Those were *supposed* to look like feathers...

This "scaly" design didn't work either—those were *still* supposed to look like feathers...

...but this boldly graphic look kept the outfit simple enough not to clash with her hair and wings, but striking enough to be memorable. We get there in the end!

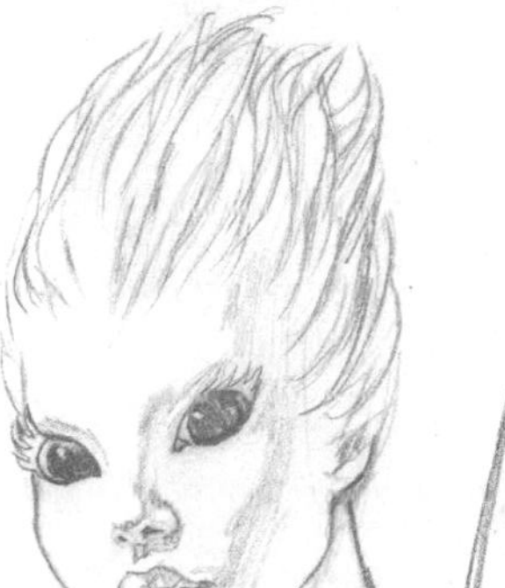

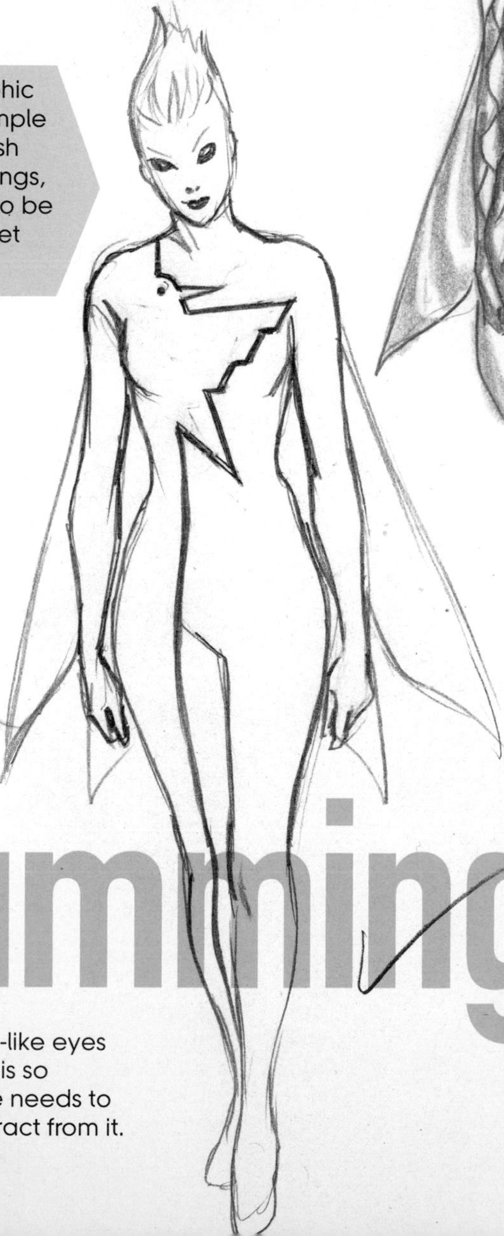

hummingbird

Her face, with the bird-like eyes and the feathery hair, is so striking that a costume needs to accentuate it, not distract from it.

the assemblyman

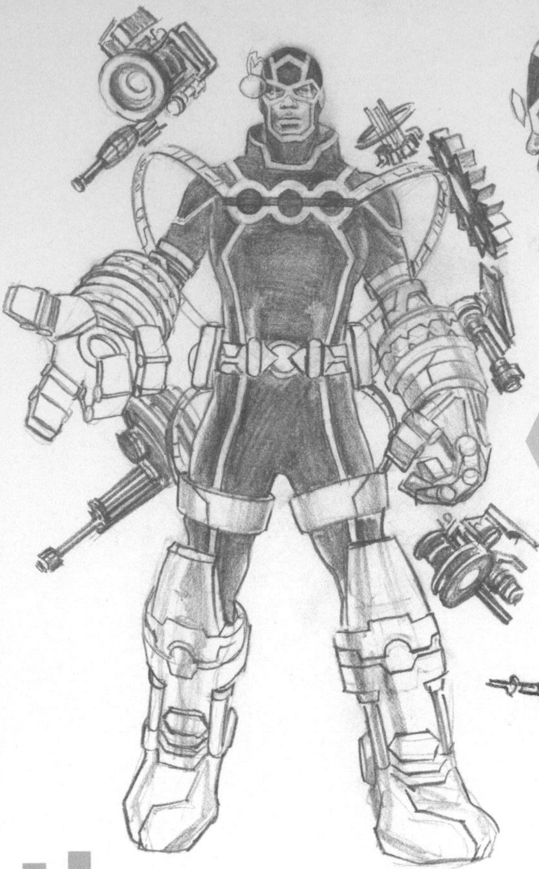

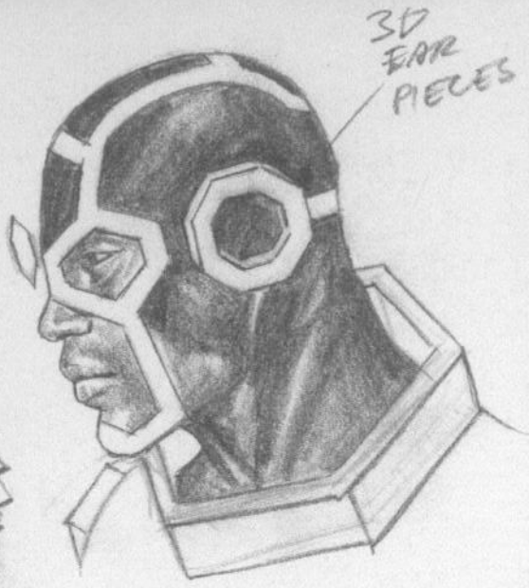
3D EAR PIECES

Alex had been wanting to give the Assemblyman a new look, and here was our chance. He, Brent and Kurt all contributed ideas.

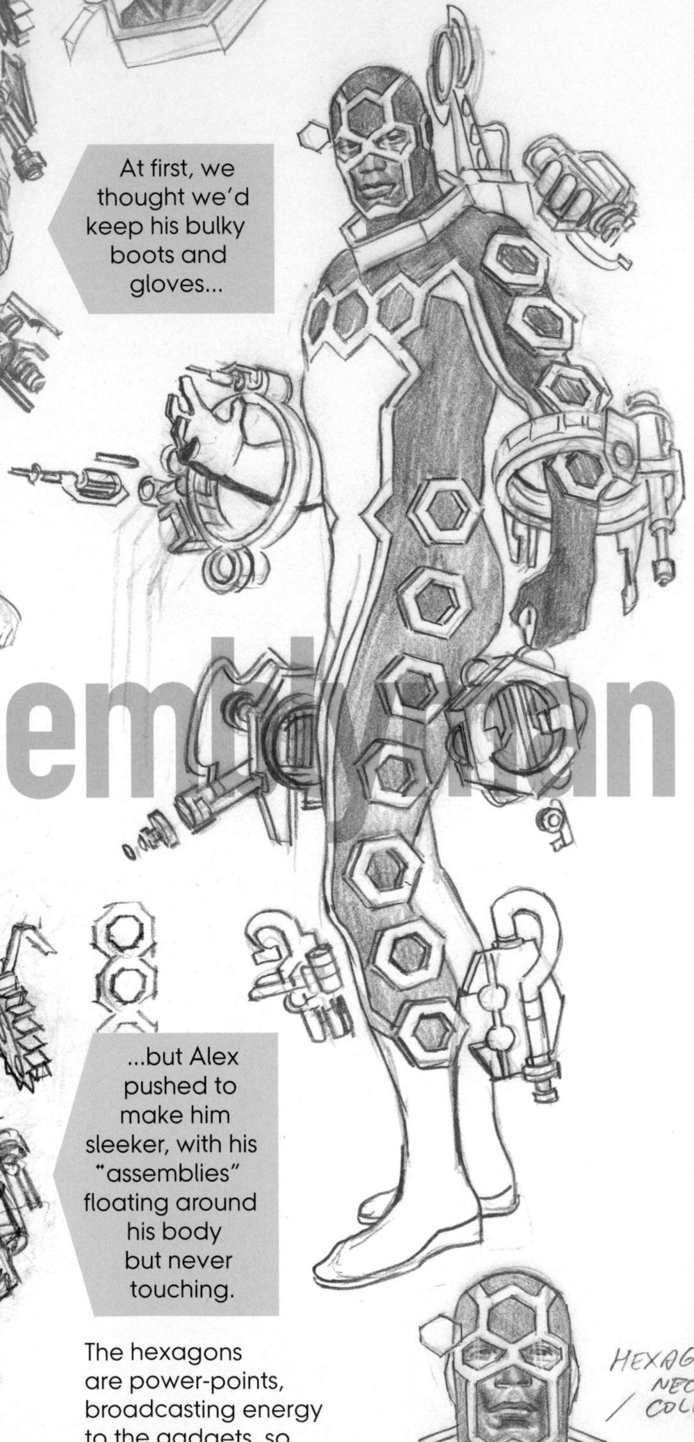

At first, we thought we'd keep his bulky boots and gloves...

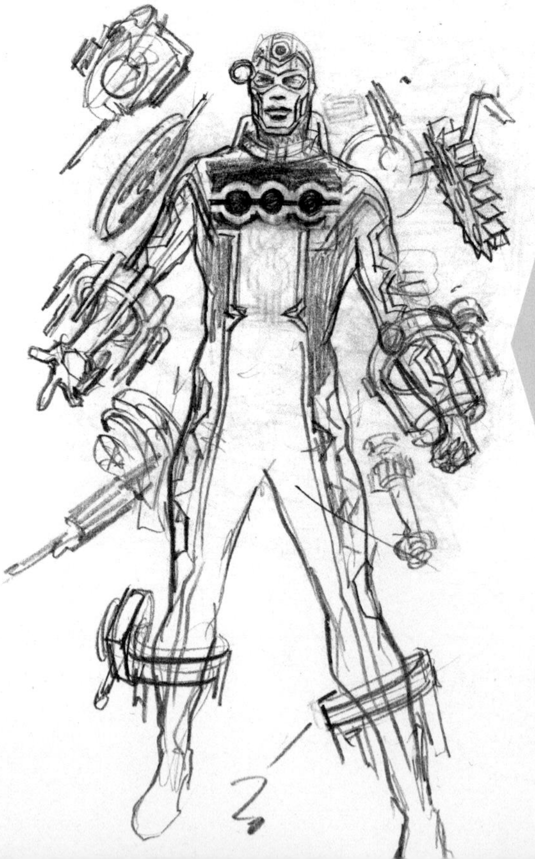

...but Alex pushed to make him sleeker, with his "assemblies" floating around his body but never touching.

The hexagons are power-points, broadcasting energy to the gadgets, so they have to hover near their power source. He's not just an engineer, but a living battery!

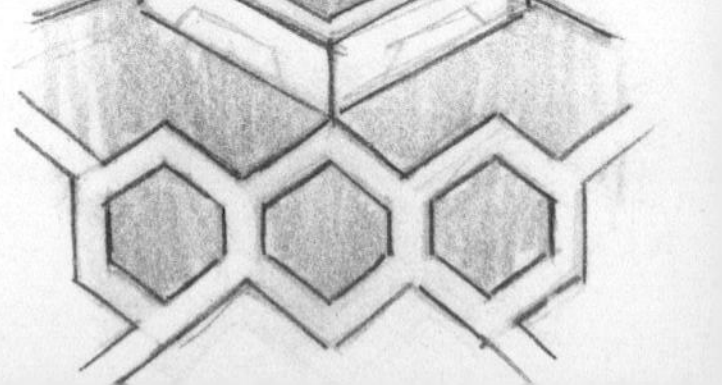

When Alex came up with a new, more modern design for the N-Forcer, there wasn't any back-and-forth. We just loved it right from the get-go.

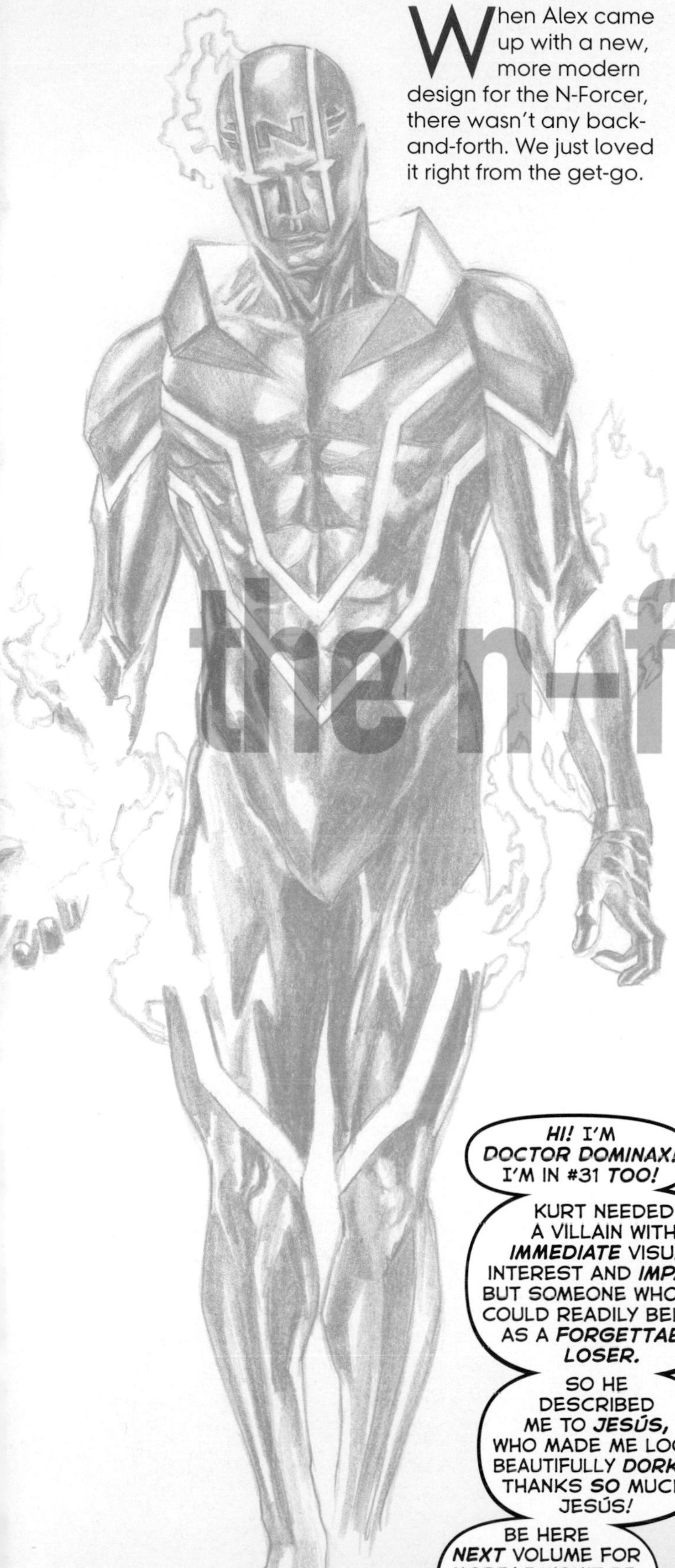

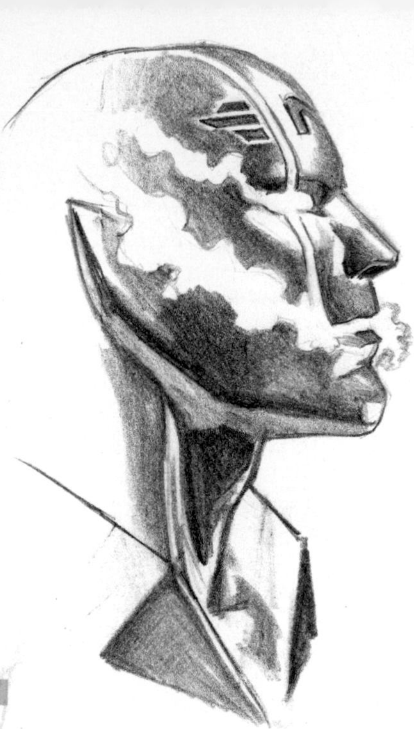

the n-forcer

He also suggested a cool plot development, that we'll get to as soon as we can...

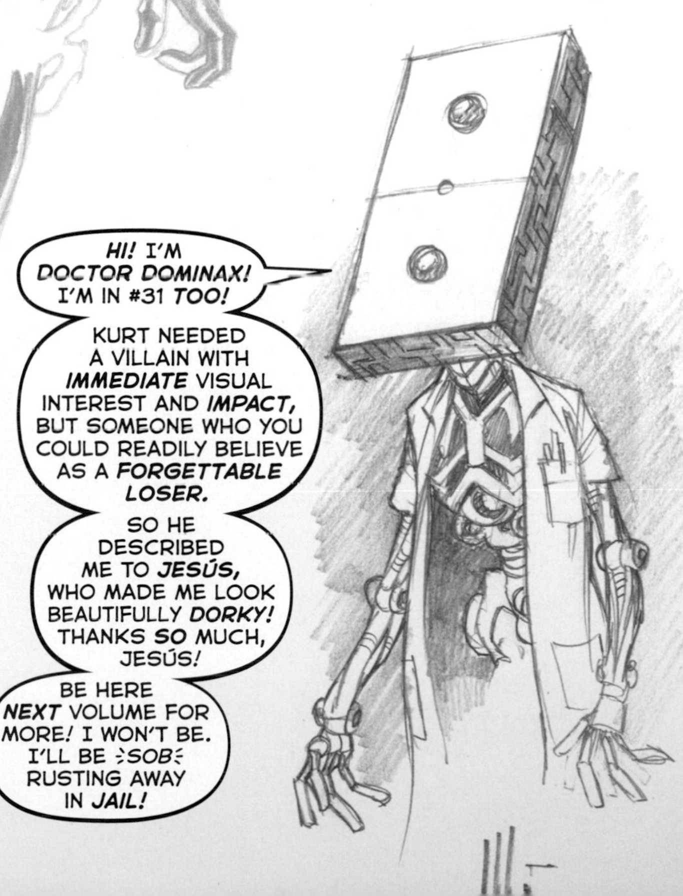
HI! I'M DOCTOR DOMINAX! I'M IN #31 TOO!
KURT NEEDED A VILLAIN WITH IMMEDIATE VISUAL INTEREST AND IMPACT, BUT SOMEONE WHO YOU COULD READILY BELIEVE AS A FORGETTABLE LOSER.
SO HE DESCRIBED ME TO JESÚS, WHO MADE ME LOOK BEAUTIFULLY DORKY! THANKS SO MUCH, JESÚS!
BE HERE NEXT VOLUME FOR MORE! I WON'T BE. I'LL BE ⋛SOB⋚ RUSTING AWAY IN JAIL!

don't miss the rest of the astro city series:

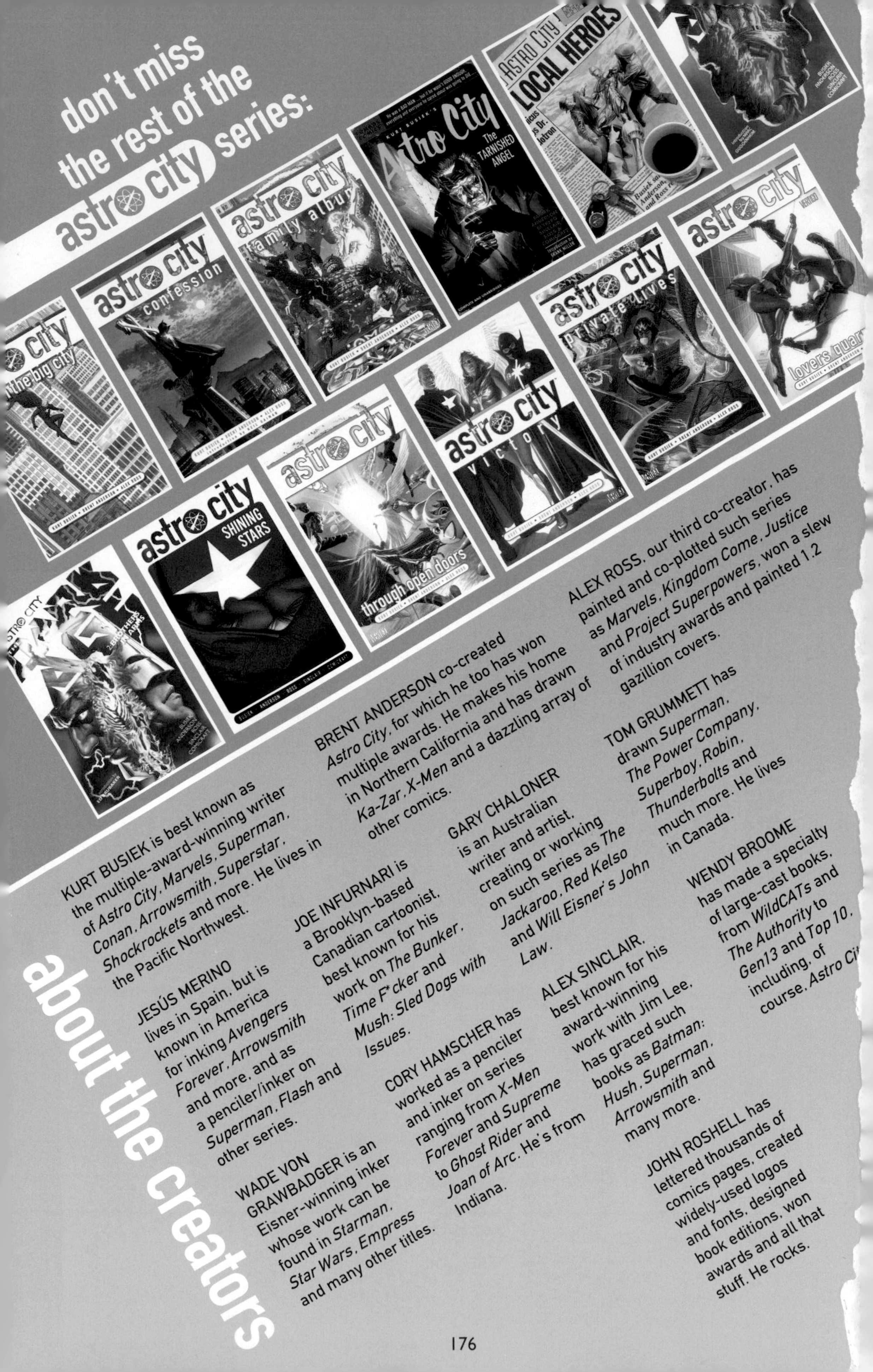
astro city
the big city
astro city
confession
astro city
family album
Astro City
The Tarnished Angel
Astro City
Local Heroes
astro city
shining stars
astro city
through open doors
astro city
victory
astro city
private lives
astro city
lovers quar

about the creators

KURT BUSIEK is best known as the multiple-award-winning writer of *Astro City*, *Marvels*, *Superman*, *Conan*, *Arrowsmith*, *Superstar*, *Shockrockets* and more. He lives in the Pacific Northwest.

BRENT ANDERSON co-created *Astro City*, for which he too has won multiple awards. He makes his home in Northern California and has drawn *Ka-Zar*, *X-Men* and a dazzling array of other comics.

ALEX ROSS, our third co-creator, has painted and co-plotted such series as *Marvels*, *Kingdom Come*, *Justice* and *Project Superpowers*, won a slew of industry awards and painted 1.2 gazillion covers.

JESÚS MERINO lives in Spain, but is known in America for inking *Avengers Forever*, *Arrowsmith* and more, and as a penciler/inker on *Superman*, *Flash* and other series.

JOE INFURNARI is a Brooklyn-based Canadian cartoonist, best known for his work on *The Bunker*, *Time F*cker* and *Mush: Sled Dogs with Issues*.

GARY CHALONER is an Australian writer and artist, creating or working on such series as *The Jackaroo*, *Red Kelso* and *Will Eisner's John Law*.

TOM GRUMMETT has drawn *Superman*, *The Power Company*, *Superboy*, *Robin*, *Thunderbolts* and much more. He lives in Canada.

WADE VON GRAWBADGER is an Eisner-winning inker whose work can be found in *Starman*, *Star Wars*, *Empress* and many other titles.

CORY HAMSCHER has worked as a penciler and inker on series ranging from *X-Men Forever* and *Supreme* to *Ghost Rider* and *Joan of Arc*. He's from Indiana.

ALEX SINCLAIR, best known for his award-winning work with Jim Lee, has graced such books as *Batman: Hush*, *Superman*, *Arrowsmith* and many more.

WENDY BROOME has made a specialty of large-cast books, from *WildCATs* and *The Authority* to *Gen13* and *Top 10*, including, of course, *Astro Ci*

JOHN ROSHELL has lettered thousands of comics pages, created widely-used logos and fonts, designed book editions, won awards and all that stuff. He rocks.

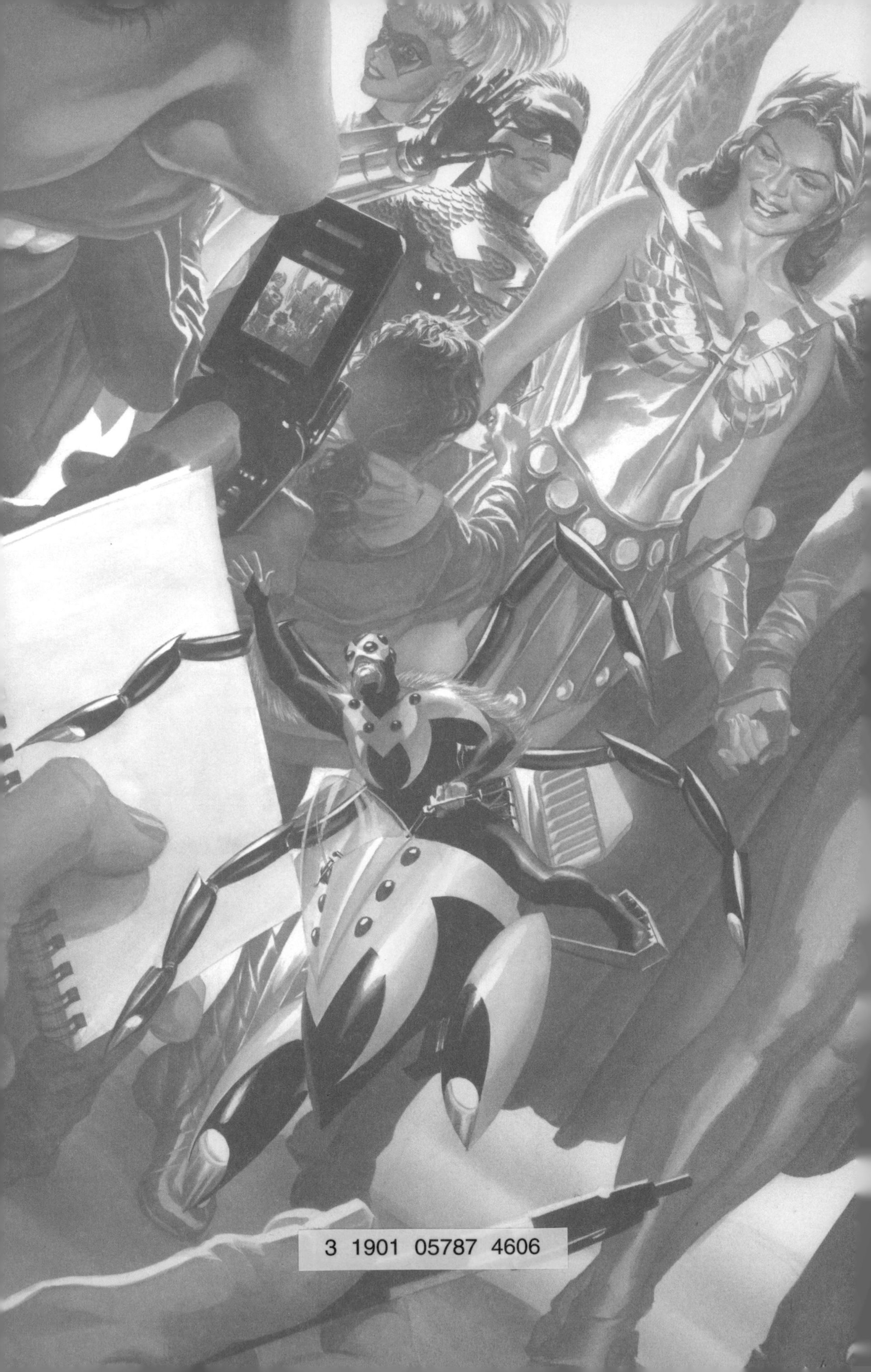